Hugh C. White is an Associate Professor in the Department of Religion, Rutgers University. *Narration and discourse in the Book of Genesis* is his first book.

This book makes an important contribution to our understanding of the Book of Genesis. Professor White shows that the traditions embodied in the narrative are essentially linguistic; and by using narratological theory he shows how each stage in the growth of the Biblical tradition is in fact an interpretation of some body of prior tradition. By relating his presentation to a general narrative typology, White hopes to demonstrate how Biblical narrative relates to the broader tradition of narrative writing in the west, and in so doing he provides a useful introduction to the work of modern narrative theorists. For this reason, his book should be of interest to literary theorists as well as to theologians, since it treats Biblical tradition as a complex literary process which projects possibilities already embedded in that tradition to successive participants in the flow of history and culture.

Narration and discourse in the book of Genesis

NARRATION AND DISCOURSE IN THE BOOK OF GENESIS

HUGH C. WHITE
Professor, Department of Religion, Rutgers University

The right of the
University of Cambridge
to print and sell
all manner of books
was granted by
Henry VIII in 1534.
The University has printed
and published continuously
since 1584.

CAMBRIDGE UNIVERSITY PRESS
Cambridge
New York Port Chester
Melbourne Sydney

Published by the Press Syndicate of the University of Cambridge
The Pitt Building, Trumpington Street, Cambridge CB2 1RP
40 West 20th Street, New York, NY 10011, USA
10 Stamford Road, Oakleigh, Melbourne 3166, Australia

First published 1991

Printed in Great Britain at the University Press, Cambridge

British Library cataloguing in publication data
White, Hugh C. (Hugh Clayton), *1936–*
Narration and Discourse in the Book of Genesis.
1. Bible. O.T. Genesis – Critical studies
I. Title
222'.1106

Library of Congress cataloguing in publication data
White, Hugh C.
Narration and discourse in the book of Genesis / Hugh C. White.
p. cm.
Includes bibliographical references.
ISBN 0–521–39020–6
1. Bible. O.T. Genesis – Criticism, interpretation, etc.
2. Narration in the Bible. I. Title.
BS1235.2.W455 1990
222'.11066 – dc20 90–31324CIP

ISBN 0 521 39020 6 hardback

WG

For my mother
Marjorie White Hancock
and in memory of my father
Otis Clayton White
(1909–1971)

Contents

Preface

Roland Barthes once wrote that the poetic Word is something which is produced and consumed with a kind of "sacred relish."[1] Certainly no less should be said of the writers and readers of the book of Genesis. It will be the underlying thesis of this work that a narrator's response to or experience of language – his or her stance toward the Word – is crucial for how s/he narrates. From this basic relation to language arises the narrator's manner of representing the narrative world and the direct discourse of the characters, as well as the way character is formed through description, analysis, action and speech. Ultimately from this system of interpretive tensions and dramatic events will erupt the unique experiences of defamiliarization which renew the reader's perceptions of self and the world, and perhaps satisfy what Barthes also refers to as the "Hunger of the Word."[2]

This thesis will be developed in the first part of this book where I attempt to create a functional narrative theory in the form of a typology of narrative functions and modes which delineate the various ways in which a narrator may relate the framing narration to the direct discourse of the characters. Within this broad context the types of discourse which characterize some of the major narratives of the book of Genesis can be determined. It may also then begin to be possible to see more exactly how narrative writing in Genesis both resembles and differs from other types of narrative literature.

This typology has grown out of my engagement with speech-act theory, but I have sought to provide an intersubjective grounding for illocutionary force chiefly in the semiotic philosophy of Edmund Ortigues. For the linguistic and literary development of the typology I have utilized primarily the work of Eugenio Coseriu, Emile Benveniste, Julia Kristeva, Lubomír Doležel and Michael Bakhtin, though I have worked it out in dialogue with some of the various theories of point of view produced by contemporary literary critics such as Franz Stanzel, Dorrit Cohn and Gérard Genette.

The second and third parts of the book then show how the overarching narrative structure of Genesis and the style of a number of separate sub-narratives relate to this typology, and how the reader is affected by the defamiliarization experience produced by the unique configuration of third-person narration and direct discourse in each narrative. The wide variety of writing styles that have come to light in this analysis lends support to the basic contention of historical criticism that the book of Genesis was written over a long period of time by a number of different authors. But within this variety, a common system of constraints upon the representation of characters and the narrative world is seen to be operating – perhaps due to a continuous tradition of narrative writing among several schools in Ancient Israel – which provides a degree of stylistic continuity and structural coherence amidst the change. Those whose interests are more exegetical and interpretive than theoretical, might begin with part II or part III which are reasonably understandable on their own, and return to part I to gain a deeper understanding of the basis of the method of analysis being used.

As a person originally trained in the disciplines of Biblical historical research I am keenly aware of the difficulty of bringing theoretical constructs developed by semioticians, linguists and literary critics to bear upon the materials of the Hebrew Bible. On the one hand, those who specialize in theory will undoubtedly be dissatisfied with the rather eclectic efforts of a newcomer to this field, and, on the other, my empirically oriented colleagues in Biblical studies will be wary of such an extensive reliance upon theory. My earlier work with form criticism, however, led me to the conclusion that narratological conceptions have always constituted significant but usually unexamined presuppositions of the historical research on Biblical narratives. It thus has not seemed possible to me to find a way into the unique subtleties of Biblical narrative writing without engaging some of the underlying theoretical issues. I view the results of this work as more supplementary than contradictory to much historical criticism, however.

With regard to the more recent literary approaches to Biblical narrative such as that especially of Robert Alter[3] and Meir Sternberg,[4] who have worked with some of the Genesis narratives, I can only say here that I am highly appreciative of their illuminating ground-breaking work, but I have had somewhat different methodological aims and interests. Alter's forthright location of Biblical narration within the field of narrative fiction, and his subtle, insightful and persuasive exposition of the stylistic art of Biblical narrators served to break the spell of historicism in which Biblical studies have been enthralled. In contrast to Alter, however, I have felt the need to place the study of Biblical narrative within a broad context of narratological theory which can account for the striking reticence on the part of the Genesis narrators to use descriptive language with regard to character and setting. And while generally supporting Sternberg's functional approach to narrative discourse, I have not sought to create a special poetics for the corpus of Hebrew Biblical narratives based on the ideology of divine and narratorial omniscience. Rather than emphasizing the universal compositional importance of the unlimited knowledge of the Biblical narrator, I have sought to describe the modes of the narrator's relation to the divine Word, and the constraints this imposes upon his expression of knowledge and his use of language. Thus in focusing in detail upon the narratives of the book of Genesis alone, I have found the stance of the narrator to change in the course of the book, and the ideology also to vary. My interpretations of specific narratives are often close to those of Gabriel Josipovici whose recent book reached me only after my work was completed, but I am inclined to see the literary influence of the Bible more at the "micro" level of the individual narrative than at the "macro" level of the Christian Bible as a whole.[5]

Many friends and colleagues, both in the United States and in Europe, have given me valuable assistance and criticism over the rather lengthy period of time taken for the research and writing of this book. The Rutgers University Faculty Academic Study Program has provided funds for both research travel in France and Germany, and indispensable periods of freedom from teaching responsibilities. I am especially indebted to Erhardt Guttgemanns, Coral Lansbury, Joseph and Anne-Marie Plagemann, Jean Sabattier, Lilo Schneider and Trudi Tate who have, in different ways, given me vital assistance in my research and manuscript preparation. Further, I will always be grateful to Martin J. Buss, Stuart Charmé, Robert Detweiler, George L. Dillon, David Jobling, Julia Kristeva, Louis Marin, Angel Medina and Roland Sublon who took time from their own heavy schedules to read and respond generously to portions of this book in first draft form. The book is stronger because of their criticisms, and would doubtless be stronger had I been able to incorporate their suggestions more adequately. They are, of course, in no way responsible for the errors and weaknesses that remain.

Thanks are also due to Scholars Press for permission to adapt materials for this new context which were first published in *Semeia* 18 and 31.

Finally, a word of tribute is due to my wife, Ann Shepard White, and my daughters, Lisa and Jessica, who have had to endure hearing of this book entirely too long, and have sustained my equilibrium through it all by keeping me joyfully aware that life is always much more significant than the books we write about it.

I

A FUNCTIONAL THEORY OF NARRATIVE

1
Toward a functional theory of narrative

One of the most anomolous, puzzling, and even mysterious features of the book of Genesis is the repeated utterance of words which are pivotal for the plot by a character who has no spatial presence in the narrative world.

I speak, of course, of the words of God, Yahweh Elohim, which issue forth not from an awesomely represented heavenly world, nor from an incarnated divine being present in the time and space of the earthly world, nor even from the psychic world of dreams and visions (though all of these occasionally do occur), but – from nowhere! They simply spring from the written page, "In the beginning ... God said," (Gen. 1:1, 3) or "And Yahweh said to Abram, "Go ..." (Gen. 12:1).

Since as readers we are very dependent upon contextual clues for understanding the meaning of utterances, the total absence of such clues from some of the most crucial utterances in the book of Genesis is no small obstacle to our understanding of this narrative. To be sure later religious tradition and theology have created contexts of their own which have so encased the Genesis narrative with theological hypostases and systems that the absence of a context for these utterances in the narrative now easily goes unnoticed, just as the absence of the mention of Satan from the narrative of the Fall of Genesis 3 is no longer perceived by many readers. But the lack of context for the divine Voice in the narrative itself must be taken very seriously by a reader who seeks (as I do) to study the style and structure of Biblical narrative writing. The work to follow is an attempt to develop a way of reading the Genesis text, drawing upon the varied resources of contemporary semiotics and literary criticism, that is responsive to the peculiarities of this mode of narrative discourse which is so restrained in its use of representative language.

Actually, the implication just conveyed that no clues were given as to the contexts of the two divine utterances is not altogether accurate. We can correct this by comparing the following utterances, which are subject to remarkably different interpretations:

(1) Let there be light.
(2) He said, "Let there be light."

(3) God said, "Let there be light."
(4) He laughed and said, "Let there be light."

Statement (1) differs from (2) – (4) in that it lacks a narrative context. To interpret the statement as it stands in terms of its denotative or conceptual content and its grammatical form leaves much unclear. "Light" is apparently an object word with a precise ostensive definition: electromagnetic radiation to which the organs of sight react. The verb "be" could be grasped in terms of more abstract sense relations meaning to exist or live as opposed to not existing or dying. The word "let" in this sentence would be an auxiliary verb conveying the modality of command; and "there" would be a kind of deictic pronoun of place used here to refer to a state of existence.

Nothing, however, has been said about whether the reference of light is to sunlight, candlelight, or electric light. The precise state of existence of such light also is not conveyed in the sentence by the verb "be." Does this mean absolute existence as opposed to non-existence, or some lesser form of existence such as is achieved by striking a match or flipping a switch? The modal auxiliary "let" only makes the meaning more obscure, since to "let" "be" an object, which presumably did not exist before, puts unusual strains on the definition of "be." But more fundamentally, convention requires that a command always be uttered by someone, and this source is not given. Without knowledge of the speaker, the contextual conditions are not known which would eliminate some of the multiple possibilities given above.

Glimmers of a context begin to appear in sentences (2) – (4), provided by introductory phrases which place the command within a discursive context. Now it is clear that these words are not, for example, a poem, a riddle or an advertisement for a public utilities company. The utterance belongs within a discursive and possibly narrative context. It is a citation. The significance of sentence (2) can be seen by comparing it to (4). The latter places the citation within a parodic context so that the meaning is not to be "taken literally." The speaker has perhaps turned on the light in a room through some hidden technical device and uttered the words for the amusement of his audience, in parody of the words of the Genesis creation story which his audience knows. Utterance (2), by comparison, relates the citation in a straightforward fashion, implying that it is to be taken literally. Of course, not knowing the "he" leaves the reader still with many interpretive uncertainties.

Sentence (3) identifies the speaker as "God." This reveals another general semantic context. To the extent that the reference of the word "God" is known, the meaning of the statement becomes more stable. If, however, very little else is known of God than that he said these words, then the words themselves become the context in which their speaker is to be understood rather than the reverse. The obscurity of the sentence's meaning would then be compounded.

Since the project before us is the meaning and analysis of the structure of the Genesis narrative from which sentence (3) was taken, it is obvious that the problem of the modal connection (that is, the predominant mood) of the narrative framework to the direct discourse of the characters is fundamental. There are numerous utterances of the divine which occur not "out of the blue" but literally out of the page. To the extent that the discursive structure is a factor in producing the meaning, the modality by which the two basic elements in that structure are related – the narrative framework and the character's speech – would have to be the starting point for the analysis.

Contemporary narratologists often choose to treat such statements as this only in terms of their conceptual content, however. The distinction between the direct discourse and narrative framework is ignored when determining the fundamental structure of a narrative and its semantic content.

Good examples of this type of approach can be found in the work of Seymour Chatman and the early work of Mieke Bal. Chatman bases his narrative theory upon Aristotle and certain derivative formalist theories influenced by the Swiss linguist Ferdinand de Saussure. The distinction between direct discourse and the narrative framework is passed over at the outset when he defines narratives as a combination of "story" (*histoire*) – "the *what* in a narrative that is depicted" (the chain of events [actions, happenings] and the existents [characters, details of setting]) – and "discourse" (*discours*) – the *how*, "the means by which the content is communicated," which may be either verbal or non-verbal.[1] Since the distinction between direct discourse and narrative framework exists only at the "discourse" level, and not at the level of "story," and the bifurcation of narrative into story and discourse has the effect of confining semantics to the story level, this precludes the possibility that any fundamental semantic distinctions can be made at the discourse level.

This division reflects the Saussurian distinction between the signifier and signified, which Chatman, utilizing the categories of the Danish linguist Hjelmslev, formulates as a distinction between the plane of expression (the "how") – the signifiers – and the plane of content (the "what") – the signifieds. He further breaks down each of these planes into substance (the material medium of verbal discourse and the material, objective content to which the words refer) and form (the common narrative structures on the expression plane, and, on the content plane, the conceptual signifieds of the narrative structure such as events, character and setting and their connections).

Similarly Mieke Bal, adhering more closely to the language of the Russian formalists, presents a three-level structure: text, fabula, and story.[2] Most of what Bal places under the two categories, text and story, Chatman includes under the category of "discourse" (i.e., the "how"), whereas the category of story for Chatman (i.e., the "what") is equivalent to what Bal means by fabula. In both the central characteristic of the narrative text is that it tells a story.[3]

It is clear that Chatman and Bal both locate the meaning of the narrative itself in the formal content, that is, the "what." Chatman raises the question, "What does narrative (or narrativizing a text) mean?", and answers that it is to be found in the formal content, the three signifieds that belong to narrative structure: "event, character, and detail of setting."[4] These three elements correspond exactly to two of the three categories which Aristotle describes as arising from "the objects of the dramatic imitation" (*Poetics*, 1450a, line 10); i.e., fable or plot (actions) and character (moral qualities). The third of Chatman's categories, the representation of the setting, is also clearly a form of imitation determined by its objects.[5] It is important to note that *these signifieds may be expressed in either the direct discourse or the narrative framework. The distinction between narration and direct discourse plays no role at the level of the "what," that is, the semantic content.*

If this mimetic theory is applied to sentence (3) (God said, "Let there be light."), and to its narrative context, a number of problems arise. While the preceding verses do provide a type of setting (i.e., time reference to the beginning, and reference to unformed chaos) and character reference (i.e., God as the subject who speaks), the signifiers of sentence (3) at the discourse level do not refer to an event, but rather constitute an event. The utterance does not refer to light, but has, as the consequence of its utterance (revealed in the succeeding phrase), the existence of light. Here the discourse does not recount a happening, but is itself a happening, and it is precisely in this happening that the meaning of the narrative is to be found, i.e., creation through speech. Such language does not fit easily into an understanding of narrative that blurs the distinction between narrative framework and direct discourse, since the words of discourse would be reduced to merely signifying instruments which refer to a signified content, and there would be no place for meaning which is inseparable from the speech act itself.

Gérard Genette illuminates this problem when he points out that the chief weakness of the mimetic theory of narrative is that there is an element in narrative that is clearly not mimetic, namely, the direct discourse passages. The problem is made clear by looking at Plato's way of defining this category in relation to mimesis. Plato distinguishes between lexis (the manner of speaking) and logos (that which is said, the thought content). Under the category of lexis he locates diegesis, or simple narration by a poet in his own words, and mimesis, which is an imitation in direct discourse of another speaking. Plato opposes mimesis to diegesis as a perfect imitation to an imperfect. In diegesis the poet only gives the words of others in indirect speech.

In Genette's view, however, direct discourse in a narrative is in fact the thing itself which supposedly is being imitated. It is thus a tautology to speak of a direct speech as a perfect imitation. A perfect imitation in the verbal medium is the thing itself. It is the imperfect which is, under the category of lexis, the actual imitation, thereby making diegesis, in fact, mimesis. As Genette says: "the very notion of imitation on the level of lexis is a pure mirage which vanishes as one approaches it; the only thing that language can imitate perfectly is language, or to be more precise, a discourse can imitate perfectly only a perfectly identical discourse; in short, a discourse can only imitate itself ... A perfect imitation is no longer an imitation; it is the thing itself, and in the end, the only imitation is an imperfect one, *mimesis* is *diegesis*."[6]

In comparing narrative to a painting, Genette says that direct discourse would be equivalent to a Dutch master placing a real oyster shell into his picture. Direct discourse is heterogeneous to the representative, mimetic context in which it stands in the narrative.[7] This suggests then that mimetic theories cannot fully account for the meaning of direct discourse in narratives. A semantic cleavage exists between these two forms of discourse.[8] Thus Genette finds the two basic components of narrative to be direct discourse and presentational narration which provides the contextual framework. The discursive context of the entire narrative work creates a final important "frontier" which impinges upon the narrative form and meaning. To the extent then that direct discourse constitutes such a fundamental, semantic feature of narrative, one cannot define a narrative in terms of the relation between the narrating discourse and the narrated, mimetic (signified) content which suppresses this distinction. This is especially true of the Biblical narrative which presents many such centrally important acts of speech in direct discourse, such as Genesis 1:3.

Some literary theorists have recognized the need for an approach to narrative which finds a point of departure within discourse rather than building upon the distinction between verbal form and semantic content.

Mary Louise Pratt has been the first to move toward a comprehensive, systematically developed theory of literature which does not rely upon this formalist dichotomy.[9] Her critique of formalist poetics, from which the narratology of Chatman and Bal stems, focuses upon its primary concern with defining the features which make literature "literary." Applied to narrative, this results in an attempt to determine the formal characteristics of narrative discourse that are approximately parallel to the formal features of ordinary discourse. In Saussurian terms, the study of narrative poetics sets out to describe the system of features observable in narrative texts as Saussure set out to observe the systematic features (*la langue*) of ordinary oral discourse. Bal describes this as the development of descriptive "tools" which make possible insight in the "abstract narrative system."[10]

This approach, Pratt argues, was slanted toward the study of certain written texts already recognized as literary. These strategies cannot work with oral narratives that are generally assumed to be non-literary because oral narrative would have to be described in terms of a host of characteristics which stem from the context of utterance which is considered beyond the scope of formal analysis. Utilizing studies of oral narratives by William Labov she concludes: "His data make it impossible to attribute the aesthetic organization of prose fiction to 'literariness', but his methodology shows us what we can attribute it to: the nature of the speech situation in which the utterance occurs."[11] This similarity between natural narrative and literary narrative is due to the fact that "most of the features which poeticians believed constituted the 'literariness' of novels are not 'literary' at all. They occur in novels not because they are novels (i.e., literature) but because they are members of some other more general category of speech acts."[12]

The pressing question to which this leads, of course, is what kind of global speech act is a likely candidate to fulfill this large role? To answer this question Pratt utilizes the work of speech-act philosopher J. L. Austin to provide a way of analyzing the context in which utterances are made, and the conventions which govern their form and reception. On this basis she is able to define the location of narrative in the context of the author/reader relationship and seeks to understand, in a broad sense, what occurs in an event of narration. In contrast to standard speech acts, such as asserting or representing, she characterizes an act of narration as "verbally displaying a state of affairs,"[13] that is, transmitting a message which has a special relevance to the hearer that exceeds that of simple assertive or representative speech acts. This special relevance requires that the narratives "represent states of affairs that are held to be unusual, contrary to expectation, or otherwise problematic."[14] This endows the narratives with the quality of "tellability" which "characterizes an important subclass of assertive or representative speech acts that includes natural narrative, an enormous proportion of conversation, and many if not all literary works." She terms this subclass of speech acts the "exclamatory assertion."[15]

Having defined the type of global speech act which gives rise to narrative, Pratt then proceeds to fill in the conventional literary context shared by authors and readers which make this type of speech act "felicitous" (i.e., effective). To do this she draws on a variety of sources. They extend from the conventional factors which shape the audience's willingness to enter into a one-way discourse with no opportunity to respond,[16] to the assumption created in the reader by the "pre-selection and pre-paration" which the publication process engenders,[17] to the "conversational maxims" of speech-act philosopher H. P. Grice which provide a means of analyzing the implications (or "implicatures" in Grice's terminology) of dialogue.[18] With this array of conventions to define the external context of the narrative speech act, Pratt can then turn to the analysis of the speech acts internal to specific narratives.

Here we find a way of approaching narrative which finds significance not merely in the referential content of the discourse, but in the speech act itself. J. L. Austin argued that utterances such as promises, vows, naming, etc., do not have meaning in the usual way; that is, they are not true or false in the referential sense. Yet they also cannot be viewed as nonsense. They are cases where "the issuing of an utterance is the performance of an action."[19] He wants to describe the significance of such speech acts in terms of their "force" rather than their meaning (understood as sense and reference). By force he means that, for example, a marriage vow, when uttered under the proper conventional circumstances (before an authorized person and in the authorized form, with the proper intentions by all parties) has the effect of marrying two persons. He terms the capacity of utterances to achieve an effect through conformity to conventions, "illocutionary force."[20] The conventions or rules link the utterance to the situation of discourse and insure the "force" of the utterance.

Thus by determining the conventions which link narrative discourse to the situation of its origin, Pratt is able to determine the character of narrative in terms of its originating act rather than in terms of its referential content. In the case of Genesis 1:3 the force of this sentence (and the narrative of which it is a part) would arise from its "tellability." A problem arises, however, with the application of this approach to such a passage as this.

A distinction has to be made at the outset between the act of narrating as evidenced in the narrative framework, and the utterance internal to the narrative. While few would dispute that Genesis 1:3 and the narrative of which it is a part could be considered an "exclamatory assertion" which is "tellable," the specific sense in which it is tellable is difficult to determine because of the time gap between its original writing and the modern world. To attempt to determine this would lead away from the specific analysis of the narrative into a veritable abyss of uncertainties entailed with the reconstruction of the worldview of the original narrator (or narrators) and audience. Moreover, such a reconstruction would say very little about the modality of the relationship of the narrator's discourse to the divine utterance – the critical question here.

In addition, the very concept of tellability is an objectification of an intersubjective process (to be explained in ch. 2 below) which is far more fundamental to human life than a communicative convention.

If one applies speech-act theory to the specific utterance of the divine Voice within the "fictive" narrative world, numerous problems also arise. Pratt views the speech acts internal to works of imaginative literature as imitative speech acts; that is, they are speech acts in which their "real world" illocutionary force has been blocked by its fictionality. Aside from the question of the generic identity of Genesis 1, can the speech act in 1:3 be understood as an imitative command?

The core of the problem is seen by looking again at the sentence from Genesis 1: "And God said, 'Let there be light'."

Although in the few preceding verses information is provided to establish that the speaker, God, is also the creator of heaven and earth, and thus would presumably satisfy the "felicity" condition which requires that a performative sentence be uttered by a speaker in the proper, authoritative position to do so, the first and most important condition is not met:

There must exist an accepted conventional procedure having a certain conventional effect, that procedure to include the uttering of certain words by certain persons in certain circumstances.[21]

But while the sentence might rely upon common knowledge among its readers of the procedure for issuing orders, the circumstances are beyond comprehension and the effect is anything but conventional. Under what circumstances governed by convention can one say these words were uttered by the divine Voice? And what convention can be said to govern the effect – "and there was light"?

To be sure, the recording of the immediate positive (obedient?) effect of the command shows a correspondence of the text with speech-act conventions, but the effect is itself highly unconventional. It is clear that the force of this utterance cannot be sufficiently grasped in terms of the correspondence of speech acts to conventional rules.

The central problem of speech-act theory which has carried over as well into the attempts to build a theory of literature upon it, is that there has not been an adequate theory of the "meaning" of illocutionary force. In Austin's writing a distinction is repeatedly made *between* meaning and force. Meaning is understood primarily in terms of Fregeian sense relations and reference, that is, the meaning associated with what John Searle (Austin's principle expositor) calls the propositional act.[22] While Searle argues that no absolute distinction can be made in literal utterances between meaning and force, the way in which they remain in some kind of unity seems to be through "deep syntactic structure, stress, intonation-contour (and, in a written speech, punctuation)."[23]

Jonathan Culler points out, however, that there are too many contextual factors which cannot be reduced to syntax and sign, and which even escape conscious intention: "Meaning is context bound, but context is boundless ... any attempt to codify context can always be grafted onto another context it sought to describe."[24] This problem points to the dimensions of the subject – of the unconscious as an inescapable factor in the force of utterances. Since the problem of the subject is not opened by Austin and Searle, force still remains basically a heterogeneous factor which is somehow perceived in addition to the propositional content of sentences.[25] It is explicitly present as a verbal marker only in the case of first-person statements such as "I promise," "I bet," etc. Where such explicit markers are missing, and the theory is stretched to apply to language which is either not directly related to genuine constitutive rules (such as is the case with "expositives" and "verdictives," i.e., sentences with clearly propositional content),[26] or cases where the meaning may derive partly from an explicit grammatical elimination of reference to the speech event,[27] it has come under considerable criticism. So long as illocutionary force is presented as a quasi-objective entity produced by other objective factors such as conventional rules, then it will be difficult to prove its existence in the absence of established rules, or in the case of grammatical barriers which exclude speech acts from direct presence in the signifying relations of the sentence (the third-person form can itself be seen as such a barrier).[28]

Although it is clear that Searle is attempting to overcome the radical bifurcation of language bequeathed by Saussure, the division of the speech act into force and meaning finally bears a close formal relation to Saussure's division between synchrony and diachrony, and more particularly to his division of the synchronic realm into the quasi-diachronic syntagmatic and the associative dimensions. The propositional features of sentences consisting of sense and reference correspond to the associative (psychological) and referential relations of Saussure's conceptual "signified." The force factor, which is relative in some cases to the grammatical case of the verb (imperative, interrogative, etc.) and in all cases to the constitutive rules rooted in the collective consciousness of the society, corresponds to the syntagmatic, grammatical axis of Saussure (which he also recognized as an abstract form concretely rooted in the particularities of individual societies and their language). This explains why Searle said that the rules belonged to *langue* and not *parole*.[29]

The reason thus becomes apparent as to why speech-act theory, as Austin and Searle have formulated it, can shed little light on a sentence such as (4) (He laughed and said, "Let there be light."). Too many of the vital conditions of "felicity" are not present to account for the "force" factor. The illocutionary dimension of language can only be established on the basis of a theory which goes beyond the dichotomies of formal thought to unite the dimensions of force and meaning.

If Saussurian linguistics and its derivative narrative theories cannot adequately account for the significance of the act of speech in direct discourse, are there other language theories which might provide a better foundation?

As early as 1958, Continental linguist Eugenio Coseriu published a thoroughgoing refutation of the central concepts of Saussurian linguistics in his book *Synchronie, Diachronie und Geschichte*.[30] In this book Coseriu brilliantly shows the superficiality of Saussure's distinction between diachronic events of speech production and the synchronic language system. In Coseriu's view, language changes, whether at the level of sound, grammar, or concepts, present no problem at all for communication. "Certainly," he writes, each change alters the system or at least its balance somewhat; but it does not overturn it: as Saussure himself observed, change is not "global." For language is a complex system, a system of many inter-connected structures, so that, for example a change within a paradigm does not touch necessarily and immediately the relation between these and the other paradigms of the same order, nor the inner relations of the last. Otherwise, each change would bring with it a revolution, and the system would have no continuity. Similarly, change does not lead to the inevitable downfall and ruin of language ... because it is not "destruction," but "production."[31]

Thus rather than beginning with the concept of language as a static system, Coseriu begins with the fact of change:

One must begin with change in order to understand the formation of the system (not to describe *one* system in *one* prescribed moment), for the reality of the system is certainly no less problematic than the reality of change. Even better, one must begin with the becoming of language in general (that also includes its production).[32]

For him, change is not the antithesis of system. Rather, "the activity through which language is made is itself systematic: that through which language is language is not only its structure (which is only the condition of its functioning), but speech as Tradition."[33] Movement is not mere successiveness, but rather a "system in motion" – a "systematization" – and "each language situation constitutes a systematic structure just because it is a moment of the systematization."[34]

Thus the cleavage between synchrony and diachrony is overcome. Languages which do not change are in fact dead languages,[35] an observation also made independently by another opponent of Saussurian linguistics, the Russian linguist, M. Bakhtin/Voloshinov. He argues that the synchronic approach to language actually originated in the study of dead languages: "At the basis of the modes of linguistic thought that lead to the postulation of language as a system of normatively identical forms lies a practical and theoretical focus of attention on the study of defunct, alien languages preserved in written monuments."[36]

The collective form of language is thus characterized by Coseriu not as a logical system, but as a tradition which, though it can be described in a systematic fashion, cannot be explained only in terms of the logical process operating in the associative relations. Rather a great many non-logical factors determine the historic configuration the language system assumes and thus participate integrally in its structure of meaning.[37]

At the center of the process of linguistic change is the speaker who relates to language, in Coseriu's view, as a field of possibilities, an open system in which to exercise his freedom[38] within the limits of the linguistic and historico-cultural constraints. With this introduction of the perspective of the speaking subject Coseriu makes a meaningful break with traditional formal thought, and raises the possibility that the force factor in language has its basis not in language convention, but in the relationship of the speaking subject to language.

Change, which is fundamental to the dynamic system of language, is also fundamental to the life and consciousness of the speaker. It is through language innovations that humans experience their freedom and actualize a historic form of subjectivity: "Freedom needs language in order to realize historically its purposive expression. Language is the *condition* or *instrument* of linguistic freedom as historical freedom, and an instrument over which man disposes is not a prison or chain."[39]

In speaking of language as a condition of historical subjectivity, Coseriu is pointing to a constitutive function of language that bears some resemblance to the illocutionary function of speech analyzed by Austin and Searle. In fact, Coseriu makes a distinction between communicative and referential language functions which closely corresponds to the distinction between performative and constative speech acts made by Austin. Coseriu says that speaking occurs at the center of the two axes, one reaching to the language tradition, and the other to the hearer. Of the two the link with the hearer is the most fundamental, "since there is no speaking which would not be communication."[40] But this communication is of two types – the "*communication-of-something*," the "Saying-this-or-that-to-Someone" – which can best be called "information," and the "essential and original communication, the *Communicating-with-*Someone, that is not external to language since it also occurs when no practical communication is achieved (or even if what is said is not understood)."[41] Every simple speech is fundamentally "*for the other*, since language is directly the 'making known of one's Self for others' [Hegel]."[42]

This speech act, which has no meaning outside of its own intersubjective function of self-disclosure to another, possesses the central attribute of the illocutionary act, i.e., an action performed *in* communication with someone (a condition of the felicity of the illocutionary act not fully explored by Austin[43] which is beyond the communication of semantic content). The "communication of something" would then correspond to the propositional act which transmits verifiable semantic content. Coseriu probes more deeply into the implication of the "constitutive" character of this dialogical dimension of speech for human consciousness than do Austin and Searle.

Coseriu develops this concept of linguistic-shaped subjectivity by saying that this communication "for the other" establishes and makes possible the expression of the subjectivity of the self as "intersubjectivity."[44] It is in this dialogical intersubjectivity that the self is able to encounter itself and to experience the relativity of its historical existence: "this self-encounter [*sich-Begegnen*] is possible only through language which forms in the speaker and hearer their historical mode of being."[45] He thus seeks to abolish the Saussurian dichotomy between synchronic and diachronic spheres by showing that historical consciousness itself grows out of the functioning of language in the speaking subject. There can thus be no antinomy finally between diachrony and synchrony because the diachronic process is at its very center a linguistic process: "Language is ... always 'synchronized' with its speaker because its historicality coincides with that of the speaker."[46] Because of the systematic nature of the historical-linguistic process, he thus proposes to replace Saussure's synchrony/diachrony opposition with a division between descriptive and historical sciences of language.[47]

In what I consider to be a telling critique of Saussurian linguistics, Coseriu points to the proper starting point for a literary method which escapes the objectifying presuppositions of such modes of thought, that is, dialogical intersubjectivity. But he did not draw out the implications of this linguistic phenomenon for a method of analysis applicable to literature. More recently, Angel Medina, working from the perspective of the phenomenology of language, has moved decisively toward developing an approach to literature which would not be entrapped by this objectifying perspective by showing how reflective thought itself, in the western philosophical tradition, arises from a communicative act. By showing how communication functions in the shaping of consciousness, he narrows the gap between force and meaning bequeathed by the Saussurian/formalist tradition. Though his work is independent of Coseriu's, his major conclusion regarding consciousness also establishes the primacy of intersubjectivity. His term for this is "communicative fusion."[48]

Medina makes a fundamental distinction between "formal reflection" and "non-formal reflection." By formal reflection he means "a concern of consciousness with its objects and a transformational formula to relate those objects that are considered fundamental, that is, the ones that are first grasped apodictically, to all other actual and possible objects."[49]Non-formal reflection, in contrast, is "the reflection of which man is capable as a thoughtfully living subject." Its concern is "a concern for limits and boundaries."[50]

Formal reflection, which began in the west with Greek philosophy, has had a problematic relationship with insight. In the Platonic system, the objects of insight – the ideas of being and truth – coincide exactly with the occurrence of insight in reflective thought.

The presupposition of this view is "the existence of a formative, transcendent insight (either of God or of nature) at work in the universe."[51] Truth is ultimately understood as *adequation*, that is, "perfect union of the being of insight to the nature of the being of things." The result is that "Our insight is ... an awakening to the sun-like splendor of necessary existence as demanded by perfection and value."[52] The ultimate end is not the representation of perfection by the soul, but intellectual or spiritual union with it. Thus consciousness is absorbed *into* its own objects of thought, the consequence being the emergence of a serious cleavage between the world of sense experience and the world of rational truth, even though this mental world was considered to be the ultimate reality *of* the material world.

With Kant came the exclusion of the "thing itself" from the sphere of possible knowledge, and, consequently, the assumption that insight could coincide with the truth of being also vanished. Insight was no longer given the prerogative to constitute true objects of thought. Rather, reflection now came into the forefront as an object of thought itself, and insight was more or less merged with reflection. The constitutive function now shifts to the process of reflection and "comes to be composed of a set of logical operations that combine consistently the given aspects of sensory experience and *signify*, that is, simply point to the world in ways dictated by the logical combinations (form)."[53] The relation of thought to the world was no longer one of *adequation*, but rather one of signification.

With Hegel, reflection became conscious of itself in a new way. Though Kant preserved a vestige of the Greek philosophical faith in the rationality of nature in his confidence in the "affinity between natural patterns and their form in consciousness," according to Medina,[54] Hegel moves far toward the complete abandonment of that belief. With Hegel insight returns to the center of reflective thought, but now as insight into the historical nature of consciousness (self-knowledge), rather than as insight into the unchanging being of nature in the Greek sense.

The result of Kantian and Hegelian thought, however, has been to show, in different ways, the priority of reflection over the objective contents of consciousness. The question to which this leads is "to ask for the conditions of the possibility of reflectiveness itself."[55] Analytic thought should aim not at a definition of the self, but at the illumination of the *conditions under which reflection occurs*, and the form of meaning which is appropriate to those conditions. In raising this question, Medina takes a decisive step away from western philosophical objectivism which sees reflection as a quasi-natural process founded upon some kind of constitutive structure, either rational, spiritual (in the sense of Hegel's *Geist*) or physiological, and toward an intersubjective, social and biographical view. This move corresponds to Coseriu's move away from Saussurian synchronism toward an understanding of language from the perspective of its function as the basis of intersubjectivity. Medina argues for the primacy of freedom rather than self-knowledge (Hegel) as the goal of reflective thought. Stated in another way, he takes freedom to be the primary condition for reflective thought. Reflection is simultaneously regressive and progressive, which makes the contents of consciousness in both operations partial and therefore open to future completion. But for consciousness to take *totality* as its object threatens the imposition of closure upon reflection. As Medina says: "If the reflective process is to show any totality under conditions of renewed openness, it cannot be the form of totality of the world which contains in its very structure and function as a horizon an exigency of ultimate closedness.''[56] This is because closedness, which opposes freedom, acts inevitably as a cause that contradicts the conditions of simultaneous progressivity and regressivity which characterize reflection.

Thus, in order to retain a view of reflection that preserves its open character, he is required to abandon two formal principles of objective consciousness: the affinity of consciousness and nature and that of the principle of logical (teleological) totality of consciousness. In place of Hegel's teleologically determined mode of progressive reflection, he sees progressive thought as concerning itself ''not at all *with* what can be thought in general, but *for* what can be done or enacted by man, *for* what individual men can be for themselves, that is, as complete courses of life that should have a shape all their own.''[57]

This non-formal reflection, characterized by Medina as ''biographical reason,'' is both narrative and symbolic in form due to the two boundaries against which it presses, that is, the physical boundaries of birth and death which give shape in consciousness to the course of life (the boundary of ''individuation''), and the boundary experiences in the encounter with other selves (the boundary of ''communication'').[58] Of these two, the more basic is the boundary of communication since, with the abandonment of the concept of consciousness as determined by objects, consciousness appears as contingent. The chief contingency is found in the encounter with other selves. As Medina more precisely puts it: ''*Contingency in this instance corresponds to the complex presentation of another self in my own consciousness*'' (his emphasis).[59]

It is through the symbolic aspect of language that this presentation of consciousnesses to one another occurs, and that human beings experience, in so doing, the meaning of life: ''The meaning of my whole life is communicative: it emerges as such, for the benefit of another consciousness when I attempt to present myself totally to it. Reciprocally, the meaning of another life becomes a totality only when received fully within my life.''[60] Here meaning and force come together in an act of communication which is constitutive of human subjectivity.

Pointing to the same plane of language which Coseriu described as ''Communicating-with-Someone'' (as opposed to ''Communication-of-something''), Medina says that it is this plane of language which actually constitutes reflective consciousness itself. In a way similar to Coseriu he argues that communication should be understood not as the simple transmission of information about the surroundings, but ''*as the active formation of a shared course of life that is intermittently recapitulated in several reflective streams*'' (his emphasis).[61] He shows how Husserl's noesis/noema distinction, Frege's sense/reference division and Saussure's signified/signifier dichotomy are all rooted in the same kind of objectification of consciousness. When self-reflection is conceived apart from its originating condition in communication, then, whether you examine it phenomenologically or in terms of behavioristic psychology, consciousness is still seen to be a function of objective processes. The question which needs clarification, however, concerns the conditions which account for the concrete appearance of reflective movement in consciousness.

When these processes are traced, they lead inevitably back to biographical events and, consequently, the fundamental symbolic act at the root of language loses its predicative character and "becomes purely narrative."[62] The narrative form of consciousness is characterized by an "interpenetration," of each consciousness by the other. In this interpenetration self-transcendence occurs. This corresponds to Coseriu's concept of the axis of language which connects the speaker and hearer and constitutes, in his view, the "original and essential" communication – the "Communicating-with-Someone." When self-consciousness is understood as arising from this communicative axis, then, according to Medina, "its *significative* focus changes from objectification and self-objectification to self-transcendence."[63] This is to say that the meaning of the self is to be found not in terms of a system of referents which can be predicated *of* the self, that is, a system which treats the self as an object of predication, but in terms of the actual attainment of self-transcendence in the communicative encounter with the other. Self-transcendence is not a natural attribute, but the effect of an act of narration. Here the concepts of force and meaning come together, meaning now being understood, however, in terms of the force/effect of the narrative act.

Self-transcendence occurs when a consciousness transcends its boundaries in order to comprehend them from the viewpoint of another. This transcendence occurs precisely in the communication of life courses, and thus in the articulation of life as story (history). Stories embody configurations arising from the boundaries of inter-individual coexistence ... symbolic transformations of love, death, suffering, and so forth.[64]

Progressive synthetic thought, then, does not understand consciousness in terms of objective, transcendent, *a priori* structures, but in terms of boundaries constituted in part by its origin and end, and in part by the "boundary of communication" with other selves.[65] Within these boundaries the apodictic structures discovered by regressive, analytic thought are rendered provisional in light of the temporal and communicative limits imposed upon consciousness by historical existence.

This perspective, which finds one of the boundaries of consciousness in the dialogical encounter with the Other, and the other in the movement from birth toward death, when applied to narrative discourse, provides a way of understanding the "force" operative in narrative acts beyond social and linguistic conventions. The force of the narrative act, understood as the interpenetration of life courses, is its capacity to make possible self-transcendence and reflectivity. Reflection itself arises from the narrative act, and thus cannot view it as an objective process which functions apart from the subjective dimension.

In literary criticism the attempt to understand literature in terms of its effect upon the subject was first developed by the early Russian formalists. The leading question of early formalist inquiry concerned the features of literature which distinguished it from ordinary speech. Shklovsky, one of the founders of this school, defined this distinctive literary quality as "defamiliarization." By this he meant that literature takes up within itself ordinary objects, states and language, and places them in a new, alien context that causes our perception of them to be renewed. Eichenbaum, an early member of this group who wrote a summary of its early theory and methods in 1925, said: "Shklovsky [advanced] the device of 'making it strange' [*ostranenie*] and the device of impeded form which augments the difficulty and duration of perception, since the process of perception in art is an end in itself, and is supposed to be prolonged."[66] The distinctiveness of literature is thus to be understood in terms of its effect upon our perceptual process. While this effect for Shklovsky is an effect of form, the experience of the renewal of perception is close to the self-transcending experience of communicative boundaries found by Medina in the narrative communication of life courses.

Practical language, conversely, was considered practical by virtue of its utilitarian bearing which made it serve, not the perceptual process of consciousness, but some other practical social or material end. The tension here seems to stem from the distinction Coseriu describes as the sign's function of communicating information, versus its function of being "Communicating-with-Someone." As we shall see below (ch. 2), form is the medium of intersubjective communication.

"Practical" language would thus be dominated by the referential orientation of the sign, whereas literary language would emphasize the intersubjective, communicative function of form. Practical language thus would come to be used automatically, with no considerations given to its form so long as it serves a mundane purpose of communicating information. Shklovsky stated the distinguishing feature of literature precisely in these terms. In his 1914 article entitled "The Resurrection of the Word," he wrote: "If we have to define specifically 'poetic' perception and artistic perception in general, then we suggest this definition: 'Artistic' perception is that perception in which we experience form – perhaps not form alone, but certainly form."[67]

It was precisely the effect which the literary text had upon consciousness – making it aware again of the power of the form as such – that lifted it from the realm of the ordinary. This gave the "formalist" a functionalist starting point. Eichenbaum, in fact, attempts to correct the misleading impression implied by the term "formalism" that the primary object of study was form itself: "the basic efforts of the Formalist were directed neither toward the study of so-called 'form' nor toward the construction of a special 'method,' but toward substantiating the claim that verbal art must be studied in its specific features, that it is essential for that purpose to take the different *functions of poetic and practical language as the starting point.*" (my emphasis).[68]

The major flaw of this early formalism was, as Pratt has pointed out, the limitation of this experience of form to "literary" language when it can also be found as well in "ordinary" language. The confusion seems to arise from the perception that all ordinary, non-literary language is fundamentally referential, a perception that empirical evidence does not support. Medina's argument regarding the self-transcending effect of the sharing of life courses also suggests that the so-called "poetic" function is not limited to "literary" texts.

Formalism, however, was ambivalent about form, since form could be understood both progressively in terms of its interaction with consciousness, and regressively, as an object existing within a system of relations.[69] This stress on the importance of the perceptual experience of the concrete linguistic form thus clearly distinguishes at least the early formalist approach from that of the later structuralists and formalists such as Lévi-Strauss[70] and Seymour Chatman, for whom abstract signification, that is, semantic content, was the exclusive focus.

The loss of the functionalist starting point of early formalism has meant that literary analysis, when it has emphasized the functional side of language, has lacked a systematic method. On the other hand, when literary studies have attempted to utilize a more scientific method, the functional dimension of language has been excluded.

The most vigorous new efforts to return to the perceptual sources of language and literature are probably to be found among such writers as Roland Barthes, Stanley Fish, and Louis Marin. In their very different ways, they illuminate within literature those inner tensions between form as meaning and content as meaning, which cause language on the communication axis actually to subvert the significance of its own referential, semantic content.[71]

It is the philosopher Jacques Derrida, however, who has brought out the implications of this approach to language the most profoundly. Derrida locates his project within the cultural movement which is bringing the era of the sign to an end, and initiating the era of writing. During the era of the sign, writing was seen only as a technical instrumentality in the service of meaning (the signifieds) to which it referred. Now, however, "writing," understood as the "signifier of the signifier," has come to be seen as that unique word where the signified is collapsed into the signifier – a kind of "black hole" in the linguistic cosmos which pulls all meanings into itself, and allows *none* to escape. The displacement of the system of language by "writing" as the center of the verbal process leads thus "to destroying the concept of the 'sign' and its entire logic."[72] This then gives rise to Derrida's project of "deconstructing" the idea of the sign.

For Derrida, the understanding of language as a differential system, in the terms of Saussure and the western philosophical tradition, has always presupposed a metaphysical basis, a full present reality beyond the system itself. Medina referred to this as the subordination of reflective thought to the object of thought in Platonic philosophy, where the end was not so much knowledge but union through insight with perfect being. It is the possibility of the presence of perfect being, or truth in consciousness beyond the signifying process, that serves as the basis of divisions between the flesh and spirit, the signifier and signified. The mental or spiritual side of this dichotomy always thus approximates an identity with the transcendent object, the absolutely real existing in an eternal present apart from time. Derrida formulates the problem in these terms:

> The *signatum* always referred, as to its referent, to a *res*, to an entity created or at any rate first thought and spoken, thinkable and speakable, in the eternal present of the divine logos and specifically its breath. If it came to relate to the speech of a finite being (created or not; in any case of an intracosmic entity) through the *intermediary* of a *signans*, the *signatum* had an *immediate* relationship with the divine logos which thought it within presence and for which it was not a trace.[73]

Against this "onto-theo-teleological" presupposition of western thought which assumes a completed totality of being – a closed horizon of the signifying process, which excludes the material realm – he poses the "trace," or "graphie," or "mark," that is, that "differ*a*nce" (neographism) which permits this dichotomy to occur. As such, however, it stands beyond existence and nonexistence, and dichotomies of presence and absence or fullness and emptiness. Temporally considered, it approximates the reality of death in its bearing upon life: "It marks the *dead time* within the presence of the living present with the general form of all presence."[74]

In terms of space, he locates it in connection with the objective spacing that occurs in the inscription of words. Thus for him writing does not imply a subject writing, but rather, "spacing as writing is the becoming absent, and the becoming-unconscious of the subject."[75] Since writing explicitly constitutes this "becoming absent" of the subject, the sign loses its expressive dimension and becomes its opposite: the nothing which is not the contrary of the awareness of something, but the material negation of something, which the subject "knows" only in death.

Thus he can say that the becoming absent of the subject is the subject's relationship to its own death: "this becoming is the constitution of subjectivity."[76] Writing thus (he considers all signification as "*a priori* written," due to the differential system upon which it depends, but which is only made explicit in writing), rather than signifying presence, is always "of testamentary essence."[77]

Apart from the anti-metaphysical polemic which runs through this project, the collapse of the signified into the signifier he speaks of corresponds to Shklovsky's understanding of the distinctive characteristic of the artistic experience as the perception of the form as the content. It is not surprising then that Derrida makes liberal use of neologisms and various other poetic and graphic devices which have the effect of heightening the reader's awareness of the form of language. In other words Derrida relies upon what the early formalists would have called devices of defamiliarization. At the level of the semantic content of his utterance, however, he denies any such subjective, perceptual purpose because the concept of consciousness as self-presence is itself being repudiated.

I would thus see Derrida's work as a philosopher's radical attempt to break through the "automatisms" of conceptual language inherited from classical philosophy so as to bring the material form of language into the center of reflection. He thus moves philosophy toward literature and begins to break down the division between philosophic writing and poetic writing. Such a project can be understood as a continuation of the impulse to elevate the importance of the material form of language which arose in early Russian formalism, though one which seems to turn back upon itself to reject the very perception that spawned it. The central problem is the absence of an intermediate category between absolute presence and its negation. But no one has posed more forcefully the tensions between intersubjectivity and the objective orientation of western thought and so radicalized those tensions that all of the assumptions which support them are placed into question. To go beyond the negations with which we are left by Derrida it will be necessary to develop a new understanding of the sign which clearly rejects that of Saussure but does not lead to the absolute negation of presence. Such a new possibility emerges from the writings of Edmond Ortigues to be discussed in the next chapter.

In conclusion, I have attempted to show how narrative theories which privilege the synchronic semantic content over the diachronic event-character of language cannot deal adequately with narrative phenomena such as the divine Voice of Genesis 1:3, the meaning of which stems largely from the effect of its utterance. The linguists and philosophers I have discussed have made significant contributions in recent years to finding ways to provide a more adequate understanding the event-character of language as a basis for linguistics as well as philosophical thought. This has resulted in a critique on many levels of the western philosophical objectification of consciousness as the cause of the semantic privileging of the synchronic over the diachronic.

It has also brought the recognition of the importance of the role of language in the formation of human consciousness, and of the fundamental status of language-based intersubjectivity. These critiques have thus made possible an approach to language which may provide the basis for a theory of narrative which will not be shaped by the dichotomies of classical thought, and which will be able to account more adequately for the important role of language events in the creation and structuring of narrative. Before this narrative theory can be formulated, however, an understanding of the sign which can bring together force and meaning is needed to serve as its foundation. For that I turn to Edmond Ortigues.

2
The functions of the sign

Medina's displacement of ontology (philosophy of being) by narratology (biographical reason) as the primary basis of reflective thought is a decisively important step toward a position from which we can understand the significance of the statement at the beginning of the Biblical story: "and he said, 'Let there be light'." This seminal utterance incorporates nature from its beginning within a narrative horizon, and thus subordinates the material facticity of nature to an act of progressive reflection embodied in an illocutionary statement. The implications (ideological, epistemological) of this cannot be seen clearly until a broader theory of sign and symbol has been developed which shows the basis of illocutionary force in the function of the language in the subject. It is here as well that we will find the roots of the experience of defamiliarization.

The foundation of the story form, according to Medina, lies in the symbolic function of language – the Communicating-with-Someone – which is simultaneously the basis of the individual reflective consciousness and the possibility of transcending that boundary into the consciousness of another. Medina's view of the symbolic function of language owes much to a theory of performative speech developed by the philosopher Edmond Ortigues in his book *Le Discours et le symbole*,[1] and this seminally important philosophy of language must now be examined.

Whereas Medina, in order to gain an understanding of "biographical reason" as a type of non-formal reflection, focuses upon the form which reflection assumes in major western philosophies, Ortigues' concern is to show the source of these reflective processes in the sign and the sentence. His analysis is thus directed toward approximately the same range of verbal phenomena as linguistics. It is here then that we can return to the question of the relation of illocutionary force and meaning in the sentence.

Medina, in his understanding of regressive and progressive movements of reflection as resulting from biographically rooted communicative events which give consciousness a narrative form, has moved far toward a theory which unites meaning with illocutionary force. But because he is speaking in terms of the process of reflection in general, the precise way in which language shapes consciousness and embodies the force of events is not made clear. Early formalism contributed to a more precise understanding of the role of language in achieving the poetic effect, but, lacking an understanding of the sign which incorporated the subject, moved toward an objective view of linguistic form. It is this need for an understanding of the sign which includes the subject that Ortigues' view of the operation of regressive and progressive thought in the sentence will fill. Medina, by showing the limitations of formal reflection in western philosophy, provides an important context for understanding the far-reaching significance of Ortigues' analysis of language.

Ortigues, at the outset, draws a firm line of distinction between his approach to the problems of signification and that of Saussure and the formalist tradition. He accuses structural linguistics of committing what Aristotle calls the "petition of principle" (or less formally, "begging the question"), that is, considering something as known for itself when it is in fact known by means of another.[2] The petition of principle also takes the form of the infinite regression or the vicious circle.

An example of how linguistics has committed the error of begging the question is seen in the attempt to isolate the phoneme as a primary unit of language more fundamental than the morpheme, and to describe its operation as being entirely independent of semantic processes. Language could then be explained as a product of strictly formal, relational processes stemming from the differential system which produced the phonemic entities. A vicious circle arises from the fact that the phonemes are able to be divided, delimited and defined only within the morphemes and syntagms which do possess meaning. Thus, he says, "one has begun by defining the phonemes as distinctive values capable of producing oppositions of meaning between words; then one relies on the distribution of phonemes in order to define the assemblages which are endowed with meaning, which evidently implies a vicious circle."[3]

By excluding the role played by the semantic context in the very recognition of the morphemes of which the phonemes are component parts, and then extending the same formal method from phonemes to the morphemes and syntagms themselves, it is possible to develop a purely formal method. But because the phonemes themselves are recognizable as units only because of their presence in the context of meaningful discourse, by treating phonemes and their combinations as if they were entities which could be analyzed apart from this context of meaning, structural linguistics commits the error of begging the question; that is, it considers these formal elements as known for themselves when they are in fact known by means of another which remains unexamined, namely, the semantic context of the word and sentence. Ortigues thus is turning away from the regressive, analytic approach to language, in order to conceive language from the perspective of progressive reflection. This achieves a synthesis between the discrete elements and the signifying end toward which the verbal process moves.

Taking the sentence as his basic verbal horizon, Ortigues sees the sentence as a manifestation of both regressive-analytic and progressive-synthetic thought. Analytic thought is manifest through the discrete terms – through the signs which constitute the material units of the sentence. The sign cannot be understood merely in the Saussurian fashion as a union of signifier and signified. To analyze the sign only in terms of its objective components neglects the question of the conditions in consciousness which the operation of the sign presupposes. Only by posing this problem can one hope to avoid begging the question.

The chief condition which the operation of the sign presupposes is the absence of the thing, or referential object. In contemporary cybernetics, the binary signifying system is based upon the possibility of the absence of information or "Hartley" – the 0/1 pair – as the primary pair.[4] The terms do not acquire signifying capacity except within the context of the absence of all objects. This makes possible the signifying or representation function of language.

Communication with signs is often described from an objectivist viewpoint as being like a tennis game, the balls constituting the message which each partner is sending to the other. This type of description is guilty of begging the question because it is assumed that a situation exists prior to the intervention of language when, in fact, language is the basic constituent of every communicative situation: "The situation completes its formation and meaning only across language ... and inversely the words pronounced take their entire signification only if one takes into account the situation in which they have been pronounced."[5]

If communication is to be compared to a game, it would be more appropriate to compare it to a game in which there is a board with empty channels down which pieces must slide in a certain order. The board with its channels he compares to the system of linguistic forms which provide the relational order of the signs, which are comparable to the pieces. The emptiness of the channels he compares to consciousness which becomes the field of possibilities that always transcends the particular things denoted by the sign: "and it is only across these possibilities which concern us that our presence to the world tends to realize itself, accomplish itself, following a logic which is veritably the logic of the whole."[6]

Thus he grounds the form of language finally in the dialectic of the full and the empty which operates in and constitutes the self-reflective consciousness: "It is absolutely necessary that 'this which permits the beginning of the game' not be a full reality but a kind of double unity as the alternance of the full and empty, of the positive and negative, as the minimum of information or Hartley of cyberneticians or as this that has always been called the 'human inquietude'."[7] It is this double possibility at the beginning of language which empiricism of all kinds lacks, assuming instead "a positive sign, one full of reality, in this which was basically only a double possibility of the full and the empty."[8]

The function of the sign in the receptive emptiness of consciousness is not a given natural capacity. Human beings born and reared outside the human community do not exhibit this mode of consciousness. The consciousness of the infant manifests a primal continuity with the world of objects to which it relates in the mode of desire. The infant reaches out to the world and wants it all. This is what Julia Kristeva terms the semiotic "chora" – the pre-linguistic matrix of consciousness.[9] Language can come to be installed in the consciousness only by the disruption of the primal continuity through the blockage of desire for the thing. A limit must be placed upon this all-encompassing desire. As Ortigues says, "language is not able to incite thought without putting into suspense the immediate satisfaction of desire;"[10] and again, "the sign obliges us to sacrifice the immediate pleasure of the thing, the animal innocence."[11]

The operation of language can thus not be properly understood apart from the dramatic trauma with which it is acquired. The way in which this initiation into language occurs can be variously described. Ortigues follows Claude Lévi-Strauss in attributing this to the installation of the child in the system of marital exchange which begins with the prohibition against incest.[12] Regardless of what dramatic outer form this installation may take, however, the essential inner event is the subjection of the child to a prohibition which disrupts the desire-driven continuity of consciousness with the world of objects. It is only through the encounter with the other that the infantile narcissism which does not distinguish self and world is interrupted, and the self is experienced as an individual sign; that is, as an "I" which simultaneously sees itself related to a "you." Through the intervention of this third party into the unbroken self–world unity, not only is the world of personal, I–you relations opened, but also the possibility of speaking of the universe of "things of which one speaks"[13] – the world of the grammatical third person.

These grammatical relations lead beyond the sign, strictly speaking, to the symbolic structures which govern the relations between signs. Before looking at the symbolic realm, we must first examine the expressive function of the sign which operates upon the basis of the division in consciousness we have now observed.

The installation of the sign in consciousness makes possible the expressive function of language.[14] When the sign comes to be used, then one can speak in terms of both a self and its expressions, since it is through the sign that self-expression occurs. The self does not exist prior to its expression, however, since it is in the act of expression that the division, self versus expression, is realized. Ortigues can thus say that: "Expression is then an act which is in itself its own result."[15] And the reverse is also true: "that every act which is in itself its own result is by the same fact expressive."[16] The sign thus becomes a place of passage from interiority to exteriority, and from exteriority to interiority.

In the expressive act, the sign is thus bound together with that which is heterogeneous to language. Unlike objects, expression implies immediate causality since it must always be the expression of someone. From this comes its formal function of individuation.[17] Objects are situated within the horizon of relations with other objects, in a system. The expression, though existing in a similar network of relations, also implies an immanent genesis since it "adheres to the living reality of which it is the actual manifestation."[18]

In the expressive act the self identifies itself with an external phenomenon (words, gestures) and thus experiences itself as divided between exterior and interior: "to exteriorize oneself consists exactly in differentiating oneself interiorly, to render possible the explicit recognition of oneself as psychological individuality."[19] Self-reflection thus presupposes the redoubling of the subject which is made possible by the division between interiority and exteriority of the subject.

This encounter by the self with itself in its expression is not solipsistic (as Derrida argues it is) since the sign is a social, intersubjective phenomenon. The reverse passage from the exterior expression back to the interior consciousness is simultaneously a response to encounter with other selves: "each consciousness returns to itself in the center of a relation to other consciousnesses where each renders perceptible to the other its own operation."[20]

It is in the form of language that subjective consciousness encounters the social order of which it is a part. Each language concretely reflects the historic particularities of its own collective life in the idiosyncratic forms which have been given to its language.

The sign in the expressive act serves as the basis of the analytic conception of truth. Thought becomes individuated in the act of expression, and through analysis, thought can establish the relations of identity and difference between separate expressions. It is the establishment of such relations of identity and difference that analytic reflection seeks. The truth thus is conceived in terms of these relations which analysis establishes. A problem arises with this understanding of truth, however, if it is applied not only to physical objects and processes, but also to phenomena which manifest an immanent genesis, that is, to other expressions. This form of truth proposes that behind objective expressions, statements with their "accidental" features, there exist relations of identity, "substances" recoverable by analytic thought, though existing apart from such thought. But the theoretical substance which analytic thought finds beneath the appearance of things is fundamentally only an analytic expression, and the unchanging truth which seems to be implied by the semantic identity of the two expressions really implies the common internal determination which all expressions have. Rather than leading to universal objects of thought, analysis should thus lead into the linguistic and social process by which speaking subjects achieve identity between discrete expressions. This leads directly to the problem of the incorporation of signs into sentences which serve to establish such relations by means of subject–predicate relations.

At this juncture, however, it is important to note that Ortigues has developed an understanding of the sign which binds the processes and passions of subjective consciousness to language at its very basis. Language understood from this viewpoint does not exist as a neutral objective system to which a heterogeneous force factor can be added as a separable component to achieve certain illocutionary effects. The sign is established in consciousness from the outset by means of a process fraught with negativity and evocative of deep passions. Language is thus always enveloped by a modality stemming from this primary drama. What Austin termed illocutionary force stems from this primary process.

But for illocutionary force to be shown as a factor in all language acts, and not only those which have linguistic markers or are governed by established conventions, requires that the objective–analytic approach to language used by Austin and Searle be supplemented by a progressive synthetic view of language that acknowledges its inseparable relations with the heterogeneous dimension of subjective consciousness at its very foundations. It is this which Ortigues has succeeded in doing with his view of the sign.

The concept of illocutionary force can thus be broadened to refer to the effect of the operation of the sign itself within the context of the expressive act. The act of expression is itself a constitutive event for the speaker. It not only expresses semantic content but establishes a polarity in consciousness between the interiority of thought and the exteriority of language which makes possible self-reflection (self-transcendence). By constituting the conditions for the relation of thought to itself, of the expressing to the expressed, the expressive act already assumes a performative function. It is through the reaction of consciousness *upon* language by means of grammatical form, style, conventions, etc., that the force is "added" to language, and that the self-consciousness of the speaker and community is "added" to the semantic content of the words. Force stems precisely from this interplay between consciousness and language and is the manifestation of the fundamental tension between language and consciousness that is at the root of all language. This will be made clearer below in Ortigues' explication of the contractual foundations of language.

In addition to expression, a second functional component of discourse is meaning (*sens*). This includes the representative function of the sign which Ortigues views in the context of the sentence. The sentence constitutes the form in which the regressive and progressive modes of reflection may occur simultaneously. Medina has shown how, in the thought of Hegel, it was the insight into the simultaneously regressive and progressive modes of reflection that illuminated the historicality of the self. Ortigues now shows the grounds of that mode of reflection in the sign and the sentence. The sign, as we have seen, presupposes the absence of the thing that is represented. It thus reflects the regressive analytic recovery of the missing object by the establishment of a relation between the signifier and signified. The sign thus constitutes the empty present where the missing (past) object may be signified in consciousness. But it not only recovers that which is no longer present (i.e., in the past), but also proposes that which will be again present (i.e., in the future). The representation made by the sign to the recipient is expected to correspond in the future to that which it purports to represent. The sign thus acquires the function of a promise. As Ortigues says, this double movement of consciousness is why "meaning is not only the 'representation' (which in itself, is the abstraction, the '*decoupage*' of the real), but it is the future of the representation; it is the representation as a promise of effective presence in veritable reality."[21]

The teleological goal of the sign endows the progressive mode of reflection with direction and thus transforms the signifier from a sign of absence to a promise of presence. As a promise of presence, however, it does not represent absolute presence. Presence here is always mediated by the subject and is thereby relative.

Here we see that this view of the sign has a place for the positive inclusion of the subjectivity of the speaker into the meaning-producing process, since, as Ortigues points out: "The *representation* of objects as being such or such is possible only on the basis of responsible *presence* of man in the world."[22] While the signifier may communicate its signified on the basis of a language system taken from the past, the relation of the signified to the object of representation rests upon a speaker's assuming responsibility for the continuation of that system into the future. This may be the underlying reason for Umberto Eco's definition of semiotics as "*the discipline studying everything which can be used in order to lie*" (his emphasis).[23] Ortigues can thus describe signification as the "becoming true of reality."[24]

What Austin says of the promise, then, holds true of the sign: "'I promise to ...' obliges me – puts on record my spiritual assumption of a spiritual shackle."[25]

Not only is there subjective uncertainty regarding the relation of the sign and its referent in progressive reflection, but in the regressive recovery of the absent object from the past, there is a parallel, though not as obvious an uncertainty. The aleatory decision which governs both the use of the sign and its creation goes more deeply than the arbitrary relation between signifier and signified described by Saussure. What determines which of the plentitude of objects and ideas attains signification? Ortigues speaks in this regard of the sign's mysterious elective contingency: "This which the sign proposes to us as the coming of light is the same that it presupposes as the past of darkness without name, from which it is torn away by a mysterious elective contingency. Who has chosen it?"[26] But the "who" of this question leads only to another sign of equally mysterious elective contingency: "I." With this the subjective roots of the semiotic process are fully disclosed. Ortigues summarizes the sign and its subjective dilemma in this way: "The sign is this elective contingency following which is effectuated the dehiscence of a present, here and now, where man takes consciousness of himself as an enigma to which things are problems."[27]

The individual sign *per se* is not capable of achieving signification apart from a discursive context, that is, apart from the sentence. In fact, in Ortigues' view, "it is in constructing a sentence that thought gives itself the means of distinguishing analytically the terms that it puts in relation by a continuous transition. The analytic individuality of each term (the possibility for it to be repeated, identified) is relative to its function in the integrating unity of discourse progressing toward its achieved expression."[28] So, the regressive analytic character of the sign is complemented by the progressive synthetic character of the sentence. The meaning of the sign thus must await the completion of the sentence. An interminable discourse would finally have no meaning (or at least a meaning which remains undecidable).

The promissory character of the sign is related to the third component of discourse, form, and to the symbolic function of language which serves as the basis of form. The symbolic function is related to two different types of formal structures. The presence of the signs in sentences already manifests the differential, lexical system of which every sign is a part. Each sign is present there because of its selection, and the exclusion of another sign. But such a differential system operates on the basis of the logical principle of oppositions which is devoid of specific referential content. This system of empty formal opposition is grounded upon the phonemes which introduce the possibility of distinctive oppositions, alternatives, choice, etc.[29] This system of oppositions does not function independently of a discursive context, however, and depends for its final meaning upon that context.

At the level of the morpheme, the syntagmatic forms of sentence grammar, which take the morphemes up into a hierarchy of symbolic functions, come into effect. Just as the sign functions by means of exclusion, the symbolic form functions as a process of inclusion, as each level in the hierarchy includes the level inferior to it and is, in turn, included by that which is superior to it, as phonemes are included in morphemes and morphemes in sentences.[30] This hierarchical process of inclusion does not occur apart from time, but rather is itself a diachronic movement equivalent to the movement of the sentence toward its completion. Thus, like Coseriu, Ortigues is critical of the absolute distinction made by Saussure between synchrony and diachrony. This distinction rests upon time as pure succession and synchronic logic as totally atemporal. Between these two extremes, he argues for a logical function of time: "a succession which is no longer real but ideal, a succession of levels defined by degrees of synthetic extension such that each structural moment shows itself at the same time integrating with regard to this which *precedes* and integrated in this which *follows* it."[31] Here one finds in the operation of the form of the sentence the same synthesis of regressive and progressive thought that was characteristic of the sign, and of historical consciousness itself.

Ortigues can thus describe language as a dynamic process possessing centrifugal and centripetal forces. The expressive sign represents the power of language turned outward to the world of objects distributing itself as a multiplicity of different elements. But this diffusion of language is balanced by the centripetal power of symbolic forms which establish a relation of language to itself. In this way the formal conventions are created by means of which the relations of signs to their referents is guaranteed, and the possibility of signifying relations between signs is established. Thus he says that: "The sign proposes a sense and presupposes a language. The symbol belongs to the genesis of this presupposition itself."[32]

He explains the primary meaning of symbols by referring to the practice by covenantal parties in the ancient world of breaking a tile (*tessera*), each party keeping one half and passing it down to their descendents. Mutual recognition of the allied parties could then be achieved later by fitting together the complementary parts into a whole: "The *sum bolon* consists then of the correlation between elements which have no value when isolated, but the reunion (*sum-ballô*) or reciprocal adjustment of which permits the two allies to recognize themselves as such, i.e., as tied between themselves (*sum-ballontes*, contractants)."[33] Whereas the sign is "a union of signifier and signified ... the symbol is operator of a relation between a signifier and other signifiers."[34] The "principle" of symbolism is thus "mutual liaison between distinctive elements whose combination is significative." The "effect" of symbolism is "mutual liaison between subjects which recognize themselves engaged, one in regard to the other in a pact, an alliance (divine or human), a convention, a law of fidelity."[35]

Instead of the unity of discourse being established upon the basis of a theoretical "substance" discovered by analytic thought, that is, unity at the level of concepts, or mental objects, it is finally grounded upon the self-reflective conventions of language which are guaranteed only by the responsible self-presence of human beings in the world. Responsible self-presence cannot be equated with the metaphysical presence Derrida attacks, however, since it is created by and contingent upon linguistic forms.[36]

Symbols fall into two major classes for Ortigues: traditional or primary symbols, and logico-mathematical or secondary symbols.[37] The logico-mathematical symbolism, which can manifest itself purely as an algorithm, is considered secondary because it is delocutionary: "It does not speak without the intermediary of a traditional language."[38] Moreover, it is a form of writing and pronunciation of characters which "presuppose before them the usage of discourse."

Traditional symbolism, on the other hand, is "the productive *source* of the possibilities of all convention, of all formative liaison of properly human societies."[39] It is the foundation of allocutive discourse. The traditional symbolism fundamentally differs from logico-mathematical symbolism in that it is inseparably connected with a material manifestation (though not reducible to it) while at the same time exhibiting an internal differential order. Ortigues divides traditional symbols into three categories which illustrate these internal tensions.

The first is the view of the symbol which he acknowledges to be the most widely accepted: "visual configurations such as emblems or fetishes."[40] This form of symbolism is linked to the psychology of the imaginary, that is, the tendency of objects to become the focal point of desire. The self projects itself into another object and falls into narcissistic fascination with this object. Ortigues calls this the "phantasmic redoubling of the consciousness in desire."[41]

The second is the symbolism which takes a social form: institutions, titled hierarchies, and so forth. This kind of symbolism embodies a system of lateral, differential relations by means of which social roles and identities may be fixed before being recognized in discourse. Distinctions of truth and falsity may be made within this differential system.

The third type of traditional symbol is found midway between these two extremes. Here, "the symbolic function is inseparable from discourse to the extent that it always implies imperatives, social rules, prohibitions, promises, and beliefs or adherences."[42] The first type he calls "symbolism of the image," and the second the "symbolism of the rule."[43] Each hides the relation which it presupposes. The material content of the symbolic image "dissimulates the intention or the system of references which makes it appear invested with this or that quality,"[44] while the symbol of the rule conceals the relations which it presupposes beneath its truth claims.

It is only the third type of symbol that discloses the full complexity of the symbolic function of language. In promissory, covenantal language both the symbolic image and rule are held in tension within the context of the intersubjective relations that are fundamental for society. Ortigues thus believes that "the essence of the symbolic function must be sought on the side of a homology between the social fact and the linguistic fact in an intermediate zone between the psychology of the imaginary and the truth of the concept."[45] He turns away from the approach of individualistic psychology, which centers upon the symbolic image and, on the other side, wants to avoid interpreting symbols in terms of society, which is itself a problematic concept. Instead he believes there is a matrix between these two extremes where language and society intersect and generate the symbolic consciousness which is the basis of the entire historic project of humankind.

This mediating language of promises and covenants or forms which function to enable consciousness through language to take language as its own object is thus the place of meeting between the individual and society, where the forms undergirding the social order are at the same time the embodiment of and foundation of the self-reflective capacities of the individual. Here we approach the linguistic basis of the experience of form described by the early formalists as "defamiliarization."

In order for language to take itself as its own object, there must exist, in language, signifiers whose function is to embody this self-reflective capacity, that is, signifiers which cannot be related to an object or idea, but only to their own occurrence as signifiers. One type of signifier which manifests this capacity is the pronoun, particularly the "I". These signifiers represent the capacity of language to conceive language itself as a signifying form. But since such a signifier would have no referent beyond itself it can only exist by virtue of the total absence of the object referent. Thus it can exist only when the inaugural continuity between human consciousness and the objects of the world is ruptured. But this signifier, which is so fundamentally detached from a material referent, will become a problem unto itself, since it will have the capacity to raise the question of its own identity but can answer it neither in normal referential terms, nor in purely formal terms. Existing by virtue of the absence of a referential object, it is nevertheless an individuating material occurrence which cannot be reduced to purely formal relations. "Who am I?" thus remains an enigmatic question for logic and empiricism, as well as philosophy and psychology. Ortigues seeks the answer to the question in discursive terms which mediate between the formal and empirical.

There is a theoretical continuity between Ortigues' analysis of the "I" and the literary experience of defamiliarization. When the "I" is treated as an object, our awareness of ourselves as subjects is dulled as the "I" becomes absorbed into a field of objects. We come to understand ourselves in terms of necessary logical and material relations with other objects. But when we focus upon the form of the "I" as a sign which occurs as an instance of discourse made possible by the absence of the thing, the "I" becomes defamiliarized in that it appears now as an uncanny mystery precariously freed from the objectivizing systems of thought, loosed to make its way upon the contingent flow of discourse.

The defamiliarizing effect of literary devices studied by Shklovsky serve a similar function by removing familiar objects and notions from the objectified network of relations into which they have fallen, so that they may be again experienced as new forms surrounded by the enigma and mystery of their uniqueness. What is being partially renewed in such literature is actually the consciousness of the self which becomes objectified along with its perceptions of the world. Ortigues thus shows the roots of this experience of enigma in the linguistic and discursive character of the "I".

To be established as an "I" in discourse requires that all of the characteristics of the sign now become characteristics of the self. Just as the sign was both an individuating event and an opening to the universe of possibility, so now the "I" serves to individuate the speaker while opening the world of representations. Just as the discursive meaning of the sign arose from the formal end – the potentiality of imposing upon this sphere of possibility a limitation, a predication, a point of view – so too the meaning of the "I" is a function of the global end of discourse itself. The "I" as a sign with no object referent discloses its own identity in the process of expression by which it manifests its presence to itself in terms of the formal object or the global end of discourse. Because of the rupture between the symbolic and material spheres that the sign requires, the global end of discourse must be that which *guarantees* the identity between the formal and material objects of discourse, the predicate and the subject. The ultimate end of discourse of the "I" which manifests its own self-presence must then be the truth: "What then is this personal presence ...? It is that the person affirms himself present *by reference to the end of discourse*, to the constitutive intention of the word, and is able to recognize himself in the coherence of his becoming only by the achievement of his discourse in the truth 'index *sui* and *falsi*'."[46] But, in light of Derrida's critique of the metaphysics of presence, it is important to see clearly that for Ortigues this form of self-presence, this "I" "is not the expression of a state of consciousness (of a state of fact which is able to be evoked in the retrospective 'myself'). The *I* is neither a record, nor a fact, nor an idea, nor the result of an ascertainment, nor the object of a concept. It marks the autoposition of the being who speaks ... With it language attests itself as such."[47]

This is accomplished by a discursive form which permits the "I" not merely to take itself as the "material" object of a verb (as in the passive voice), but to utter a verb whose utterance constitutes an expressive act in which the subject assumes the social conventions of language as her/his own. Following the study of pronouns by the French linguist, Emile Benveniste, Ortigues points out that every occurrence of "I" does not involve the semantic actualization of this self-presence. Some occurrences serve as merely description ("I suffer"); others signify a logical operation of thought ("I conclude"). In the latter group the act of speaking coincides with the realization of the content of the verb. To say, "I conclude" effects a conclusion. But there is still here a separation between the word and the thought: "The word here attempts to express an operation effectuated in thought."[48]

But there is another category of first-person utterances in which the verb signifies an action which is entirely accomplished by the utterance itself. These are expressions such as "I promise," "I judge," "I certify," "I guarantee." Since the "I" is a sign that exists only by virtue of the absence of an objective determination of consciousness, and can achieve presence to itself only by reference to the end or formal object of its discourse, then this type of statement offers the highest degree of subjective self-presence since the formal object of the predicate coincides completely with the material object. Since the material object, in this case the "I," is a sign with no content beyond its own act of utterance, it achieves presence to itself through these expressions whose signification is also inseparable from their utterance. If meaning is produced by the synthetic function which concludes the statement by bringing the formal object or qualification (predicate) into some relation of positive or negative correspondence with the material object (subject), then the meaning of the "I" is to be found in this type of statement, in which both the subject and predicate correspond or are identical as acts of speech. This is to say that the meaning of the "I" is to be found in the discursive achievement of presence to itself. But because it is a discursive achievement, it can never be permanent or absolute. Rather, it is a possibility to be continually actualized (though never absolutely) in each new discourse.

Here Ortigues is dealing with performative speech which was to be explored two years later from an English analytic viewpoint by Austin in *How to do Things with Words*, and still later in John R. Searle's book, *Speech Acts* (1969). Ortigues moves in the opposite direction from Austin and Searle, however. As we have seen they sought to ground the performative effect of this type of language upon contextual rules (rather than self-reflectivity – see Michael Hancher),[49] and extend the scope of performative language through an analysis of the contextual assumptions reducible to abstract rules. Ortigues, instead, has located the foundations of self-reflectivity in the symbolic function of language, and has shown how the symbolic function is the most clearly realized in the classical speech acts. The illocutionary dimension of language is thereby shown to depend not upon contextual rules, but upon the very foundation of language in consciousness – consciousness in language.

This achievement by the "I" of self-presence through discourse is not made in solitude of what Derrida calls "pure auto-affection."[50] Such discursive utterances are allocutionary acts which qualify formal relations of the language and values of the community and establish a formal relation of the speaker to the addressee and to the community. Thus Ortigues can say: "The oath or the pact is the act by which the person who speaks takes into his account the social function of language and is given it as his own law, the law of veridicity and of reciprocity. The oath or the pact is an act of speech which becomes for itself its own material, its proper object, and by that constitutes the fundamental law by which a person ties himself to other persons."[51]

But the question of human identity is not resolved so directly due to the problematic role of the image in the imagination. Though the symbolic forms of the oath, pact, etc., function as mediators between the image and the sign, stability is not achieved because: "It seems in effect that the formal play of symbolic relations conceals a secret violence, a conflict of contraries."[52] The conflict is between the tendency of the image to obscure or hide the relations which it assumes and the characteristic of the sign to manifest itself as a relation between terms. It is characteristic of the imagination to conjure up the immediate presence of the idea of the thing. But in the manifestation of the image in consciousness, the imagination itself is concealed. This produces a contradiction:

> each image taken itself is a *cul-de-sac*, a materialisation, a thingification where the term hides the relation, or where the subjective intention is dissimulated to itself by the quality of this which appears ... The imagination is a faculty which contradicts itself for it produces its own content but loses itself in this content.[53]

The tension between the image and the sign is rooted in the difference between the visual and auditory sense perception. The visual sense presents to consciousness a specular image which has a quality of immediacy. But the imagination which receives the specular image exists by virtue of the sacrifice of the immediate presence of the object. This emptiness which makes possible the imagination thus exists in relation to objects in the mode of desire. Ortigues can thus say: "The imagination is the form of desire."[54]

Because the sign has fundamentally ruptured the continuity between a subject's consciousness and its objective existence, so that it is installed as an "I" in the symbolic realm (a sign which must displace its objective referent), the specular images offer the possibility of filling this absence with an immediate presence, an absolute presence. In this relation the self is seeking the immediacy of its own presence in the other, the specular image. The unmediated image exercises a narcissistic fascination over the consciousness and it finds itself absorbed into a material form. This dual relation does not admit the self-reflective consciousness. It is a *cul-de-sac* which absorbs the subject into its material form without permitting the distinction between the image and the relation of the subject to it.

This dual relation can be interrupted only by a third term – the concept, the "things of which one speaks."[55] Through the concept, conscious reversible relations can be established between objects, and the closure of the dual relation broken open.

But even then the problem is not solved. In Ortigues' view: "The problem posed by the distinction between specular relation and mediate relation is inherent in all human communication. For men see themselves and speak themselves."[56] The attention given the objects, ideas, and actions offered as possibilities to consciousness postulates an immediate relation of the consciousness to those objects. The quest for the unmediated object, the absolute presence, may thus continue, though modified, in discourse. Such pursuit of unmediated presence, of absorption into the objects of reference, accounts for some forms of the experience of automatism in literature when the form is displaced by its references. Desire perpetuates an inner disquiet in its search for the unmediated presence even in discourse. Because "desire has the form of the imagination which is the thought of absence in the present,"[57] it involves itself continually in a conflict of contraries, a hidden violence, in the signifying process.

It is in the quest for self-knowledge that this inner tension in signification is the most important. Here Ortigues turns to Augustine who was the first to articulate the dilemma of self-identification. Paraphrasing Augustine he writes: "The consciousness which 'desires' to know itself is at the same time present and absent to itself."[58] It must be present in the instant when it seeks itself, yet it must ignore itself in that very instant.

The dilemma of self-knowledge is made acute because the self has gained access to the possibility of self-signification only by the displacement of the self as an object by the sign (the family name, the "I"). The desire for self-knowledge is thus an objectless desire. Again this essential insight was already present in the writings of Augustine; he says that "know yourself" does not mean look at your face. "It is not said to man 'look at your face', which is only possible in a mirror. For our face itself is absent from our sight since it is not there where vision can be directed."[59]

He notes that Hegel in the *Phenomenology of Spirit* places this same insight in the center of his dialectic and brings to light what is in fact the appropriate way of conceiving the identity of an objectless subject: "Life awakens itself to consciousness in desire, a desire without object; no object is able to suffice ... since this for which it searches is consciousness of itself."[60]

Again Ortigues finds exactly this insight in Augustine: "But when he says to the spirit 'know yourself', for *the fact alone that he comprehends this which is said*, i.e., 'yourself', he knows himself, and that for no other reason if not from the fact of a presence to himself."[61] But for Augustine this presence to himself is engendered by the presence of God mediated through the concept (*verbum, intelligentia*), the past (*memoria*), and the future (*voluntas*), which provide a meaning to time.[62]

Ortigues sees this, however, as "the proper function of language" which has been made theological too quickly.[63] Self-presence is not self-generated, however, or generated simply by language *per se*. Just as self-knowledge cannot be satisfied by knowing the objective form of the person as a living being, it also cannot be satisfied by a concept or sign which displaces that objective reality: "Living subjectivity asks for a sign, but the sign of life is not properly life, the sign is necessarily of another order than this that it signifies."[64]

Thus self-consciousness "is able to accomplish itself only if [it] is referred to itself by another consciousness of itself."[65] It is here that mutual recognition between subjects plays a central role not only in the achievement of self-identity, but in the entire linguistic process. Already it has been shown that the signification process depends not only upon the relation between signifier and signified, but also upon the lateral, differential relations between signifiers. It is from these lateral relations that linguistic forms as well as values are engendered: "To say that an expression has this or that form is to say that its composition is able to be put into relation with that of other possible expressions possessing a 'same' law of organization."[66]

But the meaning of the form does not derive from the individual act of expression itself any more than the value of a word is bestowed upon it by an individual speaker. Just as values exist by virtue of their mutual recognition by the addressor and addressee, so also do the forms of language function in and through mutual recognition between subjects: "The identification of a form by which the expression recognizes itself as such is effective only in the moment where another expression comes in effect to recognize it, to bring to it the sanction of its response. The form of language constitutes itself by this mutual sanction."[67] Thus he can say that "each distinctive unity, each forming element of expression is a form of communication."[68]

But this communication does not occur within a *given* society. It is through mutual recognition of formal relations that society conceives its own order. The linguistic structure and social structure are homologous and inseparable: "society takes form in the language it gives itself." Language is not only an institutional form as the others which subsists alongside the other institutions ... language is the form of forms."[69] Not to recognize this is to commit the error of begging the question.

At the center of society is thus the process of communication, and at the center of this process is the mutual recognition between subjects of forms that are in principle enshrined in pacts, conventions, etc. Central to this is the mutual recognition by subjects of the other's consciousness of her/himself, a recognition that occurs concretely in the giving and receiving of oaths, promises, etc., that require this recognition to be meaningful. The subject who seeks her/his identity in images of the imagination or in material objects falls victim to an eternal inquietude, the Augustinian restlessness of heart.

The process of mutual recognition between subjects of their own identity as reflective selves thus appears to be the ruling value which supports not only the individual's own true self-understanding, but the entire process of discourse.

Ortigues' view of language opens up new perspectives upon literature, particularly upon Biblical literature, and will serve as one of the chief sources of theoretical insight for the analysis of the Genesis text which will follow. Already some of the implications for his view of Biblical literature can be suggested with regard to the sentence with which we began that initiates the narrative action in Genesis. The utterance, "Let there be light," occurring as it does as the "beginning," outside of all empirical contexts, is meaningless when analyzed in terms of referential or objective content. Ortigues, however, in establishing the foundation of language and consciousness not upon the fullness of an objective reality – an objective being of some sort – but in the dialectic of the full and the empty, provides the theoretical framework within which the significance of a story of a primal word which brings something from nothing (or an unformed chaos) can begin to be understood. This, of course, does not mean that his views can be construed as in any sense "supporting" Genesis 1.

Like the sign whose signifying capacity stems from its occurrence in the emptiness of consciousness caused by the absence of the thing, the meaning of this creative word stems from its occurrence in a primal cosmic "emptiness" prior to the *existence* of all objects. In the same way that an expressive act is its own result, dividing interiority from exteriority, so the divine utterance which brings the world and its order into existence from chaos (or nothing) is a performative act which achieves its result in its utterance, setting up the major divisions of the cosmic system. Just as the progressive movement of the sign toward its teleological goal subordinates to itself the meaning of the objects of reference, so the meaning of the created objects of nature are subordinated to the teleological goal of the creative word.

Though further analysis of Genesis 1 cannot be undertaken here, these are grounds for suggesting at this point that the account of the origin of the cosmic order in this Biblical passage may be understood as a metaphorical[70] transformation and figuration of the fundamental semiotic processes which Ortigues has described. Exactly how this figuration process occurs must await development below, however. One factor profoundly affecting this process is that the direct discourse of the divine Voice appears in the framework of the narrator's discourse, and this context fundamentally affects its meaning, as we have seen above. The distinctive features of the Biblical narrative (for example, in this case, that God speaks in the narrative) can be properly assessed only in light of a general analysis of functions and modes of narrative writing which govern the relation of the characters' discourse to that of the narrator.

More cannot be said until a set of categories has been developed which can serve to link the semiotic insights of Ortigues to this discursive context. Since the fundamental sign functions may achieve figuration in personal speech as the analysis of the pronoun "I" illustrated, they may offer a possible basis for a functional typology of character and plot development.

This problem can best be pursued, however, by analyzing Genesis narratives in which there is not only divine speech but also human speech, since the particular function of the divine speech in the Biblical narrative cannot be clearly seen apart from its place within the triad of narrative voices – those of the narrator, Yahweh Elohim, and the characters. Since Genesis 1 contains only the narratorial and the divine voices, further progress can be made only by engaging in a detailed analysis of other Genesis narratives which contain all three voices. These reflections over Genesis 1 have served the purpose of bringing to light the central importance of direct performative speech and the enclosing narrator's discourse. Detailed analyses of more fully developed Genesis narratives will follow in part 3 after the development of an appropriate narrative theory.

With this we have reached one of the initial goals of this study, namely, to find a theoretical framework which would account for the meaning of the type of primal, performative utterance found in Genesis 1 by illuminating the union of force and meaning in the root functions of the sign. We will now turn to the development of a functional narrative theory which will relate the sign functions to the figuration of characters and plot in narrative writing.

3
A functional definition of narrative

The capacity of the artistic text to bring about the perception of verbal form is the common starting point of the functional approach to literature outlined above. A functional theory of Biblical narrative must be able to relate its compositional features to this functional, experiential, perceptual process and show how the structure of the narrative is organized by the dynamic tensions generated by this process.

The way in which I will seek to accomplish this is first of all by clearly establishing the definition of the narrative text as the union of the narrator's discourse and the character's discourse, and developing the semantic and semiological implications of the effacement of the narrator's instance of speech behind the third-person form of discourse. This will reveal the profound tensions at work between the narrator's discourse and character's discourse, and lead to a typology of narrative styles based upon the possible ways in which this tension affects the stance of the author toward her characters. This typology will be shown to arise from the functions of the sign which shape human consciousness.

Each function also correlates with a modality governing the author's relation to the narrative personages, and produces a certain form of character and plot development which is relative to the experience of form characteristic of that sign function. The particular features of the Genesis narrative will then be identifiable as a configuration of certain functions and modes organized around the perception of signifying forms characteristic of the dominant sign functions. Finally, the typical discursive development of these functions and modes within specific Genesis narratives will be analyzed.

An important methodological assumption should be acknowledged at the outset. I am provisionally assuming that narrative texts constitute a definable body of verbal phenomena which possesses regularly recurring features, and operates in a systematic fashion across the continuum of time. This is not to say that I am assuming that narrative has a transcendent, synchronic structure which exists in an ideal world apart from the changing fluctuations of history. Quite to the contrary, my view is that Coseriu's description of language as a "system in motion" is true also of narrative.

If, as Coseriu says, it is language which, in fact, offers to humans the possibility of freedom to transcend the past, and to create the new, that is, to experience historical subjectivity, then one would particularly expect to find in a narrative which dramatically portrays the human subject a dynamic system which embodies the historicality of human existence. The narrative system can thus embody the distinctive features of particular historical periods and yet possess a unity and continuity within its own operational structures that will enable a narrative originating in one historical period to contribute to a fuller understanding of the narrative system in all of the others.

Because of this continuity within the narrative system, it will thus be possible to use, for example, the narrative system of Dostoyevsky to illuminate certain features of the Biblical narrative, and to allow the semiotic dynamics of the Biblical narrative to deepen our understanding of the unique features of Dostoyevsky as well. The particularity of each text will always be preserved at least by the link which ties each text to the socio-political structures of its own milieu, if not by its own particular compositional configuration and unique use of form.

On the basis of the preceding discussion it is now possible to give a definition of narrative as the basis for the work to follow. What distinguishes narrative as a literary genre is its two chief compositional elements: the narrator's framework and the direct speech of the characters. Though these two features may vary widely in their relative magnitude and importance in different works, the presence of both constitutes the normative center of the spectrum of possibilities. A work which presents events and personages, but is given over to narration of their lives and circumstances in third-person discourse and recounts very little of their speech in direct discourse (such as James Agee's, *Let Us Now Praise Famous Men*) would be situated at one end of the spectrum, while a narrative which is almost totally devoted to the direct discourse of the characters and has very little if any description would be situated at the other (see the discussion of Compton-Burnett below).

Lubomír Doležel also finds the basic distinguishing features of the narrative to be the presence of the narrator's speech, and the character's speech.[1] Each has its own function and the relation between them is non-reciprocal. The two central functions of the narrator are representation and control, whereas the central function of the characters is to act and to express themselves about the action. The narrator refers to the characters, but the reverse can never occur. He thus arrives at a standard formula for the narrative text which economically defines narrative structure.

T = DN + DC (narrator's discourse plus character's discourse)

The relation is not merely a formal one, however, but is fraught with hidden passions. This was illuminated in a particularly insightful way by a recent detailed study of Dickens' use of the suspended quotation by Mark Lambert.

Lambert persuasively shows that Dickens, by interrupting the direct discourse of his characters with narrational tags and other framing devices, often reveals a form of "authorial jealousy":

> Through his early and middle years – that is, during the period in which he wrote his most widely loved novels – Dickens the novelist was (deeply if obscurely) a jealous god, not wanting admiration for his creatures to becloud or weaken or replace admiration for the creator.[2]

At other times Lambert describes the relation of the author and character as a type of "literary class warfare."[3] While not all authors are as obvious as Dickens in revealing the tensions in their relation to their characters, Dickens' work shows clearly in its expressive language and aggressive authorial intrusions into the speech of the characters what is less obvious in all narratives. It is thus this volatile, sensitive, and revealing relation between the narrator and his/her characters from which forces emanate that shape the structure of the narrative as a whole.[4]

One of the major reasons that the DN–DC relation can give rise to such forces is that a certain disruption of the normal operation of the sign must occur in order for these two forms of discourse to coexist in the same text. The sign, as we have seen, is constituted at the conjunction of the referential and communicative axes. The implication and presupposition along the communicative axis guarantee the referent–object relationship by means of which semantic content can be communicated along the referential axis. But in the narrative text, where the "real" author does not speak directly, but only indirectly through the third-person form, and where, even then, the author "implied" by this third-person form does not necessarily correspond to the "real" author, a potential semiotic cleavage occurs between these two axes.[5] The usual system of implications and presuppositions which is based upon the communicative axis of a concrete speech act between specific interlocutors who know each other does not necessarily apply.

Roland Barthes has posed the problem in this way: "who speaks (in the narrative) is not who writes (in life), and who writes is not who is."[6] In the narrational framework you are thus presented with three distinguishable subjects: the grammatical subject of the statement (s/he), the subject of the utterance (implied author), and the real subject. This means that the DC is severed from the communicative axis of the author's speech act, and thus deprived of the implicit meaning conveyed along this axis.

Julia Kristeva describes what happens to the real author in these terms: "He becomes an anonymity, an absence, a blank, in order to permit the structure to exist as such. At the origin even of narration, just in the moment where the author appears, we encounter death: the experience of nothingness."[7] Through this negation of the author, the "s/he" of the narrative personage is allowed to appear, assume a name, and begin to function as a source of direct discourse. Thus just as the sign functions only in the emptiness created by the absence of the thing, the narrative sign, the "s/he" and the instance of discourse which is its referent are able to occur only through the negation of the author's subjective presence. This negation constitutes a fundamental semantic alteration of the normal functions of the sign since it separates the narrative from the act of speech which produces it. The effect this has of decontextualizing the speech of the characters holds far-reaching implications for narrative semantics to which we must now turn.

The problem presented by decontextualizing the DC is obvious in light of the understanding of the sign already developed. We have seen that the sign consists of two axes, the communicative axis and the referential axis. The communicative axis relates the sign to the grammatical structures which embody the symbolic reflection of the community (the action of self-reflective consciousness upon language itself which endows it with a signifying order). According to Ortigues, these in turn imply agreements to which each speaker becomes a party in order to communicate within a particular language community.

A direct line thus leads from the communicative axis of language to the order of society, since acceptable grammar varies with each separate language community. Even the referential axis of terms is supported by implicit agreements between speakers regarding the object or concept which a term denotes, and these may vary for the same term with each sub-group within a single language community. It is thus obvious that decontextualizing a speech act dissolves the network of semantic constraints which normally control the meaning of words and presents the author with a semantic *tabula rasa* upon which s/he may begin to compose a new system.

This becomes clearer if we look at the complex strata of meaning "implicit"[8] in ordinary dialogue. François Flahault, in his work *La Parole intermédiaire*, more broadly describes the implicit dimension of discursive language as an "effect of place."[9] Every dialogue assumes that each partner occupies some position of power relative to the other – at least some capacity to give pleasure or inflict pain, to support and confirm the speaker's global discursive position, or disdain and reject it. As Flahault says: "Every desiring subject, in effect, bears the mark of an absolute subjection to the criteria according to which recognition is operated in the intersubjective network of which he constitutes one of the links."[10]

With the initiation of dialogue, the speaker assumes that the hearer will accede to the position which s/he assumes for her/himself. This position operates within the subject on four "registers," according to Flahault: the unconscious, the ideological (hierarchical, social system), the constraints of the situation of the specific utterance, and the circulation of signs within the dialogical interchange between the allocutory partners (which affects the previous three).[11]

Thus, in requiring accession to the first three homologous positions by the hearer, the speech act requires an implicit agreement by the hearer to these conditions. If the hearer does not accede to them in the fourth register of the dialogical process, then the conversation will soon be terminated. This implicit agreement is what Flahault calls the illocutionary effect of the implicit factors in discourse. They represent the unconscious and conscious effects of the interpersonal, social experiences of the speaker which have created in her/him a real or imaginary subjective sense of her/his place within the social and historical or cosmic system. For the speaker to accede to his/her sense of place indicates a shared world of discourse, an intersubjective bond that gives meaning to the utterances by providing their implications.

From these perspectives it is then possible to see precisely what occurs in the narrative form. By displacing the direct discourse (henceforth DD) of the narrator, the DC has been deprived of a *place* within a given network of social relations and temporal events, thereby eliminating all implicit meanings which would normally be provided by that network. As Gérard Genette says: "In discourse, someone speaks, and his situation in the very act of speaking is the focus of the most important significations; in narrative, as Benveniste forcefully puts it, *no one speaks*, in the sense that at no moment do we ask ourselves *who is speaking, where, when*, and so forth in order to receive the full signification of the text."[12]

This frees the sign/personage from all utilitarian contacts and poses him/her in a state of complete subjective openness. The narrator, speaking through the mask of the third person, returns to fill in, to one extent or another, this missing network of implications. Since, as we have seen, these implications reach along the communicative axis to the horizon of the social or cosmic system within which the personage must be accorded place, the narrative framework thus serves, epistemologically, to control the ultimate horizon of meaning within which the DC can be understood. The character becomes embedded in a close semantic system and subjective openness vanishes. Roland Barthes can thus say that in proportion to the degree that the third-person position is established in the narrative, "existence becomes fate."[13] This may also explain why third-person narration was accorded greater authority in ancient Greek texts than were first-person eye-witness accounts.[14] Existence was generally believed to be the product of fate and not the subjectivity of the individual.

This process by which the narrative personage emerges replicates, at a secondary (symbolic) level, the trauma by which language was originally established in consciousness. The posing of the "s/he" beyond the constraints of speech imposed upon the real author by her/his place in a community is an illocutionary act, the meaning of which stems from the effect of the act itself.[15] Just as the author is negated, the personage who exists in his/her absence is a purely empty form, devoid of referential content, and thus able to embody the subjective tensions produced in the actual author and his/her reader by the primary displacement which permits the operation of the sign in human consciousness. As Kristeva says: "He [the personage] appears as the refuge of subjectivity very near to zero."[16]

It becomes clear then that the way in which this narrative framework is constructed in relation to the discourse of the characters is of decisive semantic importance for the entire narrative. The narrator, in the first instance, poses his/her characters by means of a third-person pronoun, "he" or "she," which has as its object reference only an instance of speech designated by the pronoun "I," that is, the source of the direct discourse of the characters. Since the "I" as an instance of speech is a word whose meaning arises fundamentally from the expressive function of the sign, and the "he" depends primarily upon the representative function for its meaning, the juxtaposition of the "he" and the "I" in the DN–DC relation of the narrative places these two functions of the sign into tension with each other for dominance. Since both the expressive and representative functions are dependent upon the symbolic function for their form, the possibility exists as well that the conflict between these two functions in the narrator–character relation might give rise to a narrative form in which the symbolic function might mediate this opposition. One might then expect that these three sign functions operating in the narrator–character relations could produce three different types of narratives which arise directly from possibilities inherent in the three sign functions for relating narrator to character. It is to these possibilities that we now turn.

4
A typology of narrative functions and modes

In her comprehensive and insightful analysis of point of view in narrative literature, Susan Lanser argues, on the one hand, that typologies are legitimate inasmuch as "discourse features do not usually combine in total independence of one another," while, on the other hand: "Recent tendencies to dispense with typologies have surely benefited the study of point of view."[1] Part of the reason for this ambivalence toward typologies is the proliferation of categories and exotic terminology which has occurred in recent decades with apparently little progress being made toward consensus.

Before developing yet another typology it is thus useful to bring together some of the major proposals put forth in the last few decades in order to determine the extent to which some consensus may have actually been reached, and to see which problems remain outstanding that might be resolved by the typology to be offered here. The typologies to be examined are those of Norman Friedman, Franz Stanzel, Dorrit Cohn, and Gérard Genette.[2]

The fundamental issue for narrative typology is the relation of the narrator to the world of the characters, or, more precisely, the relation of the narrator's instance of speech to that of the characters. Closely related to this issue is the problem of the identity of the consciousness which mediates the narrative world to the reader. The problematic of these relations permits a wide variety of possible narrative strategies which have suggested a number of narrative types. But if the surface efflorescence of these types and their terminology is penetrated, a greater consensus may have been reached than is commonly recognized.

A relatively early attempt to create a comprehensive narrative typology was made in an article by Norman Friedman.[3] Posing the fundamental problem of the narrator to be the adequate transmission of the story to the reader,[4] he suggests two categories which assume the writer to be outside of the narrative world but with unlimited knowledge of it: Editorial Omniscience, in which the narrator makes his viewpoint known explicitly through authorial intrusions (e.g., Fielding's *Tom Jones*); and Neutral Omniscience, in which the author conveys his views only indirectly (e.g., Huxley's *Point Counter Point*). A second pair of categories place the author within the narrative world either as the protagonist of the story – "'I' as protagonist" (e.g., Dickens' *Great*

Expectations) – or as a more or less uninvolved observer of the action – "'I' as Witness" (e.g., Fitzgerald's *The Great Gatsby*). The standpoint assumed by the author here toward the narrative world is limited to what the narrator/character would be able to know and experience. A third set of categories formally dispenses with the narrator altogether and presents the story as it unfolds through the consciousness of several characters, as in Virginia Woolf's *To the Lighthouse* (Multiple Selective Omniscience), or only one character, as in Joyce's *Portrait of the Artist* (Selective Omniscience), or through the direct discourse of the characters (Dramatic Mode – James' *The Awkward Age*). Here the knowledge of the narrator is limited to the consciousness or speech of his/her characters. A final type in this category is what he terms "The Camera," in which the author has no internal knowledge of her/his characters but simply records a "slice of life" as it appears without imposing any order upon it (Isherwood's *Goodbye to Berlin*).

The use of the term omniscience in these categories is highly problematic. In Editorial and Neutral Omniscience, the narrator's knowledge is not unlimited, since, for the narrative to belong to these categories, the narrator cannot portray what is going on in the minds of the characters as it occurs – something which is required of true omniscience. Conversely, in the Multiple and Selective Omniscience narratives, the narrator, while portraying unlimited knowledge of the character's conscious life as it unfolds, cannot portray the comprehensive knowledge of the past and future or the non-conscious levels of the mind – things which also must certainly be characteristic of true omniscience.[5] If there are such generic limitations on authorial omniscience, the term becomes virtually meaningless and its use is inappropriate here.

If the term omniscience is eliminated from Friedman's categories, then, one is left with three basic categories which resemble those proposed by Franz Stanzel.[6] Stanzel's categories arise from the identity of the consciousness which mediates the story to the reader: "The present investigation takes as its point of departure one central feature of the novel – its mediacy of presentation."[7] He terms those narratives in which the author's consciousness serves this mediating function, "authorial" narratives.[8] This corresponds exactly to Friedman's category of "Editorial Omniscience." Although Friedman's "Neutral Omniscience" also refers to narratives mediated by an authorial consciousness, Stanzel does not deal with the neutral authorial role.

When the author withdraws from the narrative world and allows the story to be mediated by the characters, Stanzel terms it a "figural" narrative.[9] His "figural" narrative thus corresponds exactly to Friedman's "Multiple Selective Omniscience" and "Selective Omniscience". Further, just as Friedman includes a type (the Dramatic Mode) in which the author discloses the characters through their dialogue rather than through their consciousness, so Stanzel terms a sub-category of the figural narrative the "neutral figural" or "objective-scenic" type[10] with this same characteristic.

Stanzel's third category, the "first-person" narrative, places the author in the narrative. From his/her position within the text two different modes may be assumed: presentation of the narrating self and/or presentation of the experiencing self. To the extent that the narrating self is the focus, the first-person narrative resembles the authorial type, and to the extent that the experiencing self is placed at the center, it resembles the figural type. Friedman's "'I' as Protagonist" generally corresponds to Stanzel's type which has the experiencing self as the focus, and Friedman's "'I' as Witness" generally parallels Stanzel's type which places the focus upon the narrating self. Friedman's categories are less fundamental than those of Stanzel, however, since there is nothing to prevent the witness from also being the protagonist. The more crucial question has to do with mode of presentation which Stanzel addresses with his distinction between the experiencing/narrating self.

A more systematic analysis of this problem has been offered by Gérard Genette, who wants to make a firm distinction between the locus of focalization of the narrative, which he terms "mood" or "point of view," and the position of the narrator ("who speaks?") which he terms "voice."[11] With regard to mood, he develops a tripartite typology which resembles Stanzel's, but differs in one important respect. He argues that Stanzel's first-person narrative type is based not on point of view, but on voice, and with regard to point of view actually belongs with his figural narrative since both have "internal focalization." The distinction between the authorial and figural narratives rests upon a difference on the level of point of view which he characterizes as "zero focalization" (when the narrator knows and says more than the character) compared to "internal focalization."[12] First-person narration thus should not be the basis of a separate type with respect to mood or point of view. In addition, Stanzel's "objective-scenic" type does not share internal focalization with the figural type, as his analysis suggests, but rather has what Genette calls "external focalization," that is, only the spoken words and actions of the characters are revealed while the internal feelings and thoughts are never disclosed.[13] He thus makes narratives with "external focalization" into a third type alongside those with internal and zero focalization.

When he examines "voice" ("who speaks?") Genette proposes a different set of categories. Rather than making the more familiar distinction between authorial and first-person narratives, Genette proposes the terms "homodiegetic" and "heterodiegetic" to distinguish between narratives in which the story is narrated by one of the characters, and narratives in which the narrator is absent from the story. Reference to the first person does not, in his view, sufficiently make it clear that it can refer both to the "narrator's own designation of himself as such'' (Virgil's ''I sing of arms and the man''), and ''the identity of person between the narrator and one of his characters in the story.''[14] Since in fiction, mistakenly, only the latter is thought of as first-person narration, he proposes to use the more restricted term ''homodiegetic'' for character-narrated stories and the term ''heterodiegetic'' for those cases when the narrator's instance of speech (always implicitly in the first person) is not found in the text. Refining these categories further, he distinguishes between homodiegetic narratives in which the narrator is the protagonist, which he terms ''autodiegetic,'' and those where s/he is a witness or observer.[15]

But because it is possible to have a secondary narrator within a story recount a narrative in which he is not a character, as well as a case in which an external narrator recounts a story in which s/he is a character, without incorporating references to the instance of narration, Genette must create two additional terms which serve to locate the instance of discourse without reference to the narrator/character relation. These terms are ''intradiegetic'' and ''extradiegetic.'' Narratives which are told by a narrator within a story (who still does not have to be a character in the story) are termed ''intradiegetic,'' and those in which the narrating instance is altogether outside the story (even though the narrator may be a character in the story) are ''extradiegetic''.[16]

How satisfactory are these typological categories in accounting for the various types discovered by other analysts? Genette's categories permit a more finely tuned analysis with respect to the relation of the authorial instance of speech to the narrative world. The autodiegetic–witness/observer distinction he makes within the homodiegetic category would make more clear the distinction Friedman seems to have intended by his '''I' as Witness'' category, that is, a narrator who is within the narrative but is more of a witness than a participant in the story he relates. Similarly his terms add helpful precision to Stanzel's distinctions between authorial/figural narratives and narrating/experiencing selves. They make clearer the distinction between narratives in which the narrating and experiencing selves are unified with the narrator's instance of speech as a part of the story – homo/intradiegetic – and those in which they are unified but the narrator's instance of speech is not found in the story – homo/extradiegetic. Other, more subtle distinctions can be made which are not as clear within Stanzel's categories: for example, when the authorial position may be assumed by a narrator who tells a story within a narrative in which he is neither a participant nor observer – hetero/intradiegetic.

But Genette's categories, while helpful in making clear the various possibilities of the narrator/character relation, do not themselves illuminate the internal dynamics of the characters as such. Does the narrating of a story by a character (homo/intradiegetic) effect his/her character formation in a way that could be distinguished from the character formation of a hetero/extra-diegetic narrator?[17]

In conclusion, for a typology to be convincing and useful, it must be grounded upon a set of premises that can logically generate a finite set of types capable of linking pertinent surface features of the narrative to the underlying premises. Otherwise, the categories will be generated by the surface features of the text, and will become too numerous to be useful. Among the analysts studied thus far there is little agreement regarding premises, and an uneven development of the premises by individual authors. Already we have seen the internal contradictions within Friedman's concept of omniscience. A similar problem can be seen in Stanzel's categories. On the one hand, Stanzel elevates the authorial, first-person and figural types to a preeminent position based on the premise that narrative types arise from different forms of mediation between the story and the reader. Yet these types do not correspond to the three fundamental forms of mediation which he delineates: the authorial, figural, and neutral. The neutral form is found in the objective-scenic narrative which he categorizes as figural since it is dominated by direct discourse. But the mediation is attributed to an "imaginary witness."[18]

Two questions arise. First, why, if mediation is the central, generative feature of narrative types, do the three primary types not stem from the three forms of mediation? Second, if mediation is the fundamental generative category, why is the third form of mediation not found in the text ("imaginary witness") as are the authorial and figural? In answer to the first question, it is obvious that the first-person type is based upon surface features of the text and not upon a distinctive type of mediation. It thus should not constitute a separate type according to Stanzel's own premises. Genette also perceives the incongruity of this category on similar grounds. Then regarding the second question, the "imaginary witness" concept seems to be an attempt to explain the deviant "objective-scenic" type of narrative in terms of the basic premise when no comparable form of mediation is actually evident in the text. Genette is justified in seeing the focalization of this type of narrative to be quite different from the figural. Genette's own categories, however, uncover more subtle variations and distinctions than can be profitably utilized, especially when they are inadequately related to the problem of character formation.

Lubomír Doležel has moved the basis of his typological proposals from the anthropomorphic concepts rooted in the mimetic theory of fiction (such as omniscient, authorial, or figurative narrators) to the textual base with its underlying semiotic functions and modes. By going more deeply into the semiotic functions, he also is able to propose fewer, more fundamental terms than Genette. This approach provides a way of both seeing the common ground reached by the previous analysts, and accounting for a multitude of features which could not be satisfactorily accommodated by their systems. His analysis shows how the definition of narrative mentioned above – narrator's discourse (DN) + character's discourse (DC) – can be derived from a deep structure of functions and modes which can systematically account for the various narrative features present in the previous analyses.[19]

For Doležel the deep structure of narratives (DN + DC) is generated by a set of primary "obligatory" functions. The distinctive ("obligatory") function of the narrator – the representative function – gives rise to the DN, and the distinctive ("obligatory") function of the characters – the action function – gives rise to the DC. A second obligatory function is connected to each of the primary functions. Because the DN encompasses the DC, the representative function always occurs with a subordinate "control" function with respect to the DC. The action function must be supplemented by the "interpretation" function since the action function accounts only for the character's participation in the narrative, but not for speech. It is the interpretation function of the personages that generates their direct discourse.

At the verbal level each of these deep structure functions is articulated through one of three modes: objective, rhetorical, or subjective. All three may be found in either first- or third-person forms. The objective mode excludes personal feelings and views regarding the events being narrated. The rhetorical mode occurs where personal views and feelings are expressed by one who is not a participant in those events (that is, not a product of the action function), while the subjective mode expresses the views and feelings of a participant in the action. At the verbal level, however, the features of the rhetorical and subjective modes are the same. They are distinct only at the deeper functional level, one possessing the action function and the other not.

On the surface of a classic, realistic narrative the third-person narrative framework might be generated by the representation function in the objective mode, and the DC by the interpretation function in the subjective mode. The various narrative types then can be seen as emerging from the mediation of these two opposing poles. A mediating narrative type can be created when a third-person narrator exercises the interpretation function through the rhetorical mode ("rhetorical *Er*" [German "he"] type), thereby expressing his own views and feelings about the narrated events and characters. Such would correspond to Stanzel's authorial narrative type, and Friedman's Editorial Omniscience.

On the basis of these types Doležel can also identify transitional forms of narration such as free indirect discourse, or, as he terms it, "represented discourse." In light of his functional analysis this form of narrative discourse can be understood as the result of the "neutralization" of the opposition between the DN and DC.

This development, which he associates with modern fiction, makes it possible for a new form of discourse to emerge in which the narrative writing and the movement of consciousness coincide. The experiencing self and the narrating self approach an ambiguous unity.[20] This is the form of speech found in Friedman's Multiple Selective Omniscient type, and Stanzel's figural narrative. When the third-person narration comes to reflect the subjective language and perspective of a character, or when this type of subjective narration becomes so diffuse throughout the narrative that it is difficult to identify the boundary between the narrator's and character's discourse (seen in the use of deictics and the expression of emotion, etc.), Doležel attributes this to the presence of the action function with the narrator, and terms this the "subjective *Er* form" or "represented discourse."[21] These same subjective, stylistic features (plus others) are found in the expression of the narrator's own viewpoint in the "rhetorical *Er*" form. The question raised by his analysis of represented discourse is whether this form of narration can properly be considered a product of the action function. This question arises more acutely in connection with first-person forms to be discussed below.

Before examining first-person narration it is important to note that these categories seem to pass over the important style which Dorrit Cohn terms "psychonarration," in which the author takes the inner consciousness and perceptual experiences of the character as the primary subject matter without portraying consciousness as it happens. Cohn finds two forms of this type of narration: "dissonant psychonarration" where the authorial viewpoint upon the inner consciousness is still dominant, and "consonant psychonarration" where there is very little cognitive privilege on the part of the narrator.[22] In spite of the infiltration of stylistic features of direct discourse, the narrator, nevertheless, is still reporting and describing the contents of consciousness, and not actually portraying the verbal process of thought as it occurs. Thus time may be contracted or expanded to serve the narrator's interest. Although Doležel says that: "The technique of the subjective *Er* form is a prominent tool of profound psychological analysis,"[23] represented discourse does not enjoy the cognitive privilege needed for actual psychological interpretation.[24]

The first-person forms of Doležel's system account more logically and economically for most of the first-person types found in the previous analysts' work. Two of Doležel's first-person forms, the "rhetorical *Ich* [German "I"] form" and the "observer's *Ich* form" correspond to Stanzel's distinction between various types of first-person narratives which focus upon the "narrating self," and replicate in the first person the distinction between the "rhetorical *Er*" form and the "objective *Er*" form.[25] The "observer's *Ich*" parallels Friedman's "I as witness," but the "rhetorical *Ich*" form, in which the first-person narrator is not a participant in the events s/he narrates, but still expresses personal feelings and views regarding them, is missing from Friedman's account.[26]

But can one assume, then, that the personal or subjective *Ich* form is unequivocally generated by the action function? While it would seem self-evident that this would be so, linguistically, it is not at all clear since even in the subjective mode (i.e., when the narrating self has the action function and thus is participating in the action depicted), the relation of the narrating self to the experiencing self can still replicate all three modal possibilities.[27] Stanzel points to this when he shows that emphasis upon the narrating self at the expense of the experiencing self, even in a first-person novel where the narrating I is also the protagonist, tends to produce a narrative situation corresponding to the authorial type, that is, Doležel's objective or rhetorical *Er* form.[28] What does it mean, then, to say that the action function is present?[29]

But even when the narrating self is reduced in importance or eliminated, the presentation of the experiencing self may not produce total identification with the perspective of the character. Cohn shows how the first-person narrator, in speaking of her own self, may engage in "dissonant and consonant self-narration" and "self-quoted monologue," all of which maintain distance between the narrating and experiencing selves.[30] It is only in the "self-narrated monologue" that the retrospective stance of the narrator tends to drop away, and the narrator begins to enter fully the mental process of her character (her self!). Even here, however, the fundamentally retrospective standpoint created by the presence of the narrating self makes this a somewhat awkward and little-used form. As Cohn says: "Consonant presentation of a past consciousness is dependent on the self-effacement of the narrating voice, and few authors of autobiographical fiction have been willing or able to silence this voice completely."[31]

Full attainment of unity of the narrating self with the experiencing self, and loss of cognitive privilege is thus not achieved in the first-person form until the narrating self has dropped entirely away and the "autonomous interior monologue" is reached (as in the "Penelope" episode in Joyce's *Ulysses*, for example). This is a first-person form which corresponds to free indirect discourse (narrated monologue) in the third person. It must be distinguished from other first-person forms in the total simultaneity of the narration and the action. Cohn describes it thus: "This employment of the present tense pinpoints the simultaneity of language and happening that distinguishes the new form from 'the usual form of narrative' in the first person, where language always follows happening."[32]

The most significant "action" in this type of narration thus takes the form of verbal occurrences in the consciousness of the character which coincide with the narration. Consequently the outer action of the character becomes a secondary and relatively unimportant implication of the discourse.[33] Questions are even raised by Cohn as to whether this form can still be considered a narrative form: "When a first-person text contains no evidence of writing activity or of fictional listeners present on the scene, and yet adopts a distinct tone of oral colloquy, the narrative presentation itself becomes mysterious, is left – in Butor's phrase – 'in the shadows'."[34] Doležel does not deal with this form, but it transcends the narrative functions and modes as he defines them, and raises questions about the adequacy of the action function.

The problem with the action function is that it seems to vanish under closer examination. In the autonomous narrated monologue one would expect the highest degree of "participation" by the character in the action of the narration, but instead the outer action is displaced by verbal events. The same is true of represented discourse, the third-person form. Thus the close analysis of the action function suggests that the basis of human characters' participation in a narrative – their "obligatory function" – is not action at all, but specifically verbal events (both interior and exterior). The outer action is an implication or consequence of the speech of the characters since it is through their speech that characters define themselves and participate in the most fundamental way (more on this in chapter 5 below). A character whose presence and participation in a narrative is achieved only through action which is reported in the DN never emerges as an authentic narrative personage. This happens only through DD and its related forms.

The interpretation function, apart from the action function, cannot generate the DC, however, since it presupposes the action function for its own operation. It is through action that the characters participate in the narrated events and thus acquire a position in the narrative from which they can speak, according to Doležel. If there is no action function, then the interpretation function becomes irrelevant.

In place of the action function, I would argue that the indispensible function of the characters which gives rise to DC should be termed the expressive function. A foundation for this function is provided by Ortigues' semiotic theory which shows that expression is one of the cardinal functions of the sign. If narrative writing involves the decontextualizing of the sign, and a figurative reenactment in the narrator–character relation of the semiotic processes by which signs function, as argued above, then it follows that the functions which generate the narrative should correspond to the semiotic functions which are fundamental to the sign as such. The primary "action" of narrative personages in which they participate in the internal narrative world would thus be that of expressing themselves in DD. This is consistent with Doležel's description of the text dominated by DD as a "speaker-oriented text" as opposed to the "referent-oriented text" dominated by the DN.[35]

Narratives consisting of DN + DC may exist in which the characters may engage in virtually no action except expression, or in which the action of the characters is conveyed only through their direct discourse, as is apparently the case with *Kaliba's Crime*. In other modern narratives an even more meager narrative framework is retained, consisting of little more than minimal connecting sentences, and the passive narrative functions of censoring dangerous motifs (such as the erotic), and postponement.[36] In such narratives, an example of which will be analyzed below, the DC becomes the dominant force. This type incorporates what Friedman described as the "dramatic mode" and Stanzel called the "objective scenic" type. Neither of these types fit smoothly into the larger categories to which they were assigned by Friedman and Stanzel.

But if the action function can be eliminated and the interpretation function replaced by the expressive function as the generative source of the DC, reformulation of the other functions and modes must be made as well.

The function of representation, in contrast to the action function, is one of the cardinal functions of the sign in Ortigues' semiotic theory and it should be retained. The problem with Doležel's formulation of the representation function is that he has drawn it in opposition to the action function. If the action function is eliminated, then the representation function can be seen as generating a broader range of language than narration which is devoid of subjective views, feelings, etc. When dominant in the DN–DC relation it would generate, more broadly, narration predominated by many forms of referential, representative language. I will thus use the term "representation" to designate the entire spectrum of possibilities which reaches all the way from detached, objective narration, across the opinionated authorial narration, to the writing which enters the subjective world of the characters to report on perceptions and psychological processes (psychonarration).[37] It would reach one of its boundaries at narrated monologue, and the other at direct discourse.

These diverse styles of narration are united by their primary reliance upon the referential function of the sign to convey meaning. They constitute what Doležel in another context calls a "referent-oriented text" as opposed to a "speaker-oriented text."[38] The common feature of this style of narration is, in Genette's terms, its extradiegetic or hetero/intradiegetic character. The distance of the narrating from the experiencing selves requires the use of language which creates a closed framework of references within which the DC will inevitably be interpreted by the reader. The differences between the external and internal styles lie more at the ideological than semiotic level, as will be seen below (pp. 62–63).

Both of these functions will be expressed at the verbal level through a mode which will, in each case, reflect the relation of the DN to the DC when that function is dominant in a narrative. When the expressive mode is dominant, the relation of the DN to the DC will be passive, since the narrator's voice retires and allows the characters to define themselves in their own voices. Thus the mode will be termed the "passive" mode. Doležel also connects the quality of passivity with the objective narrator who assumes this same stance toward the narrative personages in his scheme.[39] This mode is characteristic of narratives with far less narrative framework than Doležel's objective narrative, however.

What modality, then, governs the articulation of the representation function? If the subjective and rhetorical modes are rendered problematic by the elimination of the action function, the same can be said of the objective mode, connected by Doležel to the representation function. Specifically, the characterization of the semantic content of the objective mode as lacking in subjective feelings and views is difficult to support. While the novel by Rais, which Doležel uses as his primary example of an objective/representative narrative, may convey the impression of objectivity, Doležel's own analysis makes the objective mode often seem to be a rhetorical device. At times during the course of the narrative, as well as in the final crisis and denouement, the natural conditions are used to image the inner consciousness of the protagonist. In the denouement the merging of the objective and subjective goes so far that the narrator leaves the objective mode for the subjective *Er* form.[40] The linearity of events and the circularity of nature finally merge all the more powerfully *for their previous separation.*

Even without such a correlation between the inner and outer world, and without the linguistic signs of subjective semantics, it is doubtful that there can be extensive description of natural surroundings which does not ultimately constitute an interpretive framework for understanding the speech of the characters. This is especially true when the characters are described physically.[41] Representation in the narrative framework, even though not made explicitly of the characters' inner states, nevertheless subtly places them within a system of meaning from which they cannot escape. Objectivity seems thus to be more of a rhetorical style than a genuine mode.

I would thus like to link the representation function with a new modal type midway between the objective and the subjective/rhetorical. Since any extensive DN, even the most "objective," still constitutes an important, enclosing semantic framework within which the DC will be interpreted, I am consequently proposing the term "indirect" to describe the mode of the representative narrator. Behind the mask of the third person (or even the persona of the later narrating self in first-person narration) the representative narrator is indirectly, covertly active in the formation and interpretation of the narrative personages whether the narrator be authorial, "objective," or engaging in psychonarration.

Remaining from this discussion of narrative styles is a very important range of features which do not fit into either the expressive or representative function, namely, the type of narrative in which the narrator moves into the inner world of the characters, utilizing the performative, emotive, subjective language characteristic of DD. We have already encountered this type of writing in the "figural" narration of Stanzel, the "Multiple Selective Omniscient narration" of Friedman, in the "represented narration" of Doležel, and in Cohn's "narrated monologue" and "autonomous narrated monologue." As we have seen, Doležel refers to this as "represented discourse," and describes it structurally as a "neutralization" of the opposition between the discourse of the character and that of the author.[42]

This type of language cannot occur in expressive/passive narratives since the narrator does not have access to the inner speech of his/her characters. Nor can it occur in the representative/indirect narrative since the inner thought is depicted in indirect speech, or in quoted thought which is always reported from the past. I will propose below (chapter 5) that this style of writing in both first- and third-person form emerges from the moment of the language occurrence within the author which gives rise to the narrative personage. Because this type of language event corresponds to what Ortigues terms the symbolic function of language, as I will explain below, I will term this the symbolic narrative function. It will be associated with the "active" mode since the narrator leaves the concealed position of the representative narrator and the passive mode of the expressive narrator to disclose the creative, verbal formation of the narrative personages as it occurs. This function, as well as the other two, will be developed more fully below.

This revised typology can be reduced to the schema in table 1, the form of which was developed by Doležel. The system of functions and modes constitute a closed network in which a change in one signals a change in the other.

Table 1

Mode/Function	Expressive	Representative	Symbolic
Passive	x	(x)	(x)
Indirect		x	(x)
Active			x

Note: To be read vertically only, with the bottom marker signifying the dominant function and mode, and the parentheses indicating subordinate modes which may be utilized by that function. E.g., when the symbolic function is dominant, the passive and indirect modes may be present in a subordinate position. But when the expressive function is dominant, the active and indirect modes may not occur.

The functions refer to the type of sign function which governs the semantics of the narrative as a whole, and the modes indicate the stance which the narrator assumes toward the narrative personages. Between the extremes of the purely expressive narrative and the totally symbolic narrative there may be many subtle, ambiguous gradations and configurations of these possibilities, as the presence of the passive and indirect modes in the symbolic narrative suggests. As Doležel says: "Discourse ambiguity seems to be an inherent property of the narrative text structure, resulting from the dynamic character of the opposition DN–DC."[43] In a complex, lengthy narrative there may be a fluctuation in the dominant sign function as well. Together the functions and modes establish the dynamics which will give rise to the plot structure, and account for the distinctive "voice" of the narrator.[44]

The Russian literary semiologist, Mikhail Bakhtin, developed a typology of narratives based on the author–character relation which correlates closely with that being developed here. Bakhtin comes to his types through an analysis of dialogue primarily in Dostoyevsky's works. For him dialogue is a part of a larger category which he terms "double-voiced words." Utterances of this type possess a common characteristic: "in all of them the word has a double-directedness – it is directed both toward the object of speech, like an ordinary word, and toward *another word*, toward *another person's* speech."[45] He includes in the category, along with dialogue, stylization, parody and *skaz* (a narrative produced by a fictitious narrator in a style other than that of the actual author).

The double direction of this type of utterance corresponds exactly to the two axes of the sign we have established – the referential axis and the communicative axis. A word acquires this double directedness also, according to Bakhtin, from the mode of the DN–DC relation (which he terms the author's speech and the direct speech of the characters). He describes his relation in terms of a continuum at one extreme end of which is the possibility that the author's speech and the character's speech might occupy the same plane of discourse within a single text. This would require a nearly impossible dialogue to occur (even in a first-person narrative) between the author and his/her character (unless the subject matter is the writing of the narrative). Such an occurrence, however, would remove the barrier which separates the two instances of discourse, thereby freeing the author's instance of speech from its suppression. This pole is approached by free indirect discourse, although Bakhtin, arguing for a trans-linguistic approach, is not inclined to be very specific about the linguistic features of these double-voiced utterances. The features of bi- and polyvocality he speaks of, however, are generally associated with free indirect discourse.[46]

At the other end of the continuum is what he calls the "monological" discourse in which the narrator speaks in a totally referential, object-oriented framework, and the discourse of the characters is totally subordinated to the objective semantic content of the framework.[47] This can be found in a purely scientific text where the author cites the writings of others. This pole is approached by the neutral type of representative narrator or the referent-oriented text.

Within this continuum he locates three different types of utterances: the "object-oriented word" of the narrative context, the "objectivized word" – which is the "single-voiced" direct speech of characters found in a monological narrative context – and the "double-voiced word" which occurs in a narrative context where allowance is made for the emergence of implicit meaning from relations to other instances of discourse along the communicative axis.

The analysis of Bakhtin supports the main features of the functional analysis above, but there is a lack of symmetry in the formulation of his categories which I would like to eliminate so as to integrate his insights more clearly into this perspective. Bakhtin's basic premise is that the orientation of direct speech is determined by its relation to the author's speech. In light of his premise, he actually has only two basic categories: single-voiced monological speech, and double-voiced dialogical speech. His three types, however, are not based upon this premise since two of them are direct discourse and the third, the object-oriented word, is found only in the narrative framework. But single-voiced monological speech actually includes both object-oriented narration and the objectivized speech of the character which accompanies it. In terms of the present analysis, both can be seen as stemming from the representative function which governs the DN–DC relation. Thus they can be considered as a single type of speech. Bakhtin himself comes close to this view when he says: "In words of the first and of the second types there is in fact only a single voice. These are single-voiced words."[48]

Within the second category of double-voiced speech, he finds two types which reflect two different modes in which the DC can be related to the author. Stylization and parodical double-voiced words, he says, are "passive varieties." The author acts upon the DD of the narrative to make it communicate implicit meaning along the communicative axis which extends from the author to his reader. In contrast, the dialogue and what he calls the "hidden polemic" constitute instances of speech which exert an "active influence and inspiration on the author's speech forcing it to change accordingly."[49] He thus terms this the "active type" of double-voiced word.

The formulation of these categories is problematic since he creates two separate types of speech: the object-oriented word, and the objectivized speech, which exhibit the same DN–DC relation, while constituting a third type – the double-voiced word – which must be internally differentiated on the basis of two different types of DN–DC relations. Since the initial distinction between single-voiced and double-voiced words arises from differences in the DN–DC relation, it seems that his system of three types of speech, only two of which constitute different types of DN–DC relations, does not reflect a consistent application of his fundamental criteria.

In addition he seems not to have envisioned a form of the double-voiced word so radically "active" as that found in some modern novels (such as the novels of Compton-Burnett to be discussed below), where there is virtually no narrative framework at all and the meaning of the narrative is entrusted almost entirely to the complex implicit meaning of direct speech.

For these reasons I would like to separate and redefine the active and passive types of double-voiced words and place only the most extreme form of what Bakhtin calls the active double-voiced words (the dialogue and the hidden polemic) under the category of the expressive narrative function. The active mode of this pole of the DC complements the passive mode of the DN characteristic of this function. Where the narrator is more active, transgressing the barrier between the narrator and character and merging her perspective with that of the characters, this will be identified with the symbolic function. Both the expressive function and the symbolic function are thus to be considered double-voiced but in different ways.

The second voice of the expressive narrative stems not from the author but from the other personages in the narrative and the social implications of their discourse. Where the narrative is governed by the symbolic function, the implicit meaning will arise from the relations of the personages to the narrator as well as from their relations to other personages. Here the active mode causes the dialogically shaped, subjective semantics of DD to enter the narrative framework, breaking down the barrier between the narrator and personage but still providing a different type of framework within which the characters' words and behavior can be understood. We will see the way in which this is accomplished and its consequences below (chapter 5). With this adjustment Bakhtin's analysis conforms very closely to the typology developed above. The narrator's object-oriented word with its accompanying single-voiced DD corresponds exactly to the representative narrative type (though transitional types may become somewhat double-voiced, for example, dissonant psycho-narration). The double-voiced word, characterized by a passive relation between the narrator and characters, in which meaning is conveyed implicitly through the DD of the characters, corresponds, with slight modifications, to the expressive narrative type. Lastly, the fully double-voiced word, characterized by an active relation between the narrator's speech and that of the characters, corresponds exactly to the symbolic type. The modifications thus made to Doležel's system seem to be supported by the basic features of Bakhtin's analysis.

Additional support is found for this typology in the work of V. N. Voloshinov, *Marxism and the Philosophy of Language* (attributed in large part to Bakhtin).[50] Here we are provided with the most illuminating explanation of what I am calling narrative modes, that is, the distinguishing characteristic of the narrator's relationship to the direct discourse of his characters.

Like Doležel, Voloshinov/Bakhtin finds the direct discourse in the narrative and the narrator's discourse to constitute the two basic distinguishing verbal features of the narrative form. But he goes on to argue that the particular way in which the DN and DC are related is a mirror of the pattern of speech reception that is deeply rooted in the author's subjectivity and ultimately corresponds to the sociological structures in which the author lives. It thus has ideological dimensions.

For Voloshinov/Bakhtin, the fundamental unit of speech is the dialogue. The monological utterance which is the object of linguistic investigation is thus an artificiality from the outset. The dialogue transcends even grammar since: "*There are no syntactic forms with which to build a unity of dialogue.*"[51] But, as we have seen, the narrative form establishes two instances of speech – the author's and the character's – and relates them within a more or less unified semantic context. If one then assumes that the dialogue is the fundamental, seminal context of all speech, and the patterns that govern dialogue are themselves shaped by the social environment of the discourse, then it follows that the DN–DC relation would also bear the marks of the transgrammatical dialogical patterns taken over by the author from his social environment.

In the narrative framework the author explicitly responds to another instance of discourse which he has, in a sense, received, namely, the speech of the character. We will see below (chapter 5) that in the symbolic narrative, the author may respond dialogically to his character as a "thou." Voloshinov/Bakhtin, then, terming the DN as "reporting speech," says, "what is expressed in the forms employed for reporting speech is an *active relation* of one message to another."[52] Such a reaction of one sign to another, one message to another, requires a response to the form as well as to the content. Since the linguistic form, according to Ortigues, is the aspect of language in which the society's subjective interaction with language is the most immediately disclosed, it follows that the pattern of speech reception operating within the DN–DC relation would mirror the social matrix of the author. Susan Lanser speaks similarly of a "homology between the narrative structure *within* the fictional discourse and the rhetorical structure which produced it."[53]

But disclosed as well by the manner in which the speech of the other is received is the inner speech, the inner word of the author, since the word of the other comes to be present in the author's own inner dialogue. Voloshinov/Bakhtin thus raises this question: "What is the mode of existence of another's utterance in the actual, inner-speech consciousness of the recipient? How is it manipulated there, and what process of orientation will the subsequent speech of the recipient himself have undergone in regard to it?"[54] Already we have seen in the analysis of functions the wide variety of responses which authors may make to the speech of their characters. Voloshinov/Bakhtin finds this relationship to be governed by three tendencies which correspond exactly to the three functions of the narrative sign already discussed.

The basic tendency, in his view, is for the narrative framework to "maintain its integrity and authenticity" by maintaining a fixed boundary between itself and the DC.[55] This leads the author to emphasize the cultural characteristics of the personage, and thus the content more than the form of both DN and DC.

Sociologically, this represents, in his view, a dogmatic and/or rationalistic cultural environment where messages are communicated in a depersonalized fashion which emphasizes their referential content. In a valuable analysis of indirect discourse, he notes that this type of narrative modality translates direct discourse into third-person form in such a way as to preserve the content of the speech rather than the *way* in which it was delivered. He calls this a "content analyzing"mode of indirect discourse.

In terms of the typological analysis being made here, I will refer to this type of DN–DC relation as an indirect mode, since the author is very much active in interpreting the character, creating the semantic horizon for his speech, but is effaced usually behind the third-person speech form. He thus is indirectly present.

The second tendency he notices in the DN–DC relation is when: "Language devises means for infiltrating reported speech with authorial retort and commentary in deft and subtle ways. The reporting context strives to break down the self-contained compactness of the reported speech to resolve it, to obliterate its boundaries."[56]

This process can assume a wide variety of different forms, but its essential characteristics correspond exactly to the process at work in the symbolic narrative described above, and fully realized in the novels of Dostoyevsky. I shall refer to this as the active mode, and correlate it with the symbolic function.

The social milieu which gave rise to this active mode Voloshinov/Bakhtin finds in the Renaissance (especially in France), as well as in the eighteenth and nineteenth centuries, where there was "a severe debilitation of both the authoritarian and the rationalistic dogmatism of utterance. Social value judgements were then ruled by a relativism supplying extremely favorable grounds for a positive and sensitive reception of all individualized verbal nuance of thought, belief, feeling."[57]

A third tendency is also possible since "the verbal dominant may shift to the reported speech, which in that case becomes more forceful and more active than the authorial context framing it. This time the reported speech begins to resolve, as it were, the reporting context, instead of the other way around."[58] The consequence is that the author cannot elevate a world construct in representative speech that subordinates and explains his characters. This Voloshinov/Bakhtin considers the sign of "relativistic individualism" which reflects a society no longer held together by common beliefs and assumptions.

I shall call this tendency the "passive" mode by which the DN and DC may be related in a narrative, and correlate it directly with the expressive function as described above.

Although Voloshinov/Bakhtin placed Dostoyevsky in the third category, I believe that this is because, as mentioned above, he did not envision a truly passive narrator such as Compton-Burnett's, and thus misinterpreted Dostoyevsky's polyphonic perspective as relativistic. While Dostoyevsky accords a large measure of freedom to his characters, he does not do so from a passive stance toward them. On the contrary, he is passionately involved with them to the point of entering veritably into their inner thoughts. In his construction of the micro-dialogues which serve as the final bastion of the subjective freedom of the character, a passionate affirmation of both the creative power of language and the ultimate value of the individual subject is conveyed. The micro-dialogue thus constitutes a very important interpretive context within which the character may be understood and evaluated. Dostoyevsky comes at the climax of the development of the active involvement of the narrator in the affairs of his characters that had begun, in fragmentary fashion, perhaps as early as the Renaissance, rather than as the precursor of such twentieth-century writers as Compton-Burnett, whose work is characterized by amoral passivity and thoroughly relativistic semiosis.

5

The three functional narrative types

The analyses of Doležel and Bakhtin have made possible the transition from Ortigues' foundational semiotic theory to typical narrative structures and their stylistic characteristics. The chief missing element remaining in this narrative theory is the link between the types and their plot structures. But central to this problem is the process of defamiliarization which operates at the foundation of narrative structure. Any functional theory of narrative must illuminate the defamiliarization process by which the reader is brought to a renewed perception of form. So before examining the three types of functionally based plot structures, it will be necessary first to understand the semiotic process of defamiliarization which generates them.

The semiotic basis of defamiliarization: image and sign

Since plot involves the words and actions of the characters, and the characters, as we have seen, are posited as empty signs capable of receiving the complex forces in the human psyche set in motion by the installation of language as the basis of human consciousness, the shape of the plot will be determined, in its general features, by the various fundamental ways in which the subject may deal with the tensions caused by the signifying process. At the same time, the perception of form which is central to the artistic text will also arise from the dominant signifying process at work in the narrative plot which serves to shape the characters.

In order to complete this functional theory of narrative we thus must turn again to Ortigues, who has worked out a typology of the signifying processes which shape both the relation of the subject to language and the way in which these processes are dramatically expressed through critical action. From this perspective, it will then be possible to situate properly the Genesis narrative in its relation to other types of narrative writing, and analyze its style for indications of the semantic processes which give rise to the character formation and plot structure.

According to Ortigues, consciousness manifests deep tensions within itself over signifying processes. As we have seen, the self is shaped not only by the signifying process stemming from the sign and the implicit prohibition which ruptured the continuity of the self and the material world, but it can also be shaped by the imagination. The image transmitted to consciousness through visual means offers to the emptiness of consciousness what appears to be an immediate (unmediated) contact with the material world. That is, it offers the possibility of the "restoration" of the continuity between consciousness and the material world which the sign makes impossible. In consciousness governed by the image, the imagination replaces the self-reflective consciousness maintained by the sign as the central locus of the self–world relation. For consciousness to seek to satisfy desire through immediate identification with the unmediated images of the world present in the imagination transforms the self-reflective process into a passionate drama of inner conflict between doubles representing the pair, identical/nonidentical: subjects and objects of desire that are reversed images of each other as absence differs from presence.

In the rite of sacrifice we see this dual relation operating in dramatic action. In Ortigues' view: "Sacrifice, like the prohibition, manifests the power of rupture by which the symbolic order, the Sacred Law, is shown to be of another order than the material or profane given."[1] The universality of sacrifice thus is due to the fact that it, like the prohibition, reflects the discontinuity between the symbolic and material spheres that is necessary for the operation of language and culture.

Unlike the prohibition, however, sacrifice assumes a relation of total opposition between the symbolic and material spheres. Each is the mirror image, or, in Ortigues' view, the "imaginary double" of the other.[2] The relation between the two orders is not mediated. Rather it is governed by the principle of identification, the operation of which is the chief function of sacrifice. Since these two orders are the inverse of each other, one totally material, and the other totally spiritual, identification of the material with the spiritual can only be effected by the "dematerialization" of the bodily object. This is accomplished by sacrifice. As Ortigues puts it: "it supposes two orders of existence and a passage from one to the other, in such manner that the being or object placed before us in this world, which seems not to move, leaves it mysteriously all the time, estranges itself and goes to identify itself with the supernatural being or object which corresponds to it in the beyond."[3] Thus for a vase to be transmitted to the other world it must be broken in this world. For a material object to be identified with the spiritual world, for it to exist spiritually, its material form must be destroyed. This is even seen in the material images of some of the gods of India, e.g., "the god of beginnings, Savitr, the Impulsor, has no hands."[4] The relation is also reversible. In Indian mythology, the material world, in the first instance, was created by the self-sacrifice of the creator god, Purusha, the cosmic man.

Where the relation between the symbolic and material is governed by sacrifice, the principle of duality extends into the figuration of the gods into opposing pairs. Here, however, he sees that mythology is subject to constraints which limit the free play of imaginary duality. At the basis is the psychology of the imaginary arising from objectless desire that propels consciousness into unity with an inverse projection of its own image. Beyond this are the constraints stemming from language such as social rules, imperatives, prohibitions, promises, and beliefs, and those stemming from the hierarchical order of society itself.[5] In this regard he analyzes Dumézil's study of European mythology, and finds that within each of Dumézil's mythic levels (i.e., sovereignty, the military, and reproduction) the principle of dyadic pairs operates, though it is the most clearly manifest in those myths dealing with fecundity.[6]

On the one hand, mythology is pulled toward the pole of attaining absolute unity with the divine spirit through the annihilation of the differentiating forms of the material world through sacrifice. On the other, it is drawn toward the symbolic realms of language and society which consist of differentiating systems composed of fixed, definable units manifest in the form of a hierarchical divine society. The fundamental tension stemming from the total opposition of the symbolic and material realms, resolved through sacrifice, takes the form in mythology of conflict between pairs of opposing deities locked into repetitive dramas of opposition, which duplicate in imaginary symbolism, the opposition between the symbolic and the material, and the violent act of destruction by which the two realms are temporarily reconciled.

There is a fundamental contradiction within the sacrificial process, however. While sacrifice offers to consciousness direct, unmediated access to objects of desire in the form of specular images, unity with them can only be attained through annihilating their material form. This means that the unity with the object of desire which the specular image seems to make possible can finally only be achieved through the renunciation of one's desire for the material possession of that object.

Sacrifice thus involves not only the outer sacrifice of objects, but the inner sacrifice of the desire for the material form of those objects. When this is understood, sacrifice can be reinterpreted as a purely inner, spiritual process. It becomes equivalent to the spiritual act of renouncing material goods and possessions. When this occurs, the self no longer identifies its essence with any material sacrificial object, but rather sees itself as a totally spiritual reality which stands in the same relation to the entire material realm as does the divine, that is, a relation of opposition.

This process thus leads to the rejection of outward sacrificial rites, and causes sacrifice to become the internal mode in which the individual self relates to the material world as a whole. It also opens up the possibility of the achievement of the complete identification of the spiritual essence of the human with that of the divine, and thus for the human to become "divine."

Ortigues thus provides two fundamentally different ways in which form can be perceived and experienced corresponding to the two chief physical modes of perception – the auditory and the visual – and stemming from the rupture of the inaugural continuity of consciousness with the world which permitted the installation of linguistic forms and the emergence of symbolic self-reflective consciousness. The function of the artistic text to renew our experience of the form of language, as Shklovsky described it, serves to return human beings to the linguistic foundations of consciousness itself, and thus to provide for the renewal of our entire perceptual, intellectual and spiritual powers. Since this too is the fundamental import of religious literature and ritual, we find here the common semiotic source of both religious and non-religious literature, and the necessity, as well, for treating them as a part of the same system.

The way in which the text organizes itself in terms of plot, personages, and discourse across the negation of the author's instance of speech, will arise from the stance of the author toward the original rupture at the root of consciousness, since this stance will determine the type of defamiliarization of form effected by the style and plot structure. In the act of narrative writing the orientation of the author toward the logic of the image or the logic of the sign will give rise to the motivation of the characters and the nature of the tension which generates the plot.

Since the characters are originally empty signs, there are three basic possibilities for their narrative development corresponding to the three basic functions of the sign: expression, signification, and symbolization. The deeper force generated by the author's stance toward the fundamental rupture of consciousness and the world will then provide the internal dynamics of the plot structure, the logic of the image determining the plot dynamics of the significative or "representative"[7] narrative, the logic of the sign motivating the symbolic narrative, and the expressive narrative constituting an intersection of the dynamics of both the sign and the image.

The three functional narrative types

The representative narrative

When the author's stance toward language is governed by the logic of the imagination, s/he makes the representative function dominant. The statements found in both the DN and DC take on the fundamental character of descriptive, monological statements and their meaning is ultimately determined by the referential process, the signifier/signified relation. The characters are defined by the narrator on a continuum from semantic fullness to semantic emptiness. Barthes calls this "literature that is replete: like a cupboard whose meanings are shelved, stacked, safeguarded ... like a pregnant female, replete with signifieds which criticism will not fail to deliver."[8] The semantically empty characters are posed in a state of subjective desire for those objects or states with which the author has endowed the other characters.

The author in this type of narrative assumes the rupture of the continuity of consciousness with the world to be the absence of the referential object (the specular image). The motive force of the narrative in its classic expression will thus take the form of desire in one or more of the subjects for this missing object. The field of action will be populated by personages arranged in dyadic pairs, one of each pair being portrayed as a full subject – manifesting union with the desired specular images – and the other being portrayed as empty, driven by desire for the fullness that comes from such union. Between those opposing states, there is no mediation. The signifying forms *themselves*, which have displaced their referential objects, are perceived as being empty, lacking in meaning, and are at best only instrumental. The experience of form that is characteristic of this type thus occurs in the conflicting juxtaposition of the empty form and the full presence of the image of the object in consciousness. When the image is immediately present, the form is negated and transcended.

The center of the artistic experience in a text governed by the semiotics of the image is thus the conflict between form and image in which the emptiness of the form is revealed by the power immanent in the unmediated presence of the specular image. This conflict is generally portrayed as an external conflict between full and empty personages. In any case, some form of overt or covert violence is characteristic of the experience of form in narratives of this type. Through the elimination of the representation (the empty form) consciousness attains unity with the "reality" of the object which is equated with the idea or image present in consciousness.

But this union leads to the objectification of consciousness, that is, the fall into the familiar, habitual, the material. The consciousness and perceptual numbness that result from this objectification cause the acquired objects of desire to lose their significance and the experience of emptiness to return. This leads to a renewal of the search for the full presence of being. Defamiliarization is accomplished here, not by the positive experience of form that Shklovsky described, but by its negation in the interest of the renewal of the immediate presence of the thing itself to consciousness. Ortigues believes this semiotic process to be at the root of the religious ritual of sacrifice. But these sacrificial dynamics also play themselves across the plot structure of countless narratives.

This type of narrative is the most widespread, reaching all the way from folklore to the average mystery story today. It has probably received its most lucid analysis in the work of A. J. Greimas. The functional model which

Greimas developed on the basis of earlier work on Russian folklore by Vladimir Propp depicts precisely the semiotic process described above. The typical narrative structure at the level of characters or "actants" portrays an (empty) subject/protagonist in pursuit of a missing object (person) of desire which is in the possession of the (full) opponent. The subject bests the opponent in some kind of conflict and (re)gains possession of the missing object.[9]

The experience of defamiliarization occurs when the empty representation of the object of desire in the mind is displaced by the full presence of the object when it is obtained. The experience of the form as such, while providing the active force for the protagonist's action, is perceived as wholly negative, the painful absence of the referent. The significant moment occurs when the signifying form is displaced by the immediate presence of the object. In Roland Barthes' terms, this is the "*lisible*" (readerly) text.[10] Its fundamental semantics arise from the "proairetic" code expressed in action sequences. Consequently, "by their typically sequential nature simultaneously syntagmatic and organized, they form the favored raw material for a certain structural analysis of narrative."[11]

The story within a story in Balzac's novella *Sarrasine*, analyzed by Barthes in *S/Z*, provides an ironic but illuminating play on the representational processes in this type of narrative. The aesthetic power of this novella stems initially from the artist Sarrasine's pursuit of an object of erotic desire, a beautiful singer named La Zambinella, who represents for his psyche the immediate, complete presence of the specular image, his ideal of beauty. To possess her, for Sarrasine, is to overcome the fundamental rupture which has alienated consciousness from the material world. As Barthes says: "To discover La Zambinella's body is ... to put an end to the infinity of the codes, to find at last the origin (the original) of the copies."[12] Thus the defamiliarization experience which this type of narrative seeks at this point is one in which the object of reference is possessed immediately and afresh by the mind without the interference of mediating forms. The specular image is perceived anew when it emerges from the world of the imagination and becomes identified with a "real" object, which is then possessed in some sense by the desiring subject. The form of the specular image is experienced positively only fleetingly as it disappears in the full, immediate presence of the real object of desire.

Balzac inverts the defamiliarization experience of this type of narrative by making such an identification of Sarrasine's mental image with the body of La Zambinella impossible. It is rather the illumination of the illusory character of Sarrasine's imaginary ideal of feminine beauty which provides the experience of defamiliarization. Form is experienced here, but experienced as the signifying absence at the core of this illusion. To place into question the status of the object of desire which motivates the protagonist of an otherwise representative narrative, ironically unmasks the illusions at the center of this type of narrative. Balzac thus turns the strategy of the representative narrative against itself, thereby moving the novella in the direction of what I will describe below as the symbolic narrative.

The expressive narrative

Where narratives are governed by the dynamics of the sign, as opposed to the image, union of consciousness with the imaginary object of desire is displaced as a primary motivating force by the dynamics of the signifying form experienced now as the medium of intersubjectivity. Subjective consciousness in the characters is oriented not toward union with the specular image, but toward discourse with other subjects. Through discourse, the subject comes to know itself as neither an aching void, nor an absolute, objective present being, but as a mediated, intersubjective presence wholly dependent upon the other even for its own presence to itself. The sign, as the embodiment of the self-reflective process of the society, serves, in the act of expression, both to embody the position and self-presence of the speaker, and relate her/him to the presence-to-itself of the other, and the linguistic society in which s/he speaks.[13]

When the expressive function is dominant, this prevents the development of a narrative framework which would "reduce" the personage and situation to some type of object-oriented analytical description, and "explain" the behavior of a subject in terms of an intellectual or cultural system. Rather, the subjects would articulate their own situation in DD to other personages so that the reader would learn nothing of importance about the character or setting other than that which was enclosed in and shaped by the context of DD between personages.

Since, as we have seen, the sign is fundamentally an intersubjective phenomenon which mediates the consciousness of the subject to itself only through that of another consciousness, the characters in such a narrative would come to define each other in the play of their dialogue. The tendency would be for the characters either to lose their differences and merge, or to become the inverse images of each other. These possibilities would have to be forestalled, however, to prevent the breakdown of dialogue and the premature end of the narrative.

This can be done because the narrative plot is generated at a deeper level by another polarity. The existence of the characters rests upon a negativity, that is the suppression of the author's instance of speech which creates an empty sign for the subject to occupy. This negativity is present in the narrative as the fundamental emptiness of the personage which makes it possible for the logic of the imagination to play a role in the evolution of the plot. If this logic cannot here produce a conflict between full and empty characters, it can generate internal conflict within characters. This takes the form of actions in which they engage, arising from the dark recesses of desire, that contradict or negate the content of their dialogically formed consciousness, actions which they seem driven to take even when they are inexplicable to themselves. These actions, which may be self-destructive, thus preserve their differences, the irreducible negativity at the root of their own subjectivity. The plot is thus driven by the conflict between the unspoken desires and repressed truth, and the mores which regulate conventional discourse. The oppositions which motivate the plot is that of the hidden versus the revealed, the unconscious versus the conscious, the secret versus the public, and so forth. The experience of defamiliarization occurs when the life expressed in conventional discourse is revealed by the eruption of the hidden truth to be a sea of empty forms.

Although these dynamics operate often within larger narrative contexts, there are few pure examples of this type of narrative. Some of the novels of Ivy Compton-Burnett offer the best approximations. Wolfgang Iser's study of her novel, *The Heritage and its History*, brings this to light.[14] This novel concerns the relations of persons within the Challoner family, a part of the English landed gentry, and is set on their country estate. The pivotal character is Simon Challoner, a nephew of the owner of the estate, Sir Edwin Challoner. The action centers upon young Simon's increasingly impatient desire to inherit the estate. Sir Edwin has no heir, but Simon's own father is the next in line, and Simon must thus await the death of his own father before realizing his ambition. The plot hinges upon, not what Simon does to hasten the realization of his desire, but rather what he does, in contradiction to his own wishes and judgement, to make the realization impossible, namely, he has a secret affair with Uncle Edwin's young wife which results in the birth of an heir. Negativity, driven by irrational erotic impulse, thus erupts in the plot within the pivotal character (who cannot properly be called the hero), as a mysterious force operating to defeat him.

The texture of the narrative consists almost entirely of direct discourse. As Iser says: "Instead of explaining what she [the author] has reported, as the reader will naturally expect her to do, she merely describes the appearance of some of the characters, or makes observations which add virtually nothing to what we have already deduced from the dialogue."[15] Iser goes on to explain the consequences of this: "we are confronted directly by the actual 'reality' of the characters, instead of by an edited version of that reality, so that both author and reader appear to stand at an almost identical distance from the people they are observing. By her explanations of trivialities and her silence on matters of importance the author signalizes her presence in order to highlight her self-effacement."[16]

In the absence of a unifying, interpretive perspective in the narrative framework, the meaning arises from an immensely complex network of implications of the characters' discourse which the reader must explore without assistance from the narrator. By effacing herself, the narrator thus partially restores the symbolic, communicative axis of the characters' instances of speech. Since, however, this axis leads to an intricate field of agreements, customs, etc., conscious and unconscious, which are assumed by speakers, no speech can be understood apart from these common assumptions of the interlocutors. Their speech thus is never totally their own, but is formed on the basis of the expectations and assumptions of the other and the community. If the consequence of this for the reader is that "these characters seem to us more like patterns than people", Iser says it is because "an apparently indispensable principle underlying the conception of novel characterization has in this novel been given up altogether: namely, the individual self as the focal point of reference."[17] To the extent that the reader, for cultural or other reasons, misses the implications, s/he would have no way of understanding the plot. The characters are creatures of the mediating, intersubjective sign, who exist only in their complex, dialogical interaction with others. This is why there cannot be a single governing point of view, or a hero, but rather a plurality of relative viewpoints. Critics thus fault her characters for lacking individuality. Further erosion of individuality occurs because the characters are refracted in the mirror of the other's dialogue only in a fragmentary fashion. Each responds to only some of the implications of the other's dialogue and this prevents the appearance of a complete system of implied meaning at any point in the discourse.

The way in which implied meanings shape the pattern of dialogue becomes evident as the consequence of Simon's affair. No one wants to speak of it explicitly, but many know of it. When Simon's legitimate daughter eventually wants to marry Sir Edwin's heir, Simon's illegitimate son, the pattern of concealment is threatened with total dissolution. This family secret which has obviously had to be kept from the child and his peers now appears to the young couple as a mysterious force generating opposition to their marriage on the part of Simon and the other kin who know.

This crisis thus elicits reflections from the characters over the enigmatic force operating in life which runs so much counter to human intentions and good sense. Compton-Burnett, by posing her characters in the juncture between this closed, mysterious negativity and the open intersubjectivity of dialogue, leaves unanswered the question of who the characters really are. But it is precisely in revealing the profound relativity and ambiguity of conventional characters that the narrative defamiliarizes their narrative form and provides the reader with a new perspective upon them. In his criticism of Compton-Burnett's style, Iser describes very well the central effect of this narrative strategy: "The story lifts off the camouflage, but refrains from presenting us with the reality beneath. Indeed, its most penetrating effects are achieved precisely by revealing the inexplicable inconsistencies of the characters and leaving us foundering after the all-important but ungraspable motive.''[18]

The symbolic narrative

Upon first consideration it would seem difficult if not impossible for there to be a narrative shaped by the symbolic function. As shown above, this function is made possible by those signs devoid of referential content such as the pronouns, which enable the subject to identify her/himself with a form in an expressive act. In this act, the subject enters language and experiences consciousness across the mediation of the sign which unites her/him with the other. S/he experiences her/himself thus precisely in this encounter with another consciousness in an event of mutual recognition. A positive character is given to consciousness by the articulation of those recursive speech forms whose object of reference points back to the instance of speech itself and the subjective consciousness which has been established by the expressive act. Although the ''I'' already is the minimal unit of such a speech form, a stronger positive bearing stems from the performative terms such as promises, oaths, etc.

But because the narrative form arises only through the negation of the author's own instance of speech, and the installation of a semantically empty sign personage in its place that is thereby detached from any actual instance of speech, it would seem impossible for the narrative to be dominated by the symbolic function. Even in the expressive narrative, where the personage is formed by dialogue with others across the mediation of the sign, the sign of the personage still rests upon an unmediated negativity caused by this displacement of the author's instance of speech.

The personages would thus seem to be fundamentally and inescapably objects of the narrative pronouns ''he'' or ''she.'' As such they would finally be shaped either by the representational function, in the event that the author returns indirectly in the narrative framework to describe and explain the personage and the narrative world; or they would be shaped by the expressive function in which the author is content to recount the drama of the inner conflict between the conscious conventionality of the personage's intersubjective, dialogical life, and the eruption of individuating negativity (latent in a personage's semiotic position) into that conventional life. Thus, how can a narrative be structured in such a way that the narrative personage can be invested with a positive form of intersubjectivity that overcomes the negativity inherent in his/her semiotic position?

It is obvious now that the crucial problem is the barrier which separates the narrator and the personage erected by the ''he/she.'' In both the representative and expressive narratives, that barrier remains firmly in place. The symbolic narrative arises from the possibility of providing for the personages an originating relation to the communicative axis which joins the character and author. Characters in a narrative, unlike persons in life, originate in a speech event where narrators pose an "I," or instance of speech, as the referential object of the narrational pronouns, "he" or "she." Their subjectivity thus does not initially take form in the narrative across intersubjective mediation in an event of mutual recognition with another consciousness, but rather in an event which negates and suppresses such a relationship (that is, with the author). This, consequently, prevents them from attaining genuine subjectivity, which implies genuine freedom to function as the positive source of their own utterances and actions in response to others. Even in the expressive narrative where consciousness takes form almost exclusively in the dialogical interplay with other subjects, their *actions* arise from the hidden negativity upon which their functional existence is based, which is the effaced author for whom the narrative personages are still objects of his/her analytic, manipulative thought.

It is clear, then, that for the character to acquire a primary communicative axis the barrier which separates her/him from the narrator must be lowered in some way since it is only along this axis that the character can take form through intersubjective mediation. But for this to occur requires a reordering of the surface of the text and the emergence of a new form of narrative discourse positioned midway between the DN and DC. As discussed above, Doležel finds such a reordering in the elimination of the opposition of the DN and DC, and the penetration of the character's discourse into the narration which he thinks is one of the basic characteristics of modern prose.[19] Critics have termed this new feature of discourse variously as "free indirect discourse," "represented speech," "narrated monologue," as noted above.[20]

Ann Banfield has analyzed this feature of narrative prose from a linguistic viewpoint. Referring to this element in the novel as free indirect style, she characterizes it as a form of speech that is virtually indistinguishable from the actual thought of the characters, even though it is couched in the third-person form. A statement which has one meaning in direct speech, such as: "That really killed me" has quite another meaning when transformed into regular indirect speech, such as: "That really killed him." Nevertheless, in the context of free indirect style, it is quite clear in its figurative import even though occurring in the third person.[21] Since such statements occur in narratives not possessing a first-person narrator who could convey her/his inner thoughts in this fashion to the reader, they cannot be taken as equivalent to merely surface transformations of the first-person speech of the narrator. This has given rise to the theory of what Banfield calls the "third-person subject-of-consciousness,"[22] which is unique in that it has the form of direct discourse, but does not exist in a communicative framework of an "I" and a "you."[23]

S.-Y. Kuroda finds a parallel speech form in Japanese where there is a grammatical mark for what he calls a reportive style which causes a phrase to refer indirectly to the narrator even when the content is expressive (that is, presents the inner states of a personage). This has the effect of causing the statement to convey a fact about the character's inner state rather than to express it directly. But when the mark of reporting speech is omitted, these states are conveyed as direct expressions in third-person speech. He calls this form "non-reportive speech" and argues that the elimination of the grammatical sign of reporting speech in these sentences suggests the absence of a narrator, as well as the narrator–narratee relation.[24] The result is, as Banfield puts it, a grammatical alteration which makes possible the presentation of "various unspoken consciousness."[25] Most occurrances of free indirect speech represent the consciousness of a narrative personage. Occasionally, however, the location of the consciousness becomes highly ambiguous and cannot be identified with either the character or the narrator.[26] Stanzel has found such an occurrence in the chapter, "Sirens – The Concert Room" in Joyce's *Ulysses*, where, through a montage of narrated monologue, unmarked direct discourse, indirect discourse, and interior monologue, a scene is presented as if it were the contents of someone's consciousness in the scene (not the narrator), and yet is not identifiable with any single consciousness: "None of the figures present can clearly be regarded as the medium of presentation in the chapter. The events are mirrored in an impersonal consciousness which belongs to none of the figures."[27] In keeping with the overall character of free indirect speech, the duration of the scene approximates the duration of the events taking place. Stanzel accounts for this transcending of the figures as a movement away from the mimesis of outer reality into the happening of language: "This mode of presentation is characterized by a continuous attempt to move the mimesis of reality away from the realm of the words' meanings and into the body of the word itself, into the sound and sight pattern of the language."[28]

Roland Barthes describes the same phenomenon as being an occasion where language speaks: "The more indeterminate the origin of the statement, the more plural the text. In modern texts, the voices are so treated that any reference is impossible: the discourse, or better, the language speaks: nothing more."[29]

But what is the status of these "other consciousnesses" that cannot be reduced to either the author's or character's instance of speech? Is there a basis for such a narrational phenomenon in the structure of the sign?

Ortigues has shown that there is an ambivalence in the expressive sign. At the same time that it makes possible the individuation of the self, and thus its expression, it is also the agency through which the self encounters not only the other (the interlocutor), but the community as well, in forms of language which are also the basis of the community. This means that every linguistic expression is oriented not only toward the referent, but also toward the implicit meaning associated with linguistic form which is shared by the interlocutors as members of the same linguistic community. Expression thus must presuppose and arise from an implicit event of mutual recognition between subjects in which each subject comes to self-recognition. The prototypical events of this sort which have become formalized and elevated to serve as the foundations of the social order are promises, oaths, etc., which make possible the formal embodiment of this mutual recognition associated with linguistic forms. Through such events language is experienced as a creative, founding force shaping the human subject. It is because of this illocutionary dimension of language that it is meaningful to speak of a primary prohibition (Freud) or to say that "language speaks" (Barthes).

It should be clear that this is not some form of subordination to "society," since society itself is also founded upon the same linguistic forms. As Ortigues says: "language is not merely an interpreter, a medium of exchange in society," since "society takes form in the language it gives itself," and there is no society if there is no language. To overlook this is to beg the question.[30]

It is thus in the relation of consciousness to illocutionary force associated with linguistic form and implicit meanings that we encounter this "third" dimension of consciousness, the "other" dimension which cannot be equated with the interlocutor, the society, or the speaker's own consciousness, although it is, in a sense, that to which all three are themselves subjected. It is that non-objectifiable dimension of language over against which and in terms of which a speaker shapes her/his own subjective awareness, as well as that of characters, if s/he is an author. Bakhtin refers to this phenomenon as an implicit, quite personal, third dimension of dialogue: "Each dialogue takes place as if against the background of the responsive understanding of an invisibly present third party who stands above all the participants in the dialogue (partners)."[31]

When it is a matter of not merely expressing a thought, but of giving voice to a narrative personage, more is involved than simply a referential language use. The complex fragmentation of the subject which is displayed across the figurative instances of discourse connects the imaginative process of narrative writing with the deepest conflicts and emotions in the author.[32] The speech of a narrative personage thus takes form first in a preliminary inner dialogue within the author before being shaped to fit into the semiotic system which structures the plot.[33]

Neither the expressive narrative nor the representative narrative allows this preliminary inner dialogue at the root of the character to come to expression. The symbolic narrative, however, arises from the possibility of articulating through progressive synthetic reflection within and beyond the representational semiotics of the text, the open moment when the character appears in the consciousness of the author as one who is subject to the creative occurrence of language, that is, as one who speaks. This constitutes a symbolic form of expression in Ortigues' terms, since it is a relation of a sign (personage) to a sign (author), and not a sign to a referent.[34] It can assume the appearance of direct discourse even in the absence of an interlocutor because it is a speech event which brings to "life" the subjectivity of the speaking personage. More often it involves a coalescing (though not total merging) of the subjectivity of the narrator and character as in free indirect speech.

This possibility for the narrative personage to begin to speak arises along the axis of communication with another instance of speech, namely, that of the author.[35] In the fictive character's discourse, there is a convergence of the subjective posture of the writer toward language in the act of writing with that of the character. As the author writes, s/he becomes simultaneously subject to the same inner force of language as that to which the consciousness of the character is subjected. The character also enters the subjectivity of the author since there is a complete correspondence between the verbal process at work within the character, and that at work in the author in the act in which s/he writes the character into existence on the page. In such manner is the separation of the fictive character and author effected by the third-person speech partially overcome so that the semiotic negation upon which the narrative personage is based is altered, enabling the character's speech to participate to some degree in the power and openness of the authorial instance of speech. In this way the character acquires a limited form of intersubjectivity.

This type of writing is much less likely to occur in the first person since most first-person narratives assume a temporal gap between the narrating self and the experiencing self. They thus assume a completed self which can be retrospectively described. In the symbolic narrative the experiencing self comes into existence with the occurrence of language in the moment of narration/writing. But an example of such writing in the first person is found in the "Penelope" section of Joyce's *Ulysses* which Dorrit Cohn terms an "autonomous monologue." This narrative is characterized by its lack of scenic description, reportorial observations, or even explicit references to the actions of the character. Instead there is only inner speech, or, as Dorrit Cohn says, "moments of verbalization" with no external addressee, which occur dramatically, making narrated time and time of narration perfectly correspond:

> Whereas in ordinary narration time is a flexible medium that can be, at will, speeded up (by summary), retarded (by description or digression), advanced (by anticipation), or reversed (by retrospect), an autonomous monologue – in the absence of a manipulating narrator – advances time solely by the articulation of thoughts, and advances it evenly along a one-way path until words come to a halt on the page.[36]

The logic of such a narrative style in the first person would seem to require an account of the writing itself, a frequent motif which, in fact, does occur in symbolic narratives. But even more importantly, it is illogical for symbolic narration in the first person not to concern itself exclusively with the act of writing, since the present experience of the consciousness being represented in the text in the first person is the experience of writing. The difficulties presented by this problem may account for this form of writing being found more frequently in the third person, or, as in *Ulysses*, in the context of a larger narrative.

When third person is used in symbolic narration as free indirect speech, the personage is not presented as an object, but rather as an open subject constituted in events of speech inscribed on the page even in the direct, immediate process of their occurrence. The third-person discourse takes on the features of direct discourse as it is absorbed into the inner life of the narrative personage. The personage is open almost in the same way that the author is open toward the future, since both experience themselves as arising from the same type of inner discourse. Both achieve symbolic presence to themselves as they identify with the language that awakens their consciousness, and make it their own self-expression.

Dorrit Cohn finds that narrated monologue in this type of inner discourse in Hermann Broch's *Death of Virgil* approaches lyric poetry: "here the perceiving mind belongs to a creative poet, who would naturally (professionally) transmute the reality he perceives into poetic language – at the very moment when he perceives it."[37] Stanzel sees the whole of Joyce's *Ulysses* as being ordered by the creative process itself in the mode of stream-of-consciousness normally found only in the speech of characters. He terms this a conceptual monologue:[38]

> The subject for the world of *Ulysses* is simply the author's consciousness at the moment of the process of conception ... Unlike the monologue in the drama or interior monologue, the conceptual monologue is not primarily a means of self-expression, but rather a stage in the work's development; it expresses the process of the author's objective formation of a world. It is therefore not the personal self of the monologizing author, but a dramatized self, the creative consciousness of the artist.

This does not mean that the character becomes identical with the author, but rather that s/he is able to embody and participate in the very instance of speech in the consciousness of the author which is the source of her/his own subjectivity, that is, the "other" dimension of consciousness. We cannot reduce the personage to the author, since the concept of the author is even more problematic. The "identity" of both are shrouded in the "mysterious elective contingency of the sign," since the author is no less a creature of language than are his characters. And which author? The actual author? The "implied author"?[39]

This instance of inner speech, the "other" consciousness, which can be equated with neither that of the character nor that of the author, has been the most profoundly illuminated in the novel by Dostoyevsky. Bakhtin, in his study of Dostoyevsky, finds his novels to be organized around various dialogical processes that permit the characters to define themselves in their speech rather than in the narrational framework. This installs the character in a position of freedom beyond the grasp of any objectifying system of concepts. As Bakhtin says of Dostoyevsky, the final truth of the character can only be given by him in the form of a "confessional self-utterance."[40]

But in Dostoyevsky the possibility of a confessional self-utterance arises from the character's private self which takes the form of what he calls the inner "micro-dialogue."[41] Sometimes this inner dialogue begins to penetrate the third-person barrier, and appears as a dialogical (but not the literal compositional form of the dialogue) relation between the character and the author. Bakhtin describes it in this way: "the author's word about the hero is a word about a word. It is oriented to the hero as if to a word, and therefore is *dialogically addressed* to him. By the very construction of the novel the author speaks not *about* the hero but *with* him" (his emphasis).[42] By assuming a dialogical stance toward the personage, s/he thus enables the character to gain integral force which can transcend the closure of any explanation or image which the author might wish to impose.

These possible closed interpretations are taken themselves into the self-consciousness of the character as material for inner reflection. It was this dialogization of the author–character relation that Bakhtin says constituted the "small scale Copernican upheaval" which Dostoyevsky achieved in the style of the novel. This dialogue, of course, does not take the overt form of the author explicitly, by name, entering the narrative to speak with the character. Rather, the "dialogue" occurs as the kind of material which would occur in the narrative framework in the typical "monological" novel is increasingly taken up into the inner dialogue of the personage.

This means then that the focal point of the novel's drama shifts from the external action and dialogue to the internal micro-dialogue out of which the external words and happenings generally develop. Because the irreducible subjectivity of the personage coincides with this inner dialogical process, it becomes a seminal power, a creative force which stands beyond and cannot be equated with (though at times it does coincide with) the author, the social influences, and so forth. As such it comes to occupy a dominant semantic position in the novel. Concretely, this dialogue must consist of two voices. Only one of these can be properly considered the voice of the personage.

The voice of the 'Other' in the symbolic narrative

What, then, can be said about the other pole which cannot be simply reduced to the proportions of any objective source? It is here that we encounter the operation of the "dominant idea" in Dostoyevsky. According to Bakhtin, "The 'dominant idea' was indicated already in the plan of every one of

Dostoyevsky's novels.''[43] In Dostoyevsky's words, ''the idea becomes an *object of artistic representation*, and Dostoyevsky himself became a great *artist of the idea*.''[44] But what he means by idea is not the statement in representational language of some system of thought either in the narrative framework or in the direct discourse of the personage. Rather, he is speaking of a particular mode of subjective existence characteristic of the leading personages of his works. In a very fundamental sense, Bakhtin argues, ''Dostoyevsky's hero is the man of an idea.''[45] The particular semantic content of the idea takes second place to the *function* of the idea within the process of inner dialogue that constitutes the subjective personhood of the character. For the character to be a ''man of an idea'' means that s/he exists subjectively in a state of indeterminate openness toward the idea which lives within as a vital force. This idea becomes integral and integrating for the entire person, and evokes the deepest feelings as well as thoughts.

This inner locus of indeterminate openness from which arises the dialogical response to the force of the idea, Dostoyevsky calls the ''man in man.'' The inner self can never be incorporated in any kind of equation or identity with any object or conceptual understanding. As Bakhtin says:[46]

> Man is never coincident with himself. The equation of identity A = A is inapplicable to him. In Dostoyevsky's artistic thoughts the genuine life of the personality is played out in the point of non-intersection of man with himself, at the point of his departure beyond the limits of all that he is in terms of material being which can be spied out, defined and predetermined without his will, ''at second hand'' [*zaochno*].

Thus, opposed to the pole of the idea within the subjectivity of the personage is the free, indeterminate core of personal consciousness that Dostoyevsky can call the ''holy of holies,'' or the ''man in man.''[47]

But the character's entrance into this inner state of dialogue is itself a dramatic process which shapes consciousness and changes personal being. Bakhtin describes it in this way: ''in Dostoyevsky's works man overcomes his 'thingness' [*veshchnost*] and becomes 'man in man' only by entering the pure and unfinalized sphere of the idea, i.e., only by becoming the selfless man of an idea.''[48] The self-centered desire which drives the standard narrative character toward the possession of and identity with the image/object which the imagination reveals as the solution to inner emptiness is thus overcome in Dostoyevsky's characters by their relation to this ''*full-valued*'' idea.[49] At the price of the sacrifice of the self-centered desire, they are introduced into a genuine life of intersubjectivity which they live, from the power mediated by the idea. In return for the sacrifice of the object of desire: ''The idea aids the self-consciousness in asserting its sovereignty within Dostoyevsky's artistic world and helps it triumph over every firm and stable image.''[50] Gérard Genette describes Proust's experience of writing in similar terms.[51]

The power of the idea stems from the fact that it provides the link which connects the inner private world of the character with the intersubjective sphere of the larger world of which s/he is a part. The link is partially established by the dialogical matrix in which it lives in relation to other person-ideas: "Human thought becomes genuine thought, i.e., an idea, only under the conditions of a living contact with another foreign thought, embodied in the voice of another person, i.e., in the consciousness of another person as expressed in his word. It is in the point of contact of these voice-consciousnesses that the idea is born and has its life."[52]

But this means that the idea has its own existence precisely in the dialogical process that occurs between individuals, i.e., it lives in the dialogue of a society. Bakhtin thus can say: "The idea is a *living event* which is played out in the point where two or more consciousnesses meet dialogically."[53] But this means that the leading ideas of his characters were not themselves invented by Dostoyevsky. He found them in the discourse of Russian society at that time. As Bakhtin says: "As an artist Dostoyevsky did not create his ideas in the same way that philosophers and scholars create theirs – he created living images of the ideas which he found, detected, or sometimes divined in *reality itself*, i.e., images of already-living ideas, ideas already existing as idea-forces."[54]

These may, as well, be ideas which Dostoyevsky himself perceives as *latent* words or forces which are destined to become significant in the dialogical life of the society at a future time. Bakhtin quotes Dostoyevsky as saying: "Reality is not limited to the familiar, the commonplace for it consists in huge part of a *latent*, as yet *unspoken future Word.*"[55]

Thus finding the explicit and latent idea-forces at work in the dialogue of his time, Dostoyevsky took them over and transformed them according to his artistic purpose. This involved depriving them of their monological, systematic form, and placing them in an internal subjective context where they could appear as potencies which shaped the consciousness and future of his characters. This means that the idea was not presented merely in terms of what it has been, but in terms of its potentiality, its future dimension, because, as Bakhtin says, "it is just these potentialities that are of prime importance for an artistic image."[56]

In this way the idea operating within the inner life of the character connects her/him with the actual historical forces of the time which are as vital for the author and reader as for the fictional persons. This can lead, then, to a homology between the subjective stance of the author *vis-à-vis* the idea, and that of the character. Both author and character live out of an inner dialogue with the idea-forces of the time, and the indeterminacy of this dialogical consciousness may be as real for the author as it is for the character.

The common subjective orientation of the author and character toward the same inter-individual idea-event, which has its roots not in the private literary imagination of the author but in the socio-cultural realities of the historical epoch, points clearly to the junction between religious faith and ideology in Dostoyevsky's world. For him, the ultimate goal of the ideological search was not an idea at all, but the voice of the ideal man. As Bakhtin says: "The image of the ideal man or the image of Christ represents for him the solution of ideological quests ... Precisely the image of a man and his voice (a voice not the author's own) was the ultimate ideological criterion for Dostoyevsky: not faithfulness to his own convictions, and not the merit of the convictions themselves, taken abstractly, but precisely faithfulness to the authoritative image of the man."[57]

This final grounding of subjective consciousness in the traditional symbolism of a culture corresponds exactly to what Medina called non-formal reflection which sees the primal symbolic act at the root of consciousness and language as a non-predicative narrative act, that is, an act of encounter with other consciousnesses that can be recounted only in the direct discourse of living dialogue which incorporates the traditional symbolism in which societies articulate their world views, rather than in the objectifying analytic language of the disembodied intellect. It opens out upon what he called "biographical reason."

Dostoyevsky's description of the idea stemming from the reality of the present and past, but experienced by the subject as a potentiality for the future, and his view of Christ as belonging to the past as well as being a sign of the future (his chief religious question was "What would Christ do?"[58]), indicates that this third subjective consciousness or voice embodies the properties which Ortigues argued were fundamental to the character of the sign as "reminiscence and promise." Here, however, within the context of narrative, where the semiological roots of consciousness can be recovered and articulated through the voices and actions of semantically empty subjects, Dostoyevsky has posed his subjects as inwardly and outwardly thoroughgoing creatures of the sign (understood as a medium of intersubjectivity). But the lowering of the barrier between the bifurcated instances of speech (DN–DC) established by the narrative form has permitted the recovery and articulation of a third and more fundamental speech act – that upon which the consciousness of both the character and the narrator are based. Since this foundational sign/event can take its particular substance from religious as well as ideological traditions, it is here that we find the point of junction of the polyphonic symbolic narrative form of Dostoyevsky and the Biblical narrative, which, as we shall see below in Part II, is also rooted in inner speech events which found the Biblical character upon an intersubjective relation with a sign understood as both reminiscence and promise.

It remains to be shown, however, how the artistic experience of form is made accessible through the symbolic, polyphonic narrative. Though this narrative type centers upon dialogue – as did the expressive narrative – the symbolic narrative is not totally relativistic.[59] On the other hand, it also does not submit to a unified, monological, covertly dogmatic system of ideas. It does not "represent" truth in the form of a conceptual object. The unique textual feature which enables it to avoid both of these possibilities is the inner dialogue, the inner word by means of which the communicative axis of the character's instance of speech is opened toward that of the actual narrator, so that a convergence may take place between the subjective stance of the author toward the occurrence of language within his own consciousness and that of his character.

Dorrit Cohn finds such an enigmatic inner dialogue also in Poe's story, "The Tell-Tale Heart," where

> Without overture, a listening "you" is addressed, who remains disincarnated to the end: is it a listener mutely present on the fictional scene? is it the reader? or is it an imaginary interlocutor, present only in the speaker's mind? ... Many texts have analogous narrative presentations: a first person compulsively buttonholes a second person who seems to be simultaneously inside and outside the fictional scene, inside and outside the speaking self.[60]

The effect of the intrusion of the inner word into the form of the narrative is to shift the terms of the dramatic conflict through which the primary artistic experience of the form takes place. Whereas in the representative narrative the conflict was posed in terms of full versus empty sign/personages, and in the expressive narrative between the relativized dialogical consciousnesses of the characters and the mysterious, hidden negativity which drove their action into contradiction with their words, here in the symbolic narrative, the major conflict is configured differently. On the one hand there is the inner, free, indeterminate subjectivity formed by the inner dialogue of the private center of the subject (the "man in man") with the dominant full-valued idea, and on the other, the closure which the other would impose through objectifying, analytical, descriptive, representational language.

With reference to Dostoyevsky's characters, Bakhtin says: "They all acutely feel their own inner unfinalizedness and their capacity to outgrow and make *untrue* any definition that externalizes and finalizes them ... Dostoyevsky's hero always seeks to shatter the finalizing, deadening framework of '*others*' words about him."[61]

In this way the form of representational language is itself revealed as it is brought into the context of the personage's self-consciousness. There, within the context of the subject's transcending freedom and indeterminacy, of his relation to the potency of the full-valued idea with its future possibilities, object-oriented representative language is revealed as a bearer of closure and death to the subject, as a force which he must struggle against. On the other hand, the vital idea, filled with its potentiality, comes to mediate to him his own intersubjectivity, his own personhood. It is as he comes to take upon himself the idea, as he *becomes* the bodily representation of the idea, that he experiences the fullness of his own presence to himself, and simultaneously the presence of others as well across the dialogue of living ideas embodied in others.

Bakhtin indicates that Shklovsky, in his interpretation of Dostoyevsky, was very close to this understanding of the artistic perception of form in his view that "it is precisely the *conflict*, the struggle of ideological voices, that lies at the core of the artistic *form* of Dostoyevsky's works, at the core of his *style.*"[62] But Shklovsky turned away from an analysis of the semiological implications of this conflict toward a concern with identifying their historical sources.

Shklovsky did, however, indicate one further absolutely central feature of Dostoyevsky's style which flows from the central polyphonic conflict. When the central focus shifts away from either external or internal action-oriented conflict toward this internal conflict between voices, the plot structure loses its orientation toward a decisive end. Bakhtin quotes Shklovsky as saying: "*As long as a work remained multileveled and multivoiced, as long as the people in it were still arguing, despair over the absence of a conclusion was postponed.*"[63] Here, in a sense, is the ultimate novelistic device for prolonging the artistic experience of form, since now the center of the conflict has become the forms as they strike upon each other within the inner and outer dialogical processes. The meaning of the narrative is thus realized each moment in the polyphonic interchange, and not in the achievement of some decisive action which imposes closure upon this process.[64]

The decentering of the value of the ending corresponds to the movement of the narrator himself into the horizon of the great dialogue of the novel so that he is led in his writing not by the vision of the end, but by the creative emergence of the possibilities opened by the tensions of the dialogical polarities. As Bakhtin describes it:

> For the author, the hero is not "he" and not "I," but a full-valued "thou," that is, another full-fledged "I" ("Thou art"). The hero is the subject of a profoundly serious *actual* dialogical mode of address, as opposed to a rhetorically *acted-out* or *conventional* literary one. And this dialogue – the "great dialogue" of the novel as a whole – takes place not in the past, but now, in the *present* of the creative process.[65]

This does not mean that there is no plot with a conclusion in Dostoyevsky's novels, but only that the plot structure itself is often semantically subverted by the dialogical process so that the endings are rendered ambiguous or inconclusive in some other way. Tension remains between the essentially unfinalizable hero and the closure imposed upon him by the need for a conventional plot ending.[66]

This reorientation of the plot away from the ending toward the semiotic process by which characters are formed did not first appear in the writings of Dostoyevsky as Bakhtin suggests. Marie-Paule Laden has shown that a number of eighteenth-century autobiographical novels grew out of the same type of problematic which Bakhtin has discovered in Dostoyevsky.[67] The first-person narrator in these novels has a self-conscious relationship to his/her earlier persona which corresponds to the relation of a third-person author to his/her characters. The writing of the narrative requires that the relation of the author's present writing voice to his/her earlier self/selves be defined in one way or another. These writers are not as free as Dostoyevsky was to move across the boundary separating the narrator and character, since the earlier self cannot be created out of whole cloth by the later self. Nevertheless, the boundary can be transcended in some curious and surprising ways with some of the same consequences for the plot.

In *Pamela: or, Virtue Rewarded* by Samuel Richardson, the narrative takes the form first of letters written by the heroine to her parents up to the point of her being taken prisoner; after this the diary form is used. The plot of the story centers in the efforts by Pamela, a servant girl, to protect her virtue against repeated attempts by the master of the household, Mr. B., to seduce her. Writing letters to her parents comes to play a central role in her effort, since in her letters she creates a self-image of virtue which, in turn, serves to strengthen her powers of resistance. Writing comes to occupy a large portion of her time, and leads eventually to Mr. B. and others clandestinely reading some of her letters. The image of Pamela he discovers in the letters then begins to affect his regard for her virtue. This then adds a new dimension to the act of writing as Laden points out:

> Once she knows that her letters have a growing public (first her parents, to whom they are presumably addressed, then Mr. B., and later Lady Davers and the neighbors), her sense of pride as author protects her virtue as she enlarges her sense of self through writing and being read. Through her letters Pamela becomes the author of herself under the gaze of her public, as she watches herself being watched.[68]

The unfolding of the plot then is made possible by the writing of the protagonist which recounts it: "Her story is the emerging or appearing of this second identity, both *être* and *paraître*."[69] By the incorporation of the act of writing into the plot as a central feature of it, the focus of the plot shifts away from the ending toward the process of character development which is occurring in and through the event of writing itself.

A further level of analysis reveals the nature of the self-image which Pamela is creating for herself. While Richardson portrays the act of writing as the formative influence on her character, it is not the verbal act but the referential content of her writing that gives form to Pamela's self: "What Pamela is offering here and everywhere in her text is a highly manipulated version of herself and of appearances ... objectifying herself to watch herself being watched and approved."[70] By bringing the act of writing (even though fictive) into the plot, however, Richardson makes this process of self-formation through writing the central dynamic of the narrative.

A further stage in this development can be seen in Sterne's *Tristram Shandy*. There the fictive autobiographical author exhibits an intense awareness that, although he goes into great detail recounting the remote past of his family even before he was born (and including his own birth, in great detail), his writing about his life is also a part of life and thus belongs in his narrative. This is given a humorous twist when the writer observes that his life is moving so much faster than his writing about it that he will never finish. He seeks to be so thorough in recounting his origins, that, apart from volume VII, the narrative does not carry the character beyond the age of five. Thus the mature Tristram appears in the narrative, not in retrospective accounts of his deeds, but in present-tense accounts of the writing of the text which go so far as to provide the date on which particular portions were being written and the attire of the writer. Laden thus argues that "the main story told in Tristram's memoirs is that of its coming into being, to the extent that the work becomes the chronicle of its own creation, and through it, that of the author's."[71]

But since the writing is not contemporaneous with the actions being recounted, as was the case with Pamela, how then can it contribute to the formation of Tristram's character? The intrusion of accounts of his writing into the narrative sets up a correspondence and interaction between the life in the past he is recounting, and his life in the present which is dominated by the activity of writing. In this way, as Laden says: "Tristram uses his book to define himself in relation to the other, be it the Shandy community or the writer's audience."[72] His writing thus becomes the activity through which his identity and his life are formed in the present.

This opens up a much deeper disclosure of the process of writing itself since it becomes the organizing and unifying center of the narrative. The picture Tristram paints is not one of a detached, rational intellect, serenely crafting his narrative, but of struggle with problems of evidence, with control over his material, with organization, and with writing itself. As his life and his writing have come to coincide, he becomes aware that he is not in control of his writing. As Laden explains:

> In the same way as Walter could not prevent his son's nose from being crushed by the Papist Slop's forceps during delivery, so the narrator expresses his inability to determine what he is writing: "As my pen, – it governs me, – I govern it not –" (p. 40), or "– for I begin with writing the first sentence – and trusting to Almighty God for the second" (p. 540). The narrator even calls his work "rhapsodical" (p. 35), or "a wilderness" (p. 408), a book with neither beginning, middle nor end, since the reader has to get to page 192 for the preface to it.[73]

This lack of control produces frequent digressions that have no clear bearing upon a plot development, extraordinary leaps in time, and the incorporation of diverse genres which break the surface viewpoint of the narrative. But more importantly, it evidences the drama taking place in the writing of the work which will disclose to the author his own identity. Unlike Pamela, whose identity is contained in the highly controlled, idealized self which she represents in her letters, Tristram's identity is formed in a tumultuous and ultimately mysterious encounter with the force of language in the act of writing. (Although he claims at times to be in complete control, he cannot sustain it.) As Bakhtin says of Dostoyevsky, Tristram becomes unfinalizable. No definitive end/identity can be reached because his character is taking form in an ongoing dialogical encounter with writing, with language (and with God?) that emerges from a source beyond his rational control. Genette describes the experience of the "true writer" in similar terms: "the true writer is capable of thinking only in the silence and secrecy of writing; he knows and experiences at each moment that when he writes it is not he who is thinking his language, but *his language which is thinking him* and thinking outside him" (my emphasis).[74]

It is this phenomenon at the center of a certain type of writing experience which provides a model for understanding the role of the divine Voice in the Genesis narrative.[75]

The symbolic/expressive narrative

The fundamental symbolic features of a narrative do not exclude the possibility that both the expressive and representative strategies may also be used in combination with them. Since the semantic tension of a symbolic narrative often arises from the juxtaposition of the symbolic-intersubjective self with the autonomous self, this juxtaposition may require the reliance upon the expressive or representative functions to develop the tensions of the plot. When this occurs the narrator self-consciously exposes the problematic nature of the self-constructions of the other functions and modes. As an illustration of the way in which a symbolic narrator does this we will look briefly at some examples from Dostoyevsky. The combination of functions is very widespread in the Genesis narratives to be examined below.

Bakhtin describes Dostoyevsky as an "artist of the idea" because he reworked ideas "in the very same way that an artist works with his human prototypes."[76] The artist does not simply paint what s/he sees, but portrays the stance or modality which s/he assumes when consciousness meets the perceptual field. Dostoyevsky did this by freeing ideas from the monological form in order to make them a part of a great dialogue where their "potentialities" could be explored and developed by placing them "at the vortex of dialogically intersecting consciousnesses."[77] It is these *functions* which constitute the non-logical, non-referential dimension of the inner dialogical words, and imbue them with their potentiality. Thus it is the functions which provide these inner words with force and voice requiring a response involving not simply the logical faculty of the personage, but her/his whole subjective being.

The symbolic relation of the character to the word with the expressive function takes the form of an inner dialogue with the voice of another personage. Dostoyevsky explores these possibilities in *The Double*. The difficulty with this mode of subjectivity is that increasingly the protagonist loses his ability to distinguish between his own voice and the voice of the other. This leads him finally into loss of contact with himself and to absorption into the voice of the other. As Bakhtin says: "Golyadkin lives only in the other person, he lives in his reflection in the other person: 'Will it be proper', 'will it be appropriate?' And this question is always answered from the possible, conjectured point of view of the other person."[78] Eventually Golyadkin seems to lose his mind and is institutionalized.

Though similar to the expressive narrative in that the character is permitted to define himself in direct speech about himself and acts continuously in ways that contradict his words, the expressive-symbolic mode of character development differs in that the conflict is posed in terms of the inner struggle between the subject and the voices of others. The narrative traces through the inner dialogues the process by which the subject passes into a state of self-alienation and loss of freedom. Evil here does not remain for the reader a mysterious and almost metaphysical force, but is made obvious in the character's gradual loss of contact with his own "man in man," the subjective center of his own instance of speech. His "I" is taken over by the "you," by the imaginary perspective of others upon him.

The symbolic/representative narrative

Dostoyevsky again provides us with an excellent example of character development in the symbolic-representative mode. Though this mode might be portrayed in types of inner words, in his treatment of Kirilov in *The Possessed*, he gives it the form of an idea: the idea of God and of the non-existence of God. But it is not the theoretical question of God's existence that interests Dostoyevsky. Rather, it is the existential implications which his character is able to draw out from this idea and its negation.

The central issue is the implication of the idea of God for human freedom. Kirilov perceives God exclusively in terms of absolute power. Such a God cannot coexist with human freedom. In semiological terms, we could say that he perceives God as the word-event which breaks the continuity of consciousness and the world, and establishes the individual as an empty sign filled only with illegitimate desires to regain his lost unity with the absolute presence of the thing. He sees God thus as that power which totally negates the human will and deprives the human of his freedom to act. The implication which Kirilov succinctly draws from this is that: "If God exists, then the whole will is His and I can do nothing."[79]

But Kirilov's great idea is that God does not exist, and this carries the opposite implication that "all will is mine, and I must exercise my own will, my free will."[80] By proclaiming the non-existence of God, Kirilov can thus constitute himself as an absolutely free subject, in fact, as God himself. Thus Dostoyevsky creates for us a character who exists subjectively, but does not attain intersubjectivity: he is a secular mystic who has renounced the material desires of the world, and seeks his identity in the roots of his subjective consciousness. But when he finds there the idea of God as an absolute cosmic will which is both his ultimate source as well as his negation, he refuses to accept it, that is, he refuses this form of intersubjective existence.

This, however, leaves Kirilov in a precarious position as a narrative personage. If God does not exist, there is no limiting other as a source of conflict either within his subjective consciousness or outside himself in society. The only remaining limit imposed upon him is his body, which he now perceives as the final obstacle to the attainment of absolute freedom. As he explains it: "I can't imagine that there's not one person on our whole planet who, having put an end to God and believing in his own free will, will dare to exercise that free will on the most important point."[81] He thus feels impelled to be that *one* who dares to draw out the ultimate implications of absolute freedom, and concludes: "I have an obligation to shoot myself because the supreme gesture of free will is to kill oneself."[82]

Kirilov thus must finally make himself into an object. The first-person declaration of his intention to kill himself is formulated as a deduction which he has drawn from a general truth formulated in the third person: "the supreme gesture of free will is to kill *oneself*." The individual, material reality of his own instance of speech has been consumed by the general truth since individual existence now appears to be the final limit imposed upon his freedom. But the irony is that his own *voice*, by which he exists as a subject in the first person, falls victim literally to the voiceless "oneself" of the general truth.

Kirilov destroys himself when he attempts the impossible – to become the narrator of his own life-story. When the character posits for himself a subjective existence that is beyond the limits of the intersubjective relation along the communicative axis with the author, he puts himself in the position of the author. In achieving this transcendent position, however, he must objectify himself. His inner relation to himself, like the author's relation to his characters, is then mediated by the third person. This means that his own concrete instance of speech, his "I," becomes fundamentally a "he," and his relation to himself takes the form of the free subject's struggle against objectification, closure, and loss of freedom. This logically leads to suicide since it is only through the destruction of his own instance of speech that he can then overcome objectification and attain absolute freedom. Dostoyevsky thus shows how subjectivity, when it is not grounded finally in some form of limiting intersubjectivity, consumes itself. Kirilov calls it being "swallowed up by an idea."[83]

The terms of the narrative conflict in the symbolic narrative are thus transferred into the inner dialogue of the characters where, in one way or another, they wrestle with the ambivalent and even contradictory existential implications of the sign. The form this takes is some form of inner dialogue over the issue of subjective freedom versus domination by a word which imposes limits and negates the desires of the self. The writer of the symbolic narrative thus poses his protagonists as consciously confronted with such existential oppositions.[84]

From this analysis we now can bring together some of the characteristic features of the symbolic narrative.

(1) The boundary between the author and the narrative personages is transgressed so as to make the dynamics of the act of writing, in one form or another, into a central force in the structure of the plot.
(2) The central narrative personages are, to some extent, morally ambiguous. There are no unequivocally good or evil personages.
(3) The focus of the narrative is upon the formation of the personages through some form of subjective encounter with the force of language, as opposed to desire, objective action or circumstance. The tension of the plot stems from the contradiction between the forces impinging upon the narrative personages from these various sources.
(4) The ending lacks the normal resolution of the tension, and is ambiguous, or suggests a continuation of the process of character formation begun in the narrative.

II

THE STRUCTURE OF THE GENESIS NARRATIVE

6

The divine Voice and the narrative functions

In analyzing the Genesis narrative it will be necessary to begin by determining the dominant sign function as it is disclosed in the DN–DC relation. But this cannot be accomplished as directly as for the modern narrative because of the possibility that parts of the text were composed by different authors in different historical periods and brought into a single unity by yet other writers. The possibility exists, thus, that the DN–DC relation will not itself be consistent or uniform, but will vary depending upon the historical source of the portion of the text being analyzed (i.e., whether it stems from the hypothetical source documents, J, E, P, or D).

Another possibility also exists, however. Variations in the DN–DC relation might have no consistent correlation with the documentary source established by literary-historical criticism on the basis of stylistic and theological variations, but rather might correlate with other semiotic structures. In this eventuality, it would be necessary to understand the variations first of all from within the context of semiotic, narrative systems. In this case, the actual historical narrator(s) who may be implied by the DN would have no direct bearing upon the semiotically governed intra-textual variations of the DN–DC relation.

But to the extent that the results of the typological analysis do show a positive correlation with the source documents, they would contribute valuable new stylistic data to support this hypothesis. To the degree that the results are noncorrelative, they would suggest not that the divisions are invalid, but that the text is homogeneous in its semiotic characteristics across the varied sources from which the writer(s) may have drawn in the process of its composition.

This is to say, then, that the semiotic analysis being undertaken here neither fundamentally contradicts nor supports the literary-historical methods of analysis, but rather sets out to study features of the text which do not fall under the purview of these methods. For this reason, we cannot begin by building upon the results of literary-historical criticism since we will be looking at narrative features which could well have been common to all of the Pentateuchal narrators. If such be the case, then this will not prove that the narrative had a single author, but only show that there was a certain continuity in the fundamental compositional techniques of the various authors and redactors – something which is certainly not unreasonable to hypothesize in light of the overall structural balance and coherence which the text as a whole conveys to the general reader not adept at ferreting out subtle parallels and duplications. I will refer below to the authors of Genesis in the singular, however, as a matter of stylistic felicity.

We have seen that the most distinguishing semiotic feature of the narrative is its separation of the two axes of the sign – the representative and the communicative. By posing a character, not himself, as an instance of speech, the author establishes a sign outside of any community and thus with no immediately given relation to other instances of speech along the communicative axis. The implicit meaning that customarily attaches itself to the sign by virtue of the social and temporal position of its occurrence is then restored to the narrative personages from its relation to the seminal narrator's instance of speech according to one of the three possible modes: active, passive or indirect. These modes then determine which of the three basic functions of the sign will be dominant in both the DC and DN: the expressive, the representative or the symbolic.

It should be made clear, however, that this is a highly simplified schema. Narratives are complex in their modalities, and it is possible for a writer to slide from one modality to another as an artist blends colors to achieve effects. The functions and modalities should thus be viewed in relation to narratives more as one might view a chart of primary colors in relation to a painting. The typology will, I hope, identify the fundamental potentialities of narrative writing, but the "primary colors" will not necessarily appear in their pure form in specific narratives. Every narrative will thus tend to escape the categories of analysis to some extent (some more than others), preventing the attainment of "scientific" results. Such, however, may be the nature of "biographical reason" which this analysis accepts as the most fundamental form of rationality. The aim will be to determine the *dominant* modality and sign function only, but even this modest goal cannot attain formal completeness but must be satisfied if it succeeds in continuing the dialogue begun in the narrative.

As we have seen, the symbolic, intersubjective narrative function occurs when the barrier between the author and the characters is transgressed so as to allow the language events which give rise to the narrative personages in the process of writing to become a part of the discourse. It will be the purpose of this chapter to show how this mediating language event, which occurs between the author and the characters in the Genesis narrative, takes the form of a divine Voice. It is in micro-dialogues between the characters and the Voice that the intersubjective formation of the narrative personage occurs. From these events the narrative as a whole acquires its general features.

The philosophical enigma here is how to speak of the divine Voice in the inner dialogue of a human being. Ortigues points out that Augustine clearly saw the self-presence of the human subject grounded upon the presence of God mediated through the concept (*verbum, intelligentia*), the past (*memoria*), and the future (*voluntas*).[1] Ortigues seems to turn away from this theological solution, preferring to see here the proper role of language itself.

Our primary concern, however, is not the philosophical issue but rather the way in which this issue arises and is treated within Biblical literature, and particularly the "logic" of narrative literature. The connection between the philosophical-semiotic reflection of Ortigues and the problem of the subject in literature is found in the way in which the enigma of the self arises from the semiotic character of the "I." The "I," when understood as a sign which acquires its signifying potentiality only through the absence of the signified object, remains totally enigmatic for the consciousness dominated by the representative function of the sign. As soon as consciousness attempts to represent the reality of the "I" as an object among other objects, it substantially disappears, and the mind is left with an enigma, with nothing except the fleeting awareness of a paradox.

This attempt to relate the "I" to another sign, to ask, "*who am I*?" gives rise to a concrete form of self-reflectivity that is often found explicitly in poetry. Such symbolic speech by poets may offer us the experience of the defamiliarization of the self, the experience of the self as a strange, mysterious and even unknowable sign. This kind of musing upon the self is often set in motion not by another consciousness, or another word, but by such things as a sound which acts upon the mind as a voice might act, but without the sense of any contact with any consciousness beyond the self. Robert Penn Warren offers us an excellent example of such musing in his poem, "Speleology," which focuses upon an experience in utter darkness and solitude at the bottom of a cave where there is only the bubbling sound of an underground stream:[2]

> Lulled as by a song in a dream, knowing
> I dared not move in a darkness so absolute.
> I thought: *This is me*. Thought: *Me – who am I?* Felt
> Heart beating as though to a pulse of darkness and earth, and thought
> How would it be to be here forever, my heart,
> In its beat, part of all. Part of all –
> ...
> And thought: *Who am I?* And hand on heart, wondered
> What would it be like to be, in the end, part of all.

The poet in the darkness of the cave knows only the sounds of the water, the murmuring of his own inner mind, the pulsation of his heart, the feel of the earth, and thus is thrown back intensely into himself, and the problematic relation of his "I" to the "All" – to that which is beyond himself. But here the "all" is just as mysterious as the "I." Since no mediation between consciousnesses occurs (except *in* poetic communication), there is only the symbolic rebounding of consciousness upon itself through the agency of natural sounds and the feel of the earth.

The Biblical poet, in a similar mood of self-reflectivity, while contemplating the night sky articulates the mystery of the "I" in a way that clearly reveals the Biblical mode of self-understanding:

> When I look at thy heavens, the work of thy fingers,
> the moon and the stars which thou hast established;
> what is man that thou art mindful of him,
> and the son of man that thou dost care for him? Psalm 8:3, 4

Here there is the same wonder over the mystery of the human, but the wonder begins with a sense of the presence of another transcendent consciousness of immensity and grandeur far exceeding the poet's, which he can address as "Thou." The wonder does not stem only from this sense of the insignificance of the human subject in contrast to the immensity and eternity of God, however – a feeling that would have been provoked by the experience of nature alone – but, paradoxically, comes from the knowledge that the human shares in the sublime greatness of God due to his love for human beings in spite of their insignificance within the immensity of nature.

The poet then shows that he experiences himself across the mediation of the sign which conveys to him this love, a sign which is a promise and covenant between himself and the divine Other linking them in living commitment to one another. God is "mindful": he "remembers" human beings, and he "takes care of" them by appointing them to a place of authority within the natural cosmos (Ps. 8:5–8), thereby giving them a future.

This is an excellent example of the temporal form which the defamiliarization of the self assumes within the Biblical mode of intersubjective reflectivity, a defamiliarization that stems from wonder evoked by the awareness of being linked to another consciousness – a Thou, through signs which recover the past and project a future of infinite possibilities within the conditions of the relation.

Joshua Wilner has found a similar (though more naturalized) poetic response to the sign of the rainbow in Wordsworth's poem, "My heart leaps up."

> My heart leaps up when I behold
> A rainbow in the sky:
> So was it when my life began;
> So is it now I am a man;
> So be it when I shall grow old,
> Or let me die!
> The Child is father of the Man;
> And I could wish my days to be
> Bound each to each by natural piety.

Though no explicit mention of the Biblical story of the flood and the rainbow as a sign of God's promise is found here, Wilner argues that the recollection of the Biblical story adds an important dimension of meaning:

What our recollection of scripture brings to the reading of "My Heart Leaps Up" is the sense that the speaker's response is a response to a kind of promise and also a tacit awareness of the fragility of both promise and response. The precise origin and meaning of the promise remain unspecified: the speaker's movement of response is as much a sign as the rainbow itself and the promise to which he responds is simply the promise that in the future he will be able to respond to that promise. It has no fulfillment other than in its repetition.[3]

Though the "natural piety" of Wordsworth lacks a "thou" mediated across the sign, the rainbow taken as a sign evokes an experience of the temporal form of the self similar to that of the Biblical poet.

The poet of Psalm 8 gives expression to a consciousness that has been shaped by its relation to another consciousness. It manifests itself precisely through the sign understood as a word which effects the opening of a present that remembers the past and opens the future – the sign understood as reminiscence and promise.[4] But the poem contains only the response to this word. The utterance of the word itself is presented customarily in narrative rather than poetic literature in the Bible. The Genesis narrative is particularly significant in this regard since it is here that we find what the writers consider to be the first occurrence of this divine Word to human beings. We must now seek to understand the precise way in which this dialogue with the divine Word arises within a narrative context, and particularly the context of Genesis. To do this we must define the position of the divine Voice within the DN–DC relation.

The determination of the mode of the DN–DC relation in Genesis is made complex by the presence of the divine Voice in an intermediate sphere between the narrator and the characters. Is the divine Voice a personage in this narrative, unequivocally, or does it[5] rather perform some of the functions of the narrator? The chief function of the character, as we have seen, is to constitute an instance of speech which displaces that of the narrator. So, in this sense, the divine Voice is a personage since its utterances are always the object of the narrational phrase "he said," and thus displace the direct speech of the narrator. The narrator, in contrast to the divine Voice, nowhere speaks in the first person, and is thus thoroughly effaced.

But does the divine Voice really belong to the narrative world, the world of direct discourse between personages? To answer this question we must look more carefully at the position of the narrator. The narrator, through his effacement, is not a part of the world of personages he creates. His distinctive function is to represent, typically in the third-person discourse, the characters and the circumstances in which they exist. This self-effacement by the narrator establishes a barrier along the communicative axis of the sign with personages which prevents contact between character and author. By blocking the character's access to the narrator's instance of speech, and thus to the narrator's living extra-textual world, the character is confined to the closed internal world of the narrative. The narrator endows the characters with positions within a given social, economic, cosmic order, and they act in accord with the forces at play within the closed emotional and verbal economy of that order.

Narratives arising from the passive DN–DC relation dominated by the expressive sign function convey a totally relativistic order which is disclosed primarily through the implications of the direct discourse of the characters, and in the mysterious, disruptive, negative impulses that compel the leading characters into actions that run into contradiction with the goals of their verbal discourse. No external, evaluative perspective is brought to bear upon this world. There are no real heroes, and there is no unequivocal good or evil. At the center of the narrative there is no "insight" or illumination, but only a mysterious, unresolved contradiction.

In sharp contrast, the representative narrative presents in descriptive, explanatory and interpretive discourse a given order which is grounded upon some form of absolute, objective reality. The leading characters are then posed as empty forms driven by desires toward self-objectification which will give them a secure position within that order. Conflict takes the form of a struggle between the central characters, who are in a state of conscious deficiency, and those other personages who possess the objects or states the central characters lack.

It is obvious that the divine Voice does not belong to the closed, relativistic world of the expressive narrative. The bold performative speech in Genesis 1 through which the world is established clearly shows that the divine Voice is not one among many voices in this world, but the single transcendent Voice which is the source of the world's order.

It is even more obvious that this Voice is not a personage within a representative narrative which would enclose it in an objective order conveyed in the narrator's third-person speech.[6] The given world, which the narrator provides prior to the first utterance by the divine Voice, is at most (depending upon the translation of *bārā* as a dependent relative clause or an absolute assertion) a realm of complete chaos over which the divine Voice exercises absolute supremacy. (Though in subsequent passages, such as the so-called J creation account in Gen. 2:4bff., a much more lengthy third-person framework introduces the first instance of divine speech, the priority given to the account of creation by the word (the P account) in Gen. 1 confers upon it a normative function for the narrative as a whole.)

It is perhaps significant that from the viewpoint of this analysis it does not make any difference whether Genesis 1:1 represents a creation *ex nihilo* or presupposes the existence of matter in a chaotic form. Both are related in representative speech and present an objective, referential framework that, in different ways, threatens to enclose the transcendent instance of speech of the divine subject. The *ex nihilo* interpretation moves toward a conceptual ideological framework that can be derived from the meaning of *bārā*, and the relative interpretation moves toward a given, objective, materialist framework. This threat, however, has been skillfully reduced to the minimum, perhaps in part due to calculated ambiguity and extreme economy of expression.

In the symbolic narrative we are confronted with a different configuration of subjective positions. Like the expressive and representative narratives, there is in the symbolic narrative a world apart from the writer, possessing a certain given order and peopled with characters who occupy or seek to occupy positions in it, and who are enmeshed in a network of influential relations with each other. But the symbolic narrative is not completely closed, having an opening along the communicative axis toward the extra-textual instance of speech of the actual narrator effaced behind the third person.

It is here, then, that we can discern the general location of the divine Voice in the discursive structure of the Genesis narrative. The divine Voice is presented as the voice of a personage by the narrator, since the narrator speaks of "he" when referring to the instance of the divine speech. But unlike a personage, the Voice does not speak from a recognizable position within the social structure or spatial/temporal register within which the characters exist. Neither the narrator's discourse nor the direct discourse of the characters usually provide any clues as to the outer form, or the social and physical position of the divine Voice in relation to the human spatio-temporal sphere. When the narrator says that the Egyptian Pharaoh speaks, this relates to cultural codes which spatially, temporally, and socially locate the speaker in a position internal to the referential system of the narrative world. But when a voice speaks which is only identified as "Elohim" or "Yahweh," and no referential signs are given conveying the objective form and circumstances surrounding the utterance of this word, then it appears as a symbolic event in which the signs refer to other signs, but not to things. Such a symbolic word, detached from a speaker who can be spatially and temporally located, indicates that this utterance does not occur in the closed world of the narrative but on its periphery, opening it toward its subjective source.

But while the divine Voice deviates from the standard personage since it lacks a normal position internal to the narrative world, it cannot, on the other hand, be identified with the voice of the author. Although the opening of the character along the communicative axis toward an inner instance of speech moves toward a dialogue with the author, as we have seen, it is possible for that movement to contact not the author *per se*, but that third voice which is at the basis of the author's own creative impulse. It appears that in the Genesis narrative, this inner "third" voice is represented by the narrator as the Voice of God, in a way that formally corresponds to Dostoyevsky's representation of such inner words as the "idea force" which impelled his characters to action and him to write about them.

The initial, pivotal Biblical characters are presented by the narrator as creatures of the Word; they are personages who appear in the narrative first as recipients of an inward address by the divine Word, and their personal being in the narrative is thus formed from the outset by the divine Word. Apart from the account of his creation (his entrance into the spatio-temporal sphere of the narrative world), Adam first takes form as a character in Genesis 2:16–17 as the "you" in the divine utterance: "You may freely eat of every tree of the garden, but of the tree of knowledge of good and evil you shall not eat." Though Abram is minimally located in the spatio-temporal sphere as the son of Terah prior to the initial divine address, his first appearance as a central character is as the reference of the "you" in the command in Genesis 12:1: "Go from your country and your kindred..." These personages, then, apart from the bare indication of their existence in the narrative world, take form in response to these divine words addressed to them. No clues as to their appearance or character traits – and no information at all about the source of this Voice – are given.

The divine Voice thus occurs midway between the effaced author's instance of speech, and that of his characters, and mediates the opposition between them. The negation/affirmation polarity which accounts for the position of the DC is opened toward a third inner plane of discourse which is neither the author's representation of reality in third-person speech, nor the instance of speech of a typical narrative personage. As an instance of direct speech rather than third-person discourse, it eludes the semantic closure which representative speech always entails, but as an inner subjective word (rather than one that is outward and objective), it provides a perspective from beyond the closed world of the personages in terms of which their actions can be understood, that is, it opens the personage along the axis of communication toward the verbal source which is common to both the author and character, so as to show the origin of the personage in an instance of speech which is neither his/her own, nor identical with the actual or implied author's.

This indicates that the DC–DN relation in Genesis is basically active, though the active mode has been modified in a significant way. The narrator's function has been split. Rather than either a "third-person subject-of-consciousness" (Banfield), which is ambiguously suspended between the author and character, or an "idea-force" (Bakhtin) taken from the intra-individual sphere which activates the inner dialogue of the character, there is the fully personal Voice of the divine.

The author characteristically assumes a passive stance toward the divine

Voice, though there are some exceptions for reasons which will be developed below (such as Gen. 6:6).[7] This makes the authorial position a combination of two modes. As Bakhtin (Voloshinov) has shown, the modes of the DN–DC relation reflect the dynamics of the social structure in which the author lives. To the extent that the author assumes a passive stance toward his characters and refrains from enclosing them in a representational third-person framework, his discourse would reflect a relativistic, individualistic society with no transcendent norms.

But by representing the third subject-of-consciousness as a fully independent personal divine Voice who is clearly separated from the narrator, and speaks to the characters in direct speech, the narrator provides a specific interpretive framework for understanding the characters and the events. This framework is not "objective," however. That which is "represented" is an instance of speech only, and not a personal characteristic, object or idea. The objective reality of the instance of speech itself, beyond the written words, is left totally shrouded in mystery. What is conveyed here is "insight" or even "revelation" of the primacy of the Word as a force in the formation of human existence and the fundamental intersubjective character of human consciousness. It is a form of narrative reason that operates within the terms of traditional discursive symbolism.

This is what you might call the idea-less ideology of the narrator, and it corresponds exactly to the premises of the Israelite society which was founded upon a divine Word, a divine covenant. It is objective inasmuch as the divine discourse is clearly demarcated from the DN, but as communication into the narrative world from an ambiguous place "outside" it, the objectivity breaks down. This "ideology" thus is one that does not impose closure upon its personages, since it establishes a third ambiguous locus of subjectivity beyond the narrative world to which the author himself is as much subject as his characters are. This formal independence of the third subject from the control of the author makes theoretically possible a personage which is free, without falling prey to totally relativistic individualism of the expressive narrative. The shape and extent of this freedom must be examined below.

The micro-dialogue in the symbolic narrative makes possible an extraordinary recursive movement by the central characters. The lowering of the barrier separating the author and character's instances of speech opens the possibility of the character relating to an instance of speech which mediates between the closed, self-contained narrative world, and the world beyond the story (that is, the world of the actual author, the vital idea-forces in the culture, the divine).

Since subjective freedom in the symbolic narrative is not an abstract exercise of the will, but a mode of subjectivity which is realized within a dialogical relation between the character and a third subject-of-consciousness, subjective freedom arises as a response to a specific type of word. This word is a quintessential example of a symbolic word.

In general, this must be a type of performative speech, since it is performative speech which is capable of constituting an intersubjective relation. More specifically, Ortigues has shown that the type of performative speech which embodies the highest degree of self-reflectivity, and thus the most complete freedom from objective determination, is the promise and its related forms, the oath and the pact. In the promise the "I" as the sign of the subject's instance of speech duplicates its own instance of speech in a verb – to promise – which also has no objective reference beyond its capacity to signify the act in which the "I" assumes responsibility for maintaining, in its own personal action, the unity between certain other signs (verbs of action) and their material referents (the actions themselves).

In this relation between the "I" and its predicate, the presence of the subject is manifest as responsible presence, faithfully responding to the other in continuity with the signifying conventions which are the basis of language, and not as an ontological form of presence which is not intersubjective. The promise thus perfectly embodies the symbolic and temporal features of the sign. The "I," as a symbolic sign, opens the present of intersubjective discourse, and the promissory predicate relates the "I" to other signs so as to recover the past linguistic conventions from memory and extend them into the future with modifications which open a new field of possibilities for both promisor and promisee.

Inasmuch as the system of language is the basis of the social order, as Ortigues affirms, the promisor in this act freely reaffirms her/his relation to that order. In the free response made by the promisee in accepting and believing in a promise, s/he, too, is drawn into the same field of subjective possibilities. As s/he responds to the explicit or implicit "you," and listens to the promise across the semiotic conventions, s/he finds her/his own subjectivity made present in the response to the "I" of the promisor, and in the self-reflectivity quickened by that of the promisor embodied in the conventions of the promise. The recovery of the past of language is a recovery of her/his own subjective past, and the projection of the future by the promisor opens up a future also for the promisee as it is accepted in faith. This response by the promisee is made in the same temporal, intersubjective and symbolic form as that in which the promise is extended. In the mutual recognition between promisor and promisee, the freedom of both takes form on the basis of the "mysterious elective contingency" which underlies the decision to speak and to listen, and in the implicit agreement to accept the conditions of the system of language conventions which mediate this relation.

Thus the word which most completely offers the possibility of freedom within the bipolar form of the micro-dialogue of the symbolic narrative is the promise. For the character to receive a promise (or words which can be "taken" as promises) from the mediating subject of consciousness opens up the possibility for the character to enter a thoroughgoing, intersubjective relation in which subjectivity can be formed at its center by a signifier rather than an object-oriented signifier–signified relation, freeing her/him from a closed deterministic system of signifieds.

Whether the promise must be the utterance of a fully personal subject-of-consciousness who transcends both the author's world and the narrative world, or whether language or nature may generate their own subjective form of consciousness which conveys a promissory force in certain types of micro-dialogues (as the poems by Warren and Wordsworth suggest) are questions I cannot pursue here. For the Biblical narrative, it is clear that the presence of the human character is founded upon a promissory word which establishes her/his consciousness as intersubjective, and that the source of this promise is a Voice which speaks from the boundary into the narrative world which both the character and the author share – the world of sacred history.

This changes the polarities of the conflict. Whereas in the expressive narrative it is the actions versus the words and in the representative narrative it is the full versus the empty, in the symbolic narrative it is the closed versus the open, or the determined versus the free. This means that the subject is now in a position where in the micro-dialogue s/he, as a personage open to the instance of speech which founds his/her subjectivity, may establish an inner relation with any of the sign-functions which are operative in the foundation of subjectivity. This means that the micro-dialogue will always be composed of two poles. One will be the "man in man" (Dostoyevsky) that is the irreducible center of the personages' own subjective freedom, and the other will be a word in one of the three sign-functions: expressive, representative, or symbolic. The dynamics of the micro-dialogue will then arise not from the semantic content of these inner words, but from their functions, and the possibilities for response which they imply.

The general passivity of the Genesis author toward the divine Voice indicates that this is a word to which he, as author, is as much subject as his characters. The seminal position of the Word for both the author and his character, brings them together into the same narrative world. It is this move which begins to illuminate the non-fictional character of this work, or perhaps more exactly said, it illuminates the final erosion of the barrier between the world of the character internal to the narrative and the outer "real" world of the author, so that they cannot any longer be fundamentally distinguished.

The event of word-reception, which in the modern text is more typically experienced by the narrative writer, has here been made into the primary motivating event of the lives of the narrative personages. In *Tristram Shandy* this possibility was approximated for a fictive character as writing becomes the central event of Tristram's mature life and the account of his struggle with the force of language in the present moment of writing intrudes repeatedly into his account of the past. In Genesis, however, the writer's encounter with language becomes the paradigm for the seminal event in the lives of the narrative personages – their encounter with the divine Voice. Just as the writers experience their characters and plot as coming to them from some heterogeneous source (as Tristram Shandy whimsically says, "– for I begin with writing the first sentence – and trusting to Almighty God for the second" [p. 540][8]), so here the characters receive mandates, prohibitions and promises which form an armature around which the plots of their lives will take shape. The characters write the story of their lives with their responses in word and action to the primal word events. The divine Word thus emerges as a force shaping the character of human lives and societies rather than as a force giving rise directly to narratives and poetry. Narrative writing has become the living of "sacred history."

Because the event of word-reception has become the center of the narrative account of the personages, the word-reception of the author in the act of writing is suppressed. He assumes the role of one who receives from tradition the accounts of the others who have experienced this reception of the divine Words. The Word which creates sacred history does not, at this stage, come to the writer, but rather to the actors in this ongoing drama, that is, to the prophets and through them usually to the kings. The word-reception of the author does not enter his own narrative until the emergence of apocalyptic literature in the post-exilic period when the narrative itself becomes a judgement and promise addressed directly to the readers, and the author is the channel of communication. In the period of the early monarchy the "story" writes itself in life through the direct intervention of the divine Word in the lives of the actors, and the writer is only the faceless recorder of the traditions which emerge from the process. He is in the position of being the autobiographer of a nation, a nation which he sees and which, at least in part, sees itself as being formed under the impulse of the divine Word.

7

The micro-dialogue as the matrix of the Genesis narrative

And Yahweh said to Abram:
Go from your land,
and from your kindred,
and from the house of your father,
to the land which I will show you.

And I will make you into a great nation,
and I will bless you,
and I will make great your name,
and it will be a blessing.

I will bless those who bless you,
and whoever reviles you
I will curse.

All the families of the earth
will be blessed through you. Genesis 12:1–3

Semantically, the basis, if not the beginning, of the symbolic narrative is the micro-dialogue in which the central character encounters that mediating Voice made present in the promissory sign which opens the possibility of intersubjective existence. It is this fundamental insight into the positive significance of linguistic forms as mediators of intersubjectivity which sets up the polarities – closed, object-oriented versus open, intersubjective modalities – which then generate other possibilities of narrative development.

Though the Biblical narrative begins with a divine Word, it is not a promissory word directed to a human subject, but rather a divine command which calls nature into existence. The first words directed to a human are a permission and a prohibition (2:16, 17), both important types of performative speech to which we shall return. But the permission and prohibition are not semiologically primary for this narrative, because, as we shall see below, when the prohibition is presented as the primary word of the initial micro-dialogue of a symbolic narrative, as is the case in Genesis 2:16, 17, the narrative personages must develop closed, objectively oriented modes of subjectivity if the narrative is to unfold.

When the narrative subsequently juxtaposes to this closed system a promise-initiated open mode of subjectivity, it is clear that the prohibition-based mode is only a foil against which the positive, primary, promise-based mode may be seen the more clearly. Where there is no fundamental insight into the positive role of the sign as the basis of intersubjective consciousness, there is no significant reflection over the primary role of negative language such as the prohibition in the formulation of consciousness.

The beginning of the Biblical narrative, semiologically speaking, is thus a speech act in a micro-dialogue which opens the character to a positive, free intersubjective mode of existence. The promise, as we have seen, is the type of performative word most suited to this task. It is no coincidence, then, that we also have an extraordinarily important divine promissory word at a pivotal point in the Genesis narrative in the account of the promise to Abram in Genesis 12:1–3.

Genesis 12:1–3 is generally recognized as the pivotal center of the book of Genesis. Chapters 1–11 deal with the primeval history of the world and contain material, such as the story of the universal Flood, which is common to the literature of many other archaic peoples. Genesis 12 initiates the history of a single nation, Israel, by recounting the life of the most significant ancestor, Abram, from whom, it was believed, the entire nation had descended. The narrative at this point thus shifts from general to particular history. The unifying themes of the stories in chapters 1–11 also differ sharply from those in chapters 12–50. Although much will be said below about this contrast, here it should at least be mentioned that the stories in chapters 1–11 follow a general pattern of human transgressions and divine punishments, whereas in chapters 12–50, this circular pattern is entirely displaced by a more linear, or spiral, progressive pattern of movement by the major characters toward a goal.

From the viewpoint of narrative structure, it is obvious that Genesis 12:1–3 is the end which organizes the pattern of stories in chapters 1–11 so as to provide a sharp contrast between life in these two eras, and on these two social planes. On the other hand, no end is actually reached by chapter 50. The descendents of Abram are far from the "promised land," in Egypt. In the absence of any closure which could serve to unify and structure the material in chapters 12–50, its unity is thus also provided by 12:1–3. The story in chapters 12–50 unfolds as a movement toward the unattained fulfillment of the promise given at the beginning. It is thus the promise at the outset which gives thematic unity to the stories.

This presents a curious problem for understanding the relation of the time of narration to the story time. Genette indicates that one category of narrative which he terms "predictive" locates the time of narration prior to events narrated. Another type, which he terms "simultaneous," portrays the time of narration as contemporaneous with the action. Since, however, this is not strictly possible unless the action being recounted is that of the writing of the narrative, the simultaneous type presents the problem that the narrated events will catch up with the time of narration.[1] There is a comic reversal of this problem in Sterne's *Tristram Shandy*, as we have seen, when Tristram becomes dismayed that his autobiographical writing is taking so long that he despairs of ever catching up to the present. But in Proust's *A la recherche du temps perdu* it constitutes a structurally important underlying problem since the denouement is reached when the central figure receives the insight which inspires him to write the book of which he is already the protagonist.

The book of Genesis seems to have some of the features of both the predictive and simultaneous types. The promise to Abram in Genesis projects a future which not only goes beyond the end of the book, but goes in part beyond the time in which the author was living (and for that matter is still partly a future reality). This places the author in the act of writing within the story time of the narrative, and to some extent places the author in the same relation to the promissory word as his character, that is, the event of this micro-dialogue was both prior to the time of narration and simultaneous with it since it still projected a present and future story in which the narrator was obviously a believing participant. His own act of narration is excluded from the account because his role as author, has, as we have seen, been split in order to allow the primacy to be given to the divine Voice as the source who creates the characters and plots.

From this viewpoint we can now see why Genesis 12:1–3 is the "epicenter" of the book's narrative movement, shaping what precedes it as much as what succeeds it. We must thus begin with a careful examination of its linguistic form and the implications it has for plot structure.

It has long been recognized that Genesis consists of an amalgamation of story material, some of which had a life in oral tradition prior to its fixation in writing, and some of which was provided by the authors. In the latter category especially are transitional passages which join together the often disparate material, and provide for it a unified horizon of meaning. It is these passages which reflect most directly the mentality and spirituality of the authors. The passage here is considered to be such a transitional piece by the tenth-century J writer who is now believed to be responsible for the fundamental sequential ordering of the entire book as it now stands.

But whereas the material attributed to the J writer is usually filled with very concrete detail, here, as Hermann Gunkel notes in his classic commentary on Genesis, nothing is said about how Yahweh appeared, and throughout the passage there is a general absence of representational content.[2] The more recent German commentator, Gerhard von Rad, acknowledges the possibility that some of the individual promises, blessings and curses may be derived from older cultic material, but believes they have now been placed in a broader context by the writer which alters their meaning. In fact, with regard to this passage, he says: "It was, rather, created *ad hoc* by the Yahwist as a transition from the primeval history to the new series of actual Abraham narratives. But just for this reason, it is especially important for the exegete because in it the great collector of patriarchal narratives expresses himself programmatically."[3] While this passage may lack historical information, von Rad argues that it is "all the richer in programmatic theological substance."[4]

While Rolf Rendtorff does not see in this passage such a programmatic theological statement by the Yahwist, he does see the promise as belonging to the last stages of the tradition-history of the patriarchal materials, and views the promise of blessing for all humankind which climaxes the promise here as a "motto standing at the beginning of the Abraham history which is valid for the patriarchal history as a whole."[5] The absence of references which might indicate an earlier life for this story in oral tradition further indicates that it is a direct product of the pen of the narrator. The promise is related to the oath for which there was an established ritual and some features of which are preserved in the promise of land given after Abram reaches Canaan in 12:7 (altar building). Here, however, all such externalities have been eliminated.

Thus we find at this crucial turning point of the Genesis narrative a perfect example of a micro-dialogue: a word addressed to the new protagonist by a Voice who speaks words in performative language from the position of a third subject-of-consciousness intermediate between the author and character, which evokes a response from the protagonist that will shape his own consciousness and his future.

One of the chief characteristics of the micro-dialogue is its lack of objective orientation and determination. Occurring in that indeterminate "space" between the author's world and the character's world, it loses all representational or mimetic dimensions. It does not pretend to reproduce an event in an objective setting with certain material characteristics. Rather, it coincides completely only with the act of writing, in which the distance between the author and character is overcome *through* the momentary coalescence of the author's experience of word reception and articulation and the experience of his character, which cannot be located in objective space. It is thus appropriate that von Rad speaks of this as an *ad hoc* creation of the Yahwist since the micro-dialogue is a creature of the pen and more directly expressive of the author than any other type of writing. This is not to say that it is a "fiction." Rather, in passages of this type the subjective truth of the author and of his character coincide.

The character, who does not appear as the addressor or addressee of any direct speech prior to this passage, is now introduced as the addressee of a mandate and a promise uttered by the divine Voice. The narrative framework provides only the most meager information about Abram, his genealogy, his wife and the migration of their family from Ur in Mesopotamia to Haran in Syria. Enough is said to place Abram in a temporal context – to give him a past – but nothing is recounted concerning his character traits or physical appearance. In the succeeding narrative framework we are told his age at departure and that he had possessions to take with him on his trip and perhaps servants as well. These framing details are attributed to the Priestly narrator by source criticism,[6] but serve the purpose in the present context of locating Abram in the temporal continuum of his life span – a factor that is important regarding his potentiality for producing many offspring – and in the economic scale – a factor which also at the outset gives him a certain position in the cultural world necessary for understanding his relation to his adversaries later. Abram is never presented as a pauper in search of wealth.

The most significant omission from the narrative framework is the mention of any motivation for Abram's departure. As Gunkel says, "as a motive for the migration [the narrative] tells nothing of starvation, pressure from enemies, or similar folk-relations, but only of a personal motive."[7] The narrator here, in contrast to other places (e.g., 12:10) where he gives reasons for migrating, attributes the move to no force other than the divine mandate and promise to Abram. Thus Abram is presented from the outset as a character who is opened toward and shaped by a word-event within his "inner" world. The first characterological indication which the narrator reports about Abram is then his response to the divine Word, "So Abram went, as the Lord had told him" (12:4a).

Here there is no objectification of Abram's character (such as: "he was obedient"), but only the report that he acted in accord with the divine Word. Abram's character is not described, but he is given presence in the narrative by the divine Word addressed to him, and by his positive response to it. In terms of this study, his character is founded in an intersubjective mode, grounded upon a promissory sign which detaches him from his past and opens for him an entirely new future. His positive response in faith to this Word will thus endow him with a name which will itself be transformed into a promise, since a promise of blessing will now be attached to it.

The most unusual aspect of the intersubjective relation produced by this micro-dialogue is the absence of objective content from the promise. He is commanded to go from his land and kindred, but is not told his destination. He is to go to "the land that I will show you." Rather than a promise of land, he is given a promise of future revelation of the land which will be his. Likewise, he is not specifically promised children, but only that God somehow will make of him a "great nation." Again he is promised only a future divine action. Finally he is promised a great name which will be a blessing to others, and divine protection through the blessing and cursing of his friends and enemies respectively. This too amounts to a future divine action.

This means that what is promised Abram is basically a positive relationship to the divine from which will flow great benefits. Since the specific promises of land and children are given later, their omission here must be by design. This initial move by Abram into the future is to be motivated fundamentally by the anticipation of future divine words and deeds, rather than by specific, tangible, objective benefits. The absence of specifics and the uncertainties surrounding belief in such a vision of the future have the effect of making this into, as von Rad says, "a paradigmatic test of faith."[8] Abram is thus called to surrender his future to the divine Word, trusting it to reveal to him the objective contents of this vision in the course of time. He is thus called into a primary intersubjective relation, the material consequences of which, though real, are very much secondary. Von Rad sees this as embodying the paradigmatic form of the continuing relation of the entire people to Yahweh throughout its history.[9]

The new story that begins with the founding of the central character in an open intersubjective relation to the divine Word of promise, and the narrator's scrupulous avoidance of characterological attributes and objective motives for this crucial action, discloses the concern of the narrator to locate the source of his character's action within the dynamics of his relation to the "inner" word. This simultaneously poses, as the polar opposite, the mode of subjectivity which is objectively determined. To see the development of this pattern we thus must move backward to the story of the "fall" in Genesis 2–3.

III

ANALYSIS OF GENESIS NARRATIVES

8
"Who told you that you were naked?" Genesis 2,3

The story of the "fall," attributed by source criticism to the J writer, constitutes the main focus of this writer's view of the creation. It extends from Genesis 2:4b, which portrays the creation of man and a human paradise from an arid (rather than a watery) pre-creation chaos, to the expulsion of man and woman from this paradise in 3:24. Since the initial acts of creation are deeds rather than words, this narrator must begin with a somewhat lengthy third-person account of these acts and the states which result from them. Though the structure of the human environment is represented, along with the human's physical/spiritual being (*nepeš ḥayā*), and his role within nature, no description or interpretation of human character or action is given. Man himself first appears as the object of the divine prohibition given in 2:15–17, and from that point the logic of the narrative is dominated by the tensions created by this prohibition. The turning point is reached in the DD account of the temptation of woman in 3:1,2 which throws the prohibition into question. The consequences of this temptation are then given in 3:4–24, also primarily in DD.

Unlike the narrative framework of the "call" of Abram, the narrative introduction here, with its dense representative language, provides a highly important framework for understanding the development of the characters in the DD which follows. In contrast to 11:29–33, where no concepts, but only conditions which throw into sharp relief the divinely mandated actions and the material states envisioned as a consequence of faith in the promise are mentioned, the narrative framework here describes in conceptual terms the being of man. It also creates explicit symbolic terminology which establishes the subjective model to serve as the anti-type to the subjective mode elevated in 12:1–3. Beyond this, it depicts in a way unparalleled in the remainder of the book the global topographical shape of the physical world in which the characters are to live, and the specific hierarchical relation of human beings to other forms of life within this world. Though all of this is accomplished with very great verbal economy, the scope of this representative language is astonishing in its sweep. The result of this heavy reliance upon such physical and conceptual language is to create an ideological framework which constitutes a closed system, a worldview, which the characters will not succeed in escaping when left to their own devices. It is, however, what might be called a subjective rather than an objective ideology, that is, an ideology centering not upon positive concepts but upon modal relations to the realm of knowledge. In this it remains consistent with the premises of the later narrative which elevates modality above representational content in the presentation of characters.

The literary-historical research has shown ample evidence of the narrator's reliance upon earlier traditions in the construction of this account. Since my focus here is upon the meaning produced by the stylistic characteristics of the text as it now stands, and not primarily upon its representational content, it will not be necessary here to recapitulate the previous work except where conclusions bear directly upon problems of semantic uncertainty.

The most serious problem for this approach could be presented by evidence of the fundamental disunity of the narrative. The most authoritative recent commentator, Claus Westermann, finds evidence that the text is composite but has been fused into a unity by the J writer, who created it out of two pre-existing narratives. One, found in 2:4b–14, 18–24, deals with the creation of man and woman and the paradisical garden in which they live (Story A), and the other with the prohibition, violation and subsequent punishment (Story B). While he founds the division of the independent appearance of these motifs in other ancient literature, he also grounds it upon stylistic differences.[1]

The chief of these is that Story A presents God as subject and man as object, while Story B is almost all in DD between God and man with man often the subject. He argues that this stylistic distinction already suffices to prove the original independence of both narratives.[2] This distinction corresponds almost exactly to the distinction between third person and DD in the account, placing most of the third-person discourse in Story A, and most of the DD in B. Since, as we have seen, the most fundamental characteristic of a narrative is the presence of both DD and DN, the stylistic argument which Westermann makes seems deficient.

In fact, the correspondence of the hypothetical sources to the third-person and DD passages of the narrative shows the primary and thoroughgoing unity of this passage as it now stands. While, no doubt, ancient sources were used, the present text exhibits the form of a very carefully articulated whole. The presence of the trees needed in the B account already in the introductory narrative framework is further evidence of the carefully woven unity of the story. The so-called double punishment at the conclusion (curses as well as expulsion) may well exhibit the traces of older independent traditions, but now are amply justified, as will be seen below. The same holds true for the mention of the two trees (of knowledge of good and evil and of life). Westermann is persuasive in arguing for the greater likely antiquity of the "tree of life" image and the probable origin of the "tree of the knowledge of good and evil" with the J writer: "the designation, 'tree of life' antedated the author of Gen. 2–3, but he, however, constructed anew the designation of the other tree on the basis of the narrative (3:5b)."[3] The tree, which was central to the temptation story but called there only the "tree in the midst of the garden," was then given a name with a form corresponding to the "tree of life." This means, then, that this term is a direct product of the author, and thus an undistorted embodiment of his meaning. This is most appropriate since it is also the semantic center of the entire narrative, and the place where our analysis should begin.

Typological analysis

The narrative begins in third-person narration with an extended series of dependent clauses leading up to the creation of man. These depict the condition of the world in negative terms, that is, in terms of what the world lacked, climaxing with the mention of the absence of man to till the earth.

In the day when Yahweh Elohim was making the earth and the heavens, and all plants of the field were not yet on the earth, and all grass of the field was not yet sprouted – for Yahweh Elohim had not yet caused it to rain upon the earth, and there was no man to till the ground –
2:4b–5

Here the orienting perspective of this description of the pre-creation state is an inverted description of the conditions of life necessary for agriculture. These initial lacks in 2:4b–5 are immediately liquidated in the narrative sequence 2:6–15. The first positive term occurs in verse 6 with the coming of water rising from the earth (considered by Westermann and others to be semantically and stylistically out of place), followed by the creation of man as a unified being (*nep̱eš ḥāyā*) of dust and the breath of life given him by God.

a mist rose from the earth and watered all the face of the ground, and Yahweh/Elohim fashioned man of dust from the ground, and blew into his nostrils the breath of life, and man turned into a living being.
2:5–7

The human orientation is further revealed when the vegetative content of the earth is next created in the form of a garden.

And Yahweh Elohim planted a garden in Eden, and Yahweh Elohim caused to grow from the ground every tree desirable to the sight, and good for eating, and the tree of life in the midst of the garden, and the tree of the knowledge of good and evil.
2:8, 9

But the chief virtue of trees which were planted was that they were to be "desirable (נֶחְמָד) for seeing," and "good (טוֹב) for eating." Here we find the introduction of the central terms of an interpretive framework that will be fundamental for the entire primeval narrative (chapters 2–11).

Since the assumed subject of the desiring and the judge of taste is the human being just created and the others to follow, the narrator here is establishing the sensory and subjective modalities which will govern the relation of the human subjects to the most vital objects in their environment. These objects placed here will first be seen by human beings (sensory modality), and, when seen, will evoke desire in them (subjective modality). This will then lead to the act of eating as a fulfillment of visual desire, followed by the inner judgement of taste (subjective evaluative modality). The writer has thus not described the objective physical objects in this garden as such, but rather has presented those objects in terms of their relation to human subjects as seen in their anticipated response to them. His vision is already internal to the characters. You might even think of this as a form of anticipatory psychonarration. The writer tells us how humans will internally respond to these objects: by the desire of the eyes and by sense experience of taste. Of especial importance is the fact that this same procedure is followed later by Eve in assessing the fruit (3:6)!

What the narrator has constructed here is thus a succinct model of the thought process of his characters. By linking human sight to desire, and presenting the value of the trees of the garden in terms of their power to evoke these human sensory and subjective responses, the author conveys the human condition as one of lack, deficiency, or emptiness which can be filled by obtaining and consuming these sensorially stimulating objects.

The nature of this deficiency is made considerably more important by the mention next of two particular trees, the "tree of life" and the "tree of the knowledge of good and evil." The tree of life suggests that life itself is something which man relates to through desire. Thus it is something which he does not possess, at least not in an absolute sense. This already suggests, then, the presence of death on the distant horizon of human life.

With the mention of the "tree of the knowledge of good and evil" we are faced with another ominous human deficiency. The name of this tree carries us completely beyond the realm of the physical into the sphere of the symbolic. Though it appears to stand in the narrative alongside the others, it is clear that what it seems to offer cannot be obtained by eating (or not eating) its physical fruit. Rather, it represents here the most crucial human lack of all. The same sense of deficiency which evokes desire for the material fruit of the trees will also be experienced in relation to knowledge, wisdom, or intellectual discernment.[4]

The human being is thus posed here as a symbolic creature, a creature who will know himself not merely in desire for material objects to satisfy his tastes; he will also know himself as one who lacks wisdom and universal knowledge. The Biblical writer thus founds his chief character as an empty sign, oriented by desire toward all objects, including universal knowledge and wisdom. But for the human to attain perfect wisdom as a consequence of his own efforts (taking from the "fruit" of the tree) would mean that he would be absolute and autonomous, free of all dependency for self-knowledge upon other subjects (instances of speech).

The two trees thus suggest the lines of the plot to follow. They offer human beings the chief qualities of divinity: eternal life and autonomous selfhood. Certainly humans will desire these powers as they desire the "fruit" of other trees, since desire is their fundamental mode of relating to the world in which they are to be placed. Thus the question is raised whether the Creator will allow the creature to attain equal status. We encounter here what Roland Barthes speaks of as the "hermeneutic code" – narration which arouses expectations and sets up a desire for closure (truth).[5]

In this our writer is very much in the tradition of representative narrators, departing only in that he has succeeded in posing the terms of his conflict in an abstract, subjective way. That toward which the human will be most powerfully oriented by desire is not the material fruit of the trees but the inner condition termed "knowledge of good and evil." The Biblical writer, significantly, does not pose the conflict in terms of any particular content or any system of thought but in terms of a modal relation to the field of knowledge which places the human as a deciding subject, the arbiter of what is good and what is evil in general.

The conflict thus is not posed in terms of truth versus falsehood. It is not the "Tree of Natural or Spiritual Truth," or the "Tree of knowledge of the Future." No specific content is implied here, but rather an inner subjective relation to knowledge itself which poses the human being as its ultimate judge. The focus of the narrative will not be upon the attainment of material or intellectual objects, but upon the subjective modality of the human subjects' relation to those objects.

It is here that you find the influence of the writer's symbolic perspective. His premises as a symbolic narrator require him to create subjects consciously open toward the word-events which found them. When faced then with the need to create a closed subject who is an empty sign oriented by desire, he does this by depicting the fundamental object of desire as a subjective modality ("knowing good and evil"), and subsequently imposing upon the protagonist a prohibition in DD from the divine Creator against the attainment of this mode of knowledge. In this way the narrator is able to have the central conflict of the narrative arise from the psychology of desire, as in a representative narrative. But by posing the terms of conflict as an internal tension between two modes of subjectivity provoked by the divine command, rather than in terms of an outer conflict between a full and an empty subject, he is able to preserve the primacy of the word-event. As we shall see, however, he does not totally escape the problem of closure, but rather redefines its terms.

We are then taken to a higher plane and given a view of the larger topographical context in which the garden is located:

And a river flowed from Eden to water the ground, and from there it was divided, and it became four rivers. The name of the first is Pishon, it is found throughout the land of Havilah where there is gold, and the gold of the earth is good there; bdellium and onyx stone are there. And the name of the second river is Gihon; it is found throughout the land of Cush. And the name of the third river is Tigris; it is found in the east of Assyria. And the fourth river is Euphrates. 2:10–14

The historical references of the topographical description of the earth in verses 10–14 need not detain us here. The account appears to be partly historical and partly ahistorical. The river which rises in Eden apparently divides as it flows out of the primal garden into four rivers representing the four quarters of the earth.[6] The importance of this description for the narrative development is that a distinction is created, having the poles

inside the garden vs. outside the garden.

In the same way that the tree of knowledge foreshadows the "fall," the topographical description foreshadows human life outside the garden. The metals and jewels mentioned in the distant lands will form the basis of a commercial system, eventually including monetary exchange. There is no need for gold in Eden, where all is available for the taking. But outside, people will be made secure only by a symbolic/material system of exchange which is governed by the dynamics of desire.

The first element in the narrative introduction which completes the liquidation of the initial lacks is the installation of man in the garden and the specification of his limited functions – to till it and to watch over it (*šāmar*, to guard, preserve, keep, – in a supervisory role).[7]

And Yahweh Elohim took Adam[8] and placed him in the garden of Eden to till it and to watch over it. 2:15

This delineation of human functions emphasizes the circumscribed role which the man is to play and leads to the first direct discourse in which the most important limitation of all is then propounded.

The silence of the narrative is finally and decisively broken:

And Yahweh Elohim commanded Adam saying, "From all of the trees in the garden you may surely eat, but from the tree of the knowledge of good and evil, you shall not eat of it. For on the day that you shall eat from it, you will die." 2:16

The narrator introduces the divine Voice as the subject of a performative verb – to command. The prohibition in 2:17 is uttered directly to the human by the disembodied divine Voice at an unspecified place in the garden and coupled with a prefatory mandate. The absence of representational detail in this utterance and its setting indicates that we are dealing here with a subjective micro-dialogue as the inaugural direct utterance of this narrative. Since this is the first occasion in which the protagonist attains direct presence in the narrative, this establishes him subjectively in the dual mode of the addressee – the "you" – of a positive mandate (אָכֹל תֹּאכֵל) is a permissive introduced by an infinitive which establishes an antithesis with the prohibition) and a negative prohibition.

The prohibition poses a limitation upon Adam at the very center of his being.[9] Since he has been established as an empty sign-personage, the prohibition against attaining autonomous subjectivity by a divine Word leaves him suspended between the subjective mode driven by visual desire attributed to him in the narrative framework, and the intersubjective mode which arises now from this initial micro-dialogue. This dilemma is carefully posed in the words of the divine command.

Through the illocutionary dynamics of the joint mandate and prohibition, Adam is created as a subjective presence in the narrative. As the addressee of these performative utterances he is offered the possibility of subjective actualization in the mode of obedience and limited freedom. The form of his subjective presence – or, one could say, the horizon of his consciousness – is shaped in the form of the "you" of the "you shall not eat X" and the "you" of the "you may eat Y."

Performative utterances of this type require some kind of response from the addressee to have meaning. A response of obedience to the prohibition and acceptance of the mandate would imbue Adam with intersubjective existence. To refuse the mandate or violate the prohibition would represent victory for the semantic system given in the introductory framework, but would, ironically, establish the character in an autonomous mode of subjectivity inconsistent with the symbolic premises of the narrative. For the narrator to permit this would subvert the primary intersubjective system of meaning which governs chapters 12–50. The introduction of Adam through a micro-dialogue makes a simple, straightforward violation of the prohibition received in the micro-dialogue nonsensical, since this would immediately allow the representational system in the narrative framework to triumph over the divine Voice in the micro-dialogue and reduce the human character to the simple enemy of God. The narrator thus must follow a more ambiguous and subtle course.

The prohibition customarily serves as an effective starting point for narratives because its propositional content expresses clearly two opposing semic systems which can be actualized in roles and given figuration as personages engaged in conflict. The hero embodies the values connected with obedience to the prohibition, and the villain those connected with disobedience. The hero usually receives the mandate for positive action. Here, however, the "hero" who is given the mandate is also given the prohibition, and the traditional hero/villain conflict is set up as a potential conflict *within* a single personage. As will be shown below, this internalization of the process of conflict ultimately deprives the narrative plot of any unambiguous heroes and villains.

The meaning of the violation for the subjective existence of Adam is already given in the name of the forbidden tree, the "tree of the knowledge of good and evil". As indicated above, this phrase signifies an autonomous mode of subjective existence. The act of violating the prohibition would cause a shift in Adam's mode of existence from one whose meaning stemmed from his response to the divine illocutionary utterance to one whose meaning stems from his self-projected position as the knowing subject of the oppositions: good versus evil.

Here the subjective implications of the act of violating a prohibition for one whose intersubjective consciousness has been created as an addressee of an illocutionary prohibition is unmasked. The transgressor removes himself from the position of being subject *to* limits given in the prohibition, and, in the violation, projects himself as the subject who knows – who determines for himself those limits. Grammatically, he makes himself the object reference of the subject of the phrase "knowing good and evil," that is, he would become "*one* who knows good and evil." By stepping out of the intersubjective relation, his existence would become defined in terms of the third-person narrative framework as one who desires autonomous subjectivity (knowledge of good and evil).

The result is that the barrier which in the typical narrative separates the third-person discourse of the narrator from the direct discourse of the characters comes to function as a division between two conflicting modes of subjectivity potentially available to the subject as existential possibilities: the intersubjective mode defined by the "Thou shalt" and the "Thou shalt not" of the prohibition, and the autonomous mode in which the subject would independently identify himself with a mode of subjectivity implied by the narrative framework and become "one who knows good and evil." These are the two modes which Julia Kristeva characterizes as the "subject of the enunciation," and the "subject of the statement [*énoncé*]."[10] The concrete possibility of formulating this latter mode does not arise for the subject, however, until the serpent contradicts the prohibition in 3:5.

By means of symbolic language the narrative thus succeeds in making explicit the mode of subjectivity that is fundamental to every subject who violates a prohibition, and makes that mode of subjectivity the prohibited object. This has the effect of posing the central conflict of the plot in terms of a conflict inside of the characters between two modes of subjectivity, rather than in the conflict between good and evil personages found in the typical representative narrative.

This also shows the extent to which the narrator's framework has imposed closure upon the characters. Though, by posing the conflict in terms of an inner choice between an intersubjective and an autonomous mode of subjectivity, the narrator seems to preserve the freedom of his character, this is in fact only illusory. Just as the representative narrative is generated only if there is a desiring subject who acts to fulfill his/her desire against those persons or forces who possess the object of desire, so this symbolic narrative can emerge only if the character, who is created by the divine speech with a fundamental deficiency, acts to remedy that deficiency. Though in contrast to representative narratives s/he is open toward the Voice at the boundary of the narrative which created her/him, this same Voice establishes her/him through a prohibition which creates a severe lack at the center of her/his subjective existence.

The narrative framework further indicates that her/his relationship to this prohibited object will be one of desire (2:9). This signifying structure thus requires that the character violate the prohibition and fulfill desire as in the representative narrative. Otherwise nothing meaningful would occur, and there would be no story. The openness of the narrative is evidenced not in the authentic freedom of the characters but in the constraints upon representative language and the subordination of the narrator to the divine Word and to direct discourse in general as a means of character development. This prohibits the semantic fixation of the characters as good or evil, and poses them in a state of inner conflict which retains a certain potential for change in dialogue with the divine. The achievement of this degree of openness was, however, an extraordinary development.

It is important to note at this juncture that the relationship established between the divine Voice and Adam in the utterance of the prohibition is a hierarchical relationship. The form of the prohibition does not involve necessarily the utterance of "I" by the speaker, and the divine "I" is not uttered here. The relationship is thus not one of mutuality between partners, but one involving the exercise of authority by a superior party over an inferior. Rather than an I–you relation, it is more precisely an (I)–you relation. Except for the clearly authoritarian judgement pronouncement in 3:14–29, the divine "I" is uttered only within the realm of divine self-communication to which the narrator has access, but Adam does not (2:18). This means the barrier which separates the characters from the instance of speech which founds them is only partially lowered when that instance of speech is a prohibition. A prohibition within a micro-dialogue does not provide the basis for truly open intersubjectivity, but rather creates the conditions for a bi-leveled, inner dialogical structure, one level consisting of the prohibition addressed to the prohibited "you," and one in which the prohibitor might speak his "I" to another on his own level.

Correspondingly, Adam does not utter his "I" to God before the "fall."

God is the prohibitor, and communication between them is occasioned only by the violation of that prohibition. Adam speaks his "I" to God only in his defense and admission of guilt (3:10, 12). With no one on his "level" to whom he can speak his "I," Adam is alone, and this is immediately observed by Yahweh Elohim following the prohibition:

And Yahweh Elohim said, "It is not good that Adam should be alone. I will make a helper for him corresponding to him. 2:18

The aloneness of man is underscored here by the fact that God does not address his observation concerning man's aloneness to Adam himself, but rather to the other persons of his own plural nature (see 3:22 as well as 1:26). God is apparently not alone! The use of the prohibition as the inaugural utterance of the primary formative micro-dialogue forces the symbolic narrator to motivate actions of the divine toward man, not through further discourse with him, nor through conceptual explanations in the narrative framework, but through a kind of micro-dialogue of the divine with itself within the separate world of the divine.

This, of course, opens up a new plane of discourse in the narrative world to which only the author has access which could potentially explain *all* of the actions and events on the human plane. But since the human subject would not find in his own hierarchically structured micro-dialogue with the divine any indication of these happenings, the human micro-dialogue would be reduced to insignificance, and the human character reduced to impotence. The center of the action would shift to the divine world where the same issues of narrative modality would have to be solved on that level. The Genesib narrator does not follow this line of development, but the issue of the relation between the divine and human worlds of discourse is an important one for the narrative.

This becomes an explicit issue later when in 18:17 Yahweh asks himself: "Shall I conceal from Abraham what I am about to do?" Because of Abraham's election and future greatness, he decides against this and discloses to him the forthcoming destruction of Sodom and Gomorrah. This represents a significant change in the divine–human relation that stems from the new relation established by the divine promise in 12:1–3. Thus no hidden intra-divine dialogue occurs at all in chapters 12–50, except in this one place.

Because of this a barrier thus exists which separates the inner discourse of each realm from the other. But when parties within each level speak of the other, as it is inevitable that they do, they must do so in third-person terms which transform the other party into the object reference of a predicate which attaches qualities to them. The characters are thus placed in a position where they can violate the constraints upon description and interpretation which control the content of the narrative framework. This is not a matter of a neutral stylistic option, however, for it makes possible the creation of a semantically closed interpretation of personages and events which would enable the humans to impose closure upon the divine Voice and the divine to impose closure upon the human characters. The central significance of the illocutionary dynamics of direct discourse would then be preserved only in the unlikely and perhaps impossible event that the narrator favored neither the human nor the divine interpretation and maintained them in continuous unresolved conflict.

In the first occurrence of the private discourse, the divine speech takes Adam as its object. Yahweh Elohim attributes to him the quality of aloneness, and proclaims the judgement that it is not good. In fact to be alone, לְבַדּוֹ, is to be in great peril. Life is bound up with community in the Biblical tradition.[11] Here he describes the human condition and exhibits the power to know good and evil which is forbidden to human beings. He then resolves immediately to correct the problem by exercising divine power to provide Adam with a "helper corresponding to him" (2:18). The word helper (עֵזֶר) typically occurs with reference to aid given, often by God, in a life-threatening crisis.[12]

The first third-person discourse about a man by God thus sets up the conditions for the existence of intra-human dialogue that corresponds to the intra-divine dialogue. Now Adam will not be alone, just as God is presumably not alone. This charitable concern by a transcendent personage conveys the benevolent, but manipulative, superior attitude of a parent or king toward his ignorant subject. The determinism of this act is only somewhat moderated by the choice given to Adam as to the kind of partner which pleases him.

But the central dilemma of the narrative now emerges. It is legitimate at this point for the intra-divine dialogue to take man as an object of interpretation, and to make judgements about the human character regarding good and evil which are hidden from him. This is the divine prerogative (3:22), though it is later to be partially relinquished (18:17), and obviously is problematic with regard to the genuine openness of the narrative. But this is possible within terms of the hierarchical relation created by the prohibition which conceals the "I" of God from the human character, leaving the inner realm of the divine first-person discourse inaccessible to the creature, much as the private conversation of parents is inaccessible to children.

But for human dialogue to take God and his words as objects of speculative interpretation and to make judgements with regard to their goodness or evil will place the human beings in precisely the position of judgement forbidden by the prohibition. Since the prohibition constitutes the basis of Adam's intersubjectivity, and must be the same for his partner, it is inevitable that the first human dialogue utilizing the first and second person be about "him" (God) and "it" (the prohibition). The "vertical" God–human relation which gave rise to human consciousness through the prohibition would necessarily appear alien and thus threatening to the strictly human world of discourse. Thus the third party who enters this network will inevitably create the conditions for the violation of the prohibition by making possible objectifying speech *about* God which linguistically removes humans from being immediately subject *to* God.

But since this would cast the third party into the role of a villain and externalize the conflict into a confrontation of good versus evil characters (i.e., good humans versus evil God), the narrator cannot move directly to the creation of the human partner. He first brings on stage the animal world, the realm that is anomalous regarding human speech, and neutral regarding good and evil.

> And Yahweh Elohim formed from the earth all the beasts of the field, and all the birds of the heaven, and he brought them to Adam to see what he would call them. And whatever he called each living being that was its name. Adam gave names to all the cattle, and the birds of the heavens, and all living beings of the fields. But Adam did not find a helper corresponding to him.
> 2:19, 20

Adam here speaks to animals in the most significant way, by naming them, but the animals cannot become full conversation partners to human beings. When these are rejected by Adam as suitable partners after he has shown his verbal virtuosity by naming them, God creates woman from his body.

> And Yahweh Elohim caused a deep sleep to fall upon Adam, and he slept, and he took one rib from his side, and he closed up the flesh where it was. And Yahweh Elohim constructed a woman from the rib he had taken from Adam, and he brought her to Adam. 2:21, 22

The narrator here, drawing upon old mythological traditions which have been abundantly explored, portrays the creation of woman as a division of Adam's flesh. The name Adam gives to woman – *'iššāh* – is derivative from man – *'îš* – and signifies the difference within unity which is to be the model of the male–female relation. When faced with her, Adam breaks into poetry utilizing the first-person possessive pronoun:

> This at last
> is bone of *my* bones
> and flesh of *my* flesh
>
> For this she shall be called woman (*'iššāh*),
> Since out of man (*'îš*) she was taken 2:23

Adam thus has now one to whom he can speak his "I".

Woman does not respond to this eloquent welcome, and nowhere later engages Adam in an explicit dialogue. Neither does Adam address her with the first-person pronoun "I." The first words of woman are uttered in response to the serpent. Thus woman before the "fall" is scarcely differentiated from man. Her silence means that the relation of man and woman before the "fall" remains truncated, incomplete, undeveloped. She is man's possession, united with his flesh, and shaped subjectively by the prohibition given not to her but to him. But lest Adam be the one who first speaks about God in the third person, the narrator omits any reference to how Issah learns of the prohibition. (I will use this noun, Issah, as a name hereafter to emphasize the fact that the name "Eve" is not given until much later in the narrative and the narrator treats it virtually as a name, e.g., 3:1, and especially in 3:16 where it is used in a parallel construction with Adam in 3:17; there Adam occurs without the definite article for the first time. See also 4:25.)

The ideology of the narrator is expressed here through the temporal sequence in which he introduces the male and female. While the way in which woman is introduced injects ambiguity into the role played by woman in the origin of evil, the fact that the prohibition is given by Yahweh Elohim in direct address to Adam first places him in a hierarchical position superior to that of woman. Here the writer is reflecting the common cultural assumptions of his era.[13] But since God is here the third person, and thus the inevitable object of any initial conversation between Issah and Adam, for woman to speak would have likely placed her in the subsequent role of the serpent who raises "innocent" questions about God. She would have fallen into the role of the archetypal seductress, purely and simply. By not having Issah speak first, however, with the potential for the objectification of God this implies, he avoids placing the blame for the violation of the prohibition solely upon her.

The initial response to the utterance of Adam comes in the form of a relatively rare generalizing intrusion into the narrative by the narrator. Such intrusions are a well-attested narrational device[14] which, in some cases, serves the purpose of connecting the internal narrative world to the present world of the reader to increase the plausibility of the story. While this usually takes the form of some type of philosophical comment[15] or "gnomic wisdom," here it takes the form of an etiology which serves the same purpose:

Therefore a man will leave his father and cling to his wife, and they will be as one flesh. 2:24

The comment, in the imperfect tense, indicates that the action of man in welcoming the first woman both explains and establishes a pattern of sexual behavior which continues into the present world of the writer and reader. As such it belongs to the ideological register of the narrative, building upon 2:21, 22, and serves to bring closure to the lack defined by the discourse in the divine world in 2:13 regarding Adam's lonely condition. The unity between male and female indicated by the phrase "as one flesh" (לְבָשָׂר אֶחָד)[16] is of fundamental importance with respect to the vexed question of allocation of guilt after the violation of the prohibition which follows. If the two are one flesh, then an absolute separation of responsibility cannot be made, and is not made in what follows, as will be seen below.

At this point the narrator again intrudes – violating his own constraints regarding characterization – and makes a descriptive statement about man and woman in their new unity. He describes the physical appearance of the human pair – "man and his wife were both naked" – and attributes to them a quality of consciousness that corresponds to their outer appearance – "and were not ashamed."[17]

The intrusion of the narrator has become necessary due to the particular possibilities of narrative development which emerge at this point. Further obedience by humans would not lead to direct discourse of significance for narrative development, due to the total absence of any possible significant conflict. But a conspiracy to violate the prohibition in DD between man and woman would rupture the relation with the divine, and leave man and woman as thoroughgoing opponents of Yahweh Elohim. Nothing would then remain to be said to them in direct discourse from the divine viewpoint. A violated prohibition would bring the intersubjective relation with God to an end. The narrator would then either have to develop the human characters with God as their opponent, or have God destroy the human characters and start over again.[18]

Thus an impass within the limited possibilities of this narrative has been reached. But in the same way that the account of the words of God spoken in his inner world threatens the narrative with closure, so too this kind of third-person description and interpretation of man and woman in the narrative framework seems to impose closure on the human characters. The corresponding oppositions – ashamed versus non-ashamed – and naked versus clothed – now are given as the semantic horizon within which the reader is to understand the outer and inner conditions of the characters.[19]

The outer condition of nudity emphasizes the visual presence of sexual difference as a given structure of limited creaturely existence.[20] Adam's joyful verbal acceptance of Issah cannot be interpreted as devoid of sexual emotion and consciousness. Awareness of sexual difference thus does not enter first after the violation.[21]

Closure is minimized, though not entirely escaped, by the ambivalent, subjective nature of the condition of shame. Shame indicates neither good nor evil, but inner conflict in the self-relation, in this case to the body and to the presence of sexual difference in relation to another. The condition of non-shame thus points again to a subjective modality rather than to a positive quality or power. Also by posing the inner state as a negative condition – non-ashamed – the narrator further avoids the semantic closure involved in a positive descriptive concept.

Thus human character comes to be fixed only in its subjective modality. In this way the narrator further develops an "ideology" of human subjectivity begun in 2:9. The negative character of this attribute – non-ashamed – strongly suggests its positive correlate, however, and in so doing points forward to the events to follow. With this negative description of the human condition as both a culmination of the first phase, and a foreshadowing device for the second, the narrator can now deal with the emergence of conflict on the basis of a common subjective condition shared by both man and woman.

Conflict is made to arise from the animal world:

And the serpent was more subtle that all other creatures of the field which Yahweh Elohim had made, and he said to Issah, "Did Elohim really say you shall not eat from any of the trees of the Garden?" 3:1

The animal world constitutes a third-person realm which is the symmetrical opposite of the divine realm. Both exist inside and outside of the narrative, God having a voice in the narrative but no place, and the animal world having place but no voice. If God is the subject which cannot finally be predicated by the narrator, the animal world is the archetypal predicate object which cannot normally be made the true subject of speech or action.

Permitting an animal to speak, the narrator poses a speaking subject which does not originate in discourse with the divine and is not under the prohibition. This makes possible the utterance of transgressive thoughts. Further, by permitting the transgressive thought to originate in this morally neutral personage, the source of evil is rendered totally ambiguous. Is the serpent subordinate to the human and therefore only a symbol of transgressive, inadmissable human thoughts, a principle of evil independent of both God and man, or subordinate to God and thus a sign of divine determination? The writer thus avoids creating a traditional villain, and thereby throws the emphasis of the narrative upon the inner human conflict.

The narrator portrays the serpent in the manner in which characters are presented in representative narratives, namely by means of a third-person statement providing its central character trait. Since characters formulated in this manner, with no opening toward the word-event which creates them, are given fixed traits and determined inwardly by desire, the serpent appears here as a prototypical, representative character. Its function in the narrative corresponds to its semiotic nature. As one outside the constraints of the intersubjective relations of man and woman, it both represents the desire-driven personage, and serves the function of injecting this character mode into the narrative as a possibility for man and woman.

But the narrator will not allow the serpent to become a genuine antagonist. It is given its place as one among the "creatures of the field that the Lord God made" (3:1). Thus while not having the verbal relation to God which man has, it is a part of the divinely created natural hierarchy. The trait given it by the narrator is so painfully succinct and thoroughly ambiguous as to make it impossible to extrapolate from it any power that could be identified as the fundamental source of evil. The word translated as "subtle" or "cunning" (*'ārûm*) can also mean "prudent" (Prov. 14:8). An added dimension of connotative meaning comes from the word play here between "subtle" and its homophone "naked" (*'arûmmîm*) in the previous verse. The subtle cleverness of the serpent provides an ironic contrast with the naked, unashamed innocence of man and woman. While not being itself a negative trait, it nevertheless leads the reader to anticipate the appearance of evil.

Now the first discourse outside of the constraints of the primal (I)–you relation is possible, and it is not surprising that the content of this discourse is that primary relation itself, with God now being spoken of in the third person for the first time by personages:

> And he said to the woman, "Has God really said you shall not eat of any of the trees in of the garden?" 3:1

The process is initiated by the serpent asking woman a question. Though the sentence is not grammatically marked as a question, it is implied by the interjectional use of the conjunction אַף (indeed, even, really), implying excess. A question is an illocutionary act which conventionally calls for a response from the addressee, especially one with such an oral, rhetorical style. The way in which a question is posed already dictates the terms of the answer.

The serpent is being deliberately provoctive and is seeking to put Issah on the defensive by overstating the conditions of the prohibition, implying: "You don't really mean to tell me that thus and so." This seeming show of sympathy seeks to plant in her mind the possibility that this prohibition is unjust by opening a "theological" discourse about what God has done, which is outside prior constraints. She refuses to agree with the serpent's statement, however, and attempts to give a defense of God in which she will state the truth about what God has said in the third person.

> And the woman said to the snake, "From the fruit of the trees of the garden we may eat, but from the fruit of the tree which is in the midst of the garden, God said, you may not eat from it, and you may not touch it lest you die." 3:2, 3

To represent truth against falsehood requires that she communicate meaning by means of a principle of identity and difference. She must answer the question by making a judgement as to the identity or non-identity of the serpent's restatement of the prohibition and the original formulation.

The subtlety of the serpent's question stems from its neutral position. There is no significant relationship manifest between its position and the question posed. It is neither subject to the prohibition nor a transgressor of it. It speaks as a voice from outside this intersubjective realm, a voice from the purely physical realm grammatically designated by "it."

Only a pre-philosophical symbolic narrator for whom the physical realm is not yet conceived in terms of ideas would imbue this objective realm with a personal voice in order to articulate an alternative to the intersubjective mode of human existence. Normally performative utterances gain their illocutionary force in part from the position of the speaker. The meaning of the words is clear enough, but the illocutionary force of the statement is very uncertain due to the heterogeneous character of the serpent's relation to the human and divine worlds. It is from the question's ambiguity at this level that its "seductive" power arises. Why is the serpent raising this question and taunting woman? The possibility now emerges for the first time that words might not mean what they appear to mean, that something is being withheld – that the narrative is beginning to move on two levels which are separated, not because of hierarchical stratification, but because of conflict between incompatible, mutually exclusive modes of existence.

The initial response of Issah is in the first person. She defends the truth by refuting the error in the serpent's question with a statement of the divine permission translated into the first-person plural describing what "we" may do. Here she speaks as one altogether subject to the divine words, having internalized them so that she can speak them in the first-person plural. Then follows an abbreviated citation of the prohibition, having the appearance of a direct quotation in the last phrase, but altered to fit the context. Consequently she makes both God and his words into objects of reference of a third-person statement, "but God said."

Issah here enters a new mode of subjectivity. To speak in the third person suppresses reference to the first person of the speaker, and thereby separates the speaking self from the word spoken. She assumes the position of a non-person behind the third-person statement, "God said." Further, God and his word now necessarily become the objects of Issah's speech and consequently of her judgement. She must distinguish between the true and false word of God on the basis of the principle of identity.

Issah does not cite the prohibition exactly as it is given in 2:17. She uses what appears to be a circumlocution for "tree of knowledge of good and evil," referring to it as the "tree which is in the midst of the garden." Is it to be assumed that Eve did not know the name of the tree? It is peculiar also that this phrase, "in the midst of the garden," appears to be more closely associated with the tree of life in 2:9 than the tree of the knowledge of good and evil. But stylistically, it would have deprived the following statement in verse 5 of some of its power if the phrase, "knowledge of good and evil," had appeared here.

Woman also intensifies the prohibition by adding, "neither shall you touch it." This emendation, which could be taken as a spontaneous product of Issah's agitation under the serpent's questioning, reflects already the distorting pressure of desire since the emendation extends the prohibition to avoid the temptation which would come with touching the tree. Of course, these changes also could represent distortions of the prohibition by Adam in his communication of the prohibition to Issah.

Having now been manipulated into the position of a subject detached from the divine words and a judge of their semantic content, Issah is prepared to receive a fully developed alternative interpretation of the prohibition that originates totally outside of the primary relation.

The serpent's statement begins with a flat contradiction of the threat of death: "You will surely not die" (3:4). Since this was the final element of the prohibition recounted by Issah without the time reference, it had to be contradicted at the outset. If violation will not bring death, then it would become a possibility worth considering.

But verbally contradicting the threat of death is not sufficient in itself to persuade Issah to transgress. She is then merely faced with two contradictory illocutionary utterances (a threat and denial of a threat) with no way of determining which of them has the most force. It is to this issue then that the serpent turns in its next statement.

Since the force of illocutionary utterances depends upon a transparent unity between the inner disposition (thoughts, feelings, intentions) of the speaker and his words,[22] it follows that the most effective way to undermine that force is to point to a discrepancy between the words and inner thoughts which will make the words appear to be an attempt to manipulate the addressee through deception. The serpent thus now provides a third-person interpretation of that hidden center of the divine subject to which human beings have no access. *It makes the realm of the divine first person, i.e., what God thinks to himself, the object of a third-person statement.* It becomes the narrator of a story about God.

> For God knows that in the day you have eaten from it, your eyes will be opened and you will be like Elohim knowing good and evil. 3:5

God thus becomes a typical character in the serpent's small but powerful story: he is driven by desires which he has concealed from his human creatures to preserve his own powers, when he might have made them available to them. The prohibition is made to appear not in the interest of humans, but only in the interest of the deity. This deceptive discrepancy between what "God knows" and what he says is designed to dissolve the illocutionary force of his prohibition and to attract humans to become a character in the serpent's story about divine and human conflict.

But why should Issah accept the word of the serpent as more powerful than the word of Yahweh Elohim? Here the virtue of the third-person form exhibits itself. The serpent belongs to the sphere of nature which is outside of the horizon of the prohibition – the sphere of the "it." If there is a hidden interior to the serpent, it cannot be penetrated. Issah is left, therefore, with the sheer verbal force of a plausible third-person argument. A certain illocutionary force stems from third-person statements simply because the third person so thoroughly blocks access to the subjective position of the speaker that it is impossible to point to any incongruity between the inner disposition and outer words which might throw the significance of those words into question.[23] In a direct confrontation of this sort, a third-person assertion which takes the hidden dimension of the subject of a performative statement as its object is inevitably more powerful, since it does not leave itself open to the same kind of attack. Its own subjectivity is hermetically sealed. There was thus a certain inevitability to Issah's fatal decision.

It is the content of the argument of the serpent that provides a necessary, positive basis for the decision of transgression: "your eyes will be opened and you will be like Elohim" (3:5). Transgression will lead to God-likeness, that is, autonomous subjectivity. Here we find, presented in DD, the "objective" form of human subjectivity suggested in 2:9 which may now replace relational intersubjectivity based on the permission/prohibition. Although the possibility of entering into this new mode of existence is presented in DD, it is itself not something given in direct discourse (i.e., in relation), but something which must be gained through the use of the eyes rather than the ears.[24]

It is through action that the personages will acquire experience which can then be predicated of them. They will thus exchange an outwardly limited existence in the intimacy of an intersubjective relation, for an outwardly unlimited existence in the splendid solitude of the objective self. The limit that was imposed upon external behavior will become internalized as an interior barrier which will block the open trusting relation of the "I" to other subjects. Identity will now be formed by deeds, appearance, and possessions, that is, by attributes. But now unlimited knowledge through experience will be possible. The first of these experiences, the transgression, will lead to the acquisition of the attribute "knowing good and evil."

The objective self founds its identity on likeness to other objective selves. It is God, as an objective self with the attribute "knowing good and evil" which the human characters first seek to become "like." They will determine all limits (i.e., good and evil) and will no longer be subject *to* limits. Any objective limits stemming from inescapable differences, such as sexual attributes, will become a source of acute shame. The subjective mode here corresponds to that outlined in 2:9, that humans will be oriented to the world around them through the medium of sight, and in the mode of desire. The term for desire used here in 3:6 also occurs in 2:9. The wisdom that is desired (נֶחְמָד) comes from the root חמד , meaning to look at, emphasizing the specular nature of this mode of wisdom. The limitation which the verbal prohibition, communicated through hearing, imposed upon them, is now set aside, and they move toward limitless autonomy in the pursuit of the specular image.

It is noteworthy that the serpent does not directly give Issah a mandate to transgress, but contradicts the threat of punishment and provides the verbal basis for her to make her own transgressive decision. Here the narrator enters to provide a third-person account of what went on inside the mind of Issah in response to the serpent's words.

And Issah saw that the fruit was good for eating, enticing to the eyes, and the tree was desirable for wisdom. 3:6a

What we see here is not merely the narrator's representation of her thought, but the form of the thought itself in process as she changes from a mediated, auditory mode of thought to an unmediated visual mode. Now that her *eyes* are "open," she can *view* the tree more directly, without the mediation of signs; she can see it for what it is apart from the prohibition. The attributes of the tree are then named in reverse order of importance, beginning with the material value of its fruit as food, ascending to its aesthetic, physical appearance to the eyes, and climaxing with its chief symbolic quality: "the tree was desirable for wisdom." But the thought which he attributes to Issah here takes the form of a type of inductive reasoning requiring the third-person form, arising as it does from non-verbal perceptual experience, simple awareness of possibility, and the force of desire.

This representation of an inner process takes the form of what Dorrit Cohn would call "consonant psychonarration" which includes also the "indirect thought quotation."[25] The narrator renders first two conscious points of understanding that are nevertheless very close to non-verbal experience and are probably not yet in the form of a verbalized thought: "the tree was good for eating, and was enticing to the eyes." This is followed by what must be a fully verbalized thought: "the tree was desirable for wisdom," since this represents an idea verbally communicated by the serpent, and not an experience. The narrator does not inject any ironic "dissonance" into this psychonarration, but presents it fairly from within the character's perspective.

Here the character is portrayed as thinking not in the more forthright first person, "I desire it to make me wise," but in the third person, which blunts and deflects the egocentrism of the first person statement. (The hiphil form of שׂכל here makes possible the elision of the pronominal reference, meaning, literally, to cause wisdom or make [one] wise.) To represent her thought in this fashion reveals an inner division that is now operative in her thinking. And, more significantly, the inadmissable desire for god-likeness is carefully concealed behind the more acceptable desire for "wisdom."[26] Thus a division is established in her consciousness between what she can articulate to herself as her desires and what she cannot. The serpent says: "You will be like God," but she *thinks* it is "desirable for wisdom." But beneath this is the unspeakable, possible thought: "I desire to be like God."

The decision which follows appears perfectly logical, but it reflects a shift in the mode of subjective existence. Now individual desire, rather than the illocutionary power of the word of Yahweh Elohim, has become the force behind Issah's action. Further, there is a division in her own consciousness between admissable and inadmissable desire that is the precondition for shame. Formerly she was a subject which existed fundamentally in and through a relation of discourse to another subject (though this must be assumed, since the communication of the prohibition to her is not recounted, and would exist, presumably, with Adam only, and not with Yahweh Elohim). But now she enters an objective mode of subjectivity in which she exists in terms of censured attributes that she predicates of herself as the outworking of desire. She desires the attribute of God-likeness to be attached to her.

Thus a complex, divided self emerges which is made possible by the internalization of the barrier which normally separates the third-person narrative framework from the direct discourse passages of a narrative. She is now presented by the narrator as thinking of herself in the impersonal terms of the third person. Her own instance of speech becomes hidden behind the third-person speech, enabling her to elude thinking of her relational identity formed by the prohibition, and the consequences of violation (shame, hiding) to that identity. In this way the narrator can present her as choosing the one identity without rejecting the other. She becomes a transgressor but not a villain since her inner division will give rise to shame when her action becomes known by those with whom she is bound in the primary intersubjective relation.

She has thus chosen to base her decisions about her actions, not on the divine Voice, which is the ground of Adam's and her conscious existence, but upon observation and desire.[27] The prohibition becomes not a positive connection to a transcendent Subject but an unjust limit to desires for autonomy and self-sufficiency.

The issue here is not the emergence or non-emergence of a type of knowledge which could be termed "differential knowledge,"[28] for the possibility of differential knowledge was already established by the prohibition itself which limits desire and thereby makes possible life within a system of differences. Adam uses this knowledge in naming the animals and differentiates between those acceptable and those unacceptable. Rather, the issue here is the modality of the human's *relation* to differential knowledge. The choice to eat of the fruit of the tree does not bring Adam and Issah a new type of knowledge, but it changes their relation to knowledge. In transgressing, they move from an intersubjective mode of existence, based on the prohibition in which experience and differential knowledge are arbitrarily limited, to an unlimited objective mode of existence[29] with an infinite field of experience and knowledge. In fact, by destroying the primary limit through which human beings were installed in a world of differences, the transgression represents a movement toward unity which will finally eliminate all differences. The end of this movement is illustrated by the story of the Tower of Babel.

This outwardly silent process of decision and action is complete when the narrator laconically describes how Issah provided her "husband" with some of the fruit and how he took it (without question) and ate it.

And she took of its fruit, and she ate, and she also gave to her husband, and he ate. 3:6b

Here, there is a homophonic relation of woman, *'iššāh*, and "her husband," *'îšāh*. The possessive attached previously to *'iššāh* is here attached to *'îš*, underscoring homophonically the narrator's conception of unity articulated by the "one flesh" concept in 2:24. He sees each as belonging to the other. Woman and man finally are portrayed interacting with one another for the first time since they "became one flesh." There has been no portrayal of Issah speaking to Adam, nor of Adam speaking directly to her. Both now engage in an action of absolutely crucial significance in complete silence. Issah does not offer persuasion nor does Adam seek her reasons. Silence at such a critical point cannot be without significance in a narrative that habitually places such importance upon dialogue and DD. The reasons for Issah's action – which have been given to the reader and might have been shared with Adam – are not spoken, thereby signifying a division within her between what is thought and what can be uttered.

Adam's silence here indicates that he tacitly recognizes and accepts Issah's private reasons for her action; by thus accepting Issah's right to hide a portion of herself from him, he also reserves the right to conceal from her his reasons for accepting the fruit. He thereby enters freely and voluntarily with her into a state of inner division. The silence itself betokens an unspoken and unspeakable accord to act without question and explanation. While Issah's preceding position in the sequence of actions and the internal perspective upon her thought given by the narrator has had the effect of elevating her guilt above that of Adam in the history of interpretation, it is not at all clear that the narrative embodies such a simplistic view. Not only is the chief responsibility of initiating this action placed clearly upon the enigmatic serpent, who promptly disappears from the stage, but it is Adam who has been addressed directly by God, and who thus can speak of the prohibition with authority. Issah is a mediating figure here, suspended between these two worlds. The silence of Adam is thus the most crucial event in this sequence. His passivity and silence effectively broke the network of communication which related the subjects to each other and to the divine in trustfulness and truth. Shame does not occur until *after* Adam's silent participation. His silence here is not unrelated to the fact that he is the *first* who must "answer" for this deed when Yahweh Elohim comes to walk in the garden. The act is laden with meanings which cannot be expressed because they contradict the common terms of consciousness shaped by the DD regarding the prohibition (indicated by Issah's reference to "we" in

3:2) which has implicitly occurred between them, and explicitly occurred between Adam and Yahweh Elohim.

Immediately, the effect of this action upon the consciousness of the personages is described as occurring simultaneously.

And the eyes of both of them were opened, and they knew that they were naked. 3:7

Guilt occurs at the same moment for both, at the moment of the realization of their inner division and alienation from each other. Actions that exercise an effect on the consciousness of actors who cannot articulate their meaning must be expressed then by the narrator in the third person. This is reported by the narrator again in the form of psychonarration, as a new experience of sight. This is the beginning of a process of defamiliarization which will climax in 3:11 with the interrogation by Yahweh Elohim. These reactions arise out of the friction between the original intersubjective mode and the new objective mode of consciousness which Adam and Issah are now entering. As Issah *saw* the tree differently once she was detached from the form of consciousness shaped by the prohibition, so now they *see* each other in a new light. But what they "see" is the other party as different in a new sense. The barrier which prevents the inner narcissistic desires for God-likeness from being expressed or even admitted into consciousness inwardly creates a sense of separation which produces an awareness of outer difference.

The account in the third person of this reaction to the eating of the fruit is very revealing of the narrator's point of view. The violation is itself a non-verbal action which must be recounted in the third person. The effect of the violation is to remove the characters from their intersubjective relation to the divine voice which constituted a verbal source for their action. Now as characters motivated exclusively by desire, they become inwardly divided and their actions produce unexpected consequences which arise from their inner conflict. The narrator thus reports that "they knew that they were naked." This was not the kind of knowledge which they were seeking! The narrator thus posits an inner mechanism operating in the characters, independent of their will, which produces virtually autonomic, physical reactions.

These in turn then lead them to further actions by which they think that they can compensate for or correct what has happened.

And they sewed together foliage from the fig tree, and made for themselves girdles. 3:7b

The specification of the type of covering made indicates that the sexual organs were at the center of their new awareness of nakedness. This awareness of nakedness arises from the inner division and reorientation toward a narcissistic, objectifying form of consciousness, which comes to be attached to outer sexual differences. Autonomous, narcissistic consciousness is androgynous and cannot admit binary sexual differentiation. Thus they intuitively act to cover their nakedness. But they simultaneously reveal objectively the inward concealment of those desires which has occurred. An outer symbolic division of the body into revealed and concealed areas thus corresponds to the inner division between that which can and that which cannot be thought (or said). Inner concealment spontaneously gives rise to outer concealment.

This, however, is a form of concealment that reveals precisely that which it is designed to hide, as does the hiding of Adam and Eve from God which follows.

We will see the same pattern in Cain's response to the success of Abel's sacrifice. But this only leads to a further divorce of the character's actions from his intentions. This, as we have seen, is characteristic of personages in the expressive narrative. Here, however, the reason for this is made obvious through the shift in the motive force of the character from an intersubjective relation to autonomous desire.

The narrative has now produced two alienated realms of characters, and only the narrator has access to both. Things have happened which are hidden from Yahweh Elohim. When the human subject transgresses, that transgression must be hidden from the divine subject. The line of open DD is thus broken and God can no longer speak directly to Adam as in 2:16, 17. God and the humans must then become external objects to each other. This is a critical problem for the narrative because the divine had only a voice in the narrative and no position. When the direct communication between the human and God is broken, then God is in principle excluded from the narrative.

Since that cannot be permitted, God must *act* to restore direct communication; he needs to acquire position in the narrative for the first time.

And they heard the voice of Yahweh Elohim going about in the garden like the wind of the day.
3:8

The appearance of God now as he comes to walk in the garden corresponds formally, in its transgressive character, to the speech of the serpent, that is, the serpent transgresses the barrier of language which normally excludes him from DD and confines him to the linguistic status of a third-person referent, and enters DD. Inversely, God, who normally exists *only* in DD, crosses the barrier of space and enters the objective mode of existence of his creatures.

God thus, by entering space, becomes now the object of a third-person descriptive statement. But the mode of his appearance is made as elusive and ambiguous as the statement which attributes to the serpent the quality which justifies its transgressive speech. God appears only as a *sound* of footsteps heard by man and woman. Human beings are thus still related to God through sound rather than sight. The word *kol* here can mean voice as well as sound and is thus elusively ambiguous with regard to its objective referent. Further ambiguity is seen in the phrase *l^erûaḥ hayôm* which Gunkel suggests refers to the wind in the early hours of the morning before the break of day.[30] The encounter would then be shrouded in darkness, and awareness of the dual meanings of *rûaḥ* as either wind or spirit is heightened. The narrator, mediating between these two alienated parties, reports that man and woman respond to this sound by hiding. But the Voice is inescapable, asking first of all the disarmingly simple question: "Where are you?"[31]

Adam does not answer, "Here I am," as is customarily done in response to a call, but rather begins recounting why he is hiding:

> Your sound I heard in the garden and I was afraid because I was naked, and I hid myself. 3:10

His answer leaves it unclear as to whether or not he came out of hiding for this conversation. If he did not then a reason might be provided for God's provision of clothing in 3:21, namely, to enable Adam and Issah finally to come out of hiding and to enter God's presence again after the emergence of shame (see more on this below). This would correspond to the practice reflected in the command to Moses to provide clothing for the priests who were to enter the presence of God in the temple, "to cover their naked flesh" (Ex. 28:42).

But by verbally articulating his consciousness of being naked, he ironically discloses what he is really seeking to hide: that he was not naked, but clothed with foliage from the fig tree. It was his clothing that he was hiding since the covering represented a change in consciousness. *He now perceives the world as divided between what can be disclosed and what must be concealed.*

A direct question comes from Yahweh Elohim in response:

> Who told you that you were naked? 3:11

This pivotal question points to a change in consciousness and explicitly brings to the surface of speech the issue of the cause of this change. Here the end is reached of the defamiliarization process which began with the awareness of nakedness caused by the sudden encounter of alienated worlds of blocked and suppressed discourse. Both characters see each other in a new light (as does the reader). But because one party is the divine Voice, this creates characters who are consciously aware of their inner contradictions. It is the tension caused by those contradictions which is now the focal concern of the narrative. This encounter juxtaposes the relatively open but limited mode of intersubjective existence with the object-oriented mode fueled by narcissistic desire for infinite experience and knowledge. The symbolic character of this narrative is seen in the way in which the narrator poses both of these modes in tension with each other and allows the direction of the plot to arise precisely out of the continuing unresolved friction between them.

Such questions – which penetrate communicative barriers to bring to light that which is hidden – constitute the central, recurring structural feature which characterizes the genre of narratives to be analyzed in this book. The emergence of suppressed, alienated worlds of discourse occurs time and again, always leading to these striking questions which point precisely to the lie or deception which sustains them. The recurrence of this pattern points to the breakdown and repair of the communicative process as one of the deepest concerns of the Genesis narrative. Often there is no restoration of communication pointing to a tragic dimension in history of which the narrator is painfully aware.

This striking question by Yahweh Elohim uses Adam's own words to penetrate the deception he is attempting to effect. Since the naked body was not something to be hidden from the creator of that body, there was only one possible source of the desire to hide – an alienated state of consciousness; and this could only have been caused by a transgressive act which had to be concealed. Thus the question follows immediately:

Have you eaten of the tree of which I commanded you not to eat? 3:11

This question climaxes the logical development of the narrative which began in 3:6 with the division of consciousness between the unacceptable desire for God-likeness articulated by the serpent and the more legitimate desire for wisdom articulated in the third person in the thought of Issah. It proceeded then to the totally silent transgressive sharing of the forbidden fruit with Adam, and resulted in the emergence of a divided consciousness: a consciousness of what can be disclosed and what must be concealed. This division is expressed first in a joint symbolic act – the simultaneous donning of fig leaves, then in a dramatic act – hiding from the divine presence, and finally in language – the articulation of the idea of nakedness. It is from this evidence of the change in consciousness disclosed by Adam's use of the word "nakedness" that God can draw the logical conclusion that a transgression has occurred.

The logic of this narrative sequence is thus governed by the need to portray the process through which human consciousness is changed from one of relational existence in the mode of totally open intersubjective trust (seen in obedience) based on an illocutionary utterance, to one of alienated existence in the mode of internal division and intersubjective concealment (shame). This leads then to a closed form of existence governed by binary oppositions:

unashamed versus ashamed
naked versus clothed
revealed versus concealed
truth versus deception.

Adam concedes his guilt, but only *after* defensively implicating both God and Issah in the crime:

The *woman* that *you* gave to be with me, she gave me from the tree ... 3:12

The first words uttered are defensive shields behind which Adam can hide. After taking refuge behind these words, he concedes: "I ate" (3:12). The thrust of the interrogation is thereby deflected to Issah but at the price of Adam alienating himself from her by his implicit accusation.

Woman then responds to the divine question, "What is this that you have done?" by similarly taking refuge behind a third person descriptive statement: "the serpent deceived me" (3:13). This deflects the investigation to the serpent, before she concedes: "I ate" (3:13).

The source of evil has now been transferred back to the animal world, but at the price of the alienation of woman from her source of "wisdom." The serpent who has no "I" cannot speak again and disclose the meaning of his "beguiling" words. He falls back into the silence of the animal world and the narrator's descriptive discourse. The final responsibility for the origin of evil thus remains shrouded in ambiguity. The emphasis falls then upon the *state* of alienation which has now crept into the relationship of all the characters rather than upon the determination of which party bears the responsibility for what has happened.

The "I" of man is first spoken in weakness, solitude and guilt: "I heard ... I was afraid ... I was naked ... I hid ... I ate." The "I" of woman is also first uttered in the admission of guilt to the divine judge. The words spoken by man and woman which so quickly shattered the primal unity are metonymic displacements for that which cannot be spoken or even thought – the desire to be like God, and in fact to displace God as the unlimited arbiter of good and evil. The words which create outer alienation reflect the deep inner division which has occurred in human consciousness. Now the words of man and woman have acquired a profound ambivalence. Their meaning can no longer be simply derived from their denotative content.

The situation which follows the transgression contains a dilemma. The mode of consciousness into which humankind has been installed by the prohibition required the recognition of limits, and the voluntary curtailment of desire. Now desire, in pursuit of the specular image, has triumphed over those limits; but human consciousness, rather than disappearing, as the threat of death indicated it would, has instead changed to become God-like: infinite, unlimited in scope. This reorientation of the characters presents a problem for this symbolic narrator. The transgression has changed intersubjective characters open toward the speech event which founded them into autonomous characters who are driven by visually oriented desire. Since the logic governing the action of such characters leads to the conflict pattern of the representative narrative, how can the symbolic narrator accommodate these characters within his perspective?

Human beings and God now appear to be antagonists, vying for supremacy, who must settle their differences through conflict. This, however, is the serpent's plot, not the author's. As we have seen, Adam and Issah are not presented as straightforward rebels in the Promethian sense. Issah does not consciously accept the serpent's proposal that she may become God-like. And the effect of the transgression is not the rebel's feeling of victory and liberation but, rather, shame. Thus the narrator is confronted with the task of depicting the continuing relationship of God to characters who have not openly disassociated themselves from the Word, but who have covertly done so, and, when discovered, have attempted to blame their actions on others. Their relation to the divine Word thus has become ambiguous, and correspondingly the divine communication can no longer be in the form of simple mandates and prohibitions which presuppose trust, recognition of authority, and compliance.

God responds to this situation by uttering curses. Such utterances are performative-type speech acts which are distinguished by the fact that they do not require uptake by a recipient, and do not assume the recognition of an authoritative position of the speaker. They generate their own magical rather than illocutionary force through their form, and are believed effective when properly uttered. The curse as an outer, objective word thus represents the last resort for maintaining the supremacy of the Word over the characters who have broken the intersubjective relation with the inner Word, but with whom some relation must still be maintained. Unlike the standard curse, the object of which is more often mentioned in the third person (Deut. 27:15–26),[32] these curses are uttered by the divine ''I'' to the addressee in the second person. Thus an intersubjective dimension can be maintained between God and the characters (and the serpent), though it has been inverted.

The first effect of the curse is to extend explicitly the alienation which has now appeared in all of the characters' relations into the orders of human social and natural existence. This may be formulated as a series of conflictual oppositions:

serpent versus other animals (3:14)
serpent versus woman (3:15)
woman versus man (3:16)
man versus the earth (3:17)

These conflicts will constitute limits to human (and animal) action which cannot be transgressed because they are extensions of inner states into the outer, objective circumstances of nature and society.

This new order of pairs, characterized by relations of humiliation, subordination and relentless conflict, corresponds to the condition of life which Ortigues attributes to the dominance of the imagination over consciousness. As the narrator has pointed out, man and woman now have shifted from the auditory to the visual sensorium as the source of the information upon which they will base their decisions. The full and immediate presence of visually derived objects in the imagination reveals to consciousness its own emptiness and ignites the flames of desire for the full presence of being which these specular images seem to possess. This seeking of the self in the other is narcissistic and transforms the self-reflective process into a passionate drama of conflict between doubles – subjects and objects of desire that are mirror images of each other. It was this desire to overcome their own deficiency caused by the prohibition, and to share in the unlimited fullness of objective being possessed by God, upon whom no limits have been imposed, that led to the silent transgression of man and woman together, as "one flesh."

The transgression has thus led to a mode of existence dominated by the narcissistic imagination which requires that the subjects be continually locked in a relation of narcissistic conflict with their opposites. This may be a relation of humbling inferiority in which they will desire but never attain the superiority of their opposites, as is now the situation of the serpent *vis-à-vis* the other animals. It may be a relation of permanent conflict in which each party will come to resemble the other as seems the case in the serpent's eternal conflict with the seed of woman: "He shall bruise your head, and you will bruise his heel" (3:15).

A typical narcissistic relation is one in which one partner desires unity and identity with the other to the extent that s/he will suffer at the hands of the desired partner and be perpetually dominated by her/him. Such appears to be the fate of woman *vis-à-vis* man, who will suffer in bearing her husband's children, but still, the curse says:

> your desire will be for your husband
> and he shall rule over you. 3:16

Finally, man too is given his eternal antagonist – the earth with which he must now struggle to earn the food he needs for life. This mimetic struggle with his opponent will bring man ultimately into total identification and union with it:

> In the sweat of your brow
> you will eat bread
> Until you return to the earth
> since from it you were taken;
> you are dust
> and to dust you shall return. 3:19

The effect of the curses being in direct discourse is to reassert the primacy of the illocutionary mode (now in the form, however, of magical utterances) as the basis of human subjectivity. Now, however, the limits which were originally experienced in the intersubjective relation of direct discourse are injected by the divine Voice into the material and social structures and biological necessities of human existence. Humankind will experience the limits of their subjective existence not in the dignity of a divine Word to them, but in the humiliating struggle with hostile animals, unequal social structures, the recalcitrance of nature, death, and the final elusiveness of utopia. Within the confines of these fateful limits, they will have an unlimited mode of knowledge, but this they will experience as a source of perpetual alienation from themselves, from God and from their fellow humans.

The narrative has thus achieved a type of closure in that the characters appear to be fixed in their limited roles and condition. But the absence of heroes and the ambivalence which stems from the inner division that characterizes each personage preserve a dimension of openness that will eventually make possible the recasting of the narrative upon different foundations beginning with chapter 12. The curse which determines human fate, as an illocutionary act of the divine Voice, assumes the primacy of a heterogeneous dimension from which new and different Words may come to reopen and regenerate the vitality of the narrative and its personages.

Now in the aftermath of these events, the narrator reports in third-person discourse (rather than in first-person direct address as before) that Adam again exercised his authority to name by giving woman now a new name, Eve, since, as the narrator adds in a palpably ironic explanatory, etiological comment, "she was the mother of all the living" (3:20).[33] The placement of the naming of woman after the curses thus makes clear the fateful limits imposed from birth upon all human offspring. It verbally enshrines the transformation which has occurred.

The transformation is then enshrined objectively by the report that: "Yahweh Elohim made for Adam and his wife (*'ištô*) garments of skin, and he clothed them" (3:21). The mark of the new mode of existence which Adam and Issah spontaneously developed is now given divine sanction as a permanent sign of their alienation. As Robert Oden says: "Yahweh's act in presenting clothing to the man and the woman is not a gracious concession. It is an authoritative marking of the pair as beings who belong to a sphere distinctive from that of the divine."[34]

Finally, limits are extended into the topography when God sends them out of the garden and makes it impossible for them to reenter. The single outer limit given in the prohibition for Adam's voluntary compliance is now multiplied and reimposed in such a way that transgression is impossible. Through the curses and exclusion, limits are given as an inescapable fate. The narrator has provided as a justification for this final exclusion a comment made in the divine world that concedes that the serpent was right in asserting that the transgression would make man like God.

> And Yahweh Elohim said, "Thus the man has become like one of us, knowing good and evil. And now, lest he reach with his hand and take also from the tree of life, and eat, and live forever..."
>
> 3:22

Though he now shares the unlimited divine mode of consciousness, he still inhabits a limited material body and must not be permitted to eat of the other magical tree in the garden, the tree of life (3:22). He would then also share the temporally unlimited mode of divine being and live forever. He thus must be driven from the garden and excluded from it forever.

It is significant that once again the locus shifts away from the human plane to the divine world to report in direct speech this fateful decision. This heightens the sense of paranoic alienation which has now developed between the divine and the human levels. Commands given directly to humankind are no longer of any value. If Yahweh Elohim attempted to explain to man directly why he was being excluded from the garden, this might offer him the opportunity to taste the fruit of the second tree as well, before he could be expelled. A spirit of haste prevails here, suggesting that the extraordinary breaking off of this divine discussion in mid-sentence is an aposiopesis rather than textual corruption. The completion of the thought, by showing its consequences in third-person narration, also shows the close relation of the narrator's perspective with that of the divine.

Force rather than verbal command is now the mode by which the divine relates to the human:

> And Yahweh Elohim sent him from the garden of Eden to work the earth from which he was taken. And he drove out Adam, and placed at the east of the garden of Eden, the cherubim and a flaming sword which turns itself to guard the way to the tree of life. 3:23, 24

The perpetually turning flaming sword stands at the end as a visible symbol of the suspicion, hostility and fear which now characterize the relation between humankind and the realm of the divine. As a symbol it is also consistent with the institution of sacrifice as a means of relating to the divine which occurs next at the beginning of chapter 4.

9

"Where is your brother?" Genesis 4

The move from the story of paradise to "life after" requires a significant change in the narrator's style. The chief problem which this presents is that characters must be depicted who have "fallen" away from their intersubjective matrix, and now appear as typical personages, empty signs driven by desire toward objects of their imagination. But as a symbolic narrator whose premises are that human beings are creatures of the inner Word, he cannot simply give himself over to the dynamics of the representational narrative. The style assumed in chapters 2 and 3 was able to avoid the sharpness of this dilemma since there it was possible to pose characters in relation to this Word, and by the subtle use of the third-person narrative framework to show their movement toward an objective mode. The finely drawn, economical style reflects precisely the tension between these two poles, as he depicts their ambiguous inner thoughts and reactions, and the evasive dialogue which they are still able to have with the divine. The power of this narrative to engrave itself on successive generations through the centuries doubtless stems from the extraordinary fusion of style and meaning which this manifests. In this regard it stands much closer to poetry than to prose.

But with the collapse of the intersubjective matrix of the characters, it is no longer possible to rely as heavily on direct discourse or on the tension between the third-person and direct discourse modes of expression to convey meaning. The characters have "fallen" into closure. This means that, as creatures of desire, their actions more than their words will convey meaning, and consequently the narrator must rely more heavily than before upon third-person descriptions of their actions as well as interpretations of their meaning. Since they have assumed an objective mode of existence in which their identity will be located not in their speech but in their attributes, we can expect more characterizations to be given by the narrator as well. The narrator will thus have to utilize the techniques of the representative narrator more extensively.

But herein lies his dilemma. How, during this interlude of decline before the new beginning in chapter 12, is he to maintain a role for the divine Word and yet depict his characters in the conventional closed mode? It is obvious that the positive commands and mandates are of no value. Can the micro-dialogue still be used at all? Must the divine also now reveal itself through action rather than speech if the mediating word is no longer effective, as seen already in the act of expulsion at the conclusion of chapter 3? But if the divine only acts, would not this require the narrator to describe those actions, and, more importantly, explain them somehow to the reader, thereby imposing a closed ideological framework upon the divine?

These difficult questions account for the unusual eclectic style of the narratives in chapters 4 to 11. The narrator is forced to maintain the bi-leveled narrative structure, with the divine and the human on different planes. These two planes communicate very seldom in direct speech, and the narrator, who has access to both, must serve as a mediator and interpreter for the reader. The relations between the levels is primarily one of action on the human level (usually transgressive) and reaction from the divine level (usually punitive). This pattern of conflict, typical of the representative narrative, is, at the level of action, totally closed. The source of light in this darkness is refracted, as it were, from the heart of the darkness itself, the ideology of the narrator which has totally penetrated the futility of life lived on the basis of the autonomous imagination (6:4; 8:21). While the characters may be victims of their desire, the author is not deceived by this view of life, and uses these stories, taken from the common literary heritage of the ancient Near East, to unmask totally the depraved, murderous, arrogance of this mode of existence. But the punitive God who reveals himself primarily in arbitrary, devious and horrific actions (6:7) toward mankind is scarcely more capable of eliciting the sympathy of the reader.

The conflict between the antagonists is pressed to its ultimate degree of destructiveness with no apparent basis for hope that either God or man can break this pattern. But such relentless negativism can only be conceived by a narrator who has gone beyond this cyclical system and discovered another positive basis for his characters: in this case, a way of restoring the intersubjective relation to the divine Word. From this perspective he is able to treat this system arising from the autonomous imagination as a modality, as one among other ways of human orientation to life, rather than organizing his narrative around the objects of desire themselves. The reader thus does not find here a seductive object of desire which elicits identification with the character and builds up suspense. Rather, the narrator places the emphasis quickly and repeatedly upon the negative consequences of this mode of existence so as to disclose its deficiencies and implicitly point toward the event to come in which it is transcended.

He gives a first glimpse of this new relation in the word of promise to Noah by means of which humankind is saved from total annihilation, and in the promise after the flood to refrain in the future from acts of global annihilation (8:21,22). The cycles begin again in the story of the

Tower of Babel. The movement toward an entirely new Word-based history does not begin until the promise to Abram in Genesis 12.

In moving now to a consideration of the narrative of Cain and Abel, it is obvious that a greater importance must be given to the semantic content of the narrator's descriptions. The continuity of the narrative's meaning will not be found now in the relation of the characters to the divine Word, from which they are alienated, but in what their actions imply about the structure of their inner consciousness and its relation to the divine. From this reliance upon action to convey character, we would expect that the characters would be typical of the representative narrative, but now placed by the narrator in a context where the limitations of that mode of existence would be illuminated.

The first post-expulsion event to be narrated is, unsurprisingly, the birth of children to Adam and Eve. Eve, now, rather than Adam, names this new creature Cain on the basis of her utterance after its birth, "I have gotten a man with (the help of) Yahweh."[1] Then Abel is born, no explanation being given for his name. With two new characters now on stage, new possibilities and problems for narrative development emerge. The first problem is how God is to be related to these new beings who are born outside of paradise. Certainly the prohibition violated by the parents cannot be given again. Rather, God is to be encountered chiefly through the structure of nature which manifests divine power both in its productivity and in the pain and labor involved in securing its fruits in sufficient quantity to continue life. It is through sacrifice that this material relation between human beings and God in nature is to be articulated.

Excursus on sacrifice in religion and literature

One of the most fully developed examples of sacrificial ideology is to be found in Indian religion. I will turn now to examine this phenomenon as an important background for understanding the dynamics of sacrifice assumed by the Cain and Abel narrative. This sacrifice should not be understood solely against the limited background of the developed sacrificial rites of Israel since we are dealing here with sacrifice in the service of a narrative.[2]

The central issue for this analysis is the way in which certain types of sacrifice make possible the identification of the human with the divine. In their study of sacrifice in ancient India, Madeleine Biardeau and Charles Malamoud write that the candidate for *sunnyasin* "burns all of his combustible sacrificial utensils in the fire Ahavaniya at the outset ... then places the fire in himself ... He pronounces a formula of renunciation to the world the terms of which evoke the 'abandonment' of the sacrificial victim offered to the gods by the Yajamana."[3] Mental acts designed to eradicate desire for the material world thus replace outer action as the religious obligation. Breath and speech are made focal points of this mental activity. A symbolic correspondence is developed between sacrifice and breathing, and sacrifice and speaking, breath being sacrificed in speech, and speech in breath. The continuous interaction with the world was thus understood in terms of sacrifice.[4] Such absolute renunciation of the material world leads to the identification of the individual self, Atman, with the absolute spirit, Brahman. Inner sacrifice thus abolishes all difference and supports mimetic union of the essential spiritual self with that absolute divine spirit which is beyond all differences.

The same linkage of sacrifice and mimetic union with the divine is found in the Bhakti cult in India, though the symbolic realm is more imagistic. Audrey Hayley's study of Assamese Vaishnavism describes the sacrificial service (*seva*) for Krishna in this cult. There are four components of this service: the divine Name, the God, the *Guru*, and the devotees. These four elements are all divine and exist fundamentally in the Vaikuntha heaven as aspects of the godhead. Hayley describes the purpose of the service in this way: "to induce Krishna and his heavenly company to descend from their abode and take temporary residence in the bodies of the congregation, the leader of the Prayer [*nam logowa*] is installed as Krishna, the other devotees become invested with the heavenly host and the ingredients of the offering are transformed from the produce of this world into the articles of Krishna's granary. In a literal sense the aim is to create a heaven on earth."[5] Because of the internalization of sacrifice in Indian religion, it is not necessary or desirable that the sacrificial items be destroyed. Rather, only the utterance by the prayer leader of a word, a secret *mantra* representing the internal sacrifice, is necessary to effect the transformation of ordinary food into heavenly food.

The result is the complete identification of the devotee with the divine. As Hayley says, "the opposition between gods and man is largely overcome by the belief that a man participates in the god whom he worships: 'If I worship Krishna, I become Krishna; if I worship a demon, I become a demon' ... As a *guru* said: '*Guru*, Name, all are found in the devotee. He is the embodiment of them all.'"[6] Thus symbolic words and acts of the sacrifice serve to bring about mimetic identity between the divine and the human, though in this case the images of the deity are retained in the act of union. The devotees themselves become the incarnation of the heavenly world. But because of the total spiritual identification of the human with the divine, and the eradication of the difference which the purely human element would represent (there is a "penalty offering" given at the outset to compensate for any human failings in the ritual process)[7] violence against material objects is missing from the relation to the images.

Biardeau and Malamoud provide us with another example from popular Tamoul religion that more closely resembles ancient sacrificial rites. In the cult of the goddess PacceivaLiyammaN one of the central communal rites is the sacrifice of a buffalo. Puranic mythology reveals that the identity of the Buffalo is that of an antithetical double of the Goddess. Whereas the Goddess is presented as the feminine replica of the *Trimurti* who acts in place of the *Trimurti* to maintain cosmic order, the Buffalo god is the "incarnation of total evil, enemy of the gods and of the *dharma.*"[8] The myth describes how the *Trimurti* had been defeated by this Buffalo demon, Mahisa-asura, and how the goddess, propelled by anger, emerged from these three gods, and engaged in a bloody battle with the demon's army involving the severing of many heads. In a climactic fight with the Buffalo, just before she pierced it with her trident, its real being escaped through the nostrils. This was a *purusha* figure in human form, fully armed. The goddess then decapitated this figure.[9] In the sacrificial rite, the head is cut from the Buffalo and placed before the goddess, but some of the inconography makes it clear that this Buffalo head is a surrogate for the human head of the *purusha* figure.

The vegetarian upper castes participate but only indirectly in this communal sacrifice. The sacrificed animal and its carcass are handled and consumed by the lower castes.[10] Persons holding conflicting attitudes toward sacrifice are thus able to coexist in the same system and share in the common benefits of the sacrifice.

Within Indian religion one can see the full range of possible forms which the sacrificial process may assume. At one end of the continuum the sacrificial mentality affirms an absolute discontinuity between the symbolic and the material which requires the sacrifice of materialism as a whole by means of the inner annihilation of desire. At the other end of the spectrum the symbolic and material orders assume the form of antithetical specular images. The discontinuity between the material and the symbolic must be articulated through the violent destruction of the symbol of gross materiality by the symbol of spiritual order in an act of physical sacrifice as the myth of the Goddess and Buffalo demon shows.[11]

In semiotic terms, following Ortigues, one could thus say that all sacrifice assumes a fundamental cleavage between the symbolic and material realms and serves to annihilate the chief difference between the two realms (spirituality and materiality) so as to achieve mimetic unity. But the dynamics of sacrifice may follow either of two courses. The sacrificial object may be understood as a representation of the self, the material destruction of which enables the spiritual self to attain symbolic unity with the divine; or, the object may symbolize pure materiality itself (e.g., the Buffalo demon), the irreducible difference between this world and the spiritual world. This object is the reverse image of the self, and in destroying it, the self destroys the attractive power of materiality and identifies totally with the symbolic realm in its perpetual conflict with materiality. This dynamic is culticly expressed in the scapegoat ritual. The opposition between realms, which is totally subjective at one end of the continuum becomes completely objective at the other.

Since sacrificial dynamics are so prevalent in ancient mythology it would be indeed surprising if they were not similarly important within the classical literature of the west. In the work of René Girard we find the first major attempt to show this to be the case. In his writings he produces evidence of the underlying dynamics of sacrifice in the major works of western literature from the Greek tragedies to Shakespeare and Dostoyevsky. But it is in his book, *Violence and the Sacred*, that he brings together literary, anthropological, and ethnological evidence to construct a general unified theory of culture. His thesis is that culture as a whole stems from a primal event of generative violence in the form of a ritual sacrifice. Since his theory links the phenomenon of doubles to mimetic union with the divine in the sacrifice, his theory is of great relevance to this discussion.

For both René Girard and Edmond Ortigues, sacrifice has fundamental significance for the origin and maintenance of human culture. For Ortigues, however, the prohibition is more fundamental than sacrifice since it is the primary ground of consciousness. For Girard, the ground is the surrogate sacrifice. He brings in Freud's own study, *Totem and Taboo*, to support his case, arguing that this work actually posits an event of collective sacrifice, rather than the incest prohibition, at the origin of culture.[12]

For Ortigues, it is the relation to the specular image that leads to sacrifice because of the threat to consciousness posed by the absorption of the self into a material form. The image appears to offer the fullness of presence which the empty self desires. But mimetic union with that image threatens to destroy the difference which is the ground of consciousness itself. Thus what was an object of desire is transformed into an object of hatred, or another symbolic object must arise to play the role of the despised image of gross materiality. Consciousness can renew itself only through the symbolic destruction either of the self or the self's mirror image.

Ortigues thus founds sacrifice upon the dual relation which the imagination has to the material world. The imagination seeks immediate unity with the images of the world, but because they are antithetical, such unity is possible only by the spiritualization of the material object through its physical destruction. Although Ortigues does not discuss ritual sacrifice as a replacement for unrestrained violence between doubles, it appears consistent with his views that collective sacrifice might serve this function. But he would not agree with

Girard that the origin of violence is in a primal violence hidden in the roots of human nature.[13] Rather, he would attribute it to the seduction of consciousness by the specular image into the pursuit of an impossible narcissistic unity with the world.

But leaving aside the issue of the primacy of the prohibition, Girard's view of sacrifice constitutes a significant bridge to literature. Girard sees evidence, especially in classical Greek drama, of a correlation between a decline in the practice of sacrificial rites and the emergence of generalized violence in the society. He calls this development the "sacrificial crisis."[14] The surrogate sacrifice, which he considers to be the original and basic form of sacrifice, upholds the social order by upholding a differential system. In the absence of sacrifice humans become locked in relations of conflict which eradicate their differences, making each a mirror image of the other. This erosion of differences through violence leads to the destruction of society. In his view, "the cultural order is nothing more than a regulated system of distinctions in which the differences among individuals are used to establish their 'identity' and their mutual relationships."[15]

The system of distinctions is restored by the surrogate victim who embodies the evil which the society rejects. By joining together in a collective act of rejection and annihilation of this symbol of evil, the society can establish or maintain the fundamental distinctions of the social order.[16] On this basis Girard can say that the rite of the surrogate sacrifice, "permits [people] to escape their own violence, removes them from violence, and bestows on them all the institutions and beliefs that define their humanity."[17]

This estimation agrees with that made by Biardeau and Malamoud regarding sacrifice in Indian society:

> The interdependence of the sky and the earth is then total. They maintain themselves only together. The order which permits this whole to subsist, where each has his role to play is the *dharma*; a notion fundamentally and inseparably related to sacrifice since one does not exist without the other. The cosmic drama is played then on earth in this world where one sacrifices.[18]

But the primacy given to absolute violence in human nature, and the corollary argument of the fundamental role played by violent sacrifice in human culture, does not accord with the Indian experience entirely. As we have seen, the Vedantic philosophers realized that the ultimate aim of sacrifice was a positive goal: to achieve unity with the divine. The positive goal has been devalued by Girard due to his interest in the negative, prophylactic social function of ritualized violence. This has also caused him to fail to give attention to the deeper problem this positive function entails, which Vedantic philosophy uncovered: that the material roots of the image of the sacrificial object ultimately limit its capacity to serve as a symbol for universal spiritual reality. This corresponds to Ortigues' critique of sacrifice as well, since he argues that the unformed emptiness of the imagination would prevent it from ever finding identity with any material image, thereby setting up the conditions for tension and conflict.

One of the primary tensions which would be generated by the material image stems from the desire for that image to be, in fact, ultimate reality, possessing absolute fullness of being. But its material form and its individuality set it into lateral relations with other material forms offered by others as sacrificial objects. A question would necessarily arise as to which of these forms was in fact ultimate. Such questions have generally been answered by the ordering of sacrificial objects into a system which corresponds to the social system, such as in the Tamoul society in India discussed above, where only the lower castes offered "impure" bloody sacrifices, while the vegetarian upper classes offered "pure" fruit and vegetables. The correlation of the class system with the sacrificial system is even found in the more egalitarian Biblical religion (Lev. 4). Thus, while on one hand, the sacrifice diverts individual violence into a symbolic, collective act, uniting the society around a renewed moral order, on the other hand, acts of sacrifice by individuals reinforce the differences of status, wealth, and power of the various classes within the society.

While the sacrifice itself might serve to reconcile the individual to his/her place in society, and thus to perpetuate the socio-economic order as a system of differences, a lateral glance would inevitably give rise to envy. As the anthropologist Victor Turner (cited by Girard) says: "Structural differentiation, both vertical and horizontal, is the foundation of strife and factionalism, and of struggles in dyadic relations between incumbents of positions or rivals for positions." Though Girard attributes to this statement by Turner an "anti-differential" prejudice, Girard does not seem to see that the positive mimetic presuppositions of sacrifice itself finally undermine the differential systems which it appears to establish, and lead to conflict, unless the path of Vedantic philosophy is taken.[19] In that case, however, material society itself is ultimately devalued and rejected.

While collective violence does undoubtedly serve to redirect the violent propensities within the individual into harmless symbolic acts, it simultaneously elevates violence into the means of creating and maintaining the fundamental distinction upon which the entire cultural order is based, namely the distinction between the symbolic and the material, the sacred and the profane.

Furthermore, since, apart from Vedantic philosophy, this relation to the symbolic takes the form of a relation to an imaginary image, a double, this type of relation would serve as a model for human social relations. The effect of this would be to increase the potential for an outbreak of violence within societies characterized by the sacrificial mentality. As Girard points out, in Euripides' *Heracles* the hero seizes his own wife and children at the altar, and in a fit of madness, thinking them his enemies, sacrifices them. Though

Girard attributes this to a breakdown in the "mechanism of substitution," it is a breakdown that is consistent with the sacrificial mentality which hallucinates the image of the sacrificial object into either a positive or negative psychological double. Thus, while clearly illustrating the importance of the substitutionary mechanism in sacrifice as a barrier against inter-personal violence, it also illustrates the potential of sacrifice to create the mental conditions for such violence.

Typological analysis

Against this background, it now seems obvious that our narrative should move from depicting the new state of life after the violation of the prohibition to a narrative centering upon the first sacrifice. Now that the prohibition has broken down as a mediator between the human and the divine, the flesh and the spirit, the other classical mode of maintaining the relation between the two realms must be instituted. But, significantly, Adam and Eve are not portrayed as taking this momentous step. The violation of the prohibition is depicted as being fraught with ambiguous conflicting motives. They do not explicitly pursue God-likeness, and their action which is covertly motivated by this desire produced shame and guilt. Adam and Eve, though "fallen," are still tied to the verbally mediated mode of divine–human relationship through their guilt and shame. They have not come to the point of openly exhibiting their new state of consciousness.

But what the first generation believes inwardly, the second generation expresses outwardly. Also, since this new mode of existing is to involve dual, opposing relations in place of verbally mediate relations, rival brothers offer excellent material for probing this sort of relation. The tensions of these self-limiting dual relations have begun to manifest themselves in the relations prescribed in the curses. The perpetual struggle between woman (and her offspring) and the serpent suggests the hostile conflict with the despised image of the lower material order. The relation of woman to man corresponds to the relation with an idealized specular image which requires subordination and servitude. Man, in his context with nature, encounters explicitly the hated and rejected image of his materiality: "Dust you are and to dust you shall return."

Now with the advent of brothers born outside of paradise and beyond the reach of the prohibition, the mode of existence foreshadowed in the previous story and characterized by the autonomous imagination and the relation of the self to its imaginary double may come into full expression. To make sacrifice the occasion which precipitates and exposes the dynamics of this new mode of existence goes directly to the most profound level of this problem with astonishing accuracy and economy.

The narrator begins by providing us with a succinct one-sentence characterization of each brother. Abel was a "watcher of sheep" and Cain a "worker of the ground." This has the immediate effect of posing each brother with a basic distinctive, fixed identity which contains, in its difference from the other, the seeds of rivalry and conflict. We will see the same technique used in the initial presentation of the other pair of rival brothers in Genesis, Jacob and Esau (23:27), but there with some considerable ideological modifications. No hint of preference for one vocation above the other is given at this point by the narrator.

Then follows "at the end of some days" the account of the first sacrifice. Cain, the farmer, makes an offering of "the fruit of the ground." But the narrator then adds with stress that Abel, "also he" (repeating the pronoun גַם הוּא), brought a sacrifice from his flocks. His was distinguished by being the "firstlings of the flock" and is further marked by possessing fat (the best portion) in some form (the texts are not clear here). These qualifying descriptions endow Abel's sacrifice with special characteristics missing from the simple unqualified naming of Cain's sacrifice as the "fruit of the ground." Such a difference invites comparison. Further, one is a blood sacrifice and one is not.

It is significant that the narrator orients his description of these initial sacrifices toward the rivalry between the brothers rather than toward the expiation of guilt. These first sacrifices are not portrayed as being surrogate sacrifices of the type considered primary by Girard. The sacrificial object does not represent the evil which the society rejects, but is rather an extension of the essential self of the sacrificer. Cain the farmer offers the first fruits of the land which he has produced. Abel, the herdsman, offers the products of his herds. The aim of the sacrifice is to transform these material objects which represent the sacrificers into spiritual form so as to achieve mimetic identification and unity with the divine.

But by posing these initial sacrifices as acts of fraternal rivalry, the narrator immediately exposes the most critical problem at the heart of the sacrificial system: the problem of human beings attaining mimetic union with the divine by means of materially relative symbolic representations of themselves. When the society offers only a common sacrifice, or when there is a prescribed sacrificial system for the whole society, this problem may not become overt. But here each brother represents a different cultural ethos, and in this primal situation, where there is no established hierarchical system of values, there is thus a question as to which of the symbolic expressions will correspond to the divine and be acceptable. In the light of this question, it is understandable that the divine must choose one and reject the other. If both are not rejected, then only one can be accepted since only one can meaningfully achieve identification with the divine. For both to be equally acceptable would make acceptability meaningless in this context of rivalry. Neither sacrificer would have the assurance of having achieved mimetic identification with the divine.

This unmasking of the competitive dynamics of sacrifice enables this ritual to become a narrative. Narrativization of ritual sacrifice also occurs elsewhere in the Hebrew scriptures, where it serves the positive goals of the narrator (for example, the story of Dathan and Abiram [Num. 16]; and the story of Elijah and the Baal priests [I Kgs. 18]).

The divine response to the sacrifices is recorded next. Such responses are often signaled elsewhere by the appearance of sacred fire (Gen. 15:7ff.; Judg. 16:9–24). The acceptance is described in the text, however, as a *visual* perception. Yahweh literally "gazed" on (וַיִּשַׁע) or "looked" at Abel's sacrifice. This first vital act of communication between God and man after the expulsion from paradise is thus accomplished through the medium of sight rather than language. This corresponds well to the shift from the auditory to the visual mode on the human plane which we saw in 3:6 in connection with the transgression. Just as the first expression of desire for an object is to look or gaze upon it on the human plane, so God similarly signals his desire for a sacrificial offering by looking upon it. But, as an indication of the total identification of the sacrifice and sacrificer, God looks not only upon the sacrifice, but upon Abel as well: "And Yahweh looked upon Abel *and* his sacrifice" (4:4). Conversely, the failure of the sacrifice to achieve divine acceptance is indicated by God not looking upon it or the sacrificer: "And upon Cain and his sacrifice, he did not look" (4:5).

We are not told how either the sacrificers or the narrator know God's response. Seeing is itself a subjective act. This statement thus constitutes entrance by the narrator into the inner perspective of the divine to provide a form of psychonarration. But unlike 2:18 and 3:22, no direct discourse of the divine is given which might explain the divine decision. Although it is implied that Abel's sacrifice is superior, this is not made clear. In the direct speech by God to Cain which follows, the reasons given have to do with Cain generally "making good" or "amending [his] ways" (תֵּיטִיב) (4:7) which can scarcely refer to the technical mistake of not offering "first fruits" or more desired grains, etc.

By not communicating a clear explanation for the divine, a certain arbitrariness now appears in the exercise of the divine will, and the God who came walking in the garden in the previous story now assumes a more detached posture toward the affairs of humankind. The grounds for this disparity in the treatment of equals, in Westermann's view, "lies in a decision which is withdrawn from human influence."[20] This withdrawal of God from a more direct and intimate mode of interaction serves to bring into the foreground the interaction between the human characters.

We thus find now a description of the reaction of Cain to his rejection:

"And Cain was exceedingly angry, and his countenance fell" (4:5). Just as the narrator in 3:7 provided us with a description of both the inner (awareness of nakedness) and outer responses of man and woman after the transgression (donning fig leaves), so here he tells us of Cain's inner state (great anger) and its outer manifestation (the expression of dejection on his face). As a relation existed between the state of inner conflict within Adam and Eve and the outer response of shame, so such a relation exists here. It is significant that the narrator, who is so restrained in his description of the outer appearance of his characters, has, in both of these cases, provided such a description. In both cases tangible involuntary signs of the inner states of consciousness which have produced them are given. Shame dictated the hasty apron of leaves.

The inner impact of rejection instantly changed the face of Cain. Where intersubjectivity is the basis of character, the feelings and identity of the person are embodied in his discourse, but when alienation enters, the identity and emotions are then manifest through compulsive or involuntary physical and physiological reactions (symptoms) which must then be described in third-person discourse by the narrator. Westermann speaks here of a "psychosomatic phenomenon."[21] The fig leaves as well as the "fallen" countenance are metonymic figures for inner states of consciousness. God, then, who is here related primarily by sight to the characters, responds to the fallen countenance of Cain which he apparently sees.

> And Yahweh said to Cain, "Why is there anger in you? And why has your countenance fallen? If you do well, will [it] not rise up? If you do not do well, sin is lying in wait at the door, and its desire is for you. But you will have power over it." 4:6, 7

This occurence of direct discourse from the divine comes immediately after the initial reaction of Cain is reported, but before an overt action on his part, and reveals a new mode of verbal exchange between the divine and human. In the paradise story, God speaks initially through a mandate and a prohibition, and subsequently, after the transgression, through the questions he asks when investigating the crime, and finally, through the curses which constitute the judge's verdict and sentence. Here the context has changed dramatically, and the divine utterance assumes a quite different form.

The unusual style and vocabulary of this passage has prompted much critical comment.[22] Westermann may be quite right in sensing an earlier stage of tradition beneath the present form of these verses. But it does not necessarily follow that the meaning of the verses is not congruent with the present context. Being carefully composed for this context, they may thereby reflect the writer's most considered reflections over the inner dynamics of this narrative and its relation to the previous paradise story. It is precisely by the incorporation of the term "desire" from 3:16 that the conceptual framework from the previous narrative is carried over into this story and used in a very consistent manner.

Whether this was already a part of the J narrative or the work of a late editor is probably impossible to determine, and may not be of decisive importance, in any event, in understanding the text as it now exists and affects the reader.

At the outset it should be noted that the repetition of selected terms from verse 5b and verse 6 does not suggest a duplication when the repetition is in divine speech. Their semantic context is transformed when the words move from the plane of the narrator to that of the divine, as we have seen.

The most striking aspect of this divine utterance is the understanding of the self which it conveys to Cain. Though God is speaking directly to Cain as if an intersubjective relation existed, the divine questions acutely reveal rather than ameliorate the state of alienation. For God to ask, "Why are you angry?" after choosing to favor his brother over him, though appearing formally sympathetic, only reveals the disjunction between their points of view.

Rather than waiting for a response which might have brought out the root cause of the estrangement, the divine Voice immediately adds another question which moves away from Cain's inner feelings to his outer reaction and insures that the discourse will remain at the level of external behavior. This choice was obviously made with anticipation of and indifference toward Cain's angry reaction. The questions which are posed are obviously rhetorical, and constitute a refusal to open a genuine intersubjective dialogue which might provide Cain with a just reason for one being chosen above the other. The relation to God has shifted now to an external basis, governed by mimetic identification. Where the dynamics of the God/human relation are governed by desire for identification, the differences which exist at the material level inevitably spawn rivalry which must result in only one victor. Though Abel's sacrifice is marked by the narrator as technically superior to Cain's, this is not given by God as the reason for Cain's rejection, since within this new relationship, the rejection of one of the rivals was inevitable. The decision thus is left to appear vaguely arbitrary, hidden within the mystery of divine sovereignty.

The divine Voice then can only offer somewhat feeble and general advice to mollify Cain. Even this advice is placed in the form of a question: "If you do well, [will it] not rise up?"[23] Cain appears here to be contending not with a person but with a process which will operate in his favor in exchange for some unspecified improvement in his actions.

The uncertainty of the divine Voice concerning Cain's inner life and the possibility for his future success vanishes as the divine Voice proceeds to illuminate the negative forces at work in him and their consequences if he fails now a second time to "do well." Sin is mentioned here for the first time in the Genesis narrative, and it is presented as a hypostatized force capable of being, like the serpent, the subject of its own action. Regardless of whether רֹבֵץ is translated as "demon" or as "lying in wait," sin is given the status of a quasi-independent force capable of acting against Cain. Furthermore, it acts on the basis of "desire." Cain, whose actions arise from his own desires, is about to be made subordinate to them. The anger within him is taking on the form of a desire which will have the capacity to consume the desirer as well as the desired. The incisive insight into the "logic" of desire is consistent with the concept (and terminology) of desire found in 3:16. The woman's desire for man would, in the end, consume her as she fell under his domination.

This logic of desire is also fundamental to sacrifice. The ultimate goal of desire is identification with the divine, but this cannot be attained by one with a materially differentiated human form. Sacrifice thus is two-edged, ambiguous. The dynamics are always potentially capable of turning away from the material substitute for the sacrificer to consume, literally, the body of the sacrificer itself. It is this self-destructive aspect of desire that reveals the impersonal nature of its mechanism.

Cain, who was born into a world driven by mimetic desire and limited by rival doubles, is thus given, in this brief utterance, a mirror image of the dynamics at work within him, and, by extension, within all persons who will live outside of paradise. The serpent from the previous story is no longer necessary because narcissistic desire has come to be the basis of human action, and its dynamics now constitute an impersonal force called "sin" within human beings, driving them simultaneously toward transgressive acts against others (their doubles) and toward their own self-destruction. Seduction has given way to compulsion. Now the limiting other is encountered, not in direct discourse, but as an "it" in the impersonal third-person form which operates as a non-verbal power within the subject.

The divine Voice here thus appears in the curious role of an author, analyzing and depicting the forces at work within his character. He even uses some of the same language that the narrator has used in verse 5b. But his narrative mode comes to resemble that of the representative rather than a symbolic narrator. He reveals to his character an opponent against which he must now fight. But the symbolic perspective is preserved in that he reveals this struggle to him in a direct address which appears to function as a micro-dialogue in the crucial moment before the decisive action has been taken, that is, in the moment of inner struggle and decision.

By revealing the dynamics of sin and desire to its victim in the moment before transgression occurs, the "narrator" shows that he has seen through these structures of necessity, and is not using them, as a representative narrator, to motivate his character and entice the reader's interest. It is this negative representation of the desire-driven consciousness in the micro-dialogue that manifests the fundamentally symbolic character of the divine "narrator's" perspective.

From this perspective the concluding statement can thus be made: "But you will have power over it." Our symbolic divine "narrator" has transcended the compulsive force of desire, as the later narrative will make clear. Here, also, he has not yet made sin a totally external force, though the translation of רֹבֵץ as "demon" comes very close to this. But sin is an impersonal subject of desire and, presumably, of action. While it is not yet clearly personified, it is functionally an opponent which can only be overcome through the exertion of some kind of power on Cain's part. And therein lies the illusory nature of this final reassurance that victory can be his.

Cain, lacking any prior intersubjective contact with the divine Word, is fundamentally a creature of desire. The divine Word being addressed to him at this crucial juncture is one which does not change this basic situation. As we have seen, God does not seek to elicit a real dialogue about the causes of his anger. The divine "author" essentially tells his character that he is capable, on his own, of doing what no representative character can do, that is, of overcoming this hypostatization of his own desire. The attempt is thus being made here to preserve a "theoretical" freedom for Cain which may be consistent with the perspective of the narrative as a whole, but which is not true for the character himself in this context. Such verbal "advice," while true in an abstract sense (that desire can be transcended), cannot penetrate the visually oriented, desire-driven, competitive, jealous, angry and inwardly alienated Cain. A character may escape the determination of desire only through the attainment of an intersubjectivity not offered in this divine utterance.

Appropriately, no response is recorded from Cain at all. This communication is not an authentic micro-dialogue which penetrates the internal narrative world of a character. No communication has actually occurred. Cain gives no sign that he has even heard these words. Cain, the founder of civilization, according to the later story, sees his problem not as an inner spiritual struggle with the power of sin, but as a contest on the material level with his rival double, and he proceeds without hesitation to attack this exterior problem. By destroying his brother, Cain will eliminate the Other, the one whose difference poses a permanent threat to his success in attaining mimetic identification with the divine. These are the only terms in which he understands his struggle.

The narrator shows no interest in the act of murder itself. It is possible that Cain's invitation to Abel to go into the field, given in the Samaritan Pentateuch and LXX but not in the MT, is intended to represent a literalistic response on his part to the previous warning which associates sin figuratively with the doorway. The omission of any direct speech between Cain and Abel in the Massoretic Text is preferred here: "And Cain spoke to his brother, and when they were in the field ..." (4:8). The manner in which Cain induced his rival to go into the field with him is best left to the imagination, and is consistent with the absence of verbal communication between them thus far.

The murder is recounted with excruciating brevity: "And Cain rose up against Abel his brother and he murdered him" (4:8). Even when the symbolic narrator portrays external opponents, he shows no interest in the details of their physical conflict, in contrast to the typical representative narrator. He only mentions the change in Cain's bearing as the compulsion to kill positioned his body for the act.

Immediately, the divine Voice returns, and the remainder of the narrative is given over to a micro-dialogue between God and Cain which structurally parallels the dialogue between God and Adam and Eve after their transgression. A quasi-objective divine appearance on earth is not necessary here because Cain's transgression was not an act of direct rebellion against God, but rather an attempt to *better* his relation *with* God. This will become evident as we examine the progress of the dialogue. The micro-dialogue is also necessary in order for the divine Voice to regain control of the future of the narrative which now has been assumed by the force of "sin" working in Cain.

The dialogue begins with a question by God that brings to light both the differences and similarities between his situation and that of Adam and Eve after their transgression.

> And Yahweh said to Cain, "Where is Abel, your brother? And he said, "I don't know. Am I to watch my brother?" 4:9

It is important to note first of all that Cain has not hidden from the divine presence. From the outset, he is not compelled to do so because he has openly sought identification with the divine through his sacrifice. The sacrificial order which he established makes this desire, which in his parents precipitated inner conflict and shame, a ritualized public action. The sacrificial act assumes that the differential, material factor which separates human beings from the spiritual realm of the divine can be eliminated, making possible a complete identification of the representation of the sacrificer with the divine. The narrator reveals the futility of this motive by making his fraternal rival an unexpected obstacle to the success of this enterprise. Just as the materiality of the sacrifice is an obstacle to unity with the divine, so now the materially based differentiality of the brother and his sacrifice appears to be a more fundamental obstacle. The different form of the rival Other intrudes into the narcissistic vision of unity between the sacrificer and the divine, raising the possibility that to be successful he must "do better," that is, that he must himself become different (like or better than his brother) in order to achieve his goal. But rather than turning against himself, a more direct, certain, and satisfying solution for the narcissistic mind is to eliminate his rival so that he may be the only contender for divine favor.[24] Cain thus does not seek to hide himself from God. Rather, through this murder he has sought to conceal his *brother* from God so that he may, as it were, have God "to himself," without a rival.

He gives no indication whatever of shame or guilt over his act. On the contrary, his is a consciousness ruled by desire in which there is no inner division which would lead to shame or guilt. Through the murder he has eliminated his rival, and is thus prepared for a more successful encounter with the divine than before.

Moving instantly away from the fact of the murder to the moral implications, the narrator now initiates another micro-dialogue with a question from the divine. Just as the question to Adam, "Where are you?" raised the entire issue of concealment which Adam could not answer without betraying his inner alienation, so here the question, "Where is your brother?" goes straight to the issue of inter-personal alienation.[25] Cain's response to this disturbing and unexpected question is thus not only a lie, "I do not know," but also an irritated attempt to deny the legitimacy of the question, "Am I to watch my brother?" Why should God be asking him about his brother? This question implies that Cain's relation to God does not involve his brother. He seeks an individual, exclusive relation to God, a mimetic identification with God, in which there is no room for an Other. Now that he has attained this exclusivity, and he and God are alone, why raise the question of his brother?

But, of course, it is precisely his indifference toward his brother which betrays his crime. His impertinent question reveals exactly what he intended for it to conceal. The word שׁמר means keeping, or watching (note the use of the visual sense) in the sense of protecting. It is used in relation to the task of a shepherd (Jer. 31:9), as well as in the narrator's description of the divine purpose for putting Adam in the garden (2:15). Thus, rather than letting his response remain a simple assertion of ignorance, "I don't know," he is compelled to add this (ironical) rhetorical question (since Abel was the shepherd who was supposed to be the "keeper") which, itself, suggests his guilt. If he sees no responsibility to protect his brother, then perhaps he is capable of the opposite. Cain's rejection of his role as "watcher" is another sign of this autonomous form of human subjectivity outside the garden.

The divine question which follows responds to this implied possibility: "What have you done?" (4:10). But rather than deriving the evidence altogether from the verbal formulation of Cain's response, as was done in the response to Adam's statement ("Who told you that you are naked?"), one who brings a charge of murder is required to provide more objective evidence than a change in consciousness. Since God will not come physically to search for the body of Abel, his blood is endowed with a "voice" which cries, and its cry comes to God.

The voice of the blood of your brother is crying to me from the earth. 4:10

This enables God to have a relation to these concealed physical events which is vocal/verbal rather than visual. He "hears" the evidence rather than seeing it.

The evidence of the crime consists in the fact that the cry of the blood comes "from the earth," for it is "spilled" blood.

But the word "crime" here may be much too legal in its connotation. Cain, in murdering his brother, has not violated any prohibition or law. In fact, as we have seen, the murder of Abel was consistent with the ideology of sacrifice. He was rather warned against "sin," but sin here did not have the meaning of a violation of law. Rather, it referred to the force of desire which would possess Cain and consume him. This force, empowered by the narcissistic impulse, seeks to create a world before God in which there are no threatening differences. When Cain is told that God "hears" the cry of his brother's blood, something new thus breaks into his consciousness (and that of the reader), that is, that difference cannot be eliminated by desire. The narrator's concern with the preservation of difference against the threat of narcissistic desire comes to a climax in the story of the Tower of Babel. The guilt of Cain remains ambiguous, however.

Cain acts in this situation in accord with the dynamics endemic to the network of relations in which he finds himself. The possibility of intersubjective transcendence of those dynamics is suggested but not concretely made available to him by the divine warning. Here, thus, we find an interface between the word-based mode of intersubjectivity which informs the narrator's fundamental perspective, and the visually based, desire-driven mode of subjectivity into which the characters have "fallen." Since the narrator has presented no real possibility thus far for his characters to regain this lost intersubjectivity, their guilt is left ambiguous. Cain's plea for mercy which follows his punishment thus does not fall on deaf ears.

Cain now finds himself the object of divine curses:

And now, cursed be you from the ground,
which opened its mouth
to take the blood of your brother from your hand. 4:11
For you will serve the ground
but it will not add its strength to you.
Trembling and fleeing you will exist
upon the earth. 4:12

Westermann points out that the curse itself is found only in 11a and 12b, the remaining lines constituting an expansion by the J writer.[26] He also notes significantly that this is the first direct curse of a human being, since only the serpent was directly cursed in the paradise story. Here again, however, the land is involved in the curse as it was with Adam. But whereas for Adam, the curse was placed upon the land so as to make farming difficult, here Cain is cursed "from" the land.

This is taken by Westermann and others to mean that for Cain the curse amounts to an exile or expulsion from the human community.[27] The imagery here, however, seems closely related to the imagery used elsewhere with reference to the expulsion of the Canaanites from the land. There the land "vomits out" the Canaanites because they have defiled it (Lev. 18:25). Blood, shed in violence also pollutes the land (Num. 35:33). Here, as well, the land has been endowed with a "mouth" which has received the blood of Abel. This imagery thus strongly suggests that the expulsion of Cain is accomplished by the revulsion of the land itself caused by blood pollution.[28] The alienation of human beings from the land which began with Adam is thus radicalized. Cain now is condemned to fail as a farmer, and consequently to flee, trembling across the earth as a fugitive. The separation of humans from the productive power of nature is complete.[29] The importance which Westermann places upon the absence of a direct curse of Adam seems overstated. The effect of the curse in both cases is similar and only differs in degree.

Cain now speaks to God, and his speech is an eloquent articulation of the painful consequences of the curse as he sees them. Cain first laments: "My punishment (עֲוֹנִי) is greater than I can bear" (4:13). He then explains precisely why:

Behold, you have driven me this day from the face of the earth, and from your face, I will be hidden. 4:14

As we have seen above, Adam still maintained a relation to God through the earth and his struggle with it. To be driven from a difficult but productive relation to the earth is thus seen by Cain the farmer as equivalent to being driven away from the face of God. Whereas Adam and Eve were still able to live in the presence of God because their state of shame and inner division retained an awareness of the otherness of the divine, Cain cannot. He is shameless and thus must be thrust out absolutely alone where his individuality cannot assume any pretenses of identification with the divine. When access to God leads to murder, then even that must be removed. It is significant that no further sacrifices are reported until the reinstitution of sacrifice after the universal flood, and then only because of an unusual attitude of resignation toward evil in the human heart explicitly articulated by the divine Voice. (Gen. 8:21)

Cain, who until now has never acknowledged any guilt or felt an impulse to hide from anyone, now declares: "from your face I will be hidden" (4:14). Because he has not hidden in shame over his deed, he now will "be hidden" from the face of God.

Cain then spells out what he foresees to be the ultimate consequence of this curse. The curse as such does not seem to be based on the *jus talionis*. He will be exiled but not killed. But Cain sees through the appearance of mercy in this curse. His vulnerability will lead inexorably to his death:

I will be trembling and fleeing upon the earth, and anyone who finds me will kill me. 4:14

Cain now appears as the absolute individual, stripped of all significance and the cultural protection that comes with symbolic identification. But as one for whom the different Other is an intolerable threat, he knows the fate which awaits him as a deracinated wanderer. The logic of this threat overcomes the narrational problem of the absence thus far of other characters to carry it out.

His plea proves surprisingly effective. Cain cannot be permitted to die. His death would have permanently fixed his identity as the archetypal sinner who must be deprived of any role in the unfolding story. It would have been in accord with a form of objective justice which assumes that absolute evil and good are embodied in dual, opposing, rival personages and groups, and which requires the execution of the evil by the good. A logical plot could have been developed upon these assumptions in which the good personage might have been played by Seth, the third son of Adam and Eve, and the evil personage by Cain. The defeat of Cain and his forces by Seth would have been morally instructive and dramatically satisfying. Such a plot would have conformed to the mythic, conflictive imagery of the mimetic sacrificial pattern, but it would have departed fundamentally from the assumptions of the symbolic narrative where the tension lies between open versus closed modes of subjectivity. Cain's situation represents the anguish of a personage within a symbolic narrative entrapped by the mechanism of desire and alienated from the verbal source of his identity. The divine warning holds before him a possibility of freedom to act which he has no means of attaining. Thus there is a tragic dimension to Cain's situation which requires the amelioration of the divine curse. Yahweh thus responds forcefully:

> "Because of this [לָכֵן], all who seek to kill Cain, will be avenged sevenfold." And Yahweh gave to [placed on] Cain a sign, so that all who find him would not strike him. 4:15

This immediate and dramatic response of the divine Voice to Cain's lament and complaint is striking in its role reversal. Yahweh, the cursor, becomes Yahweh, the protector. The words of the murderer have been heard with compassion, and authentic dialogue is signified by this instant agreement of Yahweh with Cain's argument, and his response.[30] The occurrence of this micro-dialogue at the end of the narrative rather than at its beginning has the effect of reasserting the primacy of the word with regard to the events which follow. The murder of Cain would have surrendered the future course of events to the circular conflict of good and evil forces. Not only would the moral ambiguity of Cain's actions have been erased, but the end of the story would have been determined by the exercise of brute power against a defenseless person. Thus, rather than seeing blood vengeance carried out against Cain, Yahweh uses blood vengeance to protect him. This strategy corresponds to the imposition of limits through the self-defeating opposition of rival doubles in the original curses. Those who seek to kill will be killed; they will become victims of their own hostility.

But there must be a mechanism by which this process will be set in motion, and this is a divine sign which is given to or placed upon Cain. The Hebrew is ambiguous (אוֹת). Westermann judiciously concludes that the antiquity of this sign even for the author was already so great that its vagueness is rooted in the author's own uncertainty as to its nature.[31] Whatever its outer form, its significance in this context is to establish a communicative relation between this character and the divine Voice. Cain will not be granted such micro-dialogues in the future. But a trace will remain of this word to him in the form of a material mark or sign apparently on his body.

And there is its chief irony. The narrative began with Cain seeking spiritual identification with the divine through the sacrifice of material representations of his person. Through the sacrifice of the material produce of the land, he could seek spiritual unity with the face of God materially manifested in the land. Now he is to be deprived of all hope of attaining such identification with the land and with the divine. The land is expelling him from its face, and as he wanders, fleeing forever homeless across the earth, his only identity will be provided by a material, differentiating sign attached somehow to his materially individuated body. Through it he will be reminded of this dialogue in the past with the divine judge which fixed his sentence as a curse, and the mercy by which he was granted this protecting mark.

The physicality of this sign, which is now the organizing center of his identity, permanently bars him from any future attempts to attain identity with the divine. His identity is forever based upon a sign which imposes upon him its own temporal and material form. The mark thus functions as a type of inverted promise, a material sign which marks Cain in an autonomous mode of existence, closing his development as a character but guaranteeing his life against attack at the price of eternal liminality, and alienation.

The repudiation of the underlying dynamics of sacrifice at the conclusion of this story explains why sacrifice is introduced at the outset as a totally human initiative. When it is reintroduced by Noah after the flood (again due to human initiative), it is accepted by God with some genuine reluctance conveyed by an extraordinary explanation by the divine Voice. A subtle but penetrating critique of sacrifice is thus conveyed by this story.

As we have seen, sacrifice, according to Ortigues, springs spontaneously from the mind ruled by the imagination. In such a mind desire orients itself toward the specular image which is hallucinated into a condition of perfect fullness of being. The self which experiences itself only as a differentiated emptiness seeks union with the image, but attainment quickly leads to satiation and insensate materiality. Sacrifice of the specular image is thus required to restore its spiritual reality. Violence and conflict between opposites are thus endemic to the specular imagination. Since these are exactly the dynamics we have witnessed operating in the Cain and Abel story, and which continue to operate in the stories leading up to the universal flood (6:1–5), how can sacrifice again be accepted by the narrator? How can sacrifice even be acceptable again to God?

This seems to have been a genuine problem for the narrator since he avoids having any sacrifices performed between the cursing of Cain and the universal flood, though he does report that at the time of Seth and Enosh, "Men began to call upon the name of Yahweh" (4:26). But after surviving the flood, Noah spontaneously offers a sacrifice of thanksgiving immediately after departing from the ark. The context of the narrative has changed since the ultimate divine punishment has now been executed. Noah, a righteous man, offers a sacrifice in thanksgiving for seeing again the face of the earth.

A dilemma is thus presented to the divine regarding the reinstitution of sacrifice after the flood. The narrator provides us with an unusually lengthy divine speech addressed to no one in particular except the reader. He reports what Yahweh "said in his heart." Here, then, we find pure hermeneutical narration designed to deal with a difficult structural problem.

The narrator reports first (in third person) that Yahweh finds the odor pleasing. He then promises in direct speech that he will never again curse the ground because of man. Why? Because "the imagination of man's heart is evil from his youth" (9:21). The condition which had led to the great flood (6:5) is now *accepted* as an inevitability about which nothing else can be done. Thus the reinstitution of sacrifice coincides with the reconciliation of God to man's evil imagination.

He promises as well never again to destroy life as he has done in the flood, but to maintain the regularity of the seasons of growth. It is thus clear that sacrifice is related to a form of identification with the productivity of the earth which the human imagination inevitably corrupts. Only by the acceptance of the "evil" nature of the human imagination with its aspiration to identity with God can the sacrificial order be reinstituted. But this compromise at the outset of the post-flood phase of the narrative reveals a moral ambiguity which will characterize practically every aspect of the life which follows.

The narrator concludes this story with a simple account of the consequences of the punishment:

> And Cain went forth from before the face of Yahweh, and he stayed in the land of Nod, east of Eden. 4:16

Thus, in summarizing the effects of the curse, the narrator emphasizes the absolute alienation of Cain from the presence of God, and uses what appears to be a metaphor to describe his new existence. The word *nod* is not the name of a place; rather it is a noun taken from the same verb stem *nud*, used in the curse, meaning wandering or flight. This concluding statement thus refers to the uprooting of Cain from any permanent relation to the earth (and its spiritual corollary, the face of God) and his entrance into the cursed, metaphorical "land of wandering," a permanently liminal state of existence. The location, east of Eden, is the same direction in which Adam and Eve were expelled from paradise (3:24). It is at the east gate of paradise that the angel is placed to block any attempt to return. To be east of Eden is thus to be in the direction from which there can be no return to paradise and the presence of God.

10

The central micro-dialogue
Genesis 12:1 – 3

And Yahweh said to Abram:
Go from your land, and from your kindred,
and from the house of your father
to the land which I will cause you to see.
And I will make you into a great nation,
and I will bless you,
and I will make great your name to be a blessing.
and I will bless whoever blesses you,
and whoever reviles you, I will curse;
and all families of the earth will be blessed through you. 12:1–3

In juxtaposition to the morbid cycles of human existence portrayed in the first eleven chapters of Genesis, the narrative now initiates a new sequence which begins with a new type of word event: the giving of a promise. This opens up the possibility of a new mode of subjectivity. The narrator cannot explicitly denote it, but it is unmistakable that the deepest meaning of this narrative is that which is *connoted* by the juxtaposition of these contrasting modes of existence. To understand this new mode initiated in Genesis 12:1–3, it will be necessary to examine the structure of the promise.

As we have seen, language comes to exist in consciousness only when the primal continuity of consciousness with the world is disrupted by the blockage of desire. Narratives which are generated by the logic of desire thus permit in one way or another the reemergence of transgressive desire into language, through the agency of the desiring character, and trace the play of conflict which that entails. Transgressive desire must be defeated so that the structure of the symbolic order can be maintained. Violence is thus a recurrent feature of these narratives.

The promise has the unusual capacity of partially readmitting desire into the signifying process. As Ortigues has shown, the sign itself is not only a signifier of the absent object of reference, but it is also a promise of the presence of that object. This promissory dimension of the sign rests on the "responsible presence" of the speaker in language utterance, that is, the subordination of the whimsy of desire to the "becoming true" of language in the signifying process. The desire of the speaker is thus brought into the signifying process and disciplined by it. When a formal promise is made into a central feature of a narrative, desire gains admission into the narrative structure in a non-transgressive way, thereby reshaping the subjectivity of the characters.

When the narrator initiates this sequence with a divine promise to Abram, he thus makes possible the portrayal of a new mode of subjective existence for the promisee (also for the promisor). Whereas the prohibition divided the subject in such a way that transgression was the only mode in which he could exist as a desiring subject (and divided the promises so that the intention was concealed behind the expression), the divine promise opens the possibility of entrance into a positive mode of subjectivity and the consequent healing of the division in the center of the subject's consciousness. The divine promise, which is given beyond the prohibition, does not negate the prohibition but opens up the possibility for the differentiated self to exist consciously as a place of desire, and to act subjectively, in some way *other* than as a transgressor. The promise to Abram is thus coupled with a positive mandate, "Go." Correspondingly, the promisor, in disclosing the future, lowers the barrier erected by the prohibition which concealed his intentions. For a valid promise there can be no reservations or hidden conditions "in the back of the mind." The promise is a verbalization of intention.

The effect of the promise upon the subjectivity of the receiver, Abram, would be to make possible his appearance in language as a desiring subject, his desire now, however, oriented toward the object values which are constitutive of society (land, nationhood – which implies children – fame, and the power to bless others).

But the fact that these desires appear in the form of a promise from another rather than as a direct expression of the self ultimately transforms the character of the desiring subject. First of all, these object values are given to Abram in advance through the signifying word. When someone promises you an object, you become, psychologically the possessor of that object upon receipt of the promise, even though you do not materially have it.[1] Your relation to the object thus is no longer one of pure desire. The flame of desire related to the object is partially quenched by the possession of the word which signifies it. This has the effect of bringing about a new and positive relationship between the desiring subject and a signifier. Initially the desiring subject stood in a relation of nonidentity with the signifier. Now, in receiving the promise, the subject gains a positive relationship of identity with it. The new relationship is expressed eventually in the giving of a new name. By accepting the promise, he *becomes* the one who will be the father of a nation, etc. This eventually results in the substitution of a new name, Abraham (father of a multitude), for the original name, Abram (exalted father). The new name directly stems from the content of the promise and is given in Genesis 17:5 just before the beginning of the fulfillment in the birth of a son.

But this identification with the signifier has an internal ambiguity: it is a composite of desire and faith. The content of the promise represents objects which Abraham doubtless desires. But the possession of these objects is *mediated* by faith in the word of promise. He will gain these objects of desire only through faith in the Word. This means that he can do nothing involving the direct use of his own power to produce these desired goods for himself. They will be given by an Other. Such desire-driven action would signify a reversion to the previous mode of subjective existence. This Word of promise is to be trusted, and it is the role now of the promisee to enter into a new mode of existence in which faith has displaced desire as the motivating factor in the character's existence. Thus the promise, as it admits desire now into language, transmutes desire in a process of "verbal alchemy" into faith, and founds the promisee in a new mode of trusting intersubjectivity which displaces fearful paranoia with confidence in the future and openness to the new. Just as the character of Adam and Eve and the subsequent structure of the narrative were direct products of the divine prohibition, so Abram's character and the events to follow will be structured by the occurrence of the divine promise.

Literarily, the divine promise to Abram constitutes an event of defamiliarization. This is not the same as the poetic defamiliarization of which Shklovsky speaks in that it is not embodied directly in the language of the text and made immediately accessible to the reader. It operates, rather, at the implicit level of the dynamics of the self revealed in the DC–DN relation, and is constituted by the experience of the self as pure form.

The heart of defamiliarization is the experience of form. Semiologically, as we have seen, this represents the experience of language as a mediator of intersubjectivity. Where such a relation to language is not attainable, defamiliarization can take the form of conflict between a full sign/subject completely assimilated into its object of reference, and the empty sign/subject which manifests its spirituality through its desire for fullness of being.

But as we have seen above, the self also can become the object of an experience of defamiliarization. In the examples of the poem, "Speleology," by Robert Penn Warren, and Psalm 8, we saw two ways in which language may mediate an experience of the self. In Psalm 8, however, the poet presupposed as the basis for his experience a relation to another Subject which was mediated by a sign in a narrative context. It is this sign which now must be analyzed. Whereas in the poem, the Hebrew Psalmist was meditating over the subjective response to this sign-based relationship, and thus capturing in his words the emotion felt in that moment of reflection, the sign that constitutes the basis of subjective experience does not itself embody the immediacy of such an emotion. Its power of defamiliarization stems from the new possibilities of characterological development which are opened and which transform the face of the narrative which follows. It is in the actions and words of the personages which reverberate with the power of a new open form of subjective existence, that the previous forms of existence are revealed as automatized. We must now turn to examine precisely how the self comes to be experienced as a form as a consequence of the micro-dialogue in 12:1–3.

As we have seen in examining Genesis 2–3, the form of the self which emerged in the transgression of the prohibition was one in which the characters became separated from the intersubjective relation which gave rise to them as narrative personages, and pursued subjective autonomy. This autonomy was to be sustained by the acquisition of infinite knowledge which could be acquired from observation and empirical experience. The self thus was reoriented from an identity grounded in intersubjectivity toward one based on objective attributes which would be gained through experience. The subjective emptiness is tolerable as the center of existence when the self understands itself symbolically as a sign through which the Other is mediated. But this emptiness becomes intolerable when the intersubjective relation is broken. The subject is then driven into a state of paranoia toward the Other and compulsive desire for the object, experience, or material state which will fill this emptiness. This compulsive desire ultimately consumes the subject, since fulfillment brings the triumph of the sensate over the symbolic, and thus the death of the self. The subject becomes the objective attributes which s/he desired, and in so doing enters a state of objectivity which constitutes the end of the symbolic self.

When the divine promise displaces the divine prohibition as the basis of the intersubjectivity of the protagonist, and the content of that promise is made future, the protagonist is confronted with the possibility of the experience of his self as a pure signifier (in a way that was not possible with the prohibition). The central function of the sign, as Ortigues has described it, is to make possible the symbolic mediation of the self to itself in and through the recognition by the other. Medina describes this mediation of the self in literature, as the communication of life courses, the act of which enables the speaker to achieve self-transcendence as s/he is forced in the act of communication to view her/himself from the standpoint of another. It is the factor of contingency that is endemic to all such communication that relativizes the subject's self-conception, and elevates the non-formal mode of reflection characteristic of biographical reason into a position of importance superior to formal reflection, whether objective or subjective.

The promise of a future given in a micro-dialogue to a narrative personage by a Voice, which is neither that of the author nor of another personage, synthesizes the most powerful features of Ortigues' view of the sign, and Medina's understanding of non-formal reflection and communicative fusion within the textual format of the micro-dialogue or inner Word. The presentation of a character with the promise of a future course for his entire life (and beyond) has the effect of enabling the character to transcend his life even more completely than communicating it to another. Rather than being forced to contemplate his past life through the eyes of another as he communicates it, he is being offered his life's future in and through another's communication to him. It is as if the act of self-transcendence in which the speaker comes to recognize his life course in the form of reminiscence and promise (that is, as having the character of a sign, of language, rather than the compulsive pursuit of objects of desire) has now become the locus or source of the Voice of another who, totally discounting the past, offers to the subject (in the form of a promise) her/his entire future. The transcendent moment in consciousness has, within the context of the symbolic narrative, become the place for the appearance of the Third Subject of Consciousness, which then offers the personage a new self upon the conditions inherent in the intersubjective relation as determined by the form of the speech act in which the communication occurred. The contingency which Medina describes as stemming from the complex presentation of another life course in my own consciousness here stems from the manner of the subject's response to the presentation of his own life course, *in advance*, within his own consciousness. Since this communication has been given the form of a promise, the contingency becomes one of faith on the part of the subject, as well as faithfulness on the part of the promisor.

It is this presentation of his future life course as a whole to Abram that enables him to experience his life as a signifying form. The automatism of desire, which drives personages toward sensate objectification and the loss of self-transcendence, has here been displaced by the presentation of the self as a whole to his consciousness, articulated from the beginning in language and subject to his own reflection and decision. Thus the divine promise achieves the defamiliarization of the self. This establishes self-presence in relation to symbolic language at a level deeper than that of the symbolism of the rule which founds identity upon the form of social roles. Here the self is given a foundation that is beyond the social order, and thus not bound by the automatism of social function.

This open form of identity corresponds closely to Bakhtin's conception of the novelistic hero whose lack of coincidence with a social role is the foundation of his/her freedom to change: "When we think away his roles, there is something left; that remainder, that non-coincidence of self and social categories, that capacity to change into different clothes, is freedom."[2] In perfect correspondence to the new position of Abraham, Caryl Emerson also notes: "Novelists rejoice in subjects that are homeless, that is, free to develop."[3]

Here, however, the verbal process by which this development is to occur has been made the central feature of the narrative discourse. Due to the absence of a descriptive representation of the divine subject at the center of the process, it remains a continuous, open dialogue.[4]

11

"Why did you say, 'She is my sister'?" Genesis 12:10–20

This story has long been important for those who have analyzed the book of Genesis, due in part to the fact that it recurs in quite similar form three times (20; 26:1–11), and in part to the difficulty of interpreting the lie which Abram has his wife tell in order to save his life. Source analysts have found little reason to question the unity of this story as it occurs in chapter 12, and have attributed it to J or a J redactor. Claus Westermann now sees the work of the final redactor as decisive in the shaping of the Abraham cycle, and thus concludes that: "It is necessary to begin with the state of the text as a whole as it has been transmitted to us."[1] This diminishes the significance of source criticism for the type of analysis being made here. The issue of its later recurrence will not be pursued here, since this question has relevance primarily within a traditio-historical investigation.[2] John van Seters has convincingly argued for the structural unity of this story and the total dependency of its parallels upon it.[3] The focus of this chapter will be the problems of interpretation which have been the occasion for widespread disagreement.

Gunkel argues that such a "necessary lie" (*Notlüge*) told by Abram to save his life was not taken as seriously in antiquity as today, and cites a similar lie told by the prophet Jeremiah to save his life (Jer. 38:24ff.).[4] He thus can conclude that it is evidence of Abram's wit that he can, with the cooperation of Sarai and the timely help of Yahweh, save his own life, acquire wealth from the Egyptians, and end up with his wife returned to his side. He thus concludes that "the story glorifies the intelligence of the patriarch, the beauty and the self-sacrifice of the mother, and especially the faithful help of Yahweh."[5]

Westermann sharply disagrees. He sees the primary emphasis of the story in the two passages of direct discourse, the conspiracy between Abram and Sarai in verses 11–13 and the accusation by the king in verses 18, 19.[6] The third-person discourse passage is extraordinarily short, by comparison, and leaves out much essential information such as how the Pharaoh discovered that the plagues were due to the presence of Sarai in his harem (a detail added to the version in chapter 20). Although he acknowledges that when a powerless individual was faced with the absolute power of an ancient monarch, "the ruse remains as his only weapon,"[7] he nevertheless sees this action by Abram as a loss of faith: "He does not think about the intervention of God: he does not show himself as one who believes."[8]

The climactic defense by the king of his innocence, which Westermann sees as having "considerable weight" for the understanding of the whole story, is then seen as completely justified, and his accusation of Abram, accurate: "The reproach of the Pharaoh is justified, and Abram is shamed through this reproach."[9] He sees this as the high point of the narrative, and finds in Abram's silence tacit admission of his guilt. He had thought only of saving his own life, and did not remember the humanity of the Pharaoh which comes eloquently to expression in his passionate reproach. He thus sees the climax of the narrative structure to be this inner acknowledgement by Abram of his own faithless selfishness, signified by his silence before the king's accusation.[10]

To choose the other path would presumably have meant death from Abram's viewpoint, but, according to Westermann, the narrative is suggesting that there were other possibilities open to Yahweh which Abram did not see. To remain faithful would have meant trusting god to rescue him from this desperate situation: "The overcoming of the fear of death in trust that God knows another open way was always the extraordinary and it will always be."[11]

This view of the culpability of Abram and the innocence of the Pharaoh raises another perhaps more serious problem regarding the action of Yahweh, however. Why does God intervene so eagerly and decisively on behalf of one who has betrayed him at the first difficulty encountered in the life of faith? Here Westermann must refer to the protective care of Yahweh which is expressed to Abram in spite of his transgression. The justice of Yahweh is then preserved only by the shamming of Abram which Yahweh apparently carries out through the agency of the Egyptian king.[12] He acknowledges, however, that this form of judgement against a patriarch for his sin is unique in the patriarchal stories. It might also be added that it is odd that the first major episode in Abram's life after entrusting himself to the promise of Yahweh should result in such a sin. The pattern here would appear to be unchanged from the sin and punishment pattern of Genesis 2–11 except for the mildness of the punishment, and the sudden appearance of an amazing new tolerance for sin on the part of Yahweh – a change which Westermann does not explain.

The story of the endangering of the patriarchal wife stands at a crucial point in the unfolding plot structure of Genesis. The stories in Genesis 2–11 have been driven by the rebellious egoistic narcissism of humans who define their identity in their rejection of divine restraints. The narratives have attempted to deal with this characterological form without forcing human beings into a position of absolute evil, but rather by presenting them in an ambiguous situation, driven by inner conflict while still existing by virtue of some vestigal divine grace (Cain's mark, the rainbow, the reinstitution of sacrifice). Beginning with Genesis 12, however, the alienation and hostility in the divine–human relation is overcome, and self-destructive, limitless, egoistic desires of an archetypal human being are taken up into the divine promises where they are transmuted into faith. The question now is how this pivotal change will affect the way in which the characters speak and act. What is the subjective form of the faith-personage? Will this new man of faith manifest a different stance toward life's crises and temptations, or will he be as prone to transgression and moral weakness as his predecessors? It is this important matter which unfolds before us in this brief but extraordinary story.

Typological analysis

It should be noted that these questions arise out of an assumption not made by literary-historical criticism, namely, that one can presuppose a high degree of internal compositional continuity in this narrative between separate narrative units, rather than viewing each narrative as being relatively self-contained, its present form having been fixed primarily by oral tradition. This assumption does not oppose an important role for oral tradition, but allows significant literary freedom to the narrator in the final shaping of the material and its syntagmatic placement. A degree of freedom for each author at the stylistic level has always been assumed in the premises of the documentary hypothesis, but this approach deepens the stylistic analysis and draws out the implications which the style has for plot and character formation across the caesuras between the narratives.

The modal stance of the symbolic narrator is one of active involvement with his characters across the boundary which normally encloses the narrative world. It is the voice of Yahweh which transgresses this boundary in Genesis 12:1–3 and reorients the perspective of the protagonist away from desire and the competitive conflict between characters, or the internal conflicts within the characters which that entails, toward the dynamics of inter-subjectivity which make the narrative tension arise from the opposition of closed and open semantic processes.

Abram has been opened to a speech event which founds his identity and discloses his future as contingent upon a promise. The question now is how will such a protagonist deal with the crises of life which have the potential to destroy him; how will he deal with opponents? Can we expect Yahweh to protect him completely from adversity? If so, there will be no true opponents and thus no story. Will faith in Yahweh's promise require of Abram a total passivity in which he will make no attempt to save himself from his opponents, or to defeat them? Is "crucifixion" inevitable for the person of faith when faced with hostility, as Westermann seems to suggest? Or are there penultimate possibilities where the person of faith may develop strategies which, though not morally pure, are less evil than those followed by her/his opponents; strategies which may prevent the reduction of conflict to the closure of violence, and the unambiguous triumph of one party over another?

The alienated subjectivity of the personages in Genesis 2–11 drove them to transgress limits which defined them as different: Adam and Eve rejected difference from God; Cain rejected difference from Abel; the builders of Babel could not accept the distinction between heaven and earth. This transgressive impulse thrust them into repeated conflict with the Other, the Different, and the logic of this conflict led to the destruction of one party by the other (Cain's murder of Abel, the destruction of the earth by God in the universal flood). The mediation of desire afforded by the promise and faith breaks down this alienated subjectivity, and opens the protagonist to the intersubjective basis of his own existence. A new logic is thus now to be expected. Abram's call to come out from his land and kindred reverses the logic of the banishment of Cain, and affirms cultural separation and difference as a blessing. Abram's power is to stem not from his capacity to destroy or subordinate those different from himself, nor to expand himself to universal dimension so as to eliminate even difference from the divine. The divine now comes to him as a differentiating power, and it is through faithfulness to this unique, differentiating vision that he is to become great.

The logic of this new character structure, in general, leads away from plots which pose sharply defined good and evil personages locked in violent conflict toward the ambiguation of characters and the symbolic mediation of conflict. More specifically, the form of the conflict is changed from one of objective, physical confrontation (the "full" personage versus the "empty"), to a more inward symbolic conflict between closed and open structures within which the personages may move and envision their own identities. In the modern novel this conflict may take place in the thought processes of the characters, as we have seen in the novels of Dostoyevsky. The division between the author and character begins to break down, and tensions arise between the novelistic personage and the authorial framework which would impose closure upon her/him. The drama shifts from external conflict, to the internal verbal struggle which comes to expression in free indirect discourse. In the Biblical narrative this is not yet possible since the internal verbal process takes only the form of divine speech events, though the account of these events becomes increasingly free and open (climaxing in the "confessions" of Jeremiah). This internal process thus comes to expression not in third-person speech, but in DD between God and the character.

The author, then, is limited in the narrative framework to providing the minimal third-person descriptions of the contexts within which these discourses occur, and recounting the external episodes in the lives of the protagonists. This is to say that, in terms of the categories being used here, the author can make only the most limited and rudimentary use of third-person free indirect discourse characteristic of the symbolic narrative in rendering these episodes which deal with human affairs where there is no intervention by the divine Voice. If he is to maintain the symbolic character of the narrative, he must find ways to combine the interests of the symbolic narrative with the strategies of the expressive and representative types.

With respect to the representative type, however, the author remains under severe constraints since he may not create a fully developed system of descriptive references in the narrative framework which would semantically fix the identity and ideology of the personage whose origin and future are produced by internal discourse with the divine.

More suitable to his own perspective is the expressive narrative in which direct discourse conveys the primary semantic content. Even here, however, he cannot remain totally passive in relation to his characters and permit the governing polarities of the narrative to remain appearance versus reality, with the concomitant determination of the plot attributed to blind unconscious forces. Within these constraints it is inevitable, however, that a subtle ideological perspective emerge in the narrative framework of some of the narratives. When it does it is designed to be compatible with the larger symbolic perspective of the whole. What one finds is the narrator using expressive and representative stylistic techniques while subordinating them to the perspective of the symbolic narrative. Emerging from this is thus what might be called symbolic/expressive and symbolic/representative narratives, or a combination of all three types. It is in the friction between the symbolic perspective and perspectives of expressive and representative narratives that the unique subtleties of the Biblical narrative style come to expression.

By way of introduction to this narrative, the narrator tells us nothing about the traits of the characters around whom the plot will center: Abram, Sarai, and the Egyptian Pharaoh. He rather describes their geographical location and a natural state of affairs which impinges upon the protagonist and his response to it.

> And Abram pulled up to go and to journey toward the Negeb. And there was a famine in the land, and Abram went down into Egypt to sojourn there since the famine was heavy in the land.
> 12:9, 10

Here the narrator poses a nomadic Abram located between the inimical forces of nature and the plenty of the settled culture of Egypt. This statement contains the terms within which the subsequent narrative will unfold – the vulnerability of the nomad to the whims of nature on the one hand, and, on the other, his desperate need for the foodstuffs of the settled culture with the implied powerlessness which goes with such dependency. This semantic framework stops short of characterizing either side of this equation, however, or even Abram's decision to move. The former thus does not, in any sense, pose Abram as a protagonist versus the Egyptians as antagonists. The absence of any divine guidance concerning the move to Egypt is particularly noteworthy since until this point, Abram had been moving under such guidance of the divine (Jacob later does not go into Egypt without seeking divine approval [46:3]). The narrator presents his character in a world where natural crises arise with no relation to the divine, and where the person of faith makes independent decisions in response to them. Nature is posed as a system of necessity within which the character must exist as best he can. But nature constitutes less a closed system of fate which exercises a determining influence upon the character than a source of blind circumstance to which he freely responds. The narrator still permits a role for desire on the part of the protagonist, but now its role is circumscribed to the need for self-preservation and limited victories over the forces and opponents who pose a threat to life.

At this juncture it is possible to begin to observe the modal stance of the narrator. The author has turned away from the stance of the realistic narrator who indirectly manipulates the behavior of the characters through third-person descriptions, explanations and qualifications. The crisis of the famine only sets the stage for the appearance of the central conflict of the plot which is disclosed altogether in the first utterance of Abram in direct discourse. This discourse is not that of the expressive narrative, however, which conceals unconscious forces at work that undermine and overthrow the conscious, verbalized intentions of the characters. On the contrary, this discourse discloses hidden forces at work beneath the surface of Egyptian society, and in so doing reveals the active perspective of the symbolic narrator.

The significant action of this plot does not begin with a crime perpetrated upon Abram by an opponent, but with Abram's anticipation of such an action. Though Abram's thought is not rendered directly by the narrator, this initial utterance presupposes an inner dialogue that has occurred in which he has imagined what the Egyptians will say about himself and Sarai upon their arrival in an Egyptian community, and is preparing to cope with it by means of a conspiracy with Sarai.

This is a new mode of behavior for a Biblical personage, and one which is consistent with the change which has occurred in Genesis 12:1–3, that is, he now lives out of his anticipation of the future. In the same way that the voice of Yahweh has created positive anticipations, he now "hears" the threatening voices of the Egyptians, and acts to forestall the evil which they suggest awaits them. His action arises out of his inner voices with all the peril of illusion and paranoic fears which that entails. It is this inner orientation to other "voice consciousnesses" (Bakhtin) that first reveals the new intersubjective, dialogical orientation of Abram's character. This indicates that the forthcoming contest will be not merely the struggle of a powerless nomad to survive the threat of the Egyptian king, but a contest between the new promise-formed, future-oriented character, and a representative of the type of existing power structure from which he was previously called to separate himself. Abram's success in this contest will foreshadow similar successes for those who follow in this path of life.

How, then, does this anticipatory dialogue relate to the other forms of the active involvement of the symbolic narrator? The basic sign of the symbolic narrator is the surrender of his transcendent omniscient, manipulative perspective to that of the character so as to present the unfolding of the plot from the point of view of the verbal events which are internal to the narrative and specifically to the character's consciousness. This may take the form of free indirect discourse, as in the modern novel, or the visionary dialogue in the Bible as in Genesis 12:1–3 just analyzed. Here, however, another possibility emerges. The narrator allows the protagonist to create his own plot, to become the narrator of his own story. As Yahweh may be considered a surrogate narrator by creating the plot through the promise to Abram, so here Abram becomes the surrogate narrator creating a fiction as a strategy for survival in Egypt. Consequently, there is no "speaking role" for Yahweh in this story. Yahweh is reduced to a secondary role which serves the interest of Abram's plot. The tension of the symbolic narrative between the openness of the protagonist to the creative verbal processes which made him and the closure of the internal narrative world is here replicated in the relation of Abram and Sarai's future-oriented perspective to that of the Egyptians. The end toward which it moves – the experience of defamiliarization – is the moment of recognition by the antagonist that he has been deceived, a moment filled with ambiguity and multiple possibilities for resolution. A strategy not too unlike that of this plot is found in Nathan's fictional discourse to David about the Bathsheba affair which reveals perhaps the ultimate potentiality of this plot structure in David's discovery of the contradictions within himself (II Sam. 12:1–14). The internal resemblance of these narrative strategies will become apparent as we uncover the internal dynamics of Abram's "fiction."

What is it then that Abram anticipates? What is his understanding of the Egyptians? Abram speaks to Sarai and constructs for her an imaginary scenario of what the Egyptians will say and do about them when they arrive.

> And when he came near to Egypt he said to Sarai his wife, "Now look, I know that you are a beautiful woman in appearance." 12:11

What Abram is beginning to reveal to Sarai is the operation of sexual desire in a society where an immigrant has no power. He does this by describing her, from his own viewpoint, as an object of beauty, and thus implicitly as an object of desire. Abram here thus makes Sarai the first character to be given attributes in this narrative, and takes the first step toward the creation of a realistic "plot" which will feature Sarai as the central figure. His description of her in these terms implies that she will be similarly perceived and sexually desired by the Egyptian men. Then he cites what he imagines they would say next:

> And it will be that the Egyptians will see you, and they will say, "This is his wife," And they will kill me, and will let you live. 12:12

This citation indicates that Abram will be seen as the obstacle blocking the fulfillment of their desire.

Abram's analysis assumes the existence of a law or practice which strictly forbids adultery, and the belief that severe consequences will follow upon one who breaks such a law. Since the royal practice of maintaining harems makes every beautiful woman subject to the king's summons, the king becomes the most likely male to lay claim upon great beauty when it appears, as is implied by Abram's words. But for the king to take a married woman would be impossible to keep secret, and would make every married male feel threatened. Far better to kill the husband first when it can be done quietly, and thus open the way for the seizure of his widow legally. Such is the logic underlying Abrams' conclusions: "and they will kill me, but they will let you live."[13]

Abram's scenario thus assumes a code which makes the open seizure of a married woman by a king for his harem taboo under penalty of severe (divine) punishment. This assumption is shared equally by the king. His angry comments later (though doubtless hypercritical) intend to convey the impression that this is something he would never do knowingly, that is, publicly.

It is here in the contradiction between knowing (public) and unknowing (covert) deeds of the Pharaoh that the fundamental polarities of this narrative are revealed which indicate its kinship with the expressive narrative. Narratives of this type are characterized by contradiction between conscious intentions and compulsive acts, between social appearances and hidden reality. It is due to this contradiction that the discourse of the characters becomes eliptical, emotional, metonymic as it plays over and around the buried truths which cannot be revealed without bringing about the collapse of the social order. Abram's lie about his wife has the effect of bringing perilously close to the surface a threatening, hidden truth about the sexual habits of the king. When he angrily asks, "Why did you say, 'She is my sister'?" he poses a question which, if answered, would shatter the facade of morality which conceals the sordid sexual practices which support his harem. A man with a beautiful wife must lie to save himself from falling victim to the murderous lust of the king. It is this contradiction between the spoken and unspoken which accounts for the tension in the dramatic accusatory question, "What have you done to me?", and the protestation of innocence, "You did not tell me that she was your wife" (12:18).

But unlike the expressive narrative where the polarities of appearance versus reality constitute a synchronic sub-structure which governs every character, one character in this narrative is not caught up in the world of appearances, but sees the whole. The scenario which Abram constructs for Sarai arises from his awareness of a fundamental cleavage between appearance and reality in Egyptian life. He instantly sees through the outer surface to the underlying dynamics of sexual desire which motivates it.

Since he, unlike his opponent, is not a blind victim of desire, he has an advantage in this conflict. When he speaks of Sarai's beauty, he speaks in the first person, "I know," revealing that he understands these desires in his opponents, because he is conscious of them in himself. His opponent is vulnerable since he is caught in a contradiction between his public appearance and his private deeds, and this contradiction can be used by Abram to gain ascendency in spite of his powerlessness. His understanding of the logic of desire and his capacity to anticipate the future on the basis of this knowledge, enable him to reverse his powerless, subordinate position *vis-à-vis* the Pharaoh.

He then proposes a solution to their dilemma:

> Please say you are my sister so that it will go well for me on your account, and my soul will live for your sake.[14] 12:13

Abram's solution is to create a fiction which is designed to cause the Pharaoh to become entrapped by his own desire. It is expressly motivated, of course, by Abram's desire to preserve his own life. The character of the new protagonist has not been altogether purged of desire, but his desire now operates within the limits imposed by the differentiating vision of the promise. This strategy is designed to reverse his situation of powerlessness and make not only the limited goal of self-preservation possible, but also a limited material victory over his opponent.

His strategy is implicit in the assumptions of Abram's original perception of the situation. The pivotal code operative in both his original scenario as well as the king's later protestation of innocence is that the abduction of a married woman was taboo. If Abram knew that the king would kill him before violating the taboo against the seizure of a married woman openly, he knew as well that as soon as Sarai entered the harem of the king while he was still alive, the king would be subject to the consequences of violating this taboo, and Abram would be the victor. When the consequences of the violation began to appear, Sarai would be returned, and both would survive. And in the interim, after they abduct her, Abram anticipates that they will treat him well on Sarai's account. And it happens exactly as he had anticipated.

And when Abram came into Egypt, the Egyptians saw the woman for she was exceptionally beautiful. When the princes of Pharaoh saw her, they commended her to Pharaoh, and the woman was taken into the house of Pharaoh. He did well by Abram for her sake, and he had sheep, oxen, he-asses, menservants, maidservants, she-asses, and camels. 12:14–16

Here the third-person description provided by the narrator simply recounts the unfolding of the plot anticipated by Abram in his initial discourse. The narrator's perspective is following that of the protagonist.

In this desperate encounter between the Pharaoh and Abram we thus have a character who exhibits all of the characteristics of the narcissistic, desire-driven, inwardly divided personality juxtaposed with the new intersubjective character type who is landless and powerless, but has been freed from the compulsions of unlimited desire, to live out of his knowing anticipation of the future and his understanding of the fallibilities of his opponents.

The dynamics of the representative narrative are present in the contest features evident here since both men are competing for the same woman, and a portion of the material goods of Egypt. But the way in which the conflict is posed lifts the plot out of the logical oppositions of the representative narrative. Abram wins this contest not by force, but because he makes use of the internal contradictions in the consciousness of the Pharaoh between public appearance and private reality, between conscious morality and unconscious physical drives. In so doing, however, his strategy appears to compromise conventional morality and prevents the conflict being drawn in the style typical of representative narratives between absolutely good versus evil personages.

The effect of Abram's deception is that the Pharaoh is maneuvered into a situation where the hidden truth of his sexual practices is miraculously disclosed, thanks to divine intervention, and astute interpretation (about which we are told nothing).

And Yahweh smote Pharaoh and his house with great plagues over the affair of Sarai, Abram's wife. 12:17

Here the narrator in third-person discourse brings Yahweh onto the stage as a decisive plot-determining character, not through speech, but through action. This is not the arbitrary action of a *deus ex machina*, however, as was the famine, but action that arises from the implications of the moral order assumed by Abram's speech to Sarai – that the appropriation of a married woman by a king violated the moral order and entailed punishment. Here the narrator's discourse does not reflect an ideology imposed upon the characters, but rather the ideology implicit in the character's own direct discourse. This ideology, however, is one in which victory is attained only through divine assistance. Without divine intervention, the clever plot of Abram would have led to the dissolution of the patriarchal family. Even human initiative driven by desire succeeds only with divine cooperation. The extraordinary brevity of this account prevents the expansion of the narrator's viewpoint beyond that of his characters. The closure operative here is that present in Abram's "plot" to entrap the Pharaoh, but in its dependence upon divine aid, it retains an open dimension.

When the Pharaoh finds himself to be the victim of a "plot," he has what might be described as an experience of defamiliarization. The meaning of Abram's previous words and deeds now appears strange and incomprehensible, and he becomes aware of their "fictional" nature. His ejaculations reflect his astonishment:

What is this you have done to me? You did not tell me she was your wife! 12:18

This experience partially corresponds to that found in expressive narratives in which there is a revelation of the unconscious forces which are driving the characters to act in ways that contradict their conscious intentions. But it is, of course, not the typical form of this experience since its subject is a character internal to the narrative world and its reference is to the "fiction" created by Abram in which he is a character.

In what form, then, does this narrative provide the reader with an experience of defamiliarization? It does this through the imponderable ambiguity cloaked behind the Pharaoh's next question to Abram:

Why did you say, "She is my sister," and I took her for myself as a wife? 12:19

Here the Pharaoh also speaks for the reader, and the absence of an answer from Abram sets the reader upon his own search. This question arises at the intersection of the private world of Abram and Sarai disclosed to us at the outset, and the public world of the king of Egypt, and it is through the friction between these two worlds and two perspectives that the narrative defamiliarizes its characters and events for the reader. The "life courses" (Medina) of the Pharaoh and Abram suddenly confront each other in a moment fraught with a potentiality for communication and self-discovery which is unrealized. It is precisely in its lack of realization that the narrative achieves a state of openness and ambiguity which causes the story to live on in the reader as a source of continuing disturbance.

On the one hand, Abram is in a contest with the Pharaoh which he ultimately wins, but, on the other, the victory does not entail the usual humiliation of the evil opponent and exaltation of the righteous hero. The usual juxtaposition of honorable hero versus dishonorable opponent is blurred by the hero's morally questionable strategy and the difficulty of finding a totally unambiguous answer to the final question raised by the Pharaoh.

When the hero, the man of faith, whose life is founded upon a mere sign and not upon power, finds himself in a situation where his survival is at stake and conflict is unavoidable, he does not go like a lamb to the slaughter. He pays the price of entering into the moral ambiguities of a situation and follows a strategy which takes advantage of the blind subservience to desire of his more powerful opponents. The end toward which the strategy moves is not to overpower the opponent and achieve an unambiguous victory over him, but to set the opponent into conflict with himself over the contradictions upon which his own existence is based. The opponent then defeats himself. But the price paid for this successful strategy is that Abram and Sarai must lie, and so cast a shadow upon their own moral rectitude. Abram's character appears unfinished, problematic, open, along with the unanswered question raised by the Pharaoh. The problem which this open ambiguity probably presented later for the Israelite traditionists can be seen in the second version of this story in Genesis 20, which is organized entirely around the question of Abram's moral justification for this type of lie, and climaxes with a lengthy answer given by Abram to the same question posed by the offended king in that story, Abimelech.

The frank but harshly insulting answer which Abram gives to Abimelech's question in the second version of the story is hardly convincing as the type of answer a powerless nomad would give to a king: "I did it because I thought, There is no fear of God at all in this place, and they will kill me because of my wife" (20:11). More in keeping with the manners of court is the deferential silence of Abram before Pharaoh, and the king's own haste to make his question rhetorical.

But even more unusual ambiguities run through this story. Sarai's total silence in the face of this strange strategy of her husband is evidence of the powerlessness of her position, and her status as property to be used for the purposes of the men in the story. As a "character" in Abram's fictive story, she is not permitted to come to speech.

But Abram, the head of the family, openly acknowledges that he owes his life to his wife and later accedes to Sarai's demands about matters of great import for him (Genesis 16:5, 6; 21:10, 11). Sarai is possibly compromised in that she becomes subject to the pleasure of the king (a suspicion which the second account in Genesis 20 is eager to dispel). Also it is certainly not plausible to think of the Pharaoh as an innocent victim of Abram's ruse, as Westermann does. In sum, all are compromised to some degree, and it becomes impossible to find in this story an unambiguous hero or villain although Sarai certainly comes out as an innocent victim. It is precisely in this polyvalent friction between individuals, classes, and circumstances that this narrative exhibits another feature of the symbolic narrative. Each character remains unfinished, open to the future and to the other characters, and it is precisely in this ambiguous communicative interaction between these distant social worlds that the story achieves its aesthetic (and religious) power. The disturbance such an open narrative causes is seen in the second version of this story, which seems anxious to close every issue which the first narrative leaves ambiguous. In so doing, it reveals the distinctive power and character of this narrative form.

The narrative does not allow Abram actually to answer the question the Pharaoh poses, but has him rush on to dismiss Abram and Sarai from his presence and from the country: "And now here is your wife. Take her and go" (12:19).

The open question and the ambiguity with which this scene ends insures the prolongation of the experiences of form characteristic of the defamiliarization process at the center of the symbolic narrative. But the story does not completely end with this question and the order for Abram and Sarai to depart. The narrator also adds a final comment which indicates that the element of contest in this narrative was won by Abram, and a certain closure achieved at least at the material level.

And Pharaoh commanded his men concerning him, and they sent him away, his wife, and all which he had with him. 12:20

The wealth which Abram had accumulated due to the assistance of the Pharaoh remained in his possession, and he left with considerably more than when he arrived. The dimension of material contest in the narrative between the Pharaoh and Abram over property (wife and goods) exhibits the dynamics of the representative narrative type. But because of the way in which the formation of the conflict itself occurs, the conflictual dynamics of the representative narrative are subordinated to those of the symbolic.

Were there any long-range consequences in the subsequent narrative to this behavior of Abram and Sarai in Egypt? According to some commentators, the assumed compromise of Sarai in the Egyptian harem may have had something to do with her infertility. But no blame is ever explicitly placed on Abram and Sarai for this. They only pay the price of the delayed birth, but even this becomes a trial of faith which has positive meaning, and ultimately is used by Yahweh for his own glory in the birth of Isaac in the old age of his parents. Thus the standpoint of the larger narrative context toward these events is itself appropriately ambiguous.

12
"Where is the lamb for the burnt offering?" Genesis 22

The story of the attempted sacrifice of Isaac is unique in the book of Genesis in that the narrator provides the reader with an interpretive frame of reference. He prefaces the story with the statement, "After these things, God tested Abraham." This has not, of course, prevented commentators from searching for additional meanings behind this extraordinary story in earlier stages of the tradition. Martin Noth finds here a reflection of an old ritual which based the substitution of a ram for a human sacrifice on this theophany.[1] Westermann finds the event of the redemption of the son to be the central event in the original story. The value of these reconstructions for an understanding of the text is very limited, however. As von Rad argues, it is a mistake to find in this story a "representation of a general historical truth" such as a protest against child sacrifice.[2] Rather, "the exposition is much more accurate when it discovers in the narrative above all the idea of a radical test of obedience."[3] The more recent tendency has thus been to turn aside from traditio-historical reconstruction of the text's earlier history, and to attempt to determine the form and meaning of the text as it stands.[4] This is facilitated by the general failure of historical critics to find any clear signs of multiple documentary sources.[5]

The meaning of the test thus constitutes the horizon within which the meaning of the narrative should be determined. This places the locus of the meaning within the inner life of Abraham, and the mysterious intentions of Yahweh. Since, however, the narrative gives us no further account of either of these dimensions, analysis and interpretation must attempt to place these events within a context which can make both God's unusual command, and Abraham's quiet acquiescence to it more comprehensible.

A variety of contexts have been used by interpreters to provide some way of absorbing these events, but the reticence of the narrator to provide an unequivocal frame of reference should be a warning to interpreters. This story is characterized above all by its polyvalent meanings, and as von Rad points out, "a story like this is basically open to interpretation and to whatever thoughts the reader is inspired."[6]

One of the contexts to which interpreters most frequently refer is the complex of ideas connected with theodicy in the book of Job. Since Abraham's suffering was explicitly caused by a divine mandate, however, this leaves both the divine and human decisions more profoundly ambiguous than is the case when suffering is caused by a circumstance which is only indirectly related to the divine will. More similar are the numerous tests God makes of the nation's obedience and faithfulness during the wilderness and conquest periods (such as Ex. 16:4; Judg. 2:22). But the expectations of God in these situations are for things such as faithfulness to the law and courage. These are significantly different from the much more intimate, emotionally complex problem of the sacrifice of one's child. A more likely religious context for such an action by a father would be the widespread rites of initiation in the ancient world which involved the symbolic murder of children, as I have shown elsewhere.[7] This is also a rite which occurs in a familial context that corresponds to the larger narrative in which the Biblical story occurs: the transition from one generation to the next. After Genesis 22, Isaac does not return to live again with his parents. The severing of the parent–child bond which is the central issue of this narrative is also a fundamental source of the dynamics of the rite of initiation.[8]

Thus I shall consider the immediate governing context of this passage to be the test between Abraham and God, but the larger context to be the deep problem of the transition from the first generation of the promise to the second. It is at the intersection of the complex tensions between these two somewhat incongruous dramatic processes that the functions of this narrative appear.

Typological analysis

And it was after these things that God tested Abraham. 22:1a

This narrative exhibits a marked shift in the relation of the narrator and the divine persona to the events transpiring in the narrative. The narrator in Genesis 2–12 allows himself the liberty to represent a decision within the hidden world of the divine before it is disclosed to the characters, thereby creating a bi-leveled narrative universe which the narrator will mediate. This division between the divine world and the human world can no longer be sustained after Genesis 12. Because of the reorientation of the protagonist toward the future, the future must be disclosed to him in every case. It is this reshaping of the topography of the internal narrative universe that accounts for the emergence of the poles – open versus closed – as the semantic model governing the characterological development. As long as the narrator represented in the narrative framework the conditions which determined the lives of the characters, their existence was experienced as an arbitrary fate, and meaningful action on their part could arise only from rebellious desire.

Now, however, in this centrally important narrative, the narrator once again gives the reader insight into divine intentions that are unknown to the protagonist. Although Abraham is not to be told, the command about to be given him in an internal micro-dialogue does not have the meaning that it will appear to have. The command for Abraham to sacrifice his son, which is about to be given, should not be placed within the general framework of cultic sacrifice that aims at achieving unity between the divine and human. Rather it is a "test." Although we are not told what the test aims at finding out, we know that it aims at establishing some truth about Abraham. The intimacy and openness between the divine and human which characterizes earlier narratives (such as Genesis 15; 18:22–33) thus is interrupted by a divine thought "in the back of the mind" which constitutes surreptitious calculation. We can thus say at the outset that the primary meaning of the narrative will stem from the third-person narration rather than from the direct discourse, though, as we shall see, the dialogue between Abraham and Isaac opens the closed structure so that certain meanings arise which escape this closure. Knowledge sought by the divine will be revealed through the action of Abraham, which in turn must be depicted in the third-person narration. The test thus installs an action sequence or proaieretic code (Barthes' term) which will be of fundamental importance for the meaning of the narrative. At the end Abraham will have acquired an objective attribute based on his depicted actions, and his character will be closed in a way that it has not been thus far.

There is a serious semantic risk involved in this narrative strategy, however. The distinctiveness of the Biblical narrative has been based on the unique function of the divine Voice in manifesting the promissory intersubjective speech event at the basis of the identity of the characters. Because of this speech event, desire in the protagonist has been transmuted into trust and faith in the future fulfillment. Now the divine Voice, which has elicited trust from Abraham, steps back outside of that trusting relation to manipulate Abraham for his own concealed ends. The divine here is taking on the role of the conventional narrator who contrives situations in order to attribute qualities to his characters at the conclusion – good or bad, successful or unsuccessful, full or empty. But unlike the conventional narrator, he too speaks and acts *within* the narrative framework, and his behavior comes back to qualify his own character. When words contradict the expectations for the future generated by his own previous dialogues with the protagonist, as is the case here, then the meaning of the previous words are placed into question, and the possibility arises that the previous words were also not to be taken at face value. The future which before seemed so clear under the light of the divine promise is now suddenly eclipsed by the arbitrary darkness of the impenetrable divine will. The issue to be resolved in this test must then be of overriding importance for such a risk to be taken.

Can we say, then, on the basis of the preface, that this narrative will not be a symbolic narrative at all, but rather a more conventional representative narrative? We will see that this comes very close to being the case because of the fundamental importance of the proaieretic code initiated by the test. It escapes complete closure only because of a dialogue emanating from Isaac, which, as we shall see, is not concluded within the context of the narrative. This dialogue is of such paramount importance that it subsumes the narrative framework and the divine dialogue which is consonant with it, thereby leaving the narrative open to some extent, and capable of being integrated into the overarching sweep of the larger symbolic narrative of which it is a part.

The narrative begins with a micro-dialogue, though it is not authentic because of the larger semantic context presented by the "test." Its function is to pose to Abraham the central semantic issues that constitute the test, and that will thus be resolved at the conclusion. After a dialogical exchange which serves to establish contact, God speaks to Abraham and says:

> "Take, I say, your son, your only son whom you love, Isaac, and go immediately to the land of Moriah, and offer him there as a sacrifice upon one of the mountains that I will declare to you."[9]
>
> 22:2

The most remarkable semantic feature of this divine discourse is the third-person reference it contains to Isaac. Isaac here is represented in the divine discourse in terms of his place within the system of familial relations. The role which defines him in this system is that of Abraham's only son, and the recipient of his love. His role and identity thus are defined altogether with respect to the powerful bonds which tie him to Abraham. Isaac is valuable to Abraham especially because he is his only (legitimate) son, and (perhaps for that reason) because he loves him.

In a few words, then, the divine discourse represents a system of subjective desire to which the protagonist is now possibly subservient. Even though the child is a miraculous fulfillment of a divine promise, as the previous narrative has made clear, when the object of desire contained in the promise takes on material form in the fulfillment, the bond of faith between the promisor and the promisee is superseded by the relation which unites the recipient with the promised object. A dilemma has thus been reached in promissory dynamics. The mediating function of the word of promise is made irrelevant by the fulfillment precisely because the tension between the spiritual and material, which the promise transmuted into a tension between the present and the future, disappears with the material fulfillment. This dilemma is avoided so long as the fulfillment is delayed, but it cannot be delayed indefinitely if the promise is to remain credible.

The other solution to this dilemma would appear to require that the fulfillment be given up after its materialization. But does this not render the preceding faith meaningless and threaten the bifurcation of the material and the spiritual dimensions? The psychology of sacrifice, as we have seen, strives to achieve a narcissistic spiritual unity with the divine by eradicating the material representation of the self. This divine command thus reflects the underlying irony to which the promissory history has come. Isaac is simultaneously the fulfillment of the promise, which has been the means by which Abraham has been delivered from the blind material compulsions of desire, and the occasion of Abraham's greatest temptation to fall back into the desire-driven mode of being.

But if the sacrifice of the fulfillment is the only way out of this inescapable dilemma, then it would seem that the promissory mode of religious subjectivity is finally being forced to submit to the principle of duality arising from the psychology of the imagination. Can the intersubjective relation of faith not ultimately accommodate the competing relation of the subject to the material fulfillment of the promise? Is Yahweh indeed a "jealous" God? But if Abraham is obedient to this Word, will absolute sacrifice of desire not also undermine his difference from the divine and transform a verbally mediated, intersubjective relation into a relation of spiritual unity (mystical absorption)? Such are the radical tensions working beneath the surface of this narrative which perhaps partly accounts for the fascination it has had for readers through the ages.

The command to sacrifice the child of the fulfillment is a final command to purge from the intersubjective faith relation the last vestige of material desire. But because the reasons for this command are not disclosed to Abraham, it does not represent a Word to which Abraham can respond verbally. A forthright answer by the divine to any question Abraham might raise would have to reveal that this situation is a contrived "test," and thus render it impossible. What the test seeks to know about Abraham cannot be disclosed in dialogue with him. It rather seeks to establish the existence of a quality within his character which can only be revealed by action. Thus Abraham is appropriately silent in the face of this monstrous mandate.

> And Abraham rose early in the morning, and he saddled his asses, and took two of his young men with him, and Isaac, his son. And he split wood for the sacrifice, and arose and went to the place of which God had told him. 22:3

Now the narrative framework assumes a much larger role than it has had in previous narratives I have analyzed. It is only through the third-person account of Abraham's subsequent actions that the reader will learn whether or not Abraham indeed possesses this trait which the test is designed to determine. An atmosphere of suspense thus hangs over the recounting of his methodical preparations for the journey, doubtless based on ritual actions connected with a pilgrimage to a holy site for a sacrifice. Each action is a sign of Abraham's inner state, and provides another clue as to what he will ultimately do.

The lack of reference to a sacrificial lamb in the detailed description of Abraham's preparations for the journey is not perceived by the reader to be a deficiency. It is obvious what the sacrificial object will be. But this lacuna in the normal preparations is a sign of division in levels of communication between the narrative personages. It is an invisible sign of a speech event which has not been and cannot be disclosed to Isaac – an absence that is heavy with unspoken significance. As such it constitutes a link between the two worlds of discourse, an emptiness which signifies. Words and actions can be effectively concealed, but an absence cannot so easily be hidden! It thus constitutes a fissure in the wall separating the inner micro-dialogue of God with Abraham, and Isaac's world of discourse. This discourse has been "about" Isaac; he has been depicted in the divine discourse. He is a character in the plot which is unfolding around him, but his role has been fixed in advance by others, and has not been disclosed to him. Except for this lacuna in the objective conditions of the ritual procedure in progress, he has no access to the speech event which is about to determine his entire existence.[10]

The report of the journey and an anticipatory sighting of the destination follows:

And during the third day Abraham lifted up his eyes and saw the place far away. 22:4

This literary technique creates a penultimate, anticipatory time frame in which events may transpire which are generated by the expectation of a specific future event. Abraham's conspiratorial conversation with Sarai took place "when they came near to Egypt," and Joseph's brothers' conspiracy to kill him occurred between the time they first saw him approaching across the pastures, and the time he arrived. To be in view of the destination before one actually arrives provides a temporal space for expectation and decision. The point has thus been reached when Abraham's final decision must be made.

With the mysterious deliberateness of a ritual action, Abraham now steadily completes the preparation for the sacrifice thus making clear his decision. He first takes leave of the *ne'arîm*.

And Abraham said to the boys, "You remain here with the ass, and I and the boy will go there, and we will worship, and return here to you." 22:5

The DD of Abraham now becomes deceptive, reflecting the division in the levels of discourse. He asserts that Isaac will also return (the verb "return" is first-person plural) with him from the sacrifice, when the mandate which has put him upon this course of action has made his return apparently impossible. (But Isaac, in spite of his reprieve, does not return with Abraham.)

The departure from the *n^e'arîm* and the beast of burden provides the narrator another occasion to depict the actions of Abraham.

And Abraham took the wood for the offering, and placed it upon Isaac, his son, and he took in his hand the fire. 22:6

The implements of sacrifice carried by others must now be borne by Abraham and Isaac, and the description of this transfer in the final minutes before the sacrifice makes the absence of the lamb more obvious. To one who does not know the hidden truth, this absence cries out for comment. It is when confronted with similar signifying absences in earlier narratives that God asked Adam and Eve, "Where are you?" and Cain, "Where is your brother?" These questions reflect the breakdown of intersubjectivity, and the presence of alienated discourse.

With this transfer complete, the narrative continues the action emphasizing now their separation from the others: "And they went, the two of them together" (22:6). Isaac, showing himself alert to the situation, speaks for the first time, and pointedly raises the crucial question:

And Isaac spoke to Abraham, his father, and he said, "My father." And he said, "Yes, my son." And he said, "Here is the fire and the wood, but where is the lamb for the sacrifice?" 22:7

That this is not merely an "innocent" question is indicated by another ellipsis. Isaac prefaces his question by listing the items present for the sacrifice – the wood and the fire – but he does not mention the knife. This is not merely due, as Gunkel said, to the desire of the narrator not to engage in "boring completeness."[11] In the context of the narrator's emphasis upon the aloneness of Abraham and Isaac, Isaac's question about the absence of the animal for the sacrifice, preceded by mention of the knife, would have allowed the unthinkable fear that he might be the sacrificial animal too close to the threshhold of expression. The elided reference to the knife thus comes to be a sign of the unspoken fear now coursing beneath the discourse of the father and son.

When Isaac then directly asks, "Where is the lamb for the sacrifice?" he seeks to bring to the level of discourse the hidden speech event which is determining his future. His own instance of speech occurs precisely in the lacunae of the over-arching plot, that is, in the absence which his own objectified body is destined to fill at the end. This question arises out of the dynamics of the symbolic narrative which bases characters upon primal speech acts which mediate between the world of the author and that of the characters. Isaac's question asks implicitly for this speech act which is determining his existence. His question thus prevents the calm unfolding of this representative narrative by pushing against its boundaries for a word of direct discourse which can be uttered about his future, signified here by the absent lamb – and the unmentionable presence of the knife.

The question, of course, cannot be answered without jeopardizing the completion of the closed plot. There is no place within the terms of the God–Abraham micro-dialogue for Isaac's question. Isaac, in this dialogue, is a "he," not a "you." His existence is defined only in terms of what he represents as an object of Abraham's desire, and not what he may himself become in dialogue with the divine Word. If his question is answered the covert plot which focuses upon this test of Abraham's faith will be revealed, and the closed structure of the narrative broken open. God's word to Abraham cannot be addressed to Isaac, and it is not possible for Abraham to convey it to him.

The function of this question is to break open the closed logic of this plot in progress, and expose it to a new reality, the lively awareness of the innocent son who will not go along with this plot in total, unthinking silence. Just as the question of the Pharaoh to Abraham brought to the surface the friction between the conflicting perspectives beneath the surface of the plot of that narrative, throwing them into a new light, so the question of Isaac defamiliarizes the conspiratorial plot of God and Abraham against him. It does not, however, bring the narrative to an end because the issue at stake in the plot has not yet been resolved. But with this question the denouement subtly begins since the actual sacrifice of such a witting son now becomes almost unthinkable.[12]

The question cannot not be answered directly. Abraham deflects the issue to God by declaring ambiguously:

And Abraham said, "God will provide for it, the lamb for the sacrifice, my son." 22:8

The narrative proceeds with no further discourse from Isaac or Abraham. With God now explicitly named as the provider of the sacrificial "lamb," Isaac is incorporated into a symbolic drama taking place between Abraham and God in which his own identity will be eclipsed by the symbolic role he has been given in that now gruesome story.

Abraham's answer clearly places the question in the hands of God. The issue at stake reaches far beyond the simple survival of Isaac. The connection between Abraham and Isaac is the link between the first and second generations of the promise. That the issue of the continuity of the promise into the future is at stake here is indicated by the link established, even if by a later redactor, between the action of Abraham in this scene and the transmission of the promises to Isaac in 26:3–5 (to be discussed below).

The central problem of achieving continuity in the history of the promise is that the child of the promise is not himself the recipient of the promise. The micro-dialogue which founded the existence of the father does not found the existence of the son. Rather he will experience the promise in the form of his father's hopes and desires for his family's future. But the promise cannot be transmitted by means of a human, biological and psychological process. To attempt to do so will cause the promissory history to descend again to the level of the psychology of desire in that what the first generation experienced as divine promise, the second generation will experience as familial ambition. It is to this quite specific and profound dilemma that this story is responding in an extraordinary way.

The dilemma is finally brought to the surface by the divine command to sacrifice physically the child of the promise. If Abraham is called upon to sacrifice his son, this will destroy the subordination of the next generation to the visionary desires of the previous generation, and purify the intersubjective faith of Abraham from its last vestige of materiality. But if he is permitted to accomplish this act, and the son actually dies, this destroys the physical continuity of the family (as well as the innocent life of the son). The succession of the promise could then be accomplished only through supernatural, spiritual means.

This possibility was already close to realization with the delay in the birth of the child of the promise beyond the period of normal child bearing so that supernatural assistance was needed for his conception. He was, nevertheless, conceived in the normal fashion. But to sacrifice the son physically would make biological succession impossible (apart from another belated pregnancy), and would so spiritualize the succession of the promise that the meaning of the promise as a mediation of desire would be fundamentally undermined. As we have seen, even the idea of an inner sacrifice of the son risks the return of the material/spiritual dualisms of the psychology of the imagination. But if a strategy can be found to sever the psychological and physiological bonds which connect the generations while allowing the son to survive physically and be present later to receive his own divine revelation, the continuity of the family can be maintained at the genealogical level, and the place of material continuity in the history of the promise is preserved.

Against this background, then, both the command to sacrifice and the mandate to halt before its culmination become understandable. The interruption, however, cannot come an instant before it is absolutely clear that the inner commitment to engage in the material sacrifice is unequivocally made. Thus the final scene of the action sequence which began with the announcement of the test is skilfully brought to a suspenseful climax in third-person narration:

> And they came to the place about which he had been told, and he built an altar there. And he arranged the wood and bound Isaac, his son, and placed him on the altar on top of the wood. And Abraham extended his hand, and took the knife to kill his son. And an angel of Yahweh called to him from heaven, and said, "Abraham, Abraham." And he said, "Here I am." And he said, "Do not extend your hand to the boy, and do not do anything to him ..."
>
> 22:9–12

The intervention of the divine messenger before the culminating act of the sacrifice makes use of the distinction between inner and outer sacrifice, which in other contexts leads to a dualism of spirit and matter. Here, however, it serves to preserve the material continuity of the family by separating physical, biological continuity from continuity through the psychology of the imagination. The physical presence of the son nourishes the psychological illusion that continuity into the future would be secured by natural succession apart from the word of promise and faith. The sacrifice of Isaac represents the end of the possibility of this "human" fantasy of the future. The continuity which arises from the psychology of the human imagination is thereby rejected.

But the interruption of the sacrifice reaffirms the place of natural succession within the future of promissory faith, divorced from imaginary fantasies. The continuity of the promise will, however, remain dependent upon divine initiative (signified by the divine Voice). Thus the distinction between inner and outer sacrifice is made horizontal, temporal, and syntagmatic, rather than vertical, eternal, and paradigmatic. It interrupts the continuity between the generations at the level of the imagination while preserving it at the level of physical, generational succession within the family.

But does this trauma not, nevertheless, leave Abraham a closed, characterologically defined entity at the conclusion? While from the divine viewpoint the physical succession is preserved, has not Abraham been required so to sever himself from material desire that his faith has fallen victim to its opposite, that is, absorption into the spiritual with the accompanying closure?

It is here that the full shock of the defamiliarization strategy of the representative plot of this narrative can be experienced. Whereas material desires were proleptically experienced in the transforming context of the promise which opened the character to the future as gift, here the material actualization of the promise is transformed into the spiritual virtue of obedience:

"... now I know that you fear Elohim, and will not withhold your son, your only one from me". 22:12

The logic governing the act of sacrifice is that of the conflict of opposites. In the context of this narrative plot, Isaac does not have presence, but represents an obstacle which prevents Abraham's attainment of a state of pure spirituality. The polarities governing this plot are the material versus the spiritual, the empty fullness of the disobedient versus the full emptiness of the obedient. The renewal of Abraham's spirituality can only be accomplished by the sacrifice of the material embodiment of his spiritual values. With this act of obedience, however, the mediating logic of the promissory faith is swept away by the unbending rigor of a world-negating spiritual demand. Abraham's material viewpoint is totally negated, and his self, as a spiritual entity, is absorbed into the divine Voice.

This sacrifice places the future for Abraham beyond the unfolding biological and cultural processes of time. The future for him is now the absolute divine Voice purged of all earthly conditions (this becomes explicit later in the narrative). A firm line is drawn here for the first time since the beginning of the history of the promise, between a form of the sacred which transcends all earthly mediated logic, and one which has a place for human experience and reason. The future which is now before Abraham has only a spiritual, supernatural continuity with the present. From this new point of view, the significance of the preceding course of events is relativized by the perception of an all-consuming absolute spirituality in which there is no place for authentic intersubjectivity.

The test which qualifies Abraham thus also imposes closure upon him. By sacrificing his son, he chooses the spiritual over the material, the eternal over the temporal, and by so doing, releases the tension of faith in the promise which began in Genesis 12.[13] Abraham's deed transcends the ambiguities and compromises of history. The unity of faith and understanding which was made possible from Genesis 12–21 by the mediating function of the Word is now broken apart by an act of absolute, incomprehending obedience in contradiction to all mediating earthly logic. Abraham's character now becomes defined at its deepest level as one who "fears God."

But the effect of this eruption of the absolute into the relative, the internal/spiritual into the external/material, is to use closure against closure, desire against desire – to achieve a double negation. This accounts partly for the dark irrational currents swirling under the surface of this narrative. In so doing a cleavage is created between the generations. This was doubtless deemed necessary because the promise has built into it the seeds of its own destruction. The future generation cannot emerge as subjects of their own discourse with the divine unless they are surrendered by the past generation. Correspondingly, the past generation falls into closure in the very moment when the future becomes a tangible object to possess, even if partial or fragmentary. As Augustine says, Abraham "teaches us not to prefer the gifts of God to God."[14] The reaction of Abraham to the divine messenger's voice (note that it is a "messenger" that delivers this announcement contradicting the previous command, a hypostatization of the semantic plurality within the divine which reflects the distance between the divine and human levels created by the idea of a surreptitious "test") is reported by the narrator as an event of sudden sight.

> And Abraham lifted his eyes and he looked, and behold a ram was caught behind in a thicket by his horns. And Abraham went and took the ram, and offered it up as a sacrifice in place of his son.
> 22:13

These events of *seeing* have a relation to the inner state of the Biblical characters. As we have seen, Adam and Eve, after eating of the fruit and removing themselves from a verbally mediated, intersubjective relation with the divine Voice to pursue immediate knowledge based on experience, "saw" something which they had not seen before – their nakedness, a sign of alienation and shame. Abraham now sees a ram caught in a thicket. His shift into a visual mode also signifies a shift from a mediated to an immediate relation to the divine. But now, rather than alienation, it is a visible sign signifying the opposite – complete union with the divine. The obsessive force driving Abraham to sacrifice his son set in motion by the divine command at the outset is now broken, and he can *see* a substitute which was doubtless there all along (though perhaps "behind" him as indicated by the M.T.'s אַחַר). The knife then swiftly falls upon the animal "in place of his son."

The sacrifice which occurs here is unusual in several respects. The animal is not a representative of Abraham's labor and productivity, that is, of his self. It is rather a simple substitute, a chance replacement for such an object, a visual symbol with the arbitrary character of a sign. It serves the logic of sacrifice, however, in that it provides a sign of the immediate presence of God, and its sacrifice, a symbol of the new unity of Abraham with God.

God has not mandated *this* sacrifice, nor does he directly provide the sacrificial animal as Abraham so interprets. The sacrifice of the ram occurs at the conjunction of two systems at work in the narrative framework, the unspent momentum built up in the narrative account of the tense procession toward the sacrifice of Isaac, and the report of Abraham's sighting of the circumstantial ensnaring of the ram. The sudden removal of Isaac as the object of sacrifice, and the explanatory statement by the divine messenger, ended the central tension stemming from the test and divine mandate at the outset. The narrative might well have ended with this event. Abraham's statement to Isaac regarding the provision of a sheep ("Yahweh will see" or "provide" יִרְאֶה) was obviously a ruse which contradicted the original divine mandate. The completion of the sacrifice thus stems from forces operating on the human level (the narrator's portrayal of human actions) which must be allowed their consummation. Corresponding to this powerful momentum of the sacrificial process conveyed by the narrator in verses 9–11a, the narrator also makes use of circumstance and the perceptual reaction of Abraham to the release of tension to bring the narrative to closure. This once again leaves the act of sacrifice itself in the status of a human undertaking or even compulsion, detached from any divine mandate. The connection is made between this event and the divine in the direct discourse of Abraham as he names the mountain, "Yahweh will see" (יִרְאֶה), making use of a word-play relating to the ambiguous answer he has earlier given Isaac ("Elohim will provide," that is "see to it" יִרְאֶה).

The visual mode, which was associated with autonomous subjectivity, and sacrifice, which was viewed with such skepticism in the primeval history, has now reached its apex of spiritual acceptability as a vehicle of Abraham's faith in its highest moment. Rather than a sign of the evil nature of the human imagination, it now serves as the human response to passing the ultimate test of faith. As such it is another indication of the radical tensions under the surface of this narrative.[15]

The narrator then turns to address the reader in an explanatory comment explicitly attempting to connect these words of Abraham with a saying with which the reader will be familiar: "On the mountain of Yahweh, it/he will be seen [or provided]." This may have been an allusion to Jerusalem as the "mount of Yahweh," and may thus be a tenuous attempt to connect Abraham's sacrifice to the sacrificial cultus in Jerusalem. In its vagueness of reference, however, it falls far short of offering a divine sanction for sacrifice.

While not providing a divine sanction for cultic sacrifice, it does provide now a new and deeper context of faith within which sacrifice may be understood. As Gregoire Rouiller argues, "the sacrificial rite is understood only in an indispensable relation to faith."[16] The object of sacrifice here is a material reality – a child – which threatens promissory faith by offering a naturalistic basis for the continuity of the family into the future. The animal sacrifices to be offered in the cult on the "mount of God" in the future can now be understood as representing the material objects in which humans are tempted to invest their trust for their future security. In this way the sacrificial cultus will be given a function in the history of the promise. Nevertheless, the passage makes clear that the inner sacrifice of the ultimate temptation to secure our future materially through our children is what is fundamentally required by God. The animal sacrifice is still of human and not divine origin. The more general concern may account for the lack of specificity regarding location, and the irregular aetiological structure it exhibits.[17]

Once again one could easily imagine the narrative ending here. All tensions seem to have been resolved. As we have seen, this narrative has brought Abraham's character to a form of closure which serves to open the future for the next generation. But several important uncertainties remain. Will there be a continuation of the promissory history to the next generation, or has the promise been subordinated to a purer form of spirituality? Will Isaac be the recipient of his own promissory revelation? And what form shall Abraham's faith take now that he has, in a sense, transcended the promise in the direction of a more immediate unity with the divine Voice? To what extent will the sacrifice be understood as the destination and end of the promise?

These questions might be answered by a divine appearance to Isaac in which the promises could be given, but this does not occur until 26:1–6. They are answered in part, however, by the "second" appearance of the divine messenger which is so often noted for its apparently unmotivated syntactical relation to the preceding scene:

A messenger of the Lord called to Abraham a second time from heaven. 22:15

The language of verses 15–18 bears many marks of late redaction due to the extensive, composite nature of the promise, the use of an unusual, probably late form of the oath, and the introduction to direct discourse associated with oracular prophecy: "By myself I have sworn, says the Lord ..." (verse 16). The evidence of late reflection here does not diminish the possibility that this passage has been constructed to play an important role in the unification and integration of this narrative into the larger context.[18]

The use of a strengthened oath form, "By myself I have sworn," as a preface to the promise serves to reestablish the importance of the promise in Abraham's relation to the divine Voice, a matter which, as we have seen, was rendered uncertain by the preceding sacrifice. It is the uncertainty which would have required a heightening of the illocutionary force of the promise, as the special ritual content of the dream accomplished after Abraham's doubts about the promise of land in 15:7–8.

But it is the incorporation now of the results of the test into the formulation of the promise as its basis that constitutes the most significant new contribution of this passage to the evolving semiology of faith in Genesis:

> Since you have done this thing, and have not withheld your son, your only one, from me [Samaritan Pentateuch], thus I will indeed bless you, and I will indeed cause your seed to multiply as the stars of the heavens ... because you have obeyed my voice. 22:16–18

Westermann notes the significant departure of this formulation of the promise from the earlier: "The promises to the fathers are by nature free promises of God. When they are grounded here through an achievement of Abraham, the understanding of the promise has been changed; the Deuteronomic theology with its qualified promise is here already presupposed."[19] But the significant function of this new formulation of the promise in a transitional context between the generations cannot be ignored by attributing it to a Deuteronomic editor. The grounding is repeated again as the basis of the promise to Isaac:

> I will be with you, and bless you ... I will multiply your descendents as the stars of the heavens ... because Abraham obeyed my voice and kept my charge, my commandments, my statutes and my laws. Gen. 26:3–5

Though the latter formulation is even more anachronistic with its mention of statutes and laws, the common bond connecting them is that Abraham has obeyed the "voice" of Yahweh in that he did not withhold his "only son" from him. The promises to Abraham are restated in an almost encyclopedic fashion and then, explicitly, because of Abraham's action, they are given to Isaac.

This passage thus places in the divine utterance descriptive qualifications based on Abraham's character, which essentially impose a climactic closure upon the dialogical, intersubjective relation of Abraham and God. *He does not speak again to Abraham in the text.* The reiteration of the promise with its heightened intensity establishes the promise as the form which will govern the future of faith beyond Abraham. This makes it clear that the promise itself is not to be spiritualized as a consequence of Abraham's sacrifice. Thus two seemingly incompatible forms are brought together into a single formulation, the descriptive qualification with its objectifying effect which forecloses future development, and the intensified promise which reaffirms the role of the promise as a mediating force in the continuing history.

There is an inner distance, however, between the absolute surrender of the future made by Abraham on the mount, and the vision of the future embodied by the promises. The repetition of the promises is often motivated by inner and outer conditions (e.g., chapters 15; 17; 25:1; 46:3). But here there is no similar circumstantial motivation. Since it is the function of the promise to mediate desire, these promises, while addressed to Abraham, no longer have a point of contact in Abraham's situation. In his decision to sacrifice Isaac he has renounced his desire for children and for the future which would stem from children. Sensing this distance commentators have repeatedly considered them to be secondary additions. Their function is more programmatic than characterological for the unfolding narrative structure.

When in 26:5 the promises are transmitted to Isaac because of Abraham's obedience, their true function is disclosed. His obedience broke the usual desire-governed relation between the generations. The other side of the spiritual closure into which Abraham has descended is the dependency upon the divine initiative to transmit the promise. The future is not to be extended simply by means of normal genealogical succession. We shall see that in dealing with this problem with each successive generation, the narrative finds ways to inject discontinuity which makes the transmission dependent upon a divine initiative that transcends earthly logic and necessity.

But with the discontinuity and closure resulting from Abraham's sacrifice of the material content of the promise, the theological question of the continuity which lies beneath the relative formulations of the promise presents itself. If Abraham is expected to sacrifice the fulfillment which, in its promissory form, had mediated his relation to the divine, to what then is Abraham related when the content of the promise has been surrendered? What is it that provides the continuity between the generations? This is a question which is crucial only for one who, like the narrator, is concerned with establishing a linkage at the spiritual level between the generations. But it is an awkward question for the narrator to answer since to answer it in third-person discourse would require that he make descriptive statements about the divine (the ontological basis for continuity).

The solution is for this continuity to be disclosed in the divine speech to the characters. We find thus that the divine now in speaking to Abraham makes reference to an aspect of its own being as the object of Abraham's transcendental obedience. Abraham has been obedient not to the person or self of God ("to me") but to "my voice". In other probably Deuteronomic writings, the Voice of Yahweh comes to be distinguished from the relative forms of his disclosure. This distinction between his Voice and his covenant law is ventured in divine speech to Moses in Exodus 19:5 where Yahweh promises, "Now therefore, if you will obey my voice and keep my covenant, you shall be my own possession among all peoples." The need to distinguish between Yahweh and the particular form of this outer manifestation is made explicit in the words of Moses in Deuteronomy 4:12: "Then the Lord spoke to you out of the midst of the fire; you heard the sound of words but saw no form; there was only a voice. And he declared to you his covenant."

The "voice" thus is treated as a transcendent theological phenomenon, separable from the divine commandments and from the physical manifestations accompanying divine appearances. Such theological or ideological thinking underlies Genesis 22:18 and 26:5. Absolute obedience to the transcendent, unqualified Voice of the divine provides both the ontological and ethical foundation of continuity between the generations. The unmediated absoluteness of this principle, qualified somewhat by its form as an enunciation by the divine Voice itself, establishes historical continuity on the basis of a dichotomy between form and content, essence and existence, which subjects history to semantic closure at its most critical juncture. The transition to the second generation is no longer a matter of the free initiative of the divine. It now is assumed by the principle of absolute obedience to the Voice by the fathers. Yet the *concept* of the Voice remains so close to the immediacy of the micro-dialogue, and so lacking in specific content, that it would seem to remain open to the possibility of new and different utterances.[20]

The primary basis of the possibility of the renewal of the divine dialogue with the next generation stems from the unanswerable question posed by Isaac. The acceptance of the spiritual virtue of obedience apart from the consummation of the obedient act establishes the closed principle of absolute obedience to the divine Voice, while permitting the physical and mental survival of Isaac. The recognition of Isaac, implied by the inclusion of his question which neither Abraham nor the divine Voice could directly answer (in terms of the original mandate to sacrifice him), forms the basis for the continuation of the divine–human micro-dialogue into the next generation. The divine–human discourse is now open to the presence of the child of the promise.

Finally, the intergenerational context of this narrative is made clear by the conclusion. Abraham returns to the young men, but no mention is made of Isaac whose presence with Abraham had been earlier reiterated at every juncture. The elision of Isaac's name indicates his absence from the return.[21]

Whereas Abraham goes to dwell in Beersheba, Isaac is next mentioned as living apart from Abraham at Beer-la-hai-roi and in the Negev. His transition to independence and adulthood (requiring this separation of males from the mother) is signaled by the death of Sarah immediately following the event on the mount (23:2), and by Abraham's arrangements for his marriage (ch. 24). The event on the mount, though a test for Abraham, was equally or perhaps more important for the narrative as the spiritual and theological basis for the transition to the second generation in the history of the promise.

The return of Abraham to his young men and to Beersheba closes the dimension of this narrative (and the Abraham cycle as a whole), that pertained to Abraham's faith, while the absence of Isaac from this return signifies an open future in which there may be a resumption of the dialogue between humans and God in the next generation.

13

"Who then is he who was hunting game... before you came?" Genesis 25:19–34; 26:34–5 and 27:1–28:9

The limits of the text to be analyzed here reach from the introductory story of the birth and early life of Esau and Jacob in 25:19–34, and the marriage of Esau in 26:34–35, to the story of Jacob and Rebekah's conspiracy to deprive Esau of his father's blessing and Jacob's departure from home in 27:1–28:9. The initial scene has been interrupted by a collection of Isaac stories which permits time to elapse so that Isaac can be old and blind at the beginning of chapter 27. Since the remainder of the Jacob cycle is controlled by the theme of his departure and return,[1] the initial phase of the story evolving from the birth of the brothers to their separation constitutes a unity.

There are few parallels and duplications which more recent commentators consider justification for a division of the text into parallel accounts. Occasional sentences with a genealogical content are attributed to P (25:19–20, 26b).[2] The most serious fissure in the story is the second justification given for the departure of Jacob at the conclusion (27:46–28:9), and its presupposition in the story of the marriage of Esau (26:34, 35). This is generally attributed to P and considered to have no connections with the plot of Genesis 27. Whether this is the case will have to be determined in the course of the detailed analysis.

The problem of moral incongruity between the Biblical and modern ages that we have already encountered in our analysis of Genesis 12 and 22 is, if possible, only heightened in the story of Jacob and Esau. It is Gunkel who has best expressed the shock of the modern reader who looks frankly at what happens in this story:

> To our sensitivity, this prank of Jacob is too immoral to be amusing: to deceive one's own blind, dying father appears to us simply repugnant. Especially offensive to us, however, is the role which religion plays in this story: a blessing of God is won through deception! The deceiver Jacob shall be at the same time a bearer of divine revelation![3]

Gunkel attempts to answer this problem through historical relativization:

> There was also a time in Israel in which morality and religion had not yet concluded a close bond which we now regard as self-evident ... the emphasis of morality in religion is a heritage for which we are indebted to ancient Israel and its prophets.[4]

Von Rad, in contrast, sees the entire process as being under the determining control of God who himself makes use of ambiguous human motives to accomplish his plans to the extent that the human characters are scarcely responsible for their roles:

> the narrator draws a powerful picture of the most extraordinary entangled guilt, but his view of what God has decreed and accomplished keeps him from being ruffled before the question of personal guilt and subjective motives of individual persons ... he intends to awaken in the reader a feeling of sympathetic suffering for those who are caught up mysteriously in such a monstrous act of God and are almost destroyed in it. For whether these subjective motives were worldly or spiritual, they go to pieces on the frightful incomprehensibility of the God who has made them the object of his saving will.[5]

For Westermann, however, the morality of the characters presents less of a problem since, in his view, the Biblical writers do not intend "to glorify the family or to idealize the familial relations; the figures of the patriarchal history are neither heroes nor archetypes."[6] Rather, for the final redactor: "Conflict belongs to human life together in all of its realms."[7] Though this is a more sensitive response to the literary character of the text, the question still remains of how the actions which transpire are to be assimilated into a theological or ethical viewpoint. But neither the historical relativism of Gunkel nor the divine determinism of von Rad offers a satisfactory resolution to this problem. More suggestive are John Gammie's proposals for a "theology of strife" which includes "empathy for Israel's antagonists" and "theonomous self-criticism" which permits reconciliation between enemies.[8] The ambiguity of the personages which these proposals assume will receive support from the analysis to follow.

Typological analysis

The narrative context within which this story occurs is once again that of the transmission of the promise from one generation to the next. The Akeda, in dealing with this process, focused upon the problems which arise in the father/son relation which would prevent a successful transmission. The problem of sibling rivalry did not arise directly, since a hierarchy was established between the two sons of Abraham based on the status of their respective mothers. The rivalry was evidenced there between the mothers rather than between the sons. Now, however, the divinely selected wife, Rebekah, gives birth to non-identical twins thereby moving into center stage the rivalry of the brothers for the position of promise-bearer. (It was the assumption of the narrative in this phase that only one son could inherit the promise, though this was to change at the end of the Joseph story because of the transition into nationhood consisting of a confederation of equal tribes with brothers as eponymous ancestors.) So long as the choice could be made on the basis of the familial status of the mother, the decision was clear, although effecting it was painful, as the stories of Hagar and Sarai made clear. But the birth of twins to Rebekah meant that grounds for favoring one son above the other could not be so objectively determined. Even the law of primogeniture is reduced to the level of a technicality in the case of twins since the oldest has that status only by a matter of minutes. This enhances the possibility that the inheritance should be determined on the basis of the qualities of the sons themselves.

This situation opens the possibility for the narrator to begin to adopt a more traditional narrative style in which he can create, through attribution, fixed character types reflecting his own ideological viewpoint and allow the possession of these values to serve as the basis for the transmission of the promise. He thus can utilize the strategies of the representative narrator and at least partially assume the indirect mode in relation to his characters which accompanies that narrative function.

Such a characterization will draw the parents in to play their roles in the discrimination process. Whereas in the Abraham story the focus was upon the creation of discontinuity between the father and his "only" beloved son, a discontinuity which would be bridged only by the divine Word, now with two brothers competing for the patriarchal blessing (which is assumed to determine also who receives the divine promise), the focus will be upon the complex interplay of character features at the human level. Now the prize, the transmission of the blessing (promise) itself, will effectively occur at the human level between father and son rather than principally in a divine–human micro-dialogue. The direct competition for divine approval which led to conflict and murder in the Cain and Abel story will not be repeated here. The conflict will be worked out between the human characters upon the basis of the developing narrative ideology. The transmission of the promise by the divine Voice to the victor (28:10–17) will only confirm what has already become actual at the human level.

If the posture of the author, then, is that of the representative narrator who encloses his characters in a framework of attributes and ideas and engineers the plot so as to allow those characters representing his own values to triumph at the expense of his opponents, it would seem then that the symbolic strategies of the previous narrative have been put aside. That this is not entirely the case can be seen by examining the oracle with which the narrative begins.

The oracle is preceded by important introductory material given in the third-person discourse of the narrator:

And these are the descendants of Isaac, son of Abraham, Abraham begetting Isaac. Isaac son of Abraham was forty years old when he took to himself Rebekah, daughter of Bethuel the Aramean from Padan Aram, sister of Laban the Aramean, for a wife. And Isaac prayed to Yahweh on behalf of his wife because of her barreness, and Yahweh let himself be entreated by him, and Rebekah his wife conceived. But the children attacked one another within her, and she said, "If this must be, why must I be?" And she went forth to inquire of Yahweh.

25:19–22

The narrator begins by providing a framing statement which, in verse 19, resembles a genealogy, but in verses 20–21, moves on to recount the marriage of Isaac at the late age of 40, and the subsequent barrenness of his wife. Yahweh, uncharacteristically (compare chapters 15, 16), "let himself be entreated" by Isaac regarding this problem, and a pregnancy immediately ensues. In verse 22 we then encounter the conflict motif with the report that the children "attacked one another" in Rebekah's womb, giving rise to her lament: "If this must be, why must I be [live]?"[9] This completes the introduction of the four central characters of this drama and delineates the crucial position which Rebekah occupies. The conflict between the brothers is a given, a part of human existence which has no external causes, and the effect upon the mother is to make her despair of her very life. She now brings her vocal lament to the divine, and seeks an answer. The answer is given in direct speech:

> Two peoples are in your womb,
> and two nations from your womb shall be divided;
> and one of the peoples shall be strong;
> and the elder shall serve the younger. 25:23

This oracular response to Rebekah's lamenting question functions as a micro-dialogue which sets up the basic tensions of the plot to follow. But as a speech act with the form of a declaration rather than a promise, no "uptake" is required by its addressee. Instead the oracle functions to make Rebekah the central figure of this narrative by disclosing to her the divine foreknowledge (and the narrator's foreknowledge) of the end toward which the narrative is moving. The eventual subordination of the elder to the younger is not promised here, but declared. The form of the oracle, unlike the promise, does not reveal an uncertain future contingent upon the faith of the addressee. The tension is not generated by the conflict between faith and doubt, but by the question of how this predetermination of the future will be actualized.

It thus is not a question of Rebekah's faith in this oracle, but of how the events will transpire, and what role, if any, she will play in its fulfillment since this foreknowledge has been given to her. But a distinction is made in this divine utterance between the two brothers that overturns the natural order of succession which would give primacy to the older.[10] Since it is the father who upholds the law of primogeniture, this revelation to the mother implicitly pits her against the father to ensure the actualization of this oracle. To endow Rebekah with the motive to take this initiative, however, the narrator must provide us with a representation of her desire. But it is not until the final hour before the succession is to occur that she takes the initiative and acts, when it is clear that no other circumstances will intervene.

Thus the oracle, though closed in its structure, makes possible the continuation of the pattern by which the end of the narrative, known by the divine (and human narrator), is also known by the principal character. Here, however, such knowledge does not make possible the subordination of the narrative to the open dialogical process. The desire of the principal character is not taken up into this oracle, as it is in a promise, where it can be transmuted into faith. Rather, the openness of the story has come to expression in the semantics of the oracle with its disruption of the law of primogeniture, and in the related but independent plot of the mother to foster the success of the younger, "quiet," "smooth" son over the rough, robust, older (by a fraction) favorite of the father.

This narrative strategy thus provides a divine utterance in a micro-dialogue which sets in motion the events, while leaving its actualization up to what appear to be independent forces operating in the dynamics of the family related in the third-person narrative framework and the dialogue between the personages. Along the divine/human axis is the performative announcement to Rebekah that injects discontinuity into the natural order of succession. At the level of human communication the subsequent discourse is redolent with marital discord and the emotions of parental favoritism as motivating factors. Thus the story appears to have two motivating systems which have little to do with each other. If one takes the oracle as dominant then a case can be made for Rebekah's sainthood due to the sacrifices she makes in order to implement it.[11] If one takes her favoritism for Jacob and manipulation of her husband as the fundamental forces in this plot, then the harsh charges of betrayal and deceit which have been leveled at her in many commentaries become justified.[12] But it is in the friction between the performative speech of the divine oracle and the representation of the characters made in the narrative framework and its related direct discourse, that the narrative will retain a degree of semantic openness, and it is in this openness that the narrative preserves its symbolic character. Though the action at the level of the human characters achieves the closure of the representative narrative, the subjective source of the action is blurred by incorporating two explanations for the events, leaving the characters and their actions shrouded in ambiguity, and semantically undecidable, as the vascillation of the commentaries illustrates.

The larger symbolic strategy of the narrator can be seen in the way in which the issues of differentiation and conflict are treated here. Differentiation of brothers by divine preference we have encountered already in the story of Cain and Abel. But there the motive force was human aspiration toward unity with the divine expressed through sacrifice. The divine choice was a response to an initial human desire. Human conflict was shown to derive from the inability to live with the state of differentiation into which they had "fallen," with the divine playing a distant, arbitrary role.

Here there is acceptance of conflict as a given part of existence (from the womb to nations), and conflict rooted in difference is now being used by the divine Word to achieve a positive end: the disruption of the closed system of primogeniture. In the Cain and Abel story, God's preference for the sacrifice of the younger above that of the older led to the murder of the younger. Here, the issue will be resolved neither by direct divine intervention (the "election" of Jacob does not occur until after the rivalry for the blessing on the human level has been resolved) nor through brute force. The younger will triumph in such a way as to enable both to survive, and some form of reconciliation between them be achieved. It is as if the problem of sibling rivalry posed in the story of Cain and Abel is now being rethought and partially resolved from the viewpoint of the history of the promise. It is in the juxtaposing of the dynamics of the micro-dialogue against those of the representative narrative that the "active" standpoint of the narrator is disclosed, and that the symbolic/representative character of this narrative emerges.

The shaping of the protagonists begins with great force in the following verses depicting the birth of the twins.

> And her days were fulfilled to bring forth, and behold there were twins in her womb. And the first came forth completely clothed in a mantel of reddish hair, so they called his name Esau. And next his brother came out, his hand holding onto the heel of Esau, and his name was called Jacob. And Isaac was sixty years old when she bore them. 25:24–26

The narrator here departs from his customary reluctance to describe appearances, and depicts the older (first from the womb) as being "completely clothed in a mantel of reddish hair" (verse 25). To deepen closure his name is fixed on the basis of this appearance, although now only through synecdochic relation of the name Esau to the place names with which he was later associated, that is, Edom (reddish), and Seir (hairy). The color red is to enter again in the story as the color of the soup for which he traded his birthright. Red thus serves as a metaphor which renders the character of Esau as robust, vigorous, passionate (S. of S. 5:10; Num. 19:2; II Kgs 3:22), and perhaps unrestrained (sins are also red, Is. 1:18).[13]

The abundant hair on his body is also taken to be a sign of physical strength and masculinity as in the story of Sampson (Judg. 16:22). Solomon was also known for the thickness and abundance of his hair (II Sam. 14:26). Jacob later is somewhat ironically forced to characterize himself, in contrast to his "hairy" brother, as "smooth" (חָלָק), associated with hairlessness. This quality is used figuratively, however, to mean one who flatters, similar to the modern colloquial expression, a "smooth talker" (Prov. 5:3; 26:28; Ps. 12:3). Thus the rough, hairy Esau emerges as one who is direct of speech, though somewhat uncouth – a description which is exemplified by his behavior in the following scene.

The only qualifying description of the second child is that he came out holding onto the heel (*'āqēb* עָקֵב) of the first. From this is the name Jacob (*ya'āqōb* יַעֲקֹב) derived. This is also closely related to the verb *'āqab* (עָקַב) which literally means "to be high" or "hill-shaped" (hence heel), but figuratively means "to deceive" or "go behind one's heels" perhaps originally as in tracking or pursuing. Though the figurative meaning is not yet suggested here, later Esau (27:36) uses the verb in this sense as signifying the meaning of the name "Jacob." The action of grasping the heel thus provides the basis of a character trait which will later be explicitly tied to Jacob. His name is a synecdoche for his character.

The chronological note providing the age of Isaac with which this scene concludes makes it clear that Isaac had waited some twenty years after his marriage to Rebekah at the age of forty (25:20) for the birth of these sons.

Then follows in verses 27–28, a finely crafted narrative transition bridging the gap between birth and young manhood. (They are now *n*^{e}*'ārîym* (נְעָרִים) which provides a further sense of the contrasting traits of the two boys, and the alignment of parental affections which that produced.)

And the boys grew up, and Esau was a man knowing the chase, a man of the field, and Jacob was a quiet man, living among tents. 25:27

These semantic features are arranged along an axis of action, and an axis of space. Along the action axis we find the pair:

A man knowing of the chase (Esau) versus a quiet man (Jacob).

Along the axis of space we find:

a man of the field (Esau) versus (a man) inhabiting tents (Jacob).

The axis of action denotes not the acts themselves, but qualities of consciousness (or character) associated with their modes of existence. Esau "knows" the chase. He is a hunter and his mind reflects the aggressive, passionate, violent, unrestrained, and unlimited qualities required in the pursuit of game. Jacob, by contrast is a "quiet man" (אִישׁ תָּם), which in this story, Gunkel says, suggests not a moral, religious ideal as it later did, but the irreproachable, upright, orderly man who remains with the tents and herds.[14]

The axis of space places these brothers in their respective locales; the hunter in the fields, and the "quiet man" near the tents. Esau roams the wilds, while Jacob remains close to the domestic scene, the realm of the women. A composite picture thus emerges of the characters of these two personages. Esau is rough, passionate, untamed, aggressive, and masculine, while Jacob is smooth, controlled, domesticated, passive and associated with the feminine.

The affections of the parents are then drawn to different children, as the writer proceeds to recount. He does this in such a way, however, as to uncover the precise dynamics operative in each relationship.

And Isaac loved Esau, because of the venison (he put) in his mouth. But Rebekah loved Jacob. 25:28

Though the phrase, "venison in his mouth," is usually translated as "his taste for venison," it is good here to notice the literal exchange described. It is in return for the venison that Isaac gives his love. In this very economical fashion, eating is lifted out as a sign of a particular mode of subjective existence. Isaac is marked as the personage in this narrative who is governed by the compulsions of desire for certain physical gratifications as was the Pharaoh in Genesis 12. This suggests a thoroughly symbiotic relation between father and son based on the father's desire for venison. It is precisely this desire and the mechanism of exchange that it creates which will be seen later by Rebekah as Isaac's point of vulnerability. The scene which follows centers upon an event of eating which betrays the inner character of the personage. The climactic scene in the episode likewise focuses upon the "blindness" of desire manifested in an act of eating. This character trait places Isaac in the same semantic field with Esau. That love could be given in exchange for venison shows that Isaac places the highest value on the satisfaction of his physical, sensory needs, and thus shares something of Esau's passionate, aggressive nature.

In contrast, the writer says simply that "Rebekah loved [lit. was loving] Jacob." Though the association of Jacob with the domestic scene might suggest a similar, natural affinity between mother and son, none is mentioned. Rebekah's love for Jacob, while perhaps being influenced by affinity, is not driven by superficial symbiotic desires. It is unqualified. Thus the narrator now "tilts" in the direction of the values of the Rebekah/Jacob pair, and begins to set the stage for the conspiracy in chapter 27.

The action finally begins in verse 29 with the statement that "Jacob 'cooked up' a pot [of lentils]" (verse 29a).[15]

The verb *yāzēd* is very ambiguous here. Although its hiphil form is related to the root *zîyḍ* or *zûd* which it shares with the noun *n āzîyd* meaning "cooked dish" (used here with it in a word-play), it is never used elsewhere in the hiphil form to mean "cook." Rather it means to act presumptiously, or with willful forethought (Deut. 1:43; 18:20). In Exodus 21:14 it refers to the act of presumption, or premeditation behind a treacherous murder. These associations could scarcely have been absent from the mind of the ancient writer or reader. The meaning seems to be similar to the colloquial expression in English "to cook up" in the sense of to scheme, though is perhaps much stronger in its negative implications. The connotation here is that Jacob presumed upon the condition of Esau when he returned from the hunt, and so "cooked up" not only a "pot" but also a plot!

Then,

Esau came from the field, and he was exhausted, and Esau said to Jacob, "Please give me to gulp from the red, this red, for I am faint." Thus his name is called Edom. 25:29b–30

This is generally regarded by commentators as crude speech. The object desired is not even named, only its color, and that repeated twice in desperation. The verb *hal^e 'îytēnîy* (הַלְעִיטֵנִי)is unique to this passage and is probably related to a noun meaning jaw.[16] This deliberately stylized direct speech is an example of what Bakhtin calls "double-voiced" speech, that is, in these words we hear not only the voice of Esau, but also the voice of the narrator who is using these words to characterize or even caricature his personage.[17] This speech embodies the qualities of impulsive passion, roughness, and untamed directness which the narrative introduction has prepared us to expect from Esau.

In the hands of this narrator, however, this is not merely crude speech, but a synecdochic expression with figurative import. The narrator uses this synecdoche for the soup, "red," immediately for etymological purposes, metonymically connecting Esau's repetition of red, *'edôm*, with the tribal/place name physically associated with him, Edom. Thus "red" is not merely a synecdoche for the soup, but through the metonymic place name becomes a metaphor for Esau himself. It "names" him in the sense of metaphorically associating his character through the place name of his region with the crude, desperate call for food, and more generally, with impulsive desire. To have derived the name merely from the earlier reference to his red color at birth would have been less damning, and thus less suited to the narrator's purposes.

Jacob then responds to the desperate vulnerability of his brother with the presumptuous proposition: "Sell now your birthright to me" (verse 31), to which Esau responds: "Behold, I am about to die, what is this to me – a birthright?" (verse 32).

Just as Esau found it difficult to name the red pottage, so here the separation of the deictic pronoun from the noun, with the noun added on at the end, indicates the extent to which the "idea" of the birthright is as hard for Esau to express as the "idea" of the pottage when his material desire is in the presence of its object.

Jacob then reveals his "quiet" (controlled, calculating) mind all the more clearly by requiring Esau, before giving him the food, to take an oath to support his declaration. The narrator then reports, not the words of Esau's oath, but their meaning.

And Jacob said, "Swear to me on this day." And he sold his birthright to Jacob, and Jacob gave bread to Esau, and a dish of cooked lentils. 25:33–34a

This referent-analyzing (Voloshinov/Bakhtin)[18] form of indirect speech interprets the oath to signify that Esau "sold" his birthright. In exchange for the birthright – a "mere" word – Jacob gives a "dish of cooked lentils" and even bread to go along with it. Then follows a series of abrupt verbs without objects:

He ate, and he drank, and he rose up, and he left. 25:34b

This style suggests the brutal simplicity of Esau's material urges which provides a basis for the following concluding interpretation: "and he despised his birthright" (verse 34b).

Nowhere has the narrator's economical style been used with more telling effect in painting the character of a personage through an account of his words and actions. The last phrase is the thematic summation of the entire story, giving it closure and structural integrity. The despising (or mocking) of the birthright to satisfy his immediate desire indicates that the intersubjective (verbal) bond that links the generations has been broken by Esau. Transgressive eating is a sign of the same desire-driven mode of subjectivity in this narrative that appeared in the story of the Garden of Eden.

The strategy that Jacob has used here upon Esau is a mirror image of the technique by which Esau himself related to his father. Just as Esau gets what he wants from Isaac through the preparation of a desired dish of venison, so now Jacob will use a pot of lentils to gain what he wants from Esau. Unlike Esau, however, for whom such action is a natural part of his character, for Jacob it is a conscious, premeditated plot. The same strategy will then be used by Rebekah against Isaac in the next scene.

The narrator has thus presented the reader for the first time in the book of Genesis with pair of opposing characters with fully developed traits fixed from birth. The source of the primal conflict between them is the implicit speech act which hovers like a fate from the past, and a future destiny: the law of primogeniture. The birth of twin sons, one born only seconds before the other, highlights the arbitrariness of the law. Posed against this implicit law is the performative utterance of the divine oracle which declares that the younger will triumph over the older. The narrator will not leave that triumph up to chance, however. He must endow the opponent brothers with traits, and show how one set of traits attains the victory. In this conflict of character traits, the passive qualities triumph over the active qualities. The narrator seeks to show the paradoxical vulnerability and weakness of the strong, and the strength of the apparently weak. This is the proairetic code of this narrative.

This choice of traits to support is consistent with the premise of the preceding Abraham narrative (the norm). The future is disclosed by the divine

Word of promise, and it is through faith in that Word that human desires will be realized. The human role is to wait with faith, and to avoid the dependence upon force and other systems of necessity to gain those ends. When the narrator thus comes to present characters who must act before the transmission of the promise, and when their action must arise out of their character traits rather than their encounter with the divine Word, he must favor a set of traits which are somewhat consistent with the deeper values implicit in the earlier narratives. These are traits on the passive side of the spectrum, which involve the use of the mind to take advantage of the opponents who are driven by force and blind desire. Cunning and even lying thus have their role to play in the victory of the weaker, passive characters who suffer disadvantage due to superior power of the opponent, and various cultural or biological systems of necessity (such as the law of primogeniture here). It is here that the courageous realism of the Biblical narrators transcends pious legalism in the interest of a deeper moral vision.

In this reliance upon predetermined character traits as the motivating force of the characters' action, however, the writer is moving into the structural field of the representative narrative. It retains its overall symbolic character only in the semantic tension which remains between the illocutionary force of the oracle, and the developing representative system of character traits and desires as competing explanations of the unfolding events.

When Esau was forty years old, he took a wife, Judith, daughter of Beeri the Hittite, and Basemath, daughter of Elon the Hittite. They brought a bitter spirit to Isaac and Rebekah."

26:34–35

The report of the marriage of Esau which comes at the conclusion of the collection of Isaac stories in 26:34–35 is generally regarded as a Priestly addition which lays the foundation for the second plan of Rebekah to have Jacob leave the household to escape Esau's wrath in 27:46. Esau is cited as being of the same age as his father at the time of his marriage, that is, 40 (26:34a), but, unlike his father, he chooses wives for himself from among the people of the land with whom there are no familial connections (Hittites). This genealogical note thus is far from being semantically neutral in the ongoing plot. Lest the reader miss the significance of these actions, the narrator tells us that "they [the wives] were a bitter spirit to Isaac and Rebekah." These marriages outside of the family with no parental consent further support the previous characterization of Esau as having no regard for the customs and laws which preserve the continuity of the familial traditions. To choose not one but two wives from among the nearby people, rather than following the more difficult course of obtaining a wife from the distant family, signifies again that Esau places immediate gratification above the more abstract cultural and spiritual values of the family. Thus both Isaac and Rebekah are united in their disapproval of Esau's wives, though they make no direct criticism of Esau for his action.

The function which this report serves in this context is to provide the immediate, negative motivation for Rebekah to act in the next scene. It is not only her love for Jacob which is behind her desire to obtain the blessing and promise for Jacob. Esau's improper marriages finally place him beyond the pale. It also provides the basis for Isaac's willingness to accept Jacob after he learns of the deception.

And it came about that Isaac was old and his eyes were dim from seeing. And he called Esau his oldest [lit. largest] son, and he said to him, "My son." And he said to him, "I am here." And he said, "Look now, I am old and I do not know when I will die. Please pick up your weapons, now, take up your quiver and your bow, and go out to the field and hunt game for me, and make for me the savory food which I love, and bring it here to me, and I will eat it, since my soul will bless you before I die." 27:1–3

The narrator sets up the temporal conditions for the development of the plot with his report at the outset that Isaac was old. The plan to transmit his blessing to Esau arises from the anticipation of his imminent death. An atmosphere of crucial finality thus hangs over this entire narrative like an impending storm (in spite of the fact that Isaac does not actually die until Jacob's return after his long sojourn in Paddam-aram, 35:29, suggesting an independent origin for this story outside of its present context).

The physical conditions assumed for the development of the plot are provided by the report that Isaac's eyesight was failing. This presents the possibility that he might be deceived as to the identity of the person he was actually blessing. In reporting this, and thereby suggesting this possibility, the narrator is also characterizing Isaac as one who relies primarily upon his sight rather than his hearing.

The phrase, "which I love," also embodies a character trait of Isaac. His desire for this particular dish reflects the symbiotic, materialistic dynamics of his personality. His relation to Esau, and thereby Esau's own identity and meaning for Isaac, have come to be mediated, not by language, but by the vocation of hunting and its products. In his instructions to Esau, he recounts, unnecessarily, and with obvious admiration, the implements of the hunt ("take up your weapons, your quiver, and your bow, and go forth to the field"). The "savory dish" is thus the quintessence of the hunt and the embodiment of the materialist, violent, desire-driven mentality that goes with it. Once his eyesight has gone, Isaac is doubly blinded by his desire for this food and by the mentality which was bound up with the hunt. In exchange for one last, evanescent taste of his precious venison stew, Isaac is about to bestow the eternal blessing. This is his vulnerability. What sexual lust is to the Pharaoh in Genesis 12, the taste of the hunt is to Isaac.

Rebekah, in contrast, makes her plans and decisions on the basis of what she hears, or rather "overhears" (she literally "listens in", שֹׁמַעַת בּ׳).

And Rebekah was listening in on the conversation of Isaac with his son Esau. And Esau went out to the field to hunt game to bring. 27:5a

The narrator presents the reader with two alienated spheres of discourse, that of Rebekah/Jacob, and that of Isaac/Esau. It is the function of the narrator to mediate between these worlds of discourse. Like the narrator, however, Rebekah has access to both through overhearing what is said by the other pair, and she takes over the mediating function. Through these words which disclose Isaac's plans and intentions, she is able to plot her own moves to thwart them, just as Abraham in chapter 12 anticipated the words of the Egyptians, and could make his plans accordingly. Both live out of the future disclosed to them by the secret voices of others. By sharing the narrator's privileged access to separate spheres of discourse, Abraham and Rebekah are able to take over the role of the narrator and create fictions of their own.

The crisis has thus been reached between the two contending perspectives. On the one hand is the desire-driven mentality of visually oriented, but blind Isaac who by elevating Esau will establish the link between the generations on the basis of primogeniture, the violent adventure of the hunt, and the taste of venison stew. On the other is the aural mentality of Rebekah, who nourishes the memory of the oracle which overturned primogeniture and loves her quiet, clever son who thinks before he acts. Two sets of character traits are thus juxtaposed in contention, and the scene of conflict through the conspiracy and deception which follow will affirm the one and negate the other. But neither is totally affirmed or totally negated, and it is in this internal ambiguity and friction between relative values that the complex symbolic perspective of the narrator will be preserved. In the scenes to follow, however, the narrative descends into the murky system of domestic passions and is able to portray them with almost brutal realism. Here we find life in its poignant uniqueness and not idealized types held up as examples of moral heroism. It is the struggle of this particular family with the force of destiny and the conflict of relative values that is the source of its universal appeal. Rebekah is now the focal point of this struggle, and it is she who must resolve it – and, like Abraham, be compromised by it.

After his initial characterization of Isaac, there is little description in the narrative framework throughout the remainder of this narrative beyond statements which recount the actualizations of Rebekah's plans. Rather, direct discourse now provides the motive force for the events. This discourse is characterized by abundant examples of ellipsis and condensation which arise from an underlying division between the speakable and the unspeakable. While these dynamics are characteristic of expressive narratives, the forces beneath the discourse have been revealed to the reader in the previous narrative framework, and in the earlier oracular utterance, as well as in the division which now fissures the world of familial discourse (as the world of discourse was divided in Gen. 12:10ff.). Thus features of both representative and expressive narration are subtly combined and subordinated to the dynamics of the symbolic narrative set in motion by the oracle.

What Rebekah discovers in her surreptitious listening are two crucial pieces of information, that is, the mechanism of exchange which will bring forth the utterance of the blessing, and the span of time before the fateful event occurs. Isaac thinks that he is upon his deathbed and is asking Esau to play the role that he has played many times in the past and that which brings pleasure to his father. Now, however, in return for Esau's success as a hunter (which role Isaac seems to delight in describing), and as a cook in the preparation of "savory food which I love", he is to give Esau his patriarchal blessing.

The critical conflict between the oracular disclosure of the future, and the system of primogeniture has now been reached. No circumstances have intervened to change the "natural" course of events, and the only circumstance remaining which may enter into the service of the oracular perspective is the desire of Rebekah. With no further hesitation Rebekah's desire, disclosed previously by the narrator's statement of her "love" for Jacob, propels her into action. But if she is to circumvent Isaac's plan, at least two capabilities are necessary: the capability of finding a substitute animal and of preparing a "savory dish" as good as Esau's. With this basis we can now examine a revealing dialogue which occurs between mother and son.

The narrator's report that Esau "went toward the field for his father to hunt some game to bring" (verse 5) gives Rebekah time to act. She summons Jacob, reports to him the contents of the conversation, and "commands" (מְצַוָּה) him to participate in a plot to deceive his father. No reasoning is given by her to justify this action, or to persuade Jacob to cooperate. The bond between the two is suggested by the way in which she selectively reports the conversation, and phrases the conspiratorial plot. Whereas Isaac says:

> Now please take up your weapons, your quiver, and your bow, and go forth to the field, and hunt game for me and make savory food which I love, and bring it here to me, and my soul will bless you before I die. 27:3–4

Through ellipsis and condensation Rebekah reduces this to:

> Bring to me game, and make for me savory food, and I will eat it, and I will bless you before Yahweh, before my death. 27:7

Rebekah, though citing Isaac's words in direct discourse, has elided all mention of Esau's hunting, one of the painful differences between himself and Esau which has attracted Isaac's affections. This omission is a sign of the covert bond between mother and son which suppresses reminders of that which estranges Jacob from his father, and in so doing signals the intimacy between mother and son. She also elides the phrase, "which I love" at this point, only to include it later. To repeat this phrase in its original context would reawaken too strongly the genuine feelings of Isaac which she is callously disregarding. To save this reference to the end of the conspiratorial proposal reverses the effect as we shall see.

She then puts forth her plot to Jacob in the strongest terms:

> And now my son, listen to my *voice* with which I am commanding you. Go please, to the flock, and take for me from there two good goat kids, and I will make them into a savory dish for your father, *like he loved.* 27:8–9

The displacement of the phrase, "like I love," to the end of Rebekah's proposition, and its transformation into third-person speech, inverts its effect. Not only does it not evoke Isaac's feelings, but it now becomes a keystone to the plot to deceive him. It now connotes Rebekah's certainty that she can prepare a "savory dish" out of kids from the flock that is indistinguishable from that prepared by Esau. The phrase reflects a cynicism about Isaac's passion for this special dish that only Esau could prepare to please him. Beneath this is the wife's suppressed resentment through the years that the husband was more pleased with the son's "savory dish" than with anything she could prepare. Now, in a perfect act of revenge, she will prove that she can make this dish so that it is indistinguishable from Esau's, and in so doing, replace Esau with her favorite as the recipient of the blessing. This phrase, as the keystone in the conspiracy, thus appeals to Jacob's love and confidence in his mother's ability to deceive Isaac, thereby inverting its original evocative power.

The blunting of the personal dimension of Isaac's words is also seen in Rebekah's recasting of the phrase "my soul will bless you before I die," to simply, "I will bless you before my death." "My soul" suggests the sacred totality of his being more forcefully than the simple first-person verbal prefix. "My death" objectifies death more than the verb "I die."

The addition of the phrase, "before Yahweh" has long puzzled commentators. Since it parallels "before I die", it is unlikely that it is a later addition. Rather, it would have the effect upon Jacob (for whom this summary has been carefully edited by Rebekah) of emphasizing the sacred finality of what is about to happen.

But Rebekah, in her enthusiasm for her culinary deception, has not thought about the other sensory signs by which Isaac identifies Esau. Recalling the narrator's description of the infants at birth, Jacob, rather than offering an objection to the plot as such, points out its weakness in its failure to consider the physical differences between the two sons. In so doing, however, his language becomes, ironically, double-voiced. He must remind his mother that: "My brother is a hairy man, and I am hairless [smooth]" (verse 11).

His collaboration with this conspiracy has thus forced Jacob, in the very first act, to describe himself in his own words as he fictively foresees himself in the forthcoming drama, as "smooth" (or in contemporary idiom "slick"), which figuratively means deceptive. He thus, ironically, is trapped into speaking of himself as a deceiver (a "slicker") in the very first act of his deception.

The ironic voice of the narrator may further be heard in the following statement of Jacob:

> If my father touches me, I will be in his eyes, as one who has lost his mind,[19] and I will bring upon myself a curse, and not a blessing.

The estrangement of father and son will be so great in the process of 27:12
this deception that one simple fatherly touch will disclose all and bring upon Jacob the opposite of what he desires.

Rebekah then hastily reassures Jacob by declaring her willingness to bear the full brunt of any reprisal by Isaac in the event of discovery, and hurries him away to get the kids. Here the time factor is shaping the discourse, since she mentions nothing of her plan to eliminate the problem which Jacob has raised: "only [אַךְ] listen to my voice, and go get them for me" (verse 13). The time for talk is over. Now there must be action.

Action requires third-person discourse, and so follows an extended description now of how the conspirators work out their plot. First comes the report of Jacob's obedience, depicted in a succession of short verb phrases reminiscent of the description of Esau's acton in 25:34. The narrator does not offer further comment on the inner feelings of the characters, but confines himself to pure action. The repeated reference to the familial relations (his mother, her son) conveys a subtle irony in light of the conspiratorial actions in which the mother and son are engaged: "And he went and he took and brought to his mother" (verse 14a).

What is described next is a clever set of stage props designed to fool the blind.

> And his mother prepared a savory dish like his father loved. And Rebekah took the most valued clothing of her eldest son Esau, which was with her in the house, and she clothed Jacob, her youngest son. And with skins of the little goat she clothed his hands and the smoothness of his neck. And she gave the savory dish, and bread which she had made into the hand of Jacob her son.
> 27:16–17

The "savory dish like his father loved" is the premier mimetic device. This phrase began in the mouth of Isaac, then was taken up ironically into the speech of Rebekah, and now the narrator repeats it, summarizing and concluding the action of the conspiracy and merging his own ironic perspective with that of

Rebekah. This "dish" is now coded, and the reference is Isaac's weakness for this meat, his vulnerability.

To answer Jacob's concern, she also takes some of Esau's valued clothing she still possesses (after his marriage?), and the skin of the young goat (from which she has prepared the stew?) and clothes Jacob with them, covering his hands and the skin upon the "*smoothness* of his neck" (verse 16). Clothing is virtually never mentioned by the narrator except where it serves as a sign of a hidden inner state, or serves to deceive. Adam and Eve clothe themselves to hide their shame, and are clothed upon leaving the garden as a sign of their permanently alienated state of existence. Joseph's robe expresses the covert favoritism of Jacob (37: 3–4), and is used later by his brothers to deceive Jacob (38:31–33). Potiphar's wife uses a robe of Joseph as the basis of her false charges against him (39:13, 15). Tamar dons the garb of a prostitute to work her will upon Jacob (38:14–15). Clothing is thus a reflection of the divided nature of corporeal existence. It conceals and reveals in the continuous interplay of intentional deception and unintentional disclosure that is characteristic of the fragmented world "east of Eden." Clothing is never mentioned as an act of simple description.

Jacob thus goes forth, dish in hand, a strange, mimetic apparition (not lost upon artists through the ages) representing the objects of the blind Isaac's sensory affections, a lure designed to play upon his sensory desires, his second blindness.

It is here that certain important parallels between this narrative and Genesis 12:10–20 begin to appear. In Genesis 12 the scene of the deception itself has been elided and emphasis given to the encounter between Pharaoh and Abram after the discovery of the deception – a scene which does not occur in this narrative.

But both narratives are structured around an underlying, implicit illocutionary event. For Genesis 12 it was the law that punishment would follow the abduction of a man's wife. Upon the basis of this certainty, the plot could involve falsifying Sarai's identity so that she would be taken into the Pharaoh's harem. The falsification of her identity would not effect the operation of the law of punishment, so that she would be freed when the punishment began, and the truth of her identity discovered. So too here there is an underlying assumption about an illocutionary event which operates regardless of the lies which may be involved. The assumption is that the transmission of the blessing from the father will be effective regardless of whether it is transmitted to the person he intends or another.[20] Because of this the possibility exists of substituting the younger favorite of the mother for the older favorite of the father. In this way the promise may be obtained by assuming a false identity in the same way that Abram obtained protection and wealth from the Pharaoh by the lie regarding the identity of Sarai.

But not only is the recipient of this blessing disguised. The giver of the blessing is also not who it appears to be. Though the words emanate from the mouth of Isaac, in reality, the effective line of communication that ends with Jacob originates with Rebekah. Isaac here is simply the vocal instrument through which Rebekah speaks. Behind Rebekah, however, is the divine oracle which forecast that "the elder shall serve the younger." Isaac is the unknowing character in a fiction Rebekah has created to make possible the fulfillment of the birth oracle, as well as her own desires.

The fiction she has created has posed two worlds of values in conflict: the man of the hunt verses the quiet man; and, ultimately, desire-driven consciousness versus faith consciousness. The transmission of the promise was about to take place on the basis of a unity between the generations existing at the physical, symbiotic level. Such a relation would violate the premise that the promise makes its own way through the generations to those who wait in confidence for the fulfillment. Rebekah, by constructing a fiction which takes advantage of Isaac's vulnerability to symbiotic relations, effects the transmissions of the blessing to the son who waits, thinks, plans, schemes; the son who embodies virtues more consonant (though certainly not identical) with faith in the divine Word, than are the desire-driven compulsions of Esau. Rebekah's fiction thus is covertly (unconsciously?) in the service of truth as disclosed to her originally in the oracle. The ambiguous role forced upon Rebekah by the declaratory form of the oracle (since the oracle declares what is to be without specifically calling Rebekah to play a role in its actualization, she must appear to act out of desire rather than faith) doubtless reflects the subordinate position of women in this religious tradition even while the narrative is affirming a woman as the intelligent protagonist and instrument of the divine will.[21] In this way not only are the conventions of primogeniture indirectly but scathingly criticized, but the absolute authority of this doubly blind male patriarch is undermined as well.

Then follows one of the most painful extended dialogues in the Biblical corpus. Though old, weak, and dim of eye, and given to his material affections, Isaac is not easily deceived. Every preparation is needed including the willingness to lie directly. The procedure which structures this encounter is a three-part ritual. The first part consists of identification of the party to receive the blessing, the second is a celebratory meal, and the third is bodily touching which can take the form of an embrace or a kiss.[22] Here all three become occasions for deception.

The natural exchange of greetings becomes the first crisis since Jacob's address, "My father," provokes the difficult question, "Who are you my son?" (verse 18). Such difficult initial questions have been found in other dialogues such as when God asks Adam, "Where are you?" and Cain, "Where is your brother?" The answer leads immediately to the heart of the issue at stake. Here it is Jacob's false identity. He can then only lie: "I am Esau, your firstborn" (verse 19a).

He then continues quickly with the plot:

> I have done as you said. Rise up, please, sit, and eat from my game. Then your soul will bless me. 27:19b

Esau repeats almost the identical words when he appears in verse 31. Time again intervenes to disturb the plot, however. Jacob has had to appear sooner than the hunt normally takes. Alert to this, Isaac is thus surprised: "How is this that you have found something so quickly my son?" (verse 20a). Not prepared in advance for this question, Jacob takes recourse to religion to end that line of questioning by saying: "Because Yahweh *your God* caused it to chance before me?" (verse 20b).

For the narrator to place a reference to an act of Yahweh in the mouth of Jacob as a part of his deception shows a remarkable secularity for an ancient writer, as well as a willingness to present the protagonist of the story in an extraordinarily realistic light.

Isaac is not content, however, and tells Jacob:

> Come near, please, and let me feel you, my son. Are you indeed my son Esau or not? 27:21

Now his doubt is directly expressed. Isaac poses his dilemma precisely after feeling Jacob, as he strangely says to no one in particular, recounting in the third-person the empirical facts confronting him:

> And Jacob came near to Isaac, his father, and he felt him, and he said, "The voice is the voice of Jacob, but the hands are the hands of Esau." 27:22

The narrator then interjects an unusual description of Isaac's non-verbal response to make clear that, in spite of this ambiguity:

> He did not recognize him, since his hands were like the hands of Esau, his hairy brother, and he blessed him. 27:23

This is to say that the plot had worked as anticipated. Isaac places more confidence in what he feels than in what he hears. This is consonant with the characterization of Isaac which the narrator has been developing. He is one who lived primarily by the visual (and now tactile) rather than the auditory sense. For one who lives primarily by hearing rather than by seeing, the voice of a person would be the final sign of his identity. Since disguising the voice is extremely difficult in this context (and was not successful if attempted), the success of the plot hangs upon Isaac's final reliance upon the deceptive tactile sense data which is being given him to establish Esau's identity. The issue is clearly stated when Isaac observes that the auditory sense tells him that it is Jacob's voice, but the tactile sense indicates that the hands are those of Esau.

But supported by Jacob's lie, which contradicts his auditory sense, he accepts the evidence of his visual/tactile sense as more valid.

This also marks the turning point in the dialogue and signals the beginning of the relaxation of the tension. The reference to the blessing in the third-person is strange since the actual blessing follows the final dialogue, and may indicate an editorial seam in the text.[23] It stands at the turning point in the dialogue, however, and serves to foreshadow the actual pronouncement of the blessing which follows.

But in light of the transition in verse 23, the additional comments of Isaac which follow appear as a sudden resurgence of doubt before the actual pronunciation of the blessing. He is still not completely satisfied, and tentatively poses the question a final time, thereby requiring Jacob to lie explicitly twice:

"You are actually my son Esau?" And Jacob said, "I am." 27:24

Now he instructs him to bring the savory dish of game in preparation for the blessing. But it seems that doubts still linger. The dish may, after all, not be as convincing as Rebekah has hoped. After he eats the desired dish and drinks some previously unmentioned wine, he again calls Jacob near to kiss him, the most intimate act thus far. And in this close proximity he smells the clothing of Esau, and his doubts seem finally to vanish as he says:

See, the smell of my son is as the scent of the field which Yahweh has especially blessed. 27:27

The use of the verb "see" by the blind Isaac accurately points to the replacement of his sight by the olfactory sense as the final basis for his decision. As Gunkel poignantly says, "with the scent he bestows the future of his son."[24] Even now, however, he omits mention of the name of Esau from his blessing, in contrast to the repeated reference to the names of the recipients in the blessing of Jacob (Gen. 49:3–27).

There follows then, in this moment of pathetic, illusioned intimacy, the long desired blessing in a series of rhythmic, poetic statements with illocutionary force. For the purposes of the plot, the most important is the last:

Be lord over your brothers, and they will bow down to you. 27:29

The narrator then returns to report the hasty exit of Jacob, just in time for the entrance of Esau from the hunt, game in hand. Such tight delimitation of his scenes within the constraints of time is further indication of the narrator's careful structuring of this narrative around a closed framework.

Esau then enters Isaac's presence with his savory dish, repeating now the words which Jacob has already uttered to his father. Isaac asked the same question, but now with a new urgency: "Who are you?" When Esau answers, the narrator reports that

Isaac trembled with an exceedingly great trembling and said, "Who then is he who was hunting game, and he brought it to me, and I ate it all before you came?" 27:33

In recording Isaac's physical reaction to his deception, the narrator incorporates within his semantic framework the violent dimension of this verbal manipulation to which he has been subjected. Isaac has not been overpowered by an opponent, but he has been "undermined" by an intimate member of the family, and he is physically shaken. A similar physical reaction has been reported by the narrator to the experiences of dismay and disillusionment when narcissistic, desire-driven actions produce unexpected consequences, for example, after the eating of the fruit by Adam and Eve (3:7), and the disregarding of Cain's sacrifice (4:5).

The rhetorical question he then poses reflects the pathetic disillusionment by which he is now engulfed as the reality of what has occurred rushes into his consciousness. In this utterance, the reader is drawn into Isaac's experience, where the two previously separate realms are flowing together, and experiences with him the new reality which has emerged from it. The reality is not only that Jacob has the blessing, but that the blessing has been obtained at the cost of disillusionment of his old, failing father. In the collision of Isaac's materialistic vulnerabilities with Rebekah's and Jacob's cleverness, occasioned by the imminent transition of the generations, the anguish and moral ambiguity at the core of historic existence is tangibly conveyed.

This is the moment of "defamiliarization" in this narrative structure which moves the reader by its complex, ambiguous vision of human reality. If the central strategy of the plots of both Genesis 12:10–20 and this story is deception through false identity, then the denouement of both is the moment of disillusionment of the antagonist. A rhetorical question posed by the antagonists in both registers this experience. For the deceived Pharaoh it is the unanswerable question posed to Abraham, "Why did you say, 'She is my sister?'" which embodied his anger while it brought close to the surface the disclosure of his hidden sexual practices. For Isaac it is the pathetic question, "Who then is he who was hunting game, and he brought it to me, and I ate it all before you came?" This question, ostensibly directed to Esau, is actually directed to those who had deceived him, and perhaps even to himself as the deceived who knows the answer even as he asks the question. At some deeper level he knew it was the voice of Jacob (and does not name Esau explicitly in the blessing). In these questions, the world hidden to the deceived rushes into consciousness, overturning the previous order and revealing to him a new state of affairs. Since the deception was in each case at least partly due to patterns of behavior of the deceived personages, this moment of disillusionment contains the potentiality of a new self-revelation. But it is lost for both Isaac and the Pharaoh in anger or self-pity.

The oracle has been fulfilled, the discontinuity in the law of primogeniture has been achieved; but for the reader there are no heroes. Nevertheless, due to the representative narrative framework, cleverness and intelligence have been affirmed as qualities more compatible with the free movement of the divine Word than are narcissitic desire and rigid cultural systems that serve only the indulgent, symbiotic interests of the powerful men who control them.

Similar interrogations which provoke disillusionment are at the center of the narratives of Adam and Eve, as well as Cain and Abel. In these narratives, however, questions are posed to the deceiver, and it is the deceiver whose illusions are destroyed by the answer he gives, Adam saying, "I was afraid because I was naked," and Cain asking, "Am I my brother's watcher?" But why has the evaluation of the roles of the deceiver and deceived been reversed?

In contrast to the earlier stories from the primeval history where desire was radically juxtaposed to the divine Word (prohibition) and deception served narcissistic goals, the promise with its legitimate mediation and discipline of desire through lengthy deferral has rendered the situation more complex and ambiguous. Deception and desire may now have positive roles to play so long as they are subservient to the contingency of the promissory Word and faith, rather than serving the interest of symbiotic personal behavior and structures of power. The "plot" here against primogeniture offers a prime example of this. Through this deception, which takes advantage of Isaac's subservience to desire, he is trapped into pronouncing the blessing upon the younger son in contradiction to his own wishes. Desire is manipulated to defeat itself, and to open a closed system. The legitimating force behind this conspiracy is the contingent oracular word to Rebekah.[25]

Upon hearing Isaac's affirmation of the irrevocability of the blessing, Esau "cried out a great and exceedingly bitter cry" (verse 34). The narrator here interprets for us the new mode of being into which Esau is thrown by the words of his father, that is, bitterness and helplessness. The strength and confidence which the relation with his father had provided him is now drawn away from him by this announcement. Esau's position is not unlike that of Saul after Samuel had taken the kingship from him and bestowed it upon David, and his reaction also resembles that of Saul in its pathos. The being of the Biblical protagonists is founded upon powerful illocutionary acts which establish their positions within the social order. Deprived of that word, Esau is reduced to illusionary thinking and pleading. He first refuses to face the finality of this act and asks his father, "Bless me *also* (גַּם־אָנִי) my father", assuming futilely that the blessing can be bestowed twice. Isaac now must explain the obvious: that the blessing that was his has been given to his deceitful brother. There was only one.

It is this moment of conscious disillusionment which determines the outcome, since it is in this moment that the antagonist (and the reader) realizes that nothing can be done to change what the deception has wrought. The Pharaoh at this point in the previous narrative cannot pursue his interrogation of Abram and realizes that there is nothing he can do but to send Abram and Sarai on their way quickly. Similarly Isaac follows his question with the statement, "I blessed him, and also blessed he will be." With this he submits to the irrevocable nature of what has occurred. But unlike the Pharaoh, who confronts his deceiver with his disillusionment, Isaac, old and blind, says nothing, and the next scene portrays him giving the deceiver a further promissory blessing. His failure to confront his deceivers, like the Pharaoh's unwillingness to pursue his question with Abram, is a sign of Isaac's inner acquiescence to the rightness of the outcome. Perhaps it also implies his awareness of the hidden dynamics that led to this outcome which might just as well be left hidden.

These words evoke from Esau a bitter question which alludes to the figurative meaning of the stem עָקַב , "to deceive," from which the name Jacob was taken: "Is not his name thus called Jacob?" This "definition" of the name and character of Jacob as a deceiver signals a break in the Jacob–Esau relation which anticipates the death-threat which follows. In a statement, the pathos of which is emphasized by its elegant parallelism,[26] Esau refers back to the initial scene when Jacob "took" (not bought) his birthright from him, as well as to what has just transpired.

> My birthright (b^{e}kōrātîy) he took,
> And look,
> Now he has taken my blessing (bir^{e}kātîy). 27:36

Having so characterized his brother to the sympathetic ears of Isaac, he then pursues a final possibility, "Have you not withheld a blessing for me?" as if Isaac saved some portion of his power, an unspent excess which still might be available. But Isaac dashes all hope, driving home the central point which could not be altered:

> Lo, a lord have I made him over you, and all his brothers; I have given to him servants, and bread, and new wine; I have sustained him. Come now, what will I do my son? 27:37

By showing him Jacob's new superior social authority and the material wealth which comes with it, he graphically illustrates to Esau that there is nothing left to give him.

In one more last desperate attempt, Esau throws aside all dignity, and even righteous anger, and makes a halting, childlike plea:

> One blessing, my father? Bless me, also me, my father!

The repetition of "my father" and "me" in these phrases conveys the pathos of this twist of fate that has cut Esau out of the rewards of his personal bond with Isaac. Reflected here is naked pleading, based on the nostalgic yearning for that which has been irrevocably lost. To fall into this mode of futile, desperate pleading again resembles the fate of Saul (I Sam. 28: 15–16). Here the LXX includes a narrator's comment that is totally in keeping with the logic of this dialogue, but which is found in no other Hebrew manuscript, "And Isaac was silent." E. A. Speiser believes that this phrase is too significant to have been added by the translators, and cites Leviticus 10:3 where a similar phrase occurs in another dialogue.[27] The final touch on the narrator's portrait of a broken Esau is his report that he "lifted up his voice and wept," perhaps in response to Isaac's silence.

This last act of abject desolation by Esau (reminiscent of Cain's last plea) finally brings a substantive response from his father. But the words which follow, rather than being a blessing, resemble more the parting words given to Cain by God. Their aim is negative, that is, to prevent the destruction of Esau by his more powerful brother:

> By your sword you will live,
> and your brothers you will serve,
> but it will be that you will break loose,[28]
> and you shall break his yoke from your neck. 27:39–40

The narrator next provides us with a plain interpretive statement of Esau's summary reaction to the previous scene:

> Esau hated Jacob because of the blessing with which his father blessed him. 27:41

But he goes further to tell us what Esau says "in his heart" in the form of quoted internal monologue. This rare device of providing a report of the internal discourse of the character is used when it is necessary for a character to formulate words for which there is no appropriate addressee – either because they are conspiratorial in nature, as is the case here, or because they contain interpretive material directed more to the reader than to a character (for example, Gen. 8:21). In either case, the perspectives of the author and of the character coincide in such moments, since these inner words always disclose the future of the plot which only the character and the narrator know. Unlike the divine/human micro-dialogue, in which the inner speech of the character is opened toward the discipline of dialogical intersubjectivity, the self-enclosed speech of a human character to himself (usually about another character) tends to arise from the dynamics of undisciplined desire. (See Eve's inner thought in 3:6, the collective conspiracies in 11:3 and 37:19.) This is why the writer of Genesis 6:5 could conclude that, from the divine viewpoint, "every imagination of the thoughts of his [the human] heart was only evil continually." So here Esau perfectly exemplifies this type of inner thought: "The days of mourning of my father are approaching, and afterward I will slay my brother Jacob'' (verse 41). His thought arises out of a passion for vengeance, undisciplined by either an encounter with the divine or authentic social discourse. The narrator's portrayal of Esau's spontaneous inner thought thus arises out of his fundamental presuppositions regarding the human heart.

This plan brings the family of Isaac to the threshhold of dissolution. The death of Isaac followed by the murder of Jacob by Esau would cause the history of the promise to be consumed by the same passion of jealous rivalry which blighted the family of Adam. But since no further children would follow (as happened with Adam and Eve after Abel's death), the consequences would be even more tragic. The plot thus has reached a major crisis.

Now we discover a peculiar thing has happened: ''it was told to Rebekah, the words of Esau, her oldest son'' (verse 42). Since we have just been told that these words were uttered in the ''heart'' of Esau, who could have heard them, and related them to Rebekah? It is here that we see the close connection between the narrator and Rebekah, and the somewhat awkward solution to the problem of narrative construction this situation presents. Rebekah can neither ''overhear'' Esau's inner thoughts nor have them conveyed by others. So how is she to learn of them? The narrator simply says that she ''was told.'' The verb נָגַד , meaning ''to declare,'' is used elsewhere in the *hophal* case with reference to an oracular announcement (Is. 21:2; 40:21), but in Genesis it usually serves as a narrative device to explain how a character learns important news conveyed by unnamed intermediaries (Gen. 20:22; 31:22; 38:13). Since here there can be none, the narrator inadvertently gives us a glimpse of his mediating function. It is only the narrator who can ''tell'' Rebekah the inner thoughts of another character. This makes all the clearer the identification of the narrator with Rebekah's viewpoint.

This revelation of Esau's intention once again gives Rebekah advance knowledge of the future, and she can construct a plan of her own to defeat Esau's. She summons Jacob, and advises him to flee and take refuge with her family in Paddam Aram, ''until the wrath of your brother will be turned aside'' (verse 44). The repetition of this phrase in slightly altered wording in verse 45 was considered by source critics to be a duplication, but rather seems more a case of parallelism (as in verse 36b above). It reiterates a reassuring thought, followed by a much desired hope for the future, ''and he will forget what you have done to him'' (verse 45).

The happy end which Rebekah projects for her scenario is that when this forgetting is accomplished, ''I will send and I will take you from there.'' The years of Jacob's sojourn extend much beyond Rebekah's apparent lifetime, however (an account of her death is curiously missing even though the death and burial of her maid is noted by the narrator in 35:8; her burial place at Machpelah is later mentioned by Jacob in 49:3 just before his death), and it is Yahweh who must call Jacob back from Paddam Aram (again showing the close identification of the narrator/God with Rebekah's viewpoint). This can hardly be considered punishment for Rebekah's role in this deception, however,[29] since Rebekah's plan works out almost exactly as she thought, with Yahweh conveniently taking her place as the instigator of Jacob's return (31:3).

Rebekah's concluding rhetorical question, "Why should I be bereaved of both of you on one day?" seems addressed more to herself (and the reader) than to Jacob, and constitutes her experience (and the reader's) of the defamiliarization of her own plot. This question embodies her awareness of the unexpected, tragic end to which their plans have come. The murderous passion of Esau was not a part of their calculations. Vengeance against Esau will immediately follow his murder of Jacob,[30] placing the entire future of the family at risk. But while this experience of defamiliarization has been shocking to her, it has not been devastating because she lives and "plots" (with the collaboration of the narrator) by anticipating the future. She has already answered this question which she poses meditatively at the end of her discourse. Her new improvised plot rescues her from the dilemma of the first, and opens a new sequence with a future. Rebekah again shows her understanding of passion: it is temporary and spends itself. Victory comes to those who strategically withdraw from confrontation and wait for those consumed by passion to bring about their own undoing, a strategy consistent with that of Abram in Genesis 12:10ff. The oracle will ultimately work its way with the future. Rebekah thus avoids the closure which Esau would have imposed upon her plot, and delays the potentially fatal encounter into the indefinite future. It is through such devices which postpone the end that the defamiliarization process of the symbolic narrative can still be seen at work here.

The concluding scene which begins in 27:46 is generally considered to be a P duplication of the previous scene since it provides another totally different rationale for Jacob's departure.

And Rebekah said to Isaac, "I will cut off my life because of the daughters of Heth. If Jacob takes his wife from the daughters of Heth, from these daughters of the land, what is my life to me?"

Isaac shows no hostility towards Jacob or Rebekah for what has happened, but tacitly concurs with Rebekah's anger at the Hittite wives of Esau and the need for Jacob to go to the family of Laban to seek a wife. El Shaddai, a divine name characteristic of P, is made the source of the blessing. The blessing given is the promise of land to Abraham, which shares phraseology with Genesis 17.[31] The giving of this different additional blessing to Jacob immediately following Esau's repeated plea for another blessing is also disturbing.

Nevertheless there are signs of sensitivity in this narrative to the motifs in the previous account. Isaac bestows the blessing upon Jacob with no explanation, unless it is *implicitly* assumed that Esau, in his marriage to the

Canaanite woman, forfeited his claim upon the blessing. This contravention of the law of primogeniture would seem to require a more *explicit* justification. It is more reasonable, thus, to think that this narrative assumes the victory of Jacob over Esau recounted in chapter 27. It further reflects the character of Esau developed in chapter 27. When Esau attempts to win the favor of his parents by marrying the Ishmaelite, it presages the same pathos of Esau's last futile pleas to Isaac for the blessing. Ishmael himself was excluded from the lineage of the promise, and to marry into his family just as firmly places Esau beyond the pale. It does, however, fix Esau ironically in relation to the history of the promise by linking him to the lineage of the rejected who enjoy some benefits of God's protection, but not the joys of positive fulfillment.

Finally, it gives a "proper" conclusion to the deception story. Since Isaac does not die at the conclusion of this sequence as it now stands, but much later, the justification for Jacob's immediate flight is diminished since Rebekah assumes that his life was to be in danger only after the death of Isaac. Also, if the larger context does not permit the death of Isaac to stand as the conclusion of this story, Jacob's departure must now be given a "proper" justification to the still living patriarch. For Jacob to depart like a thief in the night, his final words to his father having been lies, scarcely constitutes a satisfactory conclusion. Esau's marriage appears at this juncture as a common issue around which Rebekah and Isaac may unite again, and which may also serve as a positive basis for a final word from Isaac to Jacob. This story thus brings the deception narrative to a more satisfactory conclusion by bringing the alienated parties together and providing grounds for a second promissory blessing by the father in full consciousness of the identity of the recipient.

The conscious acquiescence of Isaac now to this state of affairs completes the elevation of Jacob on the human plane to his new position as promise-bearer. With this, the tension created by the divine oracle at the outset as well as by the plot of Rebekah are totally resolved, and closure has been achieved. Since, however, the closure has been achieved upon the terms initially established by the disruptive divine discourse, which is prior to the desire-driven plot of Rebekah and which is also implicitly linked to the unifying promise to Abraham, the initiative remains with the divine Voice for any major turns which the plot may take in the future. The ideological perspective of the narrator has developed density and power, however, and the latitude for innovation by the divine Voice is now considerably reduced as long as the narrative unfolds within the terms of the patriarchal history. There are, however, a number of serious tensions which are still unresolved before the fulfillment of the promise of nationhood can be realized; for example, how can the promise be transmitted to more than one son of a patriarch? How can it be transmitted without continuing to create a tradition of the rejected alongside that of the chosen? But these will be taken up by the narrator and pursued within terms of his own developing ideology in the Joseph story, with even less reliance upon the intervention of the divine Voice.

14
"Where do you come from?" Genesis 37, 39–45, 50

The critical discussion of the Joseph story has concerned itself with two central factors: the problem of unity, and the tradition-context which produced it. The two problems bear upon one another in that it is the developed narrative style and unity of the story, compared with the previous narratives of the book of Genesis, which require the assumption that the author(s) was influenced by traditions not active in the composition of the previous narratives. It is not the purpose of this analysis to pursue these central problems to a definitive resolution, but only to carry through the type of narrative analysis developed in these pages with respect to one section of the Joseph narrative. The basic contours of these problems will be sketched below, however, so that the implications which this analysis may have for the larger issues can be brought out where appropriate.

First, the question of unity must be briefly examined. Source criticism has found the Joseph narrative to be a rich source of duplications which take the form of the doubling of names (such as Jacob/Israel) and terms (*śaqq* and *'am*^{e}*tḥat* for sack in 42:27–38), recapitulations (39:10–12; 14–15; 17–18); discrepancies in the plot (37:28 and 36 compared to 37:25; 39:1); doubling of the plot episodes (two dreams of Joseph in Egypt, chapters 40, 41; two trips by the brothers to Egypt, chapters 42–44; two attempts by the woman to seduce Joseph, chapter 39). The proliferation of such duplications and inconsistencies have suggested that this story is a compilation of parallel accounts from the earlier independent J and E documents.

It has become increasingly difficult to maintain this theory for a variety of reasons, one of the most significant being the numerous literary and stylistic features of this narrative which fundamentally distinguish it from the foregoing patriarchal sagas. Gunkel had already pointed to the new "ausgeführten stil" found in the Joseph story which he feels requires the new generic designation of "novella".[1] Though he views the basic technique of collecting older sagas and incorporating them into a new Hebraic framework to be similar to that used in earlier narratives, the extent to which this earlier material has been integrated is new, and represents the final stage of the development of the narrative art in Genesis many centuries after the origin of the earliest sagas.[2]

It is at this point that an obvious problem arises which Gunkel observes but does not answer: how could this new genre and style arise independently, in what is most likely a literary form, in both J and E documents? Gunkel only comments that, "It is very important to see that J and E have reported the Joseph narrative essentially in the same way; this new narrative art has been discovered neither by E nor by J."[3] But if it did not originate with either of the authors of these two great documents, then how are we to understand the circumstances of its origin?

The problem is made more serious by the fact that the divergence from the patriarchal traditions goes far beyond the stylistic level to the center of the religious worldview. Gunkel pointedly asserts: "The narrator lives in a different religious world; there the gods appear no longer personified, but the deeper view recognizes in natural events the hand of the ruling God; in place of faith in the appearances of God has come providential faith (45:7; 50:20)."[4]

Von Rad has attempted to locate the new context of this work in the wisdom tradition which came into Israelite life in a major way during the Solomonic period.[5] A number of serious objections have been raised in recent years to this thesis, however. Whybray has pointed out that if one accepts the assumptions of both Gunkel and von Rad that the new style and form of this story did not originate with either J or E, but with a prior literary source, the dating of the J source during the Solomonic period means that an earlier common source for J and E would have had to antedate the Solomonic period. This pushes it out of the time-frame in which the wisdom tradition first flowered in Israel.[6] Beyond this is the even more difficult stylistic question which Whybray raises with respect to the literary unity of the final form of the story. To argue that the final text is a novelette of high literary merit, as von Rad describes it, seems to Whybray to be inconsistent with viewing it as a conflation of original J and E versions.[7] Thus, Whybray concludes, "we are forced to make a choice in our interpretation of the Joseph story between the documentary hypothesis on the one hand and the view that it is a 'novel' of genius belonging to the category of wisdom literature on the other."[8]

Though Whybray does not question von Rad's thesis regarding the matrix of this story in the wisdom tradition, he does show that this argument is inconsistent with use of the documentary hypothesis as an explanation of its composition. The documentary hypothesis is likewise incompatible with the high literary evaluation made of the style and unity of the final form of the text.

But if Whybray is only interested in questioning von Rad's reliance upon the documentary hypothesis in his argument, others have raised serious questions concerning his estimation of the influence of the wisdom tradition that have now led to the substantial modification or outright rejection of that thesis.[9] Redford, on the basis of a correlation of the references to Egyptian culture with our knowledge of the various periods of Egyptian history, dates the Joseph story after the seventh century B.C.E. For him, then, this story was written substantially later than either J or E, and long after the entrance of the wisdom tradition in Israelite culture. The character traits of Joseph which von Rad closely correlates with the ideal man of the wisdom tradition, and which provide him with one of his clearest evidences of wisdom influence, Redford contends, "are to be ascribed to a common, human ideal, widely disseminated throughout all ancient Near Eastern Societies."[10]

This leaves no satisfactory explanation of the matrix out of which the Joseph story emerged, with regard either to the author(s) or the intellectual context which produced such significant change in the narrative style. Redford resorts to a traditio-historical explanation, arguing for a two-stage growth of the story from an original version centering upon Reuben to a later edition which injected Judah and moved him to the center, and perhaps added what he regards as the independent stories of Joseph and Potiphar's wife (chapter 39), and Joseph's agrarian reform (47:13ff.).[11] It was then the "Genesis editor" (whom he does not more closely identify), a "compiler, loath to reject anything short of gross theological error" who added these narratives along with the remaining materials to form the conclusion of the book of Genesis.[12] Redford's traditio-historical explanation of the growth of the central Joseph narrative has not found widespread acceptance, however. (Schmitt, for example, argues persuasively for the dependency of the Reuben level upon a prior Judah level.)[13]

While there are still efforts being made to apply the source theory to the central Joseph narrative,[14] these have led to conclusions which rely finally upon intuitive perceptions of narrative continuity rather than empirical evidence, or stylistic considerations which simply assume the documentary hypothesis.[15] Coats perceived the fundamental character of this problem, and set out a new starting point for narrative analysis which reversed the traditional source-critical approach to the text. Gunkel expressed the latter approach the most clearly. After characterizing the Joseph story as a "well-organized whole" reflecting "a highly developed power to join together masses" as compared to the patriarchal sagas which stand next to each other "like strung pearls,"[16] he nevertheless takes his central task to be "to dissolve the whole again into the assumed, original component parts," rather than to uncover the structure of the whole.[17] Coats, in contrast, says that it is imperative to begin with the larger narrative context in the Pentateuch and proceed to its internal narrative structure, since to "begin with a division of the story into its component sources begs the question about structure and unity, both in the final form of the text and in the sources that may lie behind the final form."[18]

Westermann, in the recent concluding volume of his massive Genesis commentary, follows Coats in his view that the central section of the Joseph story constitutes a narrative unity which cannot be broken apart into sources. It is held together by a unifying narrative tension which reaches from the rupture of family unity in chapter 37 to the family reconciliation in chapter 45.[19] This work did not grow out of an oral background, in Westermann's view, but was a literary composition, "a work of art of the highest rank, which grew out of the conception of the writer, and served as an exposition of the history of Jacob."[20]

As an exposition, however, it had no independent life of its own, in Westermann's view, but was composed as an expansion of the Jacob story and, ultimately, inserted into the conclusion of that narrative. He thus can agree with Coats that the Jacob story as a whole constitutes a "redactional (as opposed to a structural) unity", but most of the additional materials in chapters 38 and 46–50 are not "parasites" of the Joseph story, as Coats contends,[21] but rather are the original end (though subsequently shaped again by P) of the Jacob story telling of his descent into Egypt.[22] It is this context which also provides Westermann with his framework of interpretation.

Rather than seeing this narrative as articulating the concerns and perspective of the wisdom tradition, Westermann finds in the background of this narrative the broader interest of the early monarchical period in reconciling the familial perspective of the patriarchal and tribal periods with the political perspective of the monarchical state: "Through the suspenseful involvement, opposition and cooperation of the court and the family, the narrator has wanted to indicate to his hearers that the new forms of life in existence as a state do not need to stand in unqualified opposition to the way of life in the family which was passed down from of old."[23] Joseph, a figure who is neither patriarch nor king, stands between the two epochs, and his story provides an assurance that the two ways of life can be reconciled. It is also this transitional context that provides Westermann with a way to understand the unity of the basic elements in the central Joseph narrative. Chapter 37 picks up the motifs of life in the family of Jacob; chapters 39–41 provide a relatively self-contained account of Joseph's accession to royal power in the Egyptian state, and chapters 41–45 unite the familial perspective with the political perspective. The author then repeats the scene of Joseph's interpretation of the previous events in 50:17–21 in order to join his narrative more tightly to the Jacob narrative.[24]

Both Coats and Westermann then turn away from the customary attempt to locate the matrix of the central Joseph narrative in either an oral tradition, a source document, or a recognizable social setting (such as wisdom circles in the Solomonic court). It diverges in style too sharply both from the oral characteristics of the earlier patriarchal sagas and from the literary styles of the authors of the source documents who united them. The additional rejection of von Rad's thesis regarding the narrative's locus in the wisdom setting then leaves the origin of this new style of narrative composition historically unaccounted for. Westermann attempts to place it within a historical context on the basis of the dynamics of social conflict and change which it reflects. While this argument is cogent, it is not supported by the correlations which Redford makes between the features of Egyptian culture present in the story, and our knowledge of Egyptian cultural history,[25] arguments against which Westermann offers only some general considerations.[26]

Thus we are left with a context which can only be described as literary, that is, the tradition of Hebraic historical narrative writing itself. Coats, in this regard, speaks of the "atmosphere" of the Joseph story as being that of "an artist with wide ranging experience."[27] Westermann similarly points to this narrative as an example of the blossoming of the art of narrative writing which occurred again and again in the history of Israel all the way into the post-exilic time.[28] Thus for Westermann, too, the final and most certain context within which the story should be understood is the art of narrative writing itself.

These conclusions suggest that further understanding of the Joseph story can be found through developing a method of narrative analysis which can isolate more precisely the distinguishing features of the Joseph narrative so that it can be placed with greater precision within the evolving art of narrative composition in ancient Israelite literary traditions. This type of analysis can provide not only a more thorough understanding of the structure of the Joseph narrative than the general considerations given by Coats and Westermann, but can also reveal more precisely the relation of this style to that of the patriarchal sagas. The analysis to follow will assume the correctness in almost all points of the redactional history of the narrative developed by Westermann. The focus will be upon the generally acknowledged center of the core Joseph narrative (chapters 37 and 39–45), that is the reunion of the brothers in chapter 42 and the subsequent events. The unity of this narrative will also be assumed following Coats and Westermann.

Typological analysis

In the earlier narratives analyzed from the patriarchal corpus, the future was disclosed by the divine Voice to the patriarch rather than rising out of forces depicted in the third person in the narrative framework. While the conclusions of secondary plots are not revealed in advance to the protagonist nor to the reader, the direction of future plots is known by him, and, in fact, his confidence in that future becomes the central uncertainty of the plot. This means that the narrator is effaced behind the divine–human micro-dialogue. It is in the dynamics of this micro-dialogue that the future of the plot takes form.

As the narrative progresses, however, the secondary plots become increasingly long and complex as seen in the analysis of the Jacob–Esau narrative. In the later promissory visions there is less dialogue than in the visions of Abraham, though the agon of the divine–human encounter is preserved dramatically in the struggle of Jacob with the angel at the Jabbok. In these secondary plots the representation of character and action in the narrative framework grows, and the plots exhibit a greater degree of closure, though the system of representation attempts to remain consistent with the open premises of the larger plot.

In the Joseph narrative these tendencies are allowed to develop much further. The only genuine micro-dialogue is the vision of Jacob in chapter 46 which stitches the Joseph narrative to the previous unifying theme of the history of the promise. The protagonist, Joseph, has no direct dialogue with the divine at all!

Since it has been the micro-dialogue that has effaced the narrator and prevented the imposition of closure, the question which must be raised at the outset concerns the position of the narrator *vis-à-vis* his characters. To what extent does the absence of a micro-dialogue in the presentation of the protagonist fundamentally alter the relation of the narrator and his characters, thus removing this from the category of a symbolic narrative?

The unusual nature of the narrator–character relation in the Joseph story derives from the unique position it now occupies as the link between the patriarchal sagas which were centered upon single protagonists (and their spouses) and the story of the rise of the nation which was centered upon the people as the elect of God. Whereas in the earlier patriarchal stories the promise was transmitted personally to each patriarch at the initiative of God – each receiving a distinctive promissory vision of his own, the relation of the divine to the nation is to be enshrined in a covenant made once at Sinai and continued by ritual renewals rather than by unique and discontinuous revelations to successive generations. But since a revelation to a group must be an external and social communication, rather than internal and private, does this mean that the narrator in dealing with the traditions of the nation will be forced into an external posture regarding his characters, and thus into a representative or expressive form of narrative construction?

The crucial issue in the symbolic narrative is the extent to which the barrier between the consciousness of the author and his/her character has been lowered so that the mental acts which give rise to the character in the mind of the author are present in the text, shaping the character there. The corollary of this is that the author loses his privileged temporal position, and the present of the character merges with that of the author. The narrative moves forward then by the dynamics of this mental/verbal process rather than by the necessary strictures of a closed plot structure designed from the conclusions backward.

When the Joseph narrative is analyzed from this perspective it appears that the relation of the author to his characters is both complex and changing. To see this it will be necessary to begin by attempting to delineate the perspective of the author upon his subject matter, as seen by the third-person narrative framework and by the tensions which unite the beginning and end of this narrative.

Though many scholars view the last scenes of the Joseph story as little more than a later appendix,[29] in terms of this analysis the last three verses constitute a most significant ending. They contain the transmission of the patriarchal promise of land from Joseph to his brothers (the first such transmission from one generation to the next solely by a human agent), and the extraction of an oath by Joseph from his brothers to carry his bones up from Egypt, presumably when this promise of land is fulfilled. Only the report by the narrator of Joseph's death, his age at death, and his burial follow. The transmission of a promise and the giving of an oath by the characters open a future which extends beyond the end of the narrative. Though Joseph's death and burial are reported, even this does not actually conclude the story of Joseph, since his bones will participate in the future of his people. Thus, in every sense, the narrative ends with uncertainty. Will this promise be fulfilled? Will Joseph's bones find their ultimate resting place in the land of the promise? These future-oriented words, spoken by a narrative personage, thus constitute the final horizon of meaning within which the preceding narrative should be understood.

Before assuming that this final scene is a redactional appendage we must also ask whether there is an internal connection between this event, the transmission of the promise by Joseph to his brothers, and the foregoing narrative. One of the most frequently recurring motifs throughout the narratives of Genesis has been intra-familial rivalry. The initial sin of humankind after banishment from paradise was Cain's murder of Abel. In the Abraham cycle, it is implied that the rivalry of his wives, Hagar and Sarah, extends to rivalry between their sons, Ishmael and Isaac (Gen. 21:10). The proper transmission of the promise is threatened as long as Ishmael remains in Abraham's household, in Sarah's view, and Abraham expels Hagar and Ishmael (Gen. 20:14). It is after this expulsion that the promise is transmitted by God to Isaac (Gen. 26:1–5). Similarly, in the Jacob cycle, the problem of rivalry between Jacob and his brother Esau was resolved before the promise was transmitted to Jacob. The problem of rivalry thus occupies an important position in the primeval history, and in both the Abraham and Jacob cycles. One might also conclude that it is never satisfactorily resolved. In each case the rival is simply forced outside the pale of God's blessing.

In the Joseph narrative the problem of rival brothers is placed on center stage and explored in depth. One reason for this may be the unprecedented critical problem posed by sibling rivalry for the transmission of the promise which must take place here at the end of the patriarchal history. No longer can the promise be transmitted to the chosen son, and his rival brother pushed to the sidelines of sacred history. The promise must now be transmitted to the prototypical form of the nation, the "Sons of Israel." But to transmit it to the whole body of sons poses the problem of sibling rivalry as a central obstacle, since no rival can now simply be rejected.

An additional problem arises because the promise cannot be transmitted by God to a collective entity, as he had transmitted it to Abraham, Isaac, and Jacob in private visions. It might have been transmitted by the last patriarch to all of his sons, but that would not have dealt forthrightly with the complex problem of rivalry which the Biblical writers had always acknowledged as having its roots in the parental habit of favoring one son above the other(s). Is Jacob then to be exempted from this pattern so evident in the tales of the previous patriarchal families? But if not the patriarch, then who? The brilliant solution to this problem, one which is both continuous with the previous narratives and yet boldly new, is for Jacob to choose his favorite son for the transmission of the promise, thereby precipitating the problem of sibling rivalry. Then, in the course of the narrative, a solution to the problem will be worked out that will enable the favorite son, acting as a patriarchal type figure, to transmit the promise successfully to his brothers. After this it would then be vested in traditions of each tribe and family in the nation-to-be.[30]

I would like to propose, then, that there is indeed a profound link between the concluding verses of the Joseph narrative and the events which precede it; and that in fact, it is the conclusion reached at the end of that narrative plot in 50:21 that makes possible the climactic event – the transmission of the promise – for the first time, from one brother to another. It will then be the task of the following analysis to trace the various tensions between the forces of closure operating in the narrative framework, and the open conclusion with which the plot actually ends.

The analysis below will show that this is a representative/symbolic narrative, that is, a narrative in which the style and strategy of a representative narrative has been used by and large, but the closed system of that narrative type has been finally subordinated to the open perspective of symbolic narration. The choice of values expressed in the character of the protagonist and the means by which he attains victory over his opponents are also compatible with symbolic narration.

The narrator provides at the outset of this narrative (37:1–4), a rather extensive (for the reticent Genesis narrators) explanation of the factors leading to this rupture in communication, and it is here that the analysis should begin. The narrator describes in third-person speech attributes and actions of his leading characters in such a way that he constructs a system of forces at work in the family of Jacob that leads to the subsequent events.

And Jacob dwelt in the land of the sojournings of his father, the land of Canaan. This is the generation of Jacob: Joseph, seventeen years of age, was a shepherd with his brothers' sheep, and he was a lad with the sons of Bilhah, and the sons of Zilpah, wives of his father: and Joseph brought their evil talk to their father. 37:1–2

Though verses 1–2 are considered to be from a different source than 37:3ff. (P), the framework provided by verses 1–2 is now vital to the narrative structure. The narrator provides the physical locality of the subsequent events ("Jacob dwelt in the land of the sojournings of his father, the land of Canaan"), the age of the protagonist ("Joseph, seventeen years of age"), his customary activity ("was a shepherd with his brothers' sheep"), and his generational relation with some of his brothers ("and he was a *na'ar* [lad] with the sons of Bilhah and the sons of Zilpah, wives of his father").[31] This series of qualifications moves progressively toward what is most pertinent for the dramatic development of the narrative. The reader is expected to know that Joseph was the son of Rachel, Jacob's favorite wife, whereas the others to which he was attached as a *na'ar* were the children of concubines. This suggests a significant social barrier between Joseph and the others which is then made explicit in the next phrase: "and Joseph brought their evil talk to his father".[32]

The narrator does not allow us to listen in on the brothers' "evil talk" until later when they are conspiring against Joseph. But this phrase alerts the reader to the alienation of the brothers' world of discourse from that of their father. In a very swift and economical fashion we are thus given a vivid portrayal of young Joseph, at an age when he should be submitting to the authority of his initiatory instructors and separating himself from his parents, distancing himself from these new authority figures who are his social inferiors and "tattling" to their father on their private "evil" talk. This suggests a system of social and interpersonal tensions which the following narration completes.

It also establishes Joseph in a role which he is to play consistently as the solitary hermeneut who exists between alienated realms of discourse and social positions, such as between Potiphar and his wife, between the keeper of the prison and the prisoners, between the dreamers and the divine meaning of their dreams, between the Pharaoh and the starving masses, between the royal court of Egypt and Semitic tribal life, between the Egyptian and Semitic languages, between the obvious meaning of the course of events and their hidden divine purpose, and, finally, between the role of tribal patriarch and that of national king. It should be noted already that the mediating position which Joseph has between these alienated worlds of discourse structurally corresponds to the role of an omniscient narrator. As Joseph moves from the world of the brothers to that of his father, the narrator can follow him quite naturally to give the reader insight into the inner workings of both worlds.

In verse 3 we find what is considered by source critics to be the second, independent explanation of the brothers' hatred to Joseph.

And Israel loved Joseph above all his brothers for he was to him a son of his old age. 37:3

Literarily, however, it complements the previous verse by providing Jacob/Israel's viewpoint. Joseph's unusual behavior is not to be considered in isolation from his father's attitudes. Though no causal link between them is explicitly made, the narrator is bringing to light something which would have obviously influenced Joseph's behavior toward his brothers, and that is his own likely knowledge that "Israel loved Joseph above all his brothers."

Lest the reader take this love as arbitrary, the narrator provides a reason designed to elicit sympathetic understanding of Jacob/Israel: "he was for him a son of his old age." Another material reason strangely not mentioned was that he was the oldest son of Jacob's favorite wife, Rachel. But Joseph's deceased mother's name in this narrative is entirely missing, as was the living mother's name in Genesis 22 where the focus is also on a father's relation to his favorite son; but clearly knowledge of her and her favored status in Jacob/Israel's eyes is presupposed as a factor in his favoritism toward Joseph. Another deliberate elision is reference to another, still younger son of Rachel, Benjamin, who is to play a vital role later in the narrative. These elisions leave as the dominant factor in Jacob/Israel's attitude, his subjective passion for his young son. Such a passion leads easily to excessive and unjudicious actions.

With deft economy of expression the narrator has moved from the attribution of aberrant behavior to Joseph to the grounding of that behavior in the humanly understandable passions of the father. This creates a fateful situation in which potentially destructive forces are at work in the family over which no one has control. Because it is not clear that the brothers are aware of Joseph's covert actions, no mention is yet made of the brothers' attitude toward him.

This lack of awareness is quickly overcome when the narrator reports an objective manifestation of this fatherly love. Consistent with his singular passion, he gives only Joseph a distinctive gift which will inescapably set him apart from his brothers as one especially beloved of the father: "and he made for him a striped tunic (כְּתֹנֶת פַּסִּים)." Whereas previously this father–son relation was beneath the surface, expressing itself only perhaps in the brothers' private "evil talk" and the private communications between Joseph and Jacob, now it is a *visible*, social fact: "and his brothers *saw* that it was him their father loved *above all* his brothers [LXX: sons]." Jacob's love here follows the dynamics of the psychology of imagination. A transgressive passion, as was this love which exceeds all normal, familial limits, orients itself toward a material object of desire and seeks to relate to it through sacrifice, which tends to go beyond the limits of worldly or "rational" consideration. Jacob's gift to Joseph was such a sacrifice, arising from an obsessive passion which did not recognize the limits imposed on such gift-giving by the need for emotional equilibrium in the family system. The tunic provided Jacob with the needed visual representation of his consuming love of his son.

The brothers' response can now also be summarily reported: "and they hated him" (37:4). And, consistent with the narrator's interest in communication in the family, he reports that the consequence of this hatred was that: "they were not able to speak *šalōm* to him" (37:4). Since *šalōm* was the sign which initiated and concluded trusting communication, this occurrance signaled the end of meaningful speech between Joseph and the brothers from this point on until it is restored near the end of the narrative. The visible sign (the tunic) has displaced the system of verbal communication. With Joseph's exclusion from the brothers' world of discourse, only the narrator has access to the worlds of both the father and the brothers.

In a few short sentences the narrator has sketched out an unusually complex world of fateful familial stratification, relations, and emotions: youth versus old age, intra-familial social hierarchy, concealed realms of discourse, rivalry, betrayal, obsessive love, ill-considered gifts of passion, hatred, shunning. The balance with which this system is presented leaves no heroes and no villains. The actions of each are both understandable and reprehensible so nuanced is this brief description of the "generations" of Jacob. The effect of this form of narration is not to evoke the identification of the reader with one party against another, but to convey a fundamental instability stemming from communicative alienation and unbalanced, obsessive passions.

The social divisions and passions in terms of which the narrator has defined his characters and their relations thus far appears to be a system of closed forces which might be predicted to lead directly to overt conflict between either Joseph and his brothers, or between the brothers and their father. This pattern resembles that of the representative narrative in which the experience of defamiliarization is provided by conflict, though no identification has been made of the protagonist and antagonist.

It is into this closed system that the narrator next interjects the mysterious dreams: "And Joseph dreamed a dream" (37:5). As a narrative device, the dream is placed by Dorrit Cohn in the category of psychonarration which she defines as "the narrator's discourse about a character's consciousness."[33] Dreaming is a distinctive mental state in that the dream is an occurrence in the mental life of the character and yet it does not appear to originate in the character's normal consciousness, as, for example the dreamer does not convey a dream to himself in direct discourse as he dreams it.[34] In the dream, the character's consciousness is in tension with a second pole or dimension.

Regardless of how you understand that pole psychologically, in terms of narrative structure it is one in which the perspectives of the narrator and character become quasi-unified. The third-person statement, "he dreamed," when referring to a dream and not a dream report, indicates access to events of consciousness by a second party. But since the origin of the dream is not in the normal consciousness of the character, as are perceptions, thoughts, etc., conveyed by the sympathetic narrator, the source of the dream must be sought in that mysterious middle ground between the consciousness of the narrator and the character. The opening of the closed world of the character towards its originating instance of speech in the narrator can move the narrative structure into the orbit of the symbolic narrative. The dream thus represents the covert coalescing of an aspect of the narrator's hermeneutical perspective with the deeper consciousness of the character.

When the dream content is viewed as prognosticatory, revealing the end of the narrative at its beginning, it makes it possible for the characters themselves to reflect over a central feature of the representative narrator's own strategy: his practice of structuring actions and characters to lead to a predetermined end (as is to occur at the end of this narrative). But by injecting knowledge of the end into the consciousness of the characters at the beginning, the knowledge then becomes a force which can bring about, in some way, the end which it envisions. Here the dream can have a function similar to that of the oracle to Rebekah at the outset of the previous narrative. But unlike Rebekah's oracle, the dream here is not recounted by the narrator as an occurrence in the consciousness of the protagonist. The first account of it is given by Joseph himself in DD to his brothers:

and when he told it to his brothers, they hated him even more. 37:5

It is significant that the narrator gives us the reaction to the dream by the brothers before presenting the content of the dream itself in the words of Joseph.

And he said to them, "Hear, I pray, this dream which I have dreamed. Behold, we were binding bundles in the midst of the field, and behold my bundle was standing, and was even elevated, and behold, your bundles were all around, and they bowed down to my bundle." 37:7

The social context of the disclosure of the dream, which has been carefully reconstructed in the preceding verses, insures the "double-voiced" character of this dream report and produces an explicit dialogue precisely about the polyvocal implications of the dream.

And his brothers said to him, "Will you indeed reign over us, or even rule over us?" And they hated him still more. 37:8

Their response here takes the form of a demystification of the symbolic images of the dream, and a bold statement of their view of its not too hidden meaning. The question posed by the brothers cannot be answered by Joseph since the dream imagery and its meaning do not arise from his conscious awareness and intentions. The heteroglossic character of the dream, when reported, brings to the surface of expression the cleavage in the center of the family's discourse. This question is rhetorically intensified by the hatred and resentment beneath it.

The presentation of the dream through reports in DD thus serves to dialogize and make ironical the closed systems which have now emerged in this narrative. The dream itself, if presented in third-person narration, could have represented a covert deterministic force controlling the course of events to which the conscious actions of the characters were totally unrelated. On the other hand, the system of familial passions depicted in the narrative introduction also constitute a closed system of emotions which seem destined to impel the actions of the characters toward quite different ends. Joseph's recounting of his dream serves to provoke the brothers into DD for the first time. The resentment that the narrator has described previously as a non-verbal emotion now comes to speech. This discourse then serves to precipitate the action in such a way that both of the closed determining systems are ultimately opened.

The function of the dream report here corresponds to the function of Abraham's ensnaring lie to the lustful Pharaoh, and Jacob's "offer" of a bowl of soup to the famished Esau. All are utterances which provoke action driven by unthinking passion, but provoke it in such a way that the characters are taken up into a discursive process that deprives them of their object of desire. Here the irony is more finely drawn, however. Not only is Joseph unaware, at this point, of the overall strategy (unlike in the Abraham and Jacob stories, here it is the narrator's strategy being used to manipulate all of the characters), his willingness to tell his dreams to his brothers, who hated him, and to his father, in spite of the obvious connotations of the dreams, shows a naive arrogance on his part. He is himself seduced by the dreams into these acts of disclosure by blindness to his own pride.

Here the technique of the micro-dialogue is extended from the inner life of the individual into the social dimension, where the behavior of a group may be incorporated into its dynamics. This brings about an inversion of the promissory narrative structure. If the promise depended upon the faith of its protagonist/recipient for its ultimate fulfillment, the realization of the dream announcement depends upon the passivity of its protagonist/recipient, and the active disbelief of the brothers. If the promise offered deliverance from the oppressive closure of nature and society through the protagonist's risk of faith, the dream report is a predeterminating rhetorical force that operates without faith on the part of the characters, and mocks the free, conscious efforts of opponents to defeat its realization by turning those very efforts into its means of actualization.

There is also a curious sense in which the character who brings this word becomes a quasi-narrator, that is, she plays the role *vis-à-vis* the other characters which God (or the effaced narrator) plays with relation to the protagonist in the patriarchal sagas. S/he interjects into their lives the future-mediating word, which the narrator in the symbolic narrative interjects into the protagonist's consciousness. If this word concerns only the situation of the addressees, s/he may then disappear, or play no significant role in the remainder of the narrative, as, for example, in the case of the witches in Shakespeare's *Macbeth* who virtually disappear after announcing to Macbeth his own future. The protagonist is then left with his/her own struggle with this word and its implications.

If, however, the word is one which deals with the messenger as well as his/her hearers, and, more particularly, if it deals with his/her relation to them, as is the case in the Joseph narrative, then she/he will necessarily be caught up in the actions which they take in response to this word, that is, their response to the word will take the form of a response to the messenger.

Since, however, this prognostication has come from beyond, and suggests a future already determined, the recipient may choose to assume a passive stance toward it, even though it does concern him/her (as Joseph does), or s/he may choose to act out of his/her own volition to bring this word to pass (Macbeth and especially Lady Macbeth). To the extent that s/he assumes the active posture, the narrative would be largely driven from that point on by the conflictual dynamics of the representative narrative (though the added dimension of an inner relation to this word will bring an unusual element of ambiguity and perhaps tragedy to the protagonist).

To the extent that he assumes the passive stance, however, the dynamics of the narrative must be provided by a conflict within the group itself *about* the bearer of the message since the recipient of the dream, himself, will not fill the role of an antagonist. Having no proper, aggressive opponent to contend with, their discourse and action will be formed, not by the object of their hostility, but by those issues which divide them as a group, which would necessarily, in this case, pertain to action which should be taken toward an essentially passive opponent. Under the pressure of this context, the group, which has until now spoken as a single character, will divide into contending individual parties.

Whereas the first dream suggested Joseph's future superiority over his brothers, a second dream now follows which extends the reach of his superiority to include his father and mother. He immediately recounts it as well to his brothers, and to his father.[35]

And he dreamed again another dream, and he told it to his brothers. And he said, "Behold, I have dreamed a dream again, and behold the sun and the moon, and eleven stars are bowing down to me." And he told his father, and his brothers, and his father rebuked him. 37:9–10a

This now evokes a negative response even from his father which the narrator characterizes as a rebuke (גָּעַר). Jacob also understands this dream in terms of the problematic dynamics of the family already presented, rather than seeing it as a fulfillment of his hopes for Joseph. He, like the brothers, is offended by the audacious social implications which the second dream has for him. Because the imagery of the dream is "double voiced" (the referential meaning, and the implications for the social position of the characters), he cannot respond to the implied meaning directly, and so uses the device of the rhetorical question, as did the brothers. This question recoils at the audacious implications of the dream.

And he said to him, "What is this dream which you have dreamed? Shall I and your mother, and your brothers come indeed to bow down to the earth to you?" 37:10

This "rebuke" by his father marks a turning point in the plot since it cannot be assumed hereafter that Joseph enjoys the unqualified support of his father. The dreams and Joseph's reporting of them have conveyed indirectly to the family evidence of hubris. Joseph's fortunes thus begin at this point to take a downward course. The narrator fixes the new situation for the reader in his concluding comment:

And his brothers envied him, and his father noted the thing [הַדָּבָר]. 37:11

The narrator here provides a description of the inner thoughts of his characters which point toward the future development of the plot. The brothers' envy presages their next action. The father regards or takes special note of what has happened. The term הַדָּבָר here includes both the dream report of Joseph, and the brothers' emotional reaction to it. It is probably not correct to see this phrase as similar to phrases in Luke 2:19, 51 with their focus exclusively upon the positive angelic proclamations.[36] To do so would assume a positive orientation towards Joseph's dream by Jacob which is not present in the text. Rather, Jacob's own negative reaction to the second dream now enables him to see the entire event – the dream and the negative reaction it has elicited from the brothers. It is the memory of the brothers' hatred and envy of Joseph that constitutes the indispensible background to Jacob's refusal to be comforted by the brothers when they return with Joseph's blood-stained robe. But his notice of these negative emotions also constitutes a dark and ambiguous link to the following scene. In addition, his memory of the dream also serves to alert the reader to the continuing significance which the dream, as a mystical determining force, may have for the ultimate outcome of the story.

At the conclusion of this scene, then, the reader, if attempting to anticipate the future course of the narrative, would find two contradictory factors at work. On the one hand is the familial scene in which fatherly favor and brotherly jealousy put Joseph and his brothers into a potentially fatal conflict. On the other hand is the prognosticatory dream which contradicts the outcome seemingly dictated by the familial emotions. Mediating this conflict is the emotionally warped and semantically deflected discourse between both Joseph and his brothers, and Joseph and his father. This discourse brings the occult dream into explicit verbal contact with the familial situation with the effect of inflaming sibling jealousy and provoking an alarmed patriarchal rebuke. The dream thus is taken up within the emotional logic of the familial scene, the conclusion of which is not Joseph's triumph, but his death. The reporting of the dream within the context of the fractured discourse of the family has intensified the crisis by bringing the latent emotions obliquely into expression for the first time. The question, then, is what effect this process of direct discourse will have upon the logic of the familial emotions and the contradictory determining force of the prognosticatory dream.

Following this traumatic scene we are told by the narrator that the brothers depart for Shechem to graze their sheep.

And his brothers went to graze their father's sheep in Shechem. 37:12

Joseph is not mentioned, and from the discourse of Jacob which follows, it is clear that he was not among them. The narrator here carries forward the action by relying upon the force of habitual behavior. But in light of 37:2 the absence of Joseph should be seen as a departure from his normal practice of accompanying his brothers into the pastures. It thus signals a change in their relationship. Jacob then questions Joseph: "Are not your brothers grazing in Shechem?" (37:13a).

This rhetorical question arises from the disturbance of the established pattern of family life. When Jacob then sends Joseph to his brothers – "Come, I will send you to them" (verse 13b) – Jacob's words bring into direct discourse the established pattern set forth in the introductory narrative framework where it did not require explicit utterance. The need to assert directly a customary practice reflects both the breakdown of that practice, caused by the trauma of the preceding scene, and a disregard of that change by Jacob. It conceals another, more painful question, "Why are you not with your brothers?" But Jacob knows the answer to this question as the narrator has been careful to tell us in the previous verse. Jacob's utterance is thus fateful and shrouded in ambiguity and is made in disregard of the danger for Joseph which it entails.[37] The rhetorical question itself, which reasserts a norm made untenable by the previous scene, reflects the new situation which has emerged due to the articulation for the first time of the emotions of resentment against

Joseph. In fact, the question itself, with its indifference to Joseph's fate at the hands of the brothers, participates at least minimally in that resentment. Joseph's response to his father's entreaty is a passive submission: "Behold me" (or more loosely, "I am ready").[38]

Jacob's next statement to his son stands in an ironic relation to the narrative comment in 37:4 that the brothers were unable to speak *šalōm* to Joseph:

Go now. Look into the well-being [*šalōm*] of your brothers, and the well-being [*šalōm*] of the sheep ... 37:14

Šalōm here is "double voiced" in that it is being used by Jacob in a more conventional sense to refer to how the brothers are faring in their distant work; but it also suggests to the reader the deeper problem of alienation in the family mentioned in the narrative framework. The final phrase of Jacob's command again recalls the narrative introduction: "and bring me word of them" (37:14).

The message or word (דָּבָר) which Joseph is to bring recalls the account of their evil talk (דִּבָּתָם רָעָה) which he brought before. Jacob's commission to his son thus suggests each of the sources of animosity between Joseph and his brothers, and sets Joseph on a course which will lead him directly into the hands of his jealous rivals. The ambiguity of Jacob's words here is not unlike the ambiguity of Abraham's actions in Genesis 22.

As if to underscore the new position of Joseph in the family, alienated from both father and brothers, the narrator next portrays Joseph en route through the eyes of an unnamed man who "found him ... wandering in the field" (37:15) at Shechem looking vainly for his brothers. The brothers had moved on but Joseph neither asks about their whereabouts nor returns to his father. He is the image of indecision, wandering, suspended between them, unwilling to return to his newly unsympathetic father, and lacking the desire to seek out his hostile brothers. So the man inquires of him, "What are you seeking?" and tells him where they have gone. Joseph is not acting, and it is in response to his passive inaction that discourse arises in others, propelling him toward the fateful encounter with his brothers.

As in the previous scene, the narrator portrays an encounter with Joseph dramatically in spatial and temporal terms through the eyes of characters who observe Joseph from afar. This poses Joseph again in the role of a passive recipient of the actions of others. It also emphasizes the narrator's own detachment from any single character's perspective, and his freedom to move between separate (alienated) worlds of discourse. Because they recognize Joseph (due to his robe?) coming at a distance across the pasture, a situation is created for conversation about Joseph outside of the presence of either Jacob or Joseph. The narrator then states bluntly the essence of the discussion: "they conspired against him to kill him" (37:18). With this statement the logic of the familial system of emotions comes to its predictable end. The dynamics of the roles of the characters have changed, however. Whereas in the first two settings Joseph was the actor, carrying tales to Jacob and announcing his arrogant dreams, he now has become passive as he moves, defenseless, into the hands of his brothers, knowing of their hatred. But no clear identification of hero and villain has been made so that a typical conflict between Joseph and his brothers still might occur. The murder of Joseph will be an action taken against a passive victim who no longer even enjoys the unqualified support of his father.

But the narrator does not permit the decision to kill Joseph to take form silently, as it were, in the narrative framework. Just as Joseph's dream report brought the issue of the brothers' hatred indirectly into speech, so this murder will be the result of discourse stemming from the language of that scene.

> And they said to one another, "Behold the dream lord has come." 37:19

The conspiracy to murder begins with a bitterly sarcastic comment which "names" Joseph on the basis of his identity suggested by the dream. The term "dream lord" (בַּעַל הַחֲלֹמוֹת , or "lord of dreams") expresses their deflected emotion as did the rhetorical questions in the previous scene. The dream announcements by Joseph have provided his brothers with rhetorical materials connoting transgressive egoism which can be used in their conspiratorial discourse to achieve the emotional consensus needed for their own transgressive action against him. The object of their murder is, finally, not Joseph, but the "dream lord" and "his dreams." The apparently transgressive fantasies of Joseph open the door to the articulation of the brothers' own murderous dream.

But now the sarcasm directed against the dream serves to unite the brothers emotionally for the next proposal.

> And now come, let us kill him and throw him into one of the cisterns, and we will say an evil
> beast has eaten him; then we will see what will become of his dreams. 37:20

With this conspiratorial proposal the system of family emotions and that of the dream are brought into direct confrontation in DD. For the brothers the dream is merely the disguised assertion of Joseph's arrogance. To kill Joseph is to kill his dream. But for the brothers to succeed in their conspiracy against the passive, defenseless Joseph would corrupt the family of Jacob at its center and leave the brothers in the role of unqualified villains. Having no proper opponent, the action of the plot must turn away from confrontation with Joseph and permit the emergence of a new pair of antagonists. The issue which can serve to bring about this development is, of course, whether Joseph *should* be killed, now that it is obvious that he *can* be killed. If there are divisions among the brothers relevant to the issue of family unity, this action against a defenseless brother will bring it to expression.

It is now that the solidarity of the voice of the brothers is shattered by the action and utterance of the eldest brother (knowledge of this is assumed) Reuben.

And Reuben heard and delivered him from their hand; and he said, "Let us not strike him, a living soul [נֶפֶשׁ]." And Reuben said to them, "Do not shed blood. Throw him into this cistern which is in the pasture. Do not put a hand on him" – in order to deliver him from their hand and to return him to his father. 37:21–22

The transgressive action against a passive opponent brings to the surface the internal hierarchy among the brothers, and creates a new division along the lines of responsibility, pitting the eldest son of Leah against the other brothers. Reuben acts to halt Joseph's immediate murder and poses absolute moral arguments against murder (do not strike a living soul; do not shed blood). He then offers a problematic alternative – simply to leave Joseph in the pit. But with no grammatical break, the narrator moves quickly to reveal that the inner intention of Reuben was to return Joseph to Jacob. Reuben thus is presented here as an unambiguous hero who seeks to rescue Joseph, and the brothers, correspondingly, are thrown into the villain's role.

The subtlety of this narrative can be seen especially well here when it is noted how utterly unacceptable this moral solution is to the problem which has been posed by the plot. If Reuben is successful, and Joseph returns to Jacob with a report of these happenings (as it clearly must be assumed that he would do), the communication in the family will be irreparably shattered and the moral ambiguity which has colored each of the parties until now will be overcome by the polarization of the absolutely good against the absolutely evil.

But Reuben's role is decisive, nevertheless. By breaking the solidarity of the brothers' voice, he virtually guarantees that Joseph will not be killed, since, unless they kill Reuben as well, he would be in a position to divulge their deed to Jacob.

The narrator then concludes this scene with a summary of the actions taken, adding certain significant details to the information in the preceding direct discourse. Before throwing him into the cistern the brothers "stripped" (וַיַּפְשִׁיטוּ) him of his "striped" (הַפַּסִּים) robe. This "defrocking" of Joseph is the first blow against the symbolism of Joseph's superior status. It is a spontaneous action suggesting an inner compulsion needing no verbalization and eliciting no opposition even from Reuben. The casting of Joseph into the cistern inverts the image of his elevation above them portrayed in the dream. The brothers must look no longer at either the symbol of his status, or at Joseph himself. He is visually removed from their world. But the narrator adds that there is no water in the cistern to make clear that this action alone does not threaten his life.

The plot has now posed for the brothers a serious dilemma for which there is no viable solution. Reuben's strong moral objections to murder mean that if he witnesses their action he can no longer be relied upon to maintain his silence. Further, one must assume that they suspect his intention to rescue Joseph, mentioned in the narrative framework. A decision must be made now because something must be done with him. So with no viable path of action open, the narrator reports that they did what many still do when faced with frustration: "They sat down to eat bread" (verse 25).

Since Reuben has broken with the common mentality of the group and created this dilemma, it is reasonable to assume that he did not eat with them. That Reuben maintains a certain distance from the group also seems implied by the previous scene. His intervention is prefaced by the narrator's remark, "And Reuben heard" (verse 21), implying that he was near but not in the group at the exact moment of the conspiracy. Further, the murder of Reuben along with Joseph is now a possible if not likely solution to their dilemma.

It is in this desparate situation, then, created by Reuben's action and words, that the narrator, acting as a *deus ex machina*, injects a new possibility:

and they lifted their eyes, and they looked and behold, a caravan of Ishmaelites 37:25

Judah, a middle son of Leah, now emerges from the group as a second individuated voice. Seeing the opportunity this new party provides for a solution to their dilemma, he makes a proposal:

What does it profit if we kill our brother, and conceal his blood? Come let us sell him to the Ishmaelites, and our hands will not be upon him since he is our brother, our flesh. 37:26

This proposal contains the elements of an ingenius compromise. On the one side is the powerful urge to kill Joseph, with the attendant problems of blood guilt (and the implicit danger of discovery inherent in Reuben's lack of support). On the other side is Reuben's proposal which implicitly leaves open the possibility of Joseph's escape (or his deliverance by Reuben). To sell him into servitude has the virtue of both proposals (the ridding themselves of Joseph), while neither of the disadvantages (blood guilt, or the possibility of his escape and return). There is still the possibility that they would be betrayed by Reuben, but if this can be done without his knowledge, then he will have only his suspicions. They will have their story and the facts to support it (the bloody robe – again not explicitly verbalized in their plans but emerging spontaneously at the right moment).

Judah couches his proposal in terms of a new system of motivation when he asks: "What does it profit if we kill our brother and conceal his blood?" This reference to profit sets in motion the base desire for material gain as an alternative to the motive of jealous hatred. Through a simple transaction they may exchange Joseph for silver, thereby ridding themselves of Joseph permanently (as in death), while not acquiring blood guilt. Joseph's descent into the cistern will have been only the first stage of his subsequent descent into the netherworld of Egyptian servitude where dreams of celestial rulership come to nothing. Judah's proposal thus arises from the vulnerability of the brothers to the possibility of immediate and certain profit as Jacob's offer to Esau was a response to his vulnerability for red soup. The desire for immediate material gratification overpowers deeper considerations.

Compared with the superficiality of this motive, even their jealous hatred contains a deeper element of genuine, moral outrage against Joseph's arrogance and the injustice of his position of favor in the family. But now with Joseph stripped of his robe and lowered into the pit, passive and defenseless, he can no longer be so easily seen as an object of hatred.

So the sweet reasonableness of Judah's proposal, given as they soothe their frustrations in eating, reawakens the more quotidian desire for immediate material gain. The desire, coupled with their fear of discovery, quickly overcomes their deeper moral outrage, causing them to abandon the risky but more certain course of action to rid themselves of their hated brother: "and his brothers heeded him" (37:27b).

Judah's proposal is not the *stuff* of heroism, nor can he be a "good" brother in the same sense as Reuben. His argument is not one of high moral principle but of enlightened self-interest couched in clever, manipulative rhetoric in which the effect of saving Joseph's life is only secondary. His speech begins with an appeal to their desire for "profit." Only at the end does he finally remind them that Joseph is also their own "flesh." With Judah we leave the morning light of clear moral issues and return to the twilight of grey ambiguities.

But it is precisely this ambiguity that enables Judah's proposal to be consonant with the prognosticating dimension of the dream. On the one hand, by replacing Joseph with money, a certain closure is achieved with respect to the primary emotional system of the family; Joseph has been eliminated and the brothers have achieved satisfaction for the affront they suffered at his hands. On the other, his sale to the Ishmaelites leaves his future unpromising, but relatively open. But, perhaps more significantly, the crime can be concealed from Jacob and at least the surface unity of the family preserved for the time being. The family, of course, is left with no righteous heroes (Reuben ends up as a pathetic failed hero), but also with no blood guilt.

The narrative then relates the realization of this plan. Note that by this time the names Ishmaelite and Midianite can be used interchangeably.[39]

> And the men passed through, the Midianite traders. And they [the brothers] drew up and brought out Joseph from the cistern, and they sold Joseph to the Ishmaelites for twenty sheckels of silver, and caused Joseph to go into Egypt. 37:28

The remaining uncertainty in the brothers' plan is the reaction of Reuben to what they have done. The narrator reports his later return to rescue Joseph, in accord with the previous description of his intention, and his shock in finding the cistern empty. Whereas in the first scene Reuben arrived just in time to save Joseph, now he arrives too late.

And Reuben returned to the cistern, and behold, there was no Joseph in the cistern, and he tore his garment. 37:29

The response of rending garments is often done to express grief over a death (I Sam. 1:11). He then returns to the brothers and says: "The lad is not; and I, where shall I go?" (verse 30). Rather than accusing his brothers he is overcome by anxiety for himself as he, the elder responsible brother, anticipates the encounter with Jacob. This question indicates Reuben's surrender to the brothers' treachery. Acting behind his back they have deprived him of evidence he would need to accuse them. So Reuben, who earlier heroically challenged his brothers, is now reduced to pathetic silence which will not be broken until the issue of Joseph's disappearance arises again during their unknowing encounter with him in Egypt. The solidarity of the group is regained and the concealment of the crime is made certain.

The action is now moved forward in the narrative framework by the silent logic dictated by the necessity of concealing the crime from Jacob.

And they took Joseph's robe and they slaughtered a goat, and they dipped the robe in the blood. And they sent the striped robe and caused it to come to their father. 37:31–32

The robe is taken and smeared with the blood of a slaughtered goat which substitutes for the death of Joseph (as the ram had been sacrificed in place of Isaac). They do not take but "send" this object ahead and "cause it to come" to their father, sparing themselves the trauma and the unpredictable result of confronting Jacob in his moment of discovery. Then, in their climactic encounter with Jacob, they speak collectively, Reuben now totally reabsorbed into the anonymity of the group. They do not explicitly lie, but point to the deceptive evidence of the robe:

This we have found. Examine it now to see whether it is the robe of your son or not. 37:32

It is left then to Jacob to draw the false conclusion which the evidence was designed to suggest:

And he recognized it and said, "It is the robe of my son. An evil beast has eaten him. Torn to pieces is Joseph." And Jacob tore his garments and put sackcloth on his loins, and mourned over his son many days. 37:33

In face of this event Jacob's grief becomes uncontrollable. While, on one level, a proper relation has been preserved between Jacob and the brothers because of the successful concealment of their crime, on a deeper level they are now more profoundly alienated. This is indicated by Jacob's refusal of their attempt to console him, and the declaration that he will mourn until death unites him with Joseph in sheol:

And all his sons and all his daughters rose up to comfort him, and he refused to be consoled and he said that, "I will go down to my son mourning to sheol." And his father wept for him.37:35

Jacob's refusal of their comfort relates to his memory of their hatred and envy of Joseph and to the inauthenticity of the grief of those who withhold from him the only knowledge that could truly console him – that Joseph, in fact, is not dead. He later tacitly accuses them of Joseph's murder (42:36).[40] The narrative which began with the breaking of peaceful, trusting communication between Joseph and his brothers now depicts a deep and apparently permanent emotional estrangement between Jacob and his other children. The removal of the envied Joseph (as with the death of Abel), rather than bringing the criminals into a new intimacy with their father (as Cain desired with God), has apparently made such intimacy forever impossible as Jacob prefers communion with Joseph even in death to the solace of his other living children (as Cain was driven away from the face of God to wander forever). The logic of rivalry has run its course, though it has been deflected from its murderous end by a substitution which left Joseph alive, but exiled from the family.

Chapter 37 thus closes with the initial problems raised in verses 1–4 resolved. Jacob's passion for this son of his old age has now been stifled by the bloody robe before him. The transgressive emotions which prompted this gift have now been recompensed by the hatred which it evoked in the brothers. But *šalōm* has not been restored either by the establishment of a new order or by the restoration of the old. The bloody robe is a sign which conceals the truth rather than representing it. The additional color of blood smeared across the stripes of the robe marks not the death of Joseph but the death of Jacob's desire to elevate him above his brothers. But Jacob's refusal to be comforted by the perpetrators of this deed points to the deeper alienation that now prevails between the father and his other sons.

The only way in which this alienation can be overcome is for the truth to be known. But it is here that the dilemma at this juncture in the plot is posed. So long as Joseph is assumed by Jacob to be dead, the *šalōm* between Jacob and the other brothers is undermined by their deception and his suspicion of it, making the transmission of the promise impossible. But, if the truth is known that Joseph lives, he will be reunited with Jacob and the cruel deception of the brothers revealed, thus also leading to their rejection. For the unity of the family to be preserved a way must be devised for Joseph not only to be "resurrected," but, more importantly, for this to occur in such a way that reconciliation can occur as a basis for the transmission of the promise to all the sons.

But before this dilemma can be resolved, the problem of Joseph remains. If Jacob's transgressive passion has been dispelled, Joseph's transformation from a "spoiled tattler" into a celestial ruler is not yet complete. It is this transformation that is the central concern of chapters 39–41 (chapter 38 being the digressive story of Judah and Tamar).

To move from chapter 37 to chapter 39 is to move from the world of manifest ambiguities crossed by shadows concealing unspeakable truths to a more simple world of straightforward good and evil governed by a benevolent divine will. This narrative will not be analyzed here in detail; I will note only its major features and the function it plays in the longer narrative context.

The dynamics of this narrative arise out of the hermeneutical perspective articulated in the narrative framework, and very little of decisive importance occurs in direct discourse. The narrator creates the setting of Joseph's servitude in Egypt. He recounts how Joseph is brought from the Ishmaelites/Midianites by Potiphar, a captain of the guards in the service of the Pharaoh, a stroke of good fortune indeed. Once in the house of Potiphar "Yahweh was with Joseph" and "caused him to prosper" in all that he did (37:2,3). Joseph thus is thrown again into the role of the recipient of action rather than the source of action. Seeing that Yahweh was with Joseph, Potiphar gives him more and more responsibility. The prosperity that comes to the house of Potiphar under Joseph is not the result of Joseph, *per se*, but of Yahweh working through him.

Joseph is finally called upon to act for himself only when he is tempted by Potiphar's wife. The text creates for us a setting in which Potiphar knows nothing about his own household except "the bread which he was eating" (39:6). This subtly suggests the absence of sexual relations between Potiphar and his wife. The narrator then juxtaposes the absence of Potiphar's interest in his household (of which the wife is presumably a part) with the presence of a physically appealing Joseph who has been placed in charge of it all. Joseph is described graphically as a young man of "beautiful form, and handsome in appearance". The (neglected) wife then responds visually to Joseph's appearance, "she lifted up her eyes to Joseph" and verbally entices him boldly saying, "Lie with me" (39:7).

Joseph must then decide whether Potiphar has indeed placed him in charge of *everything* in his household including his wife. He decides that marriage has at least implicitly placed the wife out of his charge. She is not to be considered simply household property. He thus spurns her request with a moral explanation which qualifies him as a person of unshakable integrity. Joseph thus defines himself not by acting, but by resisting action, and becomes unambiguously good as a consequence. The wife, by comparison, becomes the evil seductress (though perhaps with a touch of understanding implied by her apparently neglected state) drawn to him by the beauty of his physical form (one thinks here of Eve's yielding to the visual beauty of the fruit). Frustrated, she eventually presses her cause more aggressively at the appropriate time, saying again, "Lie with me," causing him to flee into the street leaving behind his garment in her grasping hands. This is an absolutely clear posing of a virtuous character against a transgressive sensualist. By deciding judiciously and acting righteously, Joseph leaves behind the egoistic, arrogant, transgressive persona he exhibited at the outset of chapter 37. He becomes an unambiguous, sympathetic protagonist with whom a somewhat moralistic (male?) reader can identify.

It should be noted that direct discourse in this scene has no effect on the course of events. Character and action are being defined by a moral struggle that takes place within (the lust of the wife, the moral decision of Joseph) which is only expressed secondarily in speech. Joseph's virtue finally was exhibited not in his speech, but in his flight (recounted in third-person discourse).

The consequence of Joseph's virtue one might expect to be a greater reward. But instead, the woman lies about what has happened using a garment of Joseph's again to serve as misleading evidence. And Joseph, quietly, passively is sent off to prison by the irate, believing husband. As a consequence of his virtuous action, he is sent even further into the depths of Egyptian servitude. His good action produces evil consequences. The lie of Potiphar's wife is now, ironically, joined to the conspiratorial discourse of the brothers to determine the fate of Joseph set in motion by the dream.

In prison, Yahweh is again "with Joseph" (39:21) and he soon finds himself in charge of the prison. Fortunately, the prisoners of the king are also kept here, and soon two persons from the court of the king are thrown into prison under Joseph's charge. The narrator has thus so arranged the action and setting as to bring Joseph, here at the nadir of his life, into contact with persons from the apex of Egyptian society. The linkage from the bottom to the top is thus made which can be the mechanism of Joseph's ascension. But how?

Again dreams intervene. This time they are not to Joseph but to the two members of the Egyptian court. Joseph, playing the role of the effective administrator, sees "how gloomy" the two officials are the morning after and asks, "Why are your faces sad today?" (41:6,7). With this a dialogue initiates the action which brings about the reversal in Joseph's descent.

They said to him, "We have dreamed a dream, and there is no interpretation of it." And he said to them, "Are there not interpretations from God? Tell me, I pray." 40:8

In this dialogue Joseph moves into the role which will define his identity for the remainder of the narrative. In response to the need of the court officials for an interpretation of their dreams, he asserts persuasively, through a rhetorical question, the availability of such interpretations from God. This links not the dreams themselves but their more crucial interpretation with the divine. But, more importantly, this statement places Joseph in the position of explaining the role of God to these men. When he then urges them to tell him their dreams, he presumes his own direct access to divine interpretations. Thus interpretations that are "from God" also may come from Joseph. In this statement he implicitly claims access to divine knowledge, while simultaneously effacing himself before the divine so that God, rather than himself, appears to be the source of the interpretation. This ambiguous coalescence of the role of Joseph with that of God (and the narrator) continues from this point on, and finally surfaces explicitly in Joseph's annoyed denial in the last scene, when he raises the rhetorical question with his brothers, "am I in the place of God?" (50:19) To the extent that he knows the meaning of the dreams, he comes to live in the same present as God (and the narrator) for whom the end is known at the beginning.

This breakthrough of Joseph into the present of God (and the narrator) brings his own inner thoughts and speech into a new importance for the progress of the narrative. His understanding and knowledge can now for the first time play a central role in the development of the plot. It is significant, then, that Joseph assumes a very aggressive stance with respect to his circumstances. After he gives the interpretation of the cup-bearer's dream, he explicitly asks him to

> remember me to the Pharaoh, and you will bring me forth from this house. For I was surely stolen from the land of the Hebrews, and also here I have not done anything that they should put me in prison. 40:14

Here Joseph takes control of his life, and attempts to use his new influence to extricate himself from prison rather than passively waiting for events to happen to him. However, the result of this self-assertion is that when the dream interpretation proves true, and the cup-bearer is again serving the Pharaoh, "he forgot him" (verse 23). His clever scheme comes to naught. There is no relation between Joseph's virtuous acts and his fate. His future is being controlled by transcendent forces. The chief butler does not tell the Pharaoh of Joseph until he sees the opportunity to be of service to the king when the Egyptian wise men are unable to interpret one of the king's own dreams. No direct connection thus remains between Joseph's scheme and the chief butler's self-serving action.

The portrayal of Joseph in this segment of the narrative thus does not seem to aim at the glorification of Joseph as an example of the wise young man.

One of the chief tenets of wisdom teaching is that wisdom is the most certain path to success. This sequence of events illustrates the opposite. Joseph's every effort proves fruitless. It is only God who is the decisive acting subject of this narrative before whom Joseph remains the effaced instrument. Thus when Joseph is asked to interpret the dreams of the Pharaoh, he again prefaces his interpretation with the statement: "Not I, God will answer the Pharaoh favorably" (41:16).

Though Joseph proposes to the king the position that he will later occupy, and suggests that it be filled by a person with his own qualities, it is nevertheless because of what God has done *through* Joseph that he is finally elevated by the Pharaoh to this high position. The king says:

> After God has caused you to know all this, there is none so intelligent and wise as you. Now you will be over my house. 41:39, 40

Thus, the direct discourse of Joseph (his interpretations offered upon request), which proves to be the turning point in his fortunes is not properly his own speech but that of God. Joseph is merely the virtuous but effaced agent through whom these interpretations may come. The effect which they have upon his fortune is thus attributable to God and not to Joseph's own efforts or brilliance as such. Joseph, the egoistic favorite son, has indeed been transformed into the opposite, a self-effacing agent of divine knowledge.

The denouement of this narrative predictably occurs when Joseph and his brothers are again united. This takes place in Egypt, and is prompted by the drought which drives the brothers to seek food there where Joseph has been given charge of drought preparation, thanks to his interpretations of the Pharaoh's dreams. But this encounter is not a straightforward reunion. The two sides of this event of recognition – Joseph's recognition of them, and their recognition of Joseph – are temporally split apart, deferring the denouement, and allowing a complex sub-plot to be developed between them. This lengthy narrative will be not be analyzed in detail. I will discuss only the major features which reveal its role in the larger narrative sequence.

The encounter of Joseph and his brothers in Egypt brings the perspective of the dream into unity with the normal consciousness of a character for the first time, that is, the future events conveyed by the dreams take place and are recognized as such by Joseph: "And the brothers of Joseph came and bowed themselves down to him, their faces to the ground, and Joseph saw his brothers and recognized them" (42:6). Since it is the dreams which convey the narrator's perspective, Joseph's realization of their fulfillment causes his knowledge of the meaning of the events to coincide with that of the narrator for the first time. Now they both occupy almost the same present. This event transforms Joseph's perspective upon the past, and defamiliarizes the events which led up to this point. But this experience is not allowed to erupt into the surface of the narrative at this early stage.

Since the brothers do not recognize him, this places him in an unusual position. He possesses knowledge of the end of the narrative before it is known by the other characters. This gives him the opportunity to orchestrate the way in which the ending will occur for them as he chooses. He can now, in effect, "write" the ending himself, and make them characters in a sub-plot of his own devising. So Joseph conceals his knowledge beneath a new deception which the narrator describes: "and he made himself strange to them, and spoke severely to them" (42:7). The deception is then expressed by Joseph specifically in the question he asks them: "where do you come from?" (42:7). But this question, while deceptive, forms the initial element in a complex plot designed now by Joseph to penetrate a more primary deception and to bring his brothers to see the past events of their lives in a new light. It is thus the beginning of the process which will lead to the climactic event of defamiliarization in chapter 45.

From this point on the course of the plot is not foreshadowed by a dream but rather is known only by Joseph. The dynamics for the reader change from uncertainty concerning how the foreshadowed end can possibly occur, to uncertainty regarding Joseph's motives and purposes. At this point the perspectives of the narrator and of Joseph almost completely coincide, with Joseph himself assuming the role of a narrator internal to the narrative. It is, in fact, through his self-conscious creation of a fiction which he compels his brothers to enact that the narrative will move toward its final, climactic denouement. Now that Joseph has understood the hidden meaning of the previous course of events, he assumes the role with respect to his brothers which the narrator (and God) had in the preceding events toward all the characters. This enables him then to imitate the pattern of the preceding narrative, putting his brothers through another sequence of events, the meaning of which will contradict their surface appearance, and only be revealed at the end.

But while Joseph is creating his fiction, the narrator is focusing upon an entirely different story – Joseph's private thoughts and especially the emotional effects of his duplicity upon Joseph himself (42:8, 9, 23, 24; 43:30, 31; 45: 1, 2). The source of tension in this plot thus becomes, in part, how long Joseph will be able to maintain his deception in the face of powerful emotions, generated by his memories and compelling him to disclose his identity to his kinsmen. This is obviously not the first time a character in Genesis has engaged in deception, but it is the first time the private anguish produced by the deception has been portrayed. Previously it has been the emotion connected with the disillusionment of the deceived (the Pharaoh, Isaac) which has been portrayed. The narrative purpose served by this portrayal is to reveal Joseph's growing feelings of compassion for his brothers behind his harsh facade, so that the reader can be aware that the meaning of Joseph's actions is not to be found in their surface appearance. This inner conflict serves to foreshadow the positive end to which this deception is leading. The duration of Joseph's self-control is the aspect of this narrative segment not known by Joseph, which prevents the total coalescence of the narrator's perspective with that of Joseph.

The impetus behind this tension in Joseph arises from the basic plot movement from alienation and the breakdown of communication in the family to reconciliation and the restoration of trusting speech. The question which now must be raised is that of the relation of Joseph's own fiction to this more basic direction of the plot.

The dilemma with which chapter 37 ended arose from the necessity yet impossibility of reintegrating Joseph into the family. For him simply to return to Jacob with the report of what had happened would cause Jacob to reject permanently the other brothers. But for him to remain outside the family would mean that the unity of the family would be based on a concealed crime. The basis of the reunion of Joseph must thus be his reconciliation with the brothers. But this can only take place authentically if the brothers themselves also now undergo a transformation, as both Jacob and Joseph have done in the preceding narrative. It is to this end that Joseph's sub-plot is directed, and as each advance is made, a corresponding weakening of Joseph's will to maintain his alien facade is registered by outbursts of private weeping. The initial and final stages of this process are specifically depicted by the narrator:

> Joseph saw his brothers, and recognized them, but made himself strange to them ... And Joseph could not restrain himself before all those standing by him, and he cried out and caused every man from around him to go out, and not a man stood with him while Joseph revealed himself to his brothers. 42:7; 45:1

The transformation is directed toward the central unresolved issue, namely, the concealment by the brothers of their crime, and the consequences that has for the relations of the brothers to Jacob (and to the process of communication in the family). The sign which betrays to Joseph the deeper problem in the family (which arose after his departure) is the absence of Benjamin. Thus he intimidates them into divulging in response to his harsh accusation that they are spies. (They later deny that they gave this information without being specifically asked for it [43:6].) The narrator reveals some of the rhetoric which has been used to conceal and to reveal Jacob's real suspicions. In his instructions to the brothers before the trip the narrator records in indirect discourse[41] Jacob's reason given to the brothers for not sending Benjamin: "For he [feared that] harm might befall him" (42:4). Later, in refusing to permit Benjamin to return with them, he explains, "if harm should befall him in the way that you will go" (42:38). At the outset of this discussion, however, he comes very close indeed to charging them directly with the murder of Joseph when he says,

"You have bereaved me. Joseph is no more... and you would take Benjamin" (42:36). The term "bereaved" (שִׁכֵּל) in the piel, characteristically refers to the murder of a child or person (Gen. 27:45; I Sam. 15:33; Ez. 14:15; Jer. 15:7).

When the brothers thus disclose to Joseph, "the youngest is this day with our father, and one is no more," the absence of Benjamin and their oblique way of speaking of Joseph's fate disclose the parameters of the familial problem. The truth about Joseph's fate has been concealed from Jacob behind equivocal words, and the result is a disappearance of trust between Jacob and the brothers. A crisis in Jacob's relation to the brothers has been avoided by the presence of Benjamin, the second and last son of Rachel, who could take Joseph's place in the father's affections. The former familial pattern could thus be continued, Jacob now doting on Benjamin. But there is one major change. Jacob does not entrust Benjamin to the brothers as he once entrusted Joseph. But no one questions this since beneath this change lies the truth which could destroy the family. The response made by Joseph goes straight to the center of this tenuous *modus vivendi* which has grown up in his absence, and extracts its key support.

Joseph's charge of spying and their denial raises the question of their truthfulness. In so doing he creates a fictional construct whose terms correspond to those of the real situation which he knows but cannot acknowledge. What he knows is that they have concealed the truth about his disappearance. When he charges them with lying about their reasons for entering Egypt he thus creates a fiction, a lie, which points to the deeper truth. The narrative from this point on thus operates on two levels, and each event has two meanings. The brothers fall blindly into his trap precisely because they passionately desire to hide the lie at the center of their existence by proving to Joseph their absolute honesty in this situation. But he has so structured the situation that for them to prove their honesty in the way he demands, it means that the deeper lie must ultimately be disclosed. Their attempt to be scrupulously honest with Joseph and their certainty of success impel them finally to agree to subordinate themselves to him. From the depth of this crisis, the truth finally emerges. It is this strategy which enables them to face themselves and their crime and purge themselves of its effects, opening the way for reconciliation with Joseph and with Jacob.

After making his demand, Joseph lets them suffer a few days of agonizing indecision in prison under the impossible demand that they send only one of their number back to Jacob to bring Benjamin (Jacob would never have let Benjamin go under such conditions, and whoever went to present such an argument would never have been believed) before softening the demand and allowing all of them save one, to return.

It is noteworthy that both of these demands are inconsistent with the charge of spying which he is making against them. To allow any of them to return would have permitted the fulfillment of their mission as spies. The demand to return and bring Benjamin is thus logically related only to the deeper issue of their honesty and credibility.

The connection between Joseph's fictitious charge and the deeper truth is perceived immediately by the brothers. The demand to deliver Benjamin up to him brings them face to face with their lack of credibility with Jacob due to their previously concealed crime. They thus confess in Joseph's hearing, but without realizing that he could understand their language (because he had been speaking through an interpreter):

> Certainly we are guilty over our brother whom we saw in the distress of his soul in his supplication to us, and we did not listen to him. Thus has this come upon us. 42:21

Joseph's demand thus returns the brothers to the primal scene of the crime as evidenced by the emotional description they make of the situation (perhaps even elaborating on Joseph's attempts to persuade them to release him, under the influence of their guilt), and evokes a collective confession of their guilt. Even Reuben, speaking up now for the first time since his final impotent lament, reminds them that he was against it from the start!

This frank acknowledgement of guilt reaches Joseph's pent-up emotions, and the narrator reports that he turns away from them to weep for the first time. This represents a break in the cold, harsh facade behind which he had chosen to hide himself at the outset, and the beginning of the process of his emotional reconciliation with them.[42]

If the first demand of Joseph was designed to open the old wound by revealing Jacob's distrust of the brothers, the second element of his strategy is to precipitate a crisis by ensnaring Benjamin, once in Egypt, thereby forcing the brothers to reveal whether they would sacrifice Benjamin as they once sacrificed him. The device he uses for this entrapment is the surreptitious return of the payment for the grain by having the money each man paid returned to his sack (42:25).

The money in this episode also has its correlate in the primal scene. Joseph is very conscious that he was "stolen" (40:15). He had been replaced by silver in the life of the family. It was for "profit" that Joseph's life had been spared. He had literally been treated as a commodity and his bodily presence exchanged for silver. Thus when the brothers come to pay Joseph in silver for the grain, the silver assumes a negative valence in relation to him. By covertly returning the money he gives them an additional means of proving their honesty to him. This attempt is even more ironically related to their dishonesty in the primal scene than the attempt to disprove the spying charge by bringing Benjamin.

Although the narrator does not take space to tell us specifically what the brothers did with this "profit," there is now a metonymic, figural (if not literal) continuity between Joseph and the family silver in the economy of this closed narrative structure. The appearance of the silver coincides with the disappearance of Joseph. The commercial transaction which began with his sale is not complete until the "profit" is used. By accepting the silver he would be participating in the closure of the commercial transaction by which he was excluded from the family, and would thus be tacitly accepting the status quo. To refuse the money prohibits this closure. Thus when the money is returned in their sacks of grain, they are indeed shocked and dismayed. The narrator says that "their hearts went out" (42:28).

The equation of Joseph and the silver becomes more explicit in the final segment of the plot when Joseph's personal silver divining cup, which, as we shall see, is a metonymic symbol of Joseph himself, is added to the silver being returned to the brothers.

But, more significantly, they see in the uncanny return of the silver the action of God: "Look what God has done to us" (42:28). Just as they immediately linked the demand that Benjamin be brought to Egypt with their guilt over the crime against Joseph, so now they link, implicitly, the return of the money with their guilt over his sale. When later, in a similar circumstance at the climax of this plot, Benjamin has been discovered with the silver cup which has been "planted" along with the money, Judah explicitly states to Joseph, "God has found the guilt of your servant" (44:16), referring indirectly to the deeper guilt from the past. In reference to the connection made here between the surface events and the deeper guilt Westermann comments: "Therein is the work of God seen here in that a connection is made in the inconceivable comings and goings of the life of a man, between guilt and punishment, and with that also a meaning."[43]

The next mention of the silver comes immediately after the brothers, at home again, have reported to Jacob the loss of Simeon in Egypt, and the necessity of bringing Benjamin with them on their next trip to obtain food. As they empty their sacks before Jacob, the silver also spills out.[44] The shocking appearance of the excess silver thus coincides in the eyes of Jacob with the report of the disappearance of another brother.

Each report of the discovery of the silver thus serves a different narrative function. For the brothers it evokes their guilt over the sale of Joseph, whereas in the encounter with Jacob it exacerbates his suspicions of the brothers and leads to the strongest accusation of their guilt in the matter of Joseph noted above: "You have bereaved me. Joseph is no more, and Simeon is no more, and now you would take Benjamin" (42:36). Due to the strategy of Joseph, the disappearance of a son from the family coincides with an increase in silver. Silver has become a mute sign of the brothers' unspeakable, subterranean commerce in Jacob's sons.

When the time has come for the second trip to obtain food (43:1,2 – Jacob resists sending Benjamin but finally has to bow to necessity, 43:6, 11), Judah gives a personal guarantee of Benjamin's safety which is reluctantly accepted by Jacob. (Reuben's earlier, more drastic, but obviously unpalatable offer to allow his own sons to be killed if he fails to return Benjamin, is ignored by Jacob, 42:37,38, again putting Reuben in the role of an ineffective moral extremist.) Jacob explicitly instructs the brothers to return to Egypt with double the required money along with some gifts (43:11,12). In spite of the brothers' insistence on Benjamin's return with them, they have made no mention of the necessity of also returning the silver. Jacob thus does not rely on the brothers' honesty in this regard.

Upon arrival in Egypt Joseph has them brought directly to his house for a feast to celebrate his reunion with Benjamin (43:16). But immediately they interpret this generous act in terms of their guilt and fear regarding the silver, and they suspect that Joseph is about to charge them with theft in order to entrap and enslave them (43:18). Of course their perception that Joseph is entrapping them with the money is ironically correct, but not in the sense they expect. The brothers are thus portrayed as vaguely sensing what is happening to them under the surface, but failing to penetrate the outer appearances.

The servant's response to the brothers' fears regarding the money mirrors their own first reaction to its discovery, that is, that God has done this (43:23). But for the brothers this divine action is a reason to fear, whereas the Egyptian official presents it as a source of comfort, thereby providing an ironic interplay of perspectives reflecting the tension between the two levels of the narrative.

But another, more significant irony is present here. The official knows that Joseph and not God is responsible for this action. His response thus deliberately plays upon the popular tendency to see in the uncanny the action of the divine (43:23). But in so doing, he offers yet another example in this narrative of the correlation of the role of Joseph with the role of God. Here, however, it is done with conscious intent by one of the characters to deceive another. This free use of the idea of divine action as a literary device shows the same type of secularity present in Jacob's similar strategy in the deception scene with Isaac (27:20).

The narrative function of the meal to which Joseph invites them provides an appropriate occasion for Joseph to encounter Benjamin. This reunion, unlike the first with the brothers, instantly evokes from Joseph an emotional reaction which he must conceal by leaving the room (43:30,31). This marks another step in the breakdown of his resistance to reconciliation. It also serves as a prelude to the climactic ruse.

In preparation for their second return, Joseph not only has their money again returned,[45] but now includes with it another piece of silver – his personal cup used, perhaps, for professional divining, in keeping with his probable reputation now as a seer (44:1,2). With the hiding of the cup, the connection between Joseph and the silver hidden in the sacks becomes more explicit. In Joseph's fictional construct, the divining cup is a metonymic figure for himself, the seer who reads the meaning of dreams and foretells the future. He is figuratively linked to silver by the brothers' initial exchange. When he hides the cup in the sacks of grain, causing the brothers to "steal" it, he forces them to reenact, figuratively, his own abduction and sale. As the result of this theft, the divining cup comes to rest in the feed sacks of Egyptian grain, just as Joseph has come to dwell in the midst of the storage bins of Egypt.

The meaning of this charade through which Joseph leads the brothers is finally made explicit when he asks Judah: "What is this deed you have done? Did you not know that a man like me will surely divine?" (44:15) To steal the divining cup from a diviner is self-defeating. So at the deeper level, the theft of Joseph, whom the brothers should have known could see the future, was foolish since his psychic powers revealed by his dreams would inevitably lead to the exposure of their crime.

The same interplay between hidden and surface meanings is also at work in his instructions to his officer as to what he should say when he caught them. He is to ask: "Why have you returned evil in the place of good?" (44:4) The brothers are being accused of committing a crime against Joseph when they intended to be acting more than honorably. Their good actions are apparently resulting in evil consequences due to the intervention of Joseph which reverses their significance. The mystifying contradiction between the intentions and their effects corresponds to the larger pattern of events which Joseph sees. Due to the actions of the divine, the evil intentions of the brothers against him are producing good effects. For the brothers to experience the evil effects of their actions, which contradict their good intentions, thus prepares them to accept the reverse proposition which Joseph offers them in the next scene regarding the meaning of the larger course of events. Nowhere can Joseph be more clearly seen to assume the role of God. But, more immediately, this charge and the investigation which follows it lead to the final denouement of the conflict between Joseph and his brothers. The brothers, blind to the hidden agenda at work, use their attempt to return the money as the basis of proving their absolute honesty. So certain are they now of their honesty in this situation that they make the ultimate vow: that the guilty person, if he be found, die, and the others be thrown into slavery (44:9). With this foolhardy declaration of their innocence, they throw themselves with blind abandon into the very teeth of Joseph's trap, and in so doing complete their absolute subjection to and humiliation before him.

The discovery of the planted cup in Benjamin's sack breaks the tenuous thread of credibility that linked the brothers with Jacob. Judah's absolute pledge to return Benjamin safely is the last bond which unites the brothers with their father. Joseph's servant again pretends to moderate their abject proposal, and requires *only* the enslavement of the guilty party (44:9). When Benjamin is discovered with the cup, the final link to Jacob is broken and their entire world falls apart (44:12, 13). The truth must now be presented concerning the family if all is not to be lost.

The crisis corresponds to the crisis in the primal scene. The brothers both then and now had responsibility for the welfare of the younger sons of Jacob. While there is no evidence that Jacob overtly flaunts his partiality toward Benjamin, as he had toward Joseph, it is obvious that he favors Benjamin above the others, as he had Joseph. The central question is, as Speiser formulates it, "Would the brothers revert to type, and welcome the opportunity to leave Benjamin, this time with a genuine excuse? This was the test."[46]

The other issue at stake is the brothers' concern over the well-being of their father. In the earlier episode they were consumed by their hatred of Joseph without any regard for the feelings of Jacob. That the effect of their action upon Jacob would be so severe that he would long to be reunited with Joseph even in death went beyond their egocentric imaginations. That deep suspicion would prevent Jacob from accepting their consolation, leaving them permanently alienated from their father, was also beyond their feverish mentality.

Judah's extraordinarily long speech to Joseph in response to this crisis first makes it clear that now the brothers have come to be keenly aware of the significance and depth of Jacob's feelings about Benjamin (44:18–34). At this point there is a divergence of opinion among commentators as to whether this represents an authentic transformation of Judah's attitude,[47] or only a submission to necessity.[48] Judah's newly found concern for Jacob's feelings and Benjamin's safety are rooted in the necessity imposed upon him by the drought and Joseph's conditions for the sale of food. In order for the family to obtain grain Benjamin must come to Egypt, and in order for him to be allowed to come, Jacob's feelings must be placated by a guarantee regarding his safety which Judah makes personally.

When Benjamin is arrested for the theft of the cup, Coats asks, "What else could he do" but offer himself in Benjamin's place? He thus sees in this action no change in character or moral awakening on the part of Judah, but only a response to the circumstances of the occasion.[49]

This, however, overlooks the fact that a commitment is always, to some extent, a free act. While circumstances engineered by Joseph put enormous pressure on Judah, they do not deprive him of freedom. But beyond that, the commitments made are effective determinants of character so long as there are no mental reservations which make them, in Austin's terms, "infelicitous." Character here is not a spiritual essence but a function of action and performative speech. The length and eloquent passion of Judah's speech makes it clear that, whatever the forces of necessity operating upon him, he speaks the truth which is decisive for this narrative. In his commitment to sacrifice himself in Benjamin's place for the sake of his old father's feelings, he undergoes a transformation (as both Jacob and Joseph had before him), and with him, to some degree, the brothers whom he represents.

Joseph's strategy has not been to revenge the wrong done him, but to create a situation in which circumstances would make it difficult for the brothers not to assume a responsible stance toward Jacob and the sons of Rachel, unless they were indeed hopelessly corrupt. The experience of assuming such a position would restore their personal dignity and parity with Joseph more than would a contrite confession to him of their sin (which he bluntly rejects when they offer it in the final scene, 50:19). Such a confession would make their status dependent upon his grace and would thus establish them in a position spiritually inferior to him.

Coats' argument that there can be no reconciliation apart from "conscious confession" to the offended party is opposed by the major thesis of the Joseph story which will be expressed in the next scene: that their "sin" served the intentions of God, and thus Joseph does not hold them guilty for their crime. The major concern of this argument is to achieve reconciliation on the basis of insight into the mysterious course of history which leaves all parties morally equal, rather than on the basis of confession and forgiveness which divides parties into the transgressors (guilty) and the transgressed (innocent). The logic of Joseph's strategy is thus to bring the brothers to the point where they can regain their self-respect so as to be able to accept moral parity with Joseph. Judah's speech eloquently achieves this aim, and evokes from Joseph the final collapse of his alien identity.

And Joseph could not restrain himself before all those standing by him, and he cried out, and caused every man from around him to go out, and not a man stood with him while Joseph revealed himself to his brothers. 45:1

With this development the narrator's story of Joseph's inner struggle to conceal his identity from his brothers comes to an end. Judah's eloquent speech reveals the suffering of his father over Joseph's assumed death and the disarray in which this sad episode has left the family. It also brings to expression Judah's capacity for noble self-sacrifice for the sake of maintaining his commitment to Jacob regarding the return of Benjamin. The basis of trust now exists for Joseph, as does the possibility that the brothers can accept themselves and their own past without undue self-incrimination. So Joseph can no longer restrain his desire for unity and reconciliation with them. This scene of reunion is not a public spectacle, however, but a restoration of familial trust at the deepest level. Joseph's expelling of the Egyptians signifies the beginning of a scene of the deepest familial intimacy. Even then, however, the narrator tells us that the Egyptians heard his weeping, so total was the breakdown of his pent-up emotions.

The normal plot structure would end at this point, with the brothers being overjoyed at discovering their brother in such a position of power and still so eager now to accept them. But the Biblical narrator is not given to glossing over the deeper complexities of human relations. As we have seen, the reunification of Joseph into the family presents serious problems for the brothers since it means that Jacob now will certainly learn the truth of what they have done to his son. Joseph's self-identification does not dispel these fears since his next statement raises this very problem:

And Joseph said to his brothers, "I am Joseph. Does my father still live?" 45:3

Rather than responding with spontaneous joy, thus, the narrator reports that the brothers, "were not able to answer him for they were terrified in his presence" (45:3). The reaction of the brothers reveals that the healing of the breach in the family and the achievement of the major goal of the plot will not be the simple consequence of Joseph's self-disclosure. This opens a new narrative episode that differs fundamentally from the foregoing scenes.

With the fulfillment of Joseph's dream now known both by Joseph and the brothers, the plot which was governed by movement toward that end has now reached its termination. Whereas in chapters 37 and 39–41 only the narrator understood how the course of events was leading to the end portrayed in the dream, and in chapters 42–44 Joseph came to share the narrator's perspective, now the brothers also know that the dream has indeed reached its end in their own abject subordination to Joseph. Thus the present of the narrator and Joseph now come together with the present of the brothers and the multi-leveled plot structure is unified into a single plane of discourse.

The narrator's report of the inability of the brothers to respond to Joseph's revelation signifies that the narrative is led by a goal deeper than that of the dream and its fulfillment. The movement of the narrative from this point on will be generated not by a revelation of the end of the story in its beginning, but by the interaction of the rhetoric of Joseph with the terrified minds and emotions of the brothers. This poses very clearly the deeper problem with which the narrative is concerned: the restoration of communication between Joseph and his brothers which was broken at the outset of the narrative by rivalry between them for the affection of the father. This problem has arisen repeatedly in the course of the Genesis narrative, and has never been adequately resolved. One rival has been consistently excluded from the history of the promise (Cain, Ishmael, Esau) with only a minimum of divine protection. Now, however, with the end of the patriarchal age coming before the settlement of the land, the promise must be a common possession of all the brothers in the lineage of Abraham.

Unless the chronic problem of rivalry is solved, the unity of the tradition will be torn apart and its future imperiled.

The narrator does not soften the problem. Joseph, seeing that they cannot respond, physically reaches out to them by saying, "Please come near to me," repeating his self-identification, "I am Joseph your brother ..." (45:4). Now, however, he proceeds to the crux of the problem – "whom you sold into Egypt." Perceiving that the central problem is with the brothers' attitude toward themselves in light of the outcome of what they had done, he says, "Do not be grieved and angry with yourselves [literally: in your eyes] that you sold me here" (45:5). Joseph does not expect from them a confession of their sin to him, nor will he offer them forgiveness. Rather he points them to a context of meaning larger than that of guilt/confession and punishment/forgiveness in which to understand what they have done.

He asks the brothers to transcend the internal world of their own life drama, and to envision the meaning of the central events of their lives from the perspective of their end, and the universal purpose served by that end. He thus invites the brothers to enter into the perspective of the transcendental Author who manipulates his characters on the stage of life to serve hidden ends as he had just manipulated them.

> God sent me before you to preserve life ... And now it was not you who sent me, yourselves, but God. 45:5, 8

These interpretive comments show the opening of Joseph to the perspective of the author. But instead of finding along this communicative axis another voice, or even the dynamic occurrence of performative language which would found his consciousness and identity, he finds third-person interpretive statements. When a character in a symbolic narrative is opened toward performative language his identity takes form in subjective dialogue with that language. It is in this free dialogue that the negativity at the basis of characters in the expressive and representative narratives is overcome. This negativity always places those characters within the determination of closed differential systems (full versus empty, hidden versus revealed), whereas in the Joseph narrative, however, an inversion of this process occurs. The language encountered in the moment of subjective reflection (not given in the narrative framework, significantly, but revealed only in Joseph's dialogue with his brothers) is itself third-person language which speaks of a hidden determination of the course of events toward an end unforeseen by any character. This is to say that the "idea-force" (Bakhtin) at the center of this narrative is itself the idea of predetermined action. It is this idea which shapes the subjectivity of Joseph who, as we have seen, after his fall from the egoistic heights of his privileged position in the family, is a largely fixed, passive character, driven by circumstance, who is made successful by the unseen presence of the divine, and who acts only according to fixed moral codes of obligation and duty. His few attempts to exert control over the course of events himself totally fail until he reaches the pinnacle of power. Once there, however, his consciousness is virtually assimilated into that of God. Knowing the future (as God does) he acquires the power to determine the present for all the other characters (he describes himself as being like a "father" to the Pharaoh, 45:8). Thus Joseph is absorbed into the negativity of the third-person subject (God) – the "He" who knows the hidden end and covertly determines the present to achieve that end.

This is the "idea-force" at work in the public world of the author which he is appropriating for his own purposes. He is still a symbolic narrator here in that he does not permit this deterministic perspective to remain global. Rather, step by step, he draws it into the narrative, first by allowing Joseph to share it with the narrator, and finally by having Joseph present it in direct discourse to his brothers as an interpretation which he seeks to persuade them to accept. As the promise was the basic "idea-force" at work in the patriarchal sagas, so here it is the concept of divine – "authorial" – determination of events. Using "social symbolic" strategy this idea is presented, not to Joseph privately, but in the social discourse he has with the brothers. The end toward which this moves is, however, not foreseen or determined, that is, the use of the idea of a divine plan to persuade the brothers to accept themselves and be reconciled with Joseph in trust. The deterministic perspective is drawn into the DD of the narrative and finally subordinated to the dialogical.

It is in this verbal encounter between Joseph and his brothers that this narrative reaches the culminating moment of defamiliarization. The interpretation of past events which Joseph offers incorporates them into a totally new context which fundamentally alters their meaning. This new context is the kernel of a new "story," the primary acting subject of which is God. Rather than seeing themselves now as guilty and defeated and Joseph as the righteous victor (as would likely be the case in the denouement of a representative narrative), in the new story which Joseph, the consummate narrator, proposes, they see themselves as playing an unknowing but indispensable role in a divine plot to save the lives of countless people. The new perspective this offers both the brothers and the reader makes possible the perception of the form of human activity apart from the content, thereby totally relativizing the form. The action that was believed to be a crime by those who perpetrated it is now perceived, in light of this new perspective, as the opposite, regardless of the intent behind the action.

The tension thus in this narrative does not stem from the conflict between Joseph and his brothers, but from their capacity at this point to perceive their own lives in a new way – as part of a larger story. But this experience is itself not the end toward which the narrative moves. This perception of form has been brought into the narrative to play a role itself in the resolution of one of the major themes of the plot. To the extent that the brothers can see their own past lives now in a new light, as Joseph does, they will be reconciled to Joseph and he to them. This new insight will thus provide the basis for overcoming the communicative estrangement that had arisen at the outset of the story (37:4). As the dialogue between Joseph and his brothers resumes, the present of the narrator will come to coincide with that of his characters, and the narrative will open toward a future spontaneously shaped by this dialogue.

But the fact that the brothers do not verbally respond in direct discourse to the words of Joseph in this encounter shows that this full dialogical openness is not reached here. Rather, the narrator simply states that after Joseph wept before them and kissed them, "his brothers spoke with him" (45:15). This third-person statement brings closure to the motif of communicative estrangement which began at the outset, and might be considered a suitable conclusion to the narrative – with "loose ends" such as the transportation of Jacob to Egypt, the final blessing of the brothers by Jacob, etc., left to be taken care of in the concluding chapters.

But for the brothers silently to acquiesce in this third-person interpretive statement would have significant implications for the narrative as a whole. This interpretation presents the past events as a closed, predetermined process, the motivating subject of which is a divine "He." Joseph has, in fact, presumed to be able to read divine intentions beneath a sequence of events which contradicts their apparent meaning. This strangely corresponds to the process used by the serpent to seduce Eve into eating the fruit! In this case, of course, the intention attributed to the divine by Joseph was positive rather than self-serving and deceptive, but the presumption to be able to penetrate the divine intentions hidden beneath his statements is the same.

The effects of being taken up into this mode of understanding history fundamentally alters the position and role of the self. The human agent is no longer a dialogue partner with the divine jointly creating an open future. Rather, the opening toward the communicative axis which this reference to the divine potentially offers quickly leads to the absorption of the characters into the negativity of the mysterious divine "He" whose actions can only be understood retrospectively from the end to which they lead. The human actors become mere cyphers who are moved about arbitrarily at the will of the transcendent "Author" to fulfill his mysterious purposes. The absence of direct discourse from the brothers' response to Joseph's interpretation suggests the negation of their own viewpoint and their absorption into the divine (authorial) perspective.

It is thus of considerable significance that the brothers finally respond in DD to Joseph, even though it is not until the final scene of the book. The sequence of events immediately following the reconciliation scene follow logically and predictably from this new state of affairs, and need not be analyzed in detail. The brothers are given wagons, clothing, and an abundance of gifts by Joseph and they return to their father prepared to bring his household to Egypt. Jacob's spirit revives when he hears the news of Joseph upon their return, and he secures approval for this migration from God in "visions of the night" (46:2). There is a grand meeting between Jacob and the Pharaoh, the establishment of the household on good land in Egypt, and continued growth in the economic power of Joseph. Finally, Jacob, nearing death, secures by oath the guarantee from Joseph that he will be buried in Canaan (which, after embalming the body, he fulfills in 50:1–14), and finally passes down to Joseph and his sons, Ephraim and Manasseh, the promise of multiplicity and land (48:16,21) which has been transmitted to him from Abraham and Isaac. In so doing he elevates the younger son over the older. This imparting of the promise of land to Joseph and his sons leaves some questions as to whether it is given to the other brothers, especially in light of the exclusion of the brothers from possession of the one specific parcel of land which Jacob claims to have taken from the Amorites (48:22). Blessings of lesser importance are given to the other brothers (chapter 49). While some of these blessings seem related to their later life in Canaan, only Joseph has been given the traditional patriarchal promises and blessings. This leaves an element of uncertainty about the future status of the other brothers in the unfolding history of the promise. The brothers thus are left in a position of inferiority to Joseph, who now, as the recipient of the traditional blessings and promises, assumes patriarchal authority upon the death of Jacob. Another scene is thus required to resolve the tensions created by this new situation.

After the death of Jacob, there follows in chapter 50:15–25 a final encounter between Joseph and his brothers in which the brothers now reveal the unexpressed feelings about the reconciliation that has been achieved with Joseph. Many interpreters have viewed this as anti-climactic and superfluous. From the perspective of the central problem of broken communication around which this narrative revolves, however, the last encounter does not appear to be at all superfluous since it provides a highly illuminating revelation of the continuing perspective of the brothers upon Joseph's earlier interpretive statement to them. Their acceptance of his viewpoint had been very qualified. They had not been "taken in" to the divine perspective of these events at all, but view Joseph's words as strictly political.

> When the brothers saw that their father was dead, they said, "Joseph will hate us; he will return to us all the evil which we have recompensed him. 50:15

Implicit in this final response to Joseph was the opinion that Joseph's kind words to them were only designed to obtain their cooperation in bringing their father to Egypt so that he could live out his life in pleasant surroundings with his favorite son. There would be no retribution upon them during Jacob's life because it would have grieved him in his last days. But after his death they again become terrified of Joseph. This reopening of the old pain and suspicion has the effect of prolonging the experience of this narrative form. The closure which was attempted in the narrative framework does not hold.

This shows clearly that the brothers' own perspective has not been collapsed into Joseph's cosmic "story." Rather, this story merely serves to suppress temporarily their anxieties, and to make civil discourse among them again possible. But the keystone in this new family structure is Jacob, and his death means that nothing can any longer be assumed.

So terrified are they that they send a messenger to convey their request, hoping, apparently, to deflect Joseph's anger before he sees them. This message reflects both the success and the failure of Joseph's strategy with them.

> Your father commanded before his death saying: "Thus say to Joseph, Please forgive, I pray, the sin of your brothers, and their transgressions due to the evil they recompensed you, and now forgive I pray the transgression of the servants of the God of Your Fathers." And his brothers also went and fell before his face and said, "Behold us, your servants." 50:17

Joseph's strategy has minimally succeeded in that they are entering into dialogue with him, but fails in that they still insist on seeing their deed within the framework of guilt and punishment. They reveal their perception of the weakness of their position by couching their request in the form of an unverifiable command from Jacob before his death, rather than simply asking forgiveness for themselves. This again reveals that, in their perception, it was only Jacob that had stood between them and the vengeful wrath of Joseph.

To this Joseph again responds with tears. In spite of all that he has now done to restore some dignity to the other brothers and to dispel their fear and guilt, his efforts are largely ineffective. They still insist on elevating him to a position of absolute righteousness, and denigrating themselves before him in fear and guilt. He thus reprimands them for placing him in the postion of God over them: "Be not afraid, since am I in the place of God?" (50:19)

By refusing to forgive them, he also refuses to judge them for what they have done, and thus refuses to play the traditional role of God over them. Ironically, however, insight into the transcendental perspective he has attained upon the events of their lives places him all the more in the position of God.

He then offers the most lengthy statement thus far which interprets the meaning of the past, giving special emphasis to the irrelevance of their own intentions, and the pertinence only of the intentions of God:

> You intended evil upon me; God intended good in order to make it possible that today the lives of many people will be preserved. 50:20

After reporting further assurances from Joseph about his wish to sustain them physically, the narrator concludes by saying, "He spoke of the concerns of their heart'' (50:21). This culminates the motif of restored communication, and brings the theme of alienation to conclusion. The rupture of the previous closure by the brothers' scepticism, however, makes this newly attained closure tentative and ambiguous. The perspective of the brothers has obviously not been totally eclipsed by Joseph's theory of a cosmic plot, but a sufficient peace has been established to make possible the transmission to his brothers of the promise of Abraham which Jacob had given to him (and his sons) but not to them. This event follows just prior to his death, with Joseph acting in a manner reminiscent of a patriarch, and using words very similar to those used by Jacob to transmit the promise of land to him just prior to his death.

> And Joseph said to his brothers, ''I am dying, but God will surely remember you, and will cause you to come up from this land, to the land which was sworn to Abraham, Isaac and Jacob.'' And Joseph swore with the sons of Israel saying, ''Surely God will remember you, and you shall bring up my bones from here.'' 50:24–25

Following again the patriarchal pattern of Jacob, Joseph has his brothers promise to bring his bones up from Egypt to Canaan when the promise of land is fulfilled. Joseph, though not a patriarch, thus plays the role of patriarch to his brothers, as Jacob has played that role to him. While the problem of rivalry has not been completely expunged from the relation of Joseph to his brothers, the basis for peaceful dialogue has been established sufficiently between the guilt-ridden, fearful perspective of the brothers, on the one hand, and Joseph's benign interpretation of the universal intentions of God, on the other, to permit an authentic transmission of the promise from Joseph to the collective entity of the brothers who prefigure the nation (''the sons of Israel'').

But it cannot be assumed, after this final scene, that the brothers have totally accepted Joseph's viewpoint. An interpretive conclusion is imposed by the narrator upon this dialogue to indicate that Joseph's words finally related to their personal anxieties. This characterization must serve as the basis of the final promissory statements and oaths regarding the future, rather than a direct expression by them of their own feelings.

But what will be the future of this promise, and of these mistrustful brothers? Joseph's final promissory utterances, which have been made possible by the restoration of some measure of trust and dialogue, open a future which is certain only to the eyes of faith. Every system utilized by the narrator to explain the actions of the characters, including the drive toward the restoration of broken communication between Joseph and his brothers, is finally subordinated to the transmitted promise and its open future. Not even the death of Joseph will bring complete closure to his story.

And Joseph died, the son of a hundred and ten years. And they embalmed him, and he was placed in a coffin *in Egypt*. 50:26

This final reference by the narrator to the embalming and encoffinment – not interment – of Joseph *in Egypt*, while decisively ending the dreams, suffering and glory of Joseph, is itself a metonymic reference to his uncertain promised future to follow *in Canaan*.

Notes

Preface

1 Roland Barthes, *Writing Degree Zero and Elements of Semiology*, trans. Anette Lavers and Colin Smith (Boston: Beacon Press, 1970), p. 48.
2 *Ibid.*
3 Robert Alter, *The Art of Biblical Narrative* (New York: Basic Books, 1981).
4 Meir Sternberg, *The Poetics of Biblical Narrative: Ideological Literature and the Drama of Reading* (Bloomington: Indiana University Press, 1985).
5 Gabriel Josipovici, *The Book of God: A Response to the Bible* (New Haven: Yale University Press, 1988).

1 Toward a functional theory of narrative

1 Seymour Chatman, *Story and Discourse: Narrative Structure in Fiction and Film* (Ithaca NY: Cornell University Press, 1978), p. 19.
2 By text Bal means a structured whole consisting of language signs, roughly equivalent to the substance of the expression plane along with formal features of narrative structure; by fabula, events caused or experienced by actors in a logical or chronological series roughly equivalent to both the substance of the content plane and formal content: events, actors, time and location; and by story the arrangements of the fabula into a pre/non-verbal communicative structure designed to achieve a certain effect – equivalent to the form of the expression plane. Mieke Bal, *Introduction to the Theory of Narrative*, trans. C. van Boheemen (University of Toronto Press, 1985), pp. 5–10.
3 Bal differs only in that the story for her is already the recounting of a fabula, i.e., the story already represents the "how" at a pre-textual, non-verbal level. Bal's more recent work presents a more complex and subtle expansion of her earlier narratology. The premises of the earlier work, however, seem to be by and large carried over, though considerably enriched by other methods into the later work; see e.g., *Death and Dyssymetry: The Politics of Coherence in the Book of Judges* (University of Chicago Press, 1988), Appendix I.
4 Chatman, *Story and Discourse*, p. 25.
5 This type of mimesis did not come into Aristotle's purview since tragic drama, the focus of his analysis, did not have a separate element devoted to representing the setting.
6 Gérard Genette, *Figures of Literary Discourse*, trans. A. Sheridan, introd. M. Logan (New York: Columbia University Press, 1982), pp. 132, 133.
7 *Ibid.*, p. 155.
8 Also see Ann Banfield, *Unspeakable Sentences: Narration and Representation in the Language of Fiction* (Boston: Routledge and Kegan Paul, 1982), p. 164; and Emile Benveniste, *Problems in General Linguistics*, trans. Mary E. Meek (Coral Gables FL: University of Miami Press, 1971), pp. 208, 209.

9 Mary Louise Pratt, *Toward a Speech Act Theory of Literary Discourse* (Bloomington: Indiana University Press, 1977).
10 Bal, *Theory of Narrative*, p. 4.
11 Pratt, *Toward a Speech Act Theory*, p. 73.
12 *Ibid.*, p. 69.
13 *Ibid.*, p. 136.
14 *Ibid.*
15 *Ibid.*
16 *Ibid.*, p. 100.
17 *Ibid.*, p. 116.
18 *Ibid.*, p. 152ff.
19 John L. Austin, *How to do Things With Words*, 2nd ed. (Cambridge MA: Harvard University Press, 1975), p. 6.
20 *Ibid.*, p. 100.
21 *Ibid.*, p. 14.
22 John Searle, *Speech Acts* (Cambridge University Press, 1969), p. 30.
23 John Searle, "Austin on Locutionary and Illocutionary Acts," in *Essays on J. L. Austin*, ed. I. Berlin, G. J. Warnock, *et al.* (Oxford: Clarendon Press, 1973), p. 154.
24 Jonathan Culler, "Convention and Meaning: Derrida and Austin," *New Literary History* 13 (1981), p. 24. On context see François Flahault, *La parole intermédiaire* (Paris: Editions du Seuil, 1978), p. 57.
25 For a different critique of the problem of meaning and force see Jonathan L. Cohen, "Do Illocutionary Forces Exist?" *Philosophical Quarterly* 14 (1964), pp. 118–137.
26 G. J. Warnock, "Some Types of Performative Utterance" in *Essays on J. L. Austin*, ed. Isaiah Berlin, G. J. Warnock, *et al.* (Oxford: Clarendon Press, 1973), p. 76.
27 S.-Y. Kuroda, "Where Epistemology, Style and Grammar Meet: A Case Study from Japanese," in *Festschrift for Morris Halle*, ed. Stephen R. Anderson and Paul Kiparsky (New York: Holt, Rinehart and Winston, 1973), pp. 377–391.
28 Hugh C. White, "A Theory of the Surface Structure of the Biblical Narrative," *Union Seminary Quarterly Review* 34 (1979), p. 164.
29 Searle, *Speech Acts*, p. 17.
30 Eugenio Coseriu, *Synchronie, Diachronie, und Geschichte: Das Problem des Sprachwandels* (Munich: Wilhelm Fink Verlag, 1958, 1974).
31 *Ibid.*, p. 221.
32 *Ibid.*, p. 236.
33 *Ibid.*
34 *Ibid.*
35 *Ibid.*, p. 237.
36 V. N. Voloshinov (a pseudonym for M. Bakhtin), *Marxism and the Philosophy of Language*, trans. L. Matejka and I. R. Titunik (New York and London: Seminar Press, 1930, 1973), p. 71.
37 Coseriu, *Synchronie, Diachronie und Geschichte*, pp. 102–119.
38 *Ibid.*, pp. 70, 169.
39 *Ibid.*, p. 61.
40 *Ibid.*, p. 66.
41 *Ibid.*
42 *Ibid.*
43 Austin, *Words*, p. 22.
44 Coseriu, *Synchronie, Diachronie und Geschichte*, p. 60.
45 *Ibid.*, p. 60.

46 *Ibid.*, p. 246.
47 *Ibid.*, p. 245.
48 Angel Medina, *Reflection, Time and the Novel: Toward a Communicative Theory of Literature* (London and Boston: Routledge and Kegan Paul, 1979).
49 *Ibid.*, p. 26.
50 *Ibid.*
51 *Ibid.*, p. 6.
52 *Ibid.*
53 *Ibid.*, p. 8.
54 *Ibid.*, p. 10.
55 *Ibid.*, p. 19.
56 *Ibid.*, p. 22.
57 *Ibid.*, p. 26.
58 *Ibid.*, p. 30.
59 *Ibid.*, p. 26.
60 *Ibid.*, p. 30.
61 *Ibid.*, p. 87.
62 *Ibid.*
63 *Ibid.*
64 *Ibid.*, pp. 102, 103.
65 *Ibid.*, p. 30.
66 Boris Eichenbaum, "The Theory of Formal Method," in Ladislav Matejka and Krystyna Pomorska, eds., *Readings in Russian Poetics: Formalist and Structuralist Views* (Cambridge MA: MIT Press, 1971), p. 12.
67 Quoted from an untranslated article by Victor Shklovsky, "The Resurrection of the Word," in Lee T. Lemon and Marion J. Reis, eds., *Russian Formalist Criticism: Four Essays* (Lincoln: University of Nebraska Press, 1965), p. 112.
68 Matejka and Pomorska, *Readings*, p. 14; see also Victor Erlich, *Russian Formalism* (The Hague: Mouton, 1965), pp. 178, 179.
69 See also Fredric Jameson, *The Prison-House of Language: A Critical Accoaunt of Structuralism and Russian Formalism* (Princeton University Press, 1972), p. 75; Matejka and Pomorska, *Readings*, p. 14; also Erlich, *Russian Formalism*, p. 184.
70 Josué V. Harari, ed., *Textual Strategies: Perspectives in Post-Structuralist Criticism* (Ithaca NY: Cornell University Press, 1979), pp. 20–22.
71 See Roland Barthes, *S/Z: An Essay*, trans. R. Miller, preface R. Howard (New York: Hill and Wang, 1974); Stanley Fish, "Structuralist Homiletics," *Modern Language Notes* 19 (1976), pp. 1208–1221; Louis Marin, "On the Interpretation of Ordinary Language," in Harari, ed., *Textual Strategies*, pp. 239–259.
72 Jacques Derrida, *Of Grammatology*, trans. G. C. Spivak (Baltimore: Johns Hopkins University Press, 1977), p. 7.
73 *Ibid.*, p. 73.
74 *Ibid.*, p. 68.
75 *Ibid.*, p. 69.
76 *Ibid.*
77 *Ibid.*

2 *The functions of the sign*

1 Edmund Ortigues, *Le Discours et le symbole* (Paris: Aubier, Editions Montaigne, 1962).
2 *Ibid.*, p. 19.
3 *Ibid.*, p. 21.
4 *Ibid.*, p. 19.
5 *Ibid.*, p. 17.
6 *Ibid.*, p. 18.
7 *Ibid.*, p. 19.
8 *Ibid.*
9 Julia Kristeva, *La révolution du langage poétique* (Paris: Editions du Seuil, 1974), p. 23.
10 Ortigues, *Discours*, p. 210.
11 *Ibid.*, p. 53.
12 *Ibid.*, p. 210.
13 *Ibid.*, p. 212.
14 "expression ... tends ... to take the form of a sign." Ortigues, *Discours*, p. 31.
15 *Ibid.*, p. 28.
16 *Ibid.*
17 *Ibid.*, p. 129.
18 *Ibid.*, p. 29.
19 *Ibid.*, p. 30.
20 *Ibid.*, p. 31.
21 *Ibid.*, p. 53.
22 *Ibid.*
23 Umberto Eco, *A Theory of Semiotics* (Bloomington: Indiana University Press, 1979), p. 7.
24 Ortigues, *Discours*, p. 53.
25 Austin, *Words*, p. 10.
26 Ortigues, *Discours*, p. 54.
27 *Ibid.*
28 *Ibid.*, p. 37.
29 *Ibid.*, p. 92.
30 *Ibid.*
31 *Ibid.*, p. 99.
32 *Ibid.*, p. 65.
33 *Ibid.*, p. 60.
34 *Ibid.*, p. 61.
35 *Ibid.*
36 For a critique of Husserl's concept of unmediated self-presence see: Jacques Derrida, *Speech and Phenomena* (Evanston: Northwestern University Press, 1973), pp. 60–69.
37 Ortigues, *Discours*, pp. 60, 61.
38 *Ibid.*, p. 171.
39 *Ibid.*, p. 66.
40 *Ibid.*, p. 190.
41 *Ibid.*, p. 195.
42 *Ibid.*, p. 190.
43 *Ibid.*, p. 198.
44 *Ibid.*, p. 203.
45 *Ibid.*, p. 191.
46 *Ibid.*, p. 163.
47 *Ibid.*

48 *Ibid.*, p. 167.
49 Michael Hancher, "Performative Utterance, the Word of God, and the Death of the Author" *Semeia* 41 (1988), pp. 27–40.
50 Derrida, *Speech and Phenomena*, p. 79.
51 Ortigues, *Discours*, p. 167.
52 *Ibid.*, p. 203.
53 *Ibid.*, p. 204.
54 *Ibid.*
55 *Ibid.*, p. 205.
56 *Ibid.*
57 *Ibid.*, p. 206.
58 *Ibid.*, p. 208.
59 *Ibid.*
60 *Ibid.*, p. 209.
61 *Ibid.*, pp. 208, 209.
62 *Ibid.*, p. 209.
63 *Ibid.*
64 *Ibid.*
65 *Ibid.*
66 *Ibid.*, p. 3.
67 *Ibid.*, p. 31.
68 *Ibid.*
69 *Ibid.*, p. 25.
70 See Mary Sirridge on metaphorical speech acts in, "Donkeys, Stars, and Illocutionary Acts," *Journal of Aesthetics and Art Criticism* 45 (1987), pp. 381–388.

3 A functional definition of narrative

1 Lubomír Doležel, *Narrative Modes in Czech Literature* (University of Toronto Press, 1973), p. 6. For a comparable, though considerably more developed definition of narrative, see Ann Banfield, *Unspeakable Sentences*, pp. 164, 165.
2 Mark Lambert, *Dickens and the Suspended Quotation* (New Haven: Yale University Press, 1981), p. 85.
3 *Ibid.*, p. 70.
4 For a discussion of the fundamental character of the linguistic distinction between narration and discourse see Ann Banfield, *Unspeakable Sentences.*
5 Wayne Booth, *The Rhetoric of Fiction* (University of Chicago Press, 1961), p. 71.
6 Roland Barthes, "Introduction à l'analyse structurale des récits," *Communications* 8 (1966), p. 20.
7 Julia Kristeva, *Le Texte du roman* (The Hague: Mouton, 1970), p. 82.
8 For an explanation of this term see: Oswald Ducrot, *Dire et ne pas dire: principes de sémantique linguistique* (Paris: Herman, 1972), p. 10.
9 François Flahault, *La Parole intermédiaire*, p. 50.
10 *Ibid.*, p. 48.
11 *Ibid.*
12 Gérard Genette, *Figures of Literary Discourse*, p. 140. Emile Benveniste says of historical narration, "there is no longer even a narrator. The events are set forth chronologically, as they occurred. No one speaks here; the events seem to narrate themselves. The fundamental tense is the aorist which is the tense of the event outside the person of the narrator." *Problems of General Linguistics*, p. 208.

13 Roland Barthes, *Writing Degree Zero*, p. 36.
14 Robert Scholes and Robert Kellogg, *The Nature of Narrative* (Oxford University Press, 1966), p. 243.
15 Barthes, "Introduction", p. 21.
16 Kristeva, *Le Texte du roman*, p. 84.

4 A typology of narrative functions and modes

1 Susan Lanser, *The Narrative Act* (Princeton University Press, 1981), p. 35.
2 Norman Friedman, "Point of View in Fiction: The Development of a Critical Concept," *PMLA* 70 (1955), pp. 1160–1184; Franz Stanzel, *Narrative Situations in the Novel*, trans. James P. Pusak (Bloomington: Indiana University Press, 1971); Dorrit Cohn, *Transparent Minds* (Princeton University Press, 1978); Gérard Genette, *Narrative Discourse*, trans. Jane E. Lewin (Ithaca NY: Cornell University Press, 1980).
3 Friedman, "Point of View in Fiction: The Development of a Critical Concept."
4 *Ibid.*, p. 1168.
5 Chatman says the narrative's capacity to skip from one scene to the other should be termed omnipresence, and argues that a narrator cannot be both omnipresent and omniscient. *Story and Discourse*, p. 212.
6 Stanzel, *Narrative Situations.*
7 *Ibid.*, p. 6.
8 *Ibid.*, p. 38.
9 *Ibid.*, p. 92.
10 *Ibid.*, pp. 23, 27, 96.
11 Genette, *Narrative Discourse*, p. 196.
12 *Ibid.*, pp. 187, 189.
13 *Ibid.*, p. 190.
14 *Ibid.*, p. 244.
15 *Ibid.*, pp. 244, 245.
16 *Ibid.*, p. 228.
17 See also Shlomith Rimmon, "A Comprehensive Theory of Narrative: Genette's *Figures III* and the Structuralist Study of Fiction," *Poetics and Theory of Literature* 1 (1976), p. 57.
18 Stanzel, *Narrative Situations*, p. 22.
19 Lubomír Doležel, *Narrative Modes*, pp. 6–7.
20 On the dispute regarding the unity of perspectives in free indirect discourse see Brian McHale, "Free Indirect Discourse: A Survey of Recent Accounts," *Poetics and Theory of Literature* 3 (1978), pp. 268–269; 278–280.
21 Doležel, *Narrative Modes*, p. 54.
22 Cohn, *Transparent Minds*, pp. 26–33.
23 Doležel, *Narrative Modes*, p. 107.
24 It is worth noting as well that neither Friedman nor Stanzel have a place for this important form of narrative discourse (though Friedman's "neutral omniscience" approaches it), but with their categories of multiple/selective omniscience and the figural narrative, they move directly to the mode in which the narrator's perspective wholly coincides with that of the character, i.e., free indirect speech, or as Doležel terms it, represented discourse.
25 *Ibid.*, pp. 68, 94.
26 *Ibid.*, p. 59.
27 This problem also arises in autobiographical writing and in psychoanalysis where the retrospective representation of the self as a unified subject of action seems to contradict the

experiencing self, and has led to more diffuse forms of self-representation which allow a greater role for the creative power of language; see Paul Jay, *Being in the Text: Self-Representation from Wordsworth to Roland Barthes* (Ithaca NY: Cornell University Press, 1984), pp. 21–38.

28 Stanzel, *Narrative Situations*, p. 68.

29 See also Ann Banfield who finds first-person narration to belong with third-person narration in its linguistic features; *Unspeakable Sentences*, pp. 144, 145.

30 Cohn, *Transparent Minds*, pp. 145–165.

31 *Ibid.*, p. 171.

32 *Ibid.*, p. 173.

33 *Ibid.*, pp. 221, 222.

34 *Ibid.*, p. 178.

35 Doležel, *Narrative Modes*, pp. 16, 17.

36 *Ibid.*, pp. 87, 88.

37 Ann Banfield incorporates represented perceptions along with represented thought/speech in the single category of representation of consciousness (*Unspeakable Sentences*, p. 199). This avoids the difficulty of distinguishing perceptions from non-verbalized thoughts, and the further difficulty of separating the narrator's viewpoint, which can be seen in the cognitive privilege which this narration of the pre-conscious contents of consciousness implies, from that of the character's viewpoint. The approach being taken here allocates all the narration of subverbal states to the representative narrative function since it is only in the verbal form of free indirect speech and direct discourse that the character as subject begins to emerge from the interpretive perspective of the narrator.

38 Doležel, *Narrative Modes*, p. 16.

39 *Ibid.*, p. 94.

40 *Ibid.*, pp. 85, 89.

41 *Ibid.*, p. 82.

42 *Ibid.*, p. 18.

43 *Ibid.*, p. 12.

44 Paul Hernadi has recently developed a typology of human experience which closely corresponds to the three functions just described: "At any particular time we typically experience ourselves in just one of three ways: as objectively existing bodies, as bearers of intersubjectively assigned roles, or as subjective selves." These closely parallel the representative, expressive, and symbolic sign functions which govern the formation of characters: "Doing, Making and Meaning: Toward a Theory of Verbal Practice," *PMLA* 103 (1988), p. 754. Ann Banfield's conclusions regarding basic narrative sentences also correspond in general to these three categories. She terms them narration, discourse, and representation of consciousness. Her distinction between narration and representation of consciousness rests upon the use in narration of the aorist (Fr.), or simple past (Eng.) with no connection to the present. The analysis of these forms in this work depends upon semiotic functions which assign both the representation of sub-verbal contents of consciousness and the narration of external phenomena to the representative function (narration). Banfield finds the coming together of these two forms of speech to be the mark of modern fictional writing. *Unspeakable Sentences*, p. 257.

45 Mikhail Bakhtin, *Problems of Dostoyevsky's Poetics*, trans. R. W. Rotsel (n.p.: Ardis, 1973), p. 153.

46 See Brian McHale, "Free Indirect Discourse," pp. 272–273.

47 Bakhtin, *Poetics*, p. 156.

48 *Ibid.*, p. 156.

49 *Ibid.*, p. 164.

50 M. M. Bakhtin, *The Dialogic Imagination: Four Essays*, ed. Michael Holquist, trans. C. Emerson and M. Holquist (Austin: University of Texas Press, 1981), p. xxvi.

51 V.N. Voloshinov, *Marxism and the Philosophy of Language*, p. 116.
52 *Ibid.*, p. 116.
53 Susan Lanser, *Narrative Act*, p. 102.
54 Voloshinov, *Marxism*, p. 117.
55 *Ibid.*, p. 119.
56 *Ibid.*, p. 120.
57 *Ibid.*, p. 121.
58 *Ibid.*

5 The three functional narrative types

1 Ortigues, *Le Discours et le symbole*, p. 212.
2 *Ibid.*, p. 213.
3 *Ibid.*, p. 214.
4 *Ibid.*, p. 215.
5 *Ibid.*, p. 190.
6 *Ibid.*, p. 193.
7 Since the sign function of signification concerns in part the relation of the sign to its referent, and it is this representative function which is of central importance in this analysis, the term "representative" will be used here to describe this function in place of the term "significative."
8 Barthes, *S/Z*, pp. 200, 201.
9 A.-J. Greimas, *Sémantique structurale: recherche de méthode* (Paris: Librairie Larousse, 1966), pp. 192–203. There are many more subtle possibilities between the representative and symbolic narrative types to which the method of Greimas can profitably be applied. A useful method for exploring representative language is also provided by David Lodge in *The Modes of Modern Writing: Metaphor, Metonymy and the Typology of Modern Literature* (Ithaca NY: Cornell University Press, 1977). The distinction Lodge makes between metonymy and metaphor often parallels the distinction made here between the representative and symbolic, though he does not raise the question of the author's relation to the narrative world which is central here.
10 Barthes, *S/Z*, p. 10.
11 *Ibid.*, p. 204.
12 *Ibid.*, p. 225.
13 Chatman discusses this type, terming it "pure speech records," but extends it to include internal speech. *Story and Discourse*, pp. 173–178.
14 Wolfgang Iser, *The Implied Reader* (Baltimore: Johns Hopkins University Press, 1974), p. 234.
15 *Ibid.*, p. 238.
16 *Ibid.*, p. 239.
17 *Ibid.*, p. 250.
18 *Ibid.*, p. 254.
19 Doležel, *Modes*, p. 11.
20 For a discussion of terminology see Roy Pascal, *The Dual Voice* (Manchester University Press, 1977), pp. 8–32.
21 Ann Banfield, "Narrative Style and the Grammar of Direct and Indirect Speech," *Foundations of Language* 10 (1973), p. 13. For a more extensive and thoroughgoing development of her position see *Unspeakable Sentences*.
22 Banfield, "Narrative Style," p. 33. The status of the consciousness presupposed by free indirect speech has been the subject of considerable debate with some arguing for exclusive identification with the character, and others for bivocality which includes both author and character, and others for a "double-voiced," dialogical character (for a discussion of this

problem see Brian McHale, "Free Indirect Discourse," pp. 278–284.)

Dorrit Cohn argues against Banfield's "third person subject-of-consciousness" because of the problem of the continuity which appears to exist between passages in FIS and regular authorial commentary (*Transparent Minds*, p. 294, n. 30). I am not certain that there is *always* a continuity of voice between these types of discourse; i.e., we may be dealing with a continuum, one end of which preserves some degree of continuity, with the other transcending the voice of the narrator as in the case of Joyce's *Ulysses* to be discussed below. Thus it is necessary to account theoretically for the discourse of this type which does transcend the voice of the narrator. It is at this point that Banfield's concepts are useful, along with the observations of Kuroda below. Banfield convincingly refutes the dual voice argument in *Unspeakable Sentences* by pointing out the absence of expressive language emanating from the narrator in the passages in question, and the critics' question-begging assumption that "if it doesn't represent the character's, it must represent the narrator's voice." (p. 189)

23 *Ibid.*, p. 33.

24 S.-Y. Kuroda, "Where Epistemology, Style and Grammar Meet," pp. 377–391.

25 Banfield, "Narrative Style," p. 35. Banfield also finds this type of narratorless narrative in both third- and first-person narratives that utilize forms of the past tense which do not relate it to a now. *Unspeakable Sentences*, p. 164. I prefer to speak of this as the suppression of the narrator who then returns indirectly for reasons given above.

26 Chatman indicates that it is fairly common for the narrative voice to be so ambiguous that "it is difficult to know whose voice speaks." *Story*, p. 203. He attributes this to a "covert narrator." More recently Banfield has analyzed instances of free indirect speech which cannot be identified with any character or narrator. She speaks of this as the apotheosis of the impersonalized consciousness comparable to Russell's "unobserved sensibilia" or to a photographic plate: "This vision, this sensation is blind, insensible, silent, unconscious – only the gathering of appearances into a 'prehensive' unity around a centre in a sensitive instrument which has no human eye, *no human mind*, behind it" (my emphasis). "Describing the Unobserved: Events Grouped Around an Empty Centre", in *The Linguistics of Writing: Arguments between Language and Literature*, ed. Nigel Fabb *et al.* (New York: Methuen, 1987), p. 279. This mechanistic view seems largely inappropriate in light of the creative role played by language in this form of speech, as will be seen below. The experience of the trans-subjective dimension of language itself may be variously evaluated as, for example, in the case of the Buddhist nirvana to which Banfield's description of this impersonalized form of consciousness bears not a little resemblance.

27 Stanzel, *Narrative Situations*, p. 127.

28 *Ibid.*

29 Barthes, *S/Z*, p. 41.

30 Ortigues, *Discours*, p. 25.

31 M. M. Bakhtin, *Speech Genres and Other Late Essays*, ed. C. Emerson and M. Holquist, trans. Vern W. McGee (Austin: University of Texas Press, 1986), p. 126.

32 See M. Lambert, *Dickens and the Suspended Quotation*, p. 35, n. 34. For a semiological analysis, see Julia Kristeva, *La Révolution du langage poétique* (Paris: Editions du Seuil, 1974), pp. 315–335.

33 For an excellent description of this process by a novelist see John Gardner, *On Moral Fiction* (New York: Basic Books, 1978), pp. 84, 85. For a description of a similar private dialogue between the author and his characters during the writing process, see Stephen Connor, *Charles Dickens* (Oxford: Basil Blackwell, 1985), p. 109; Bakhtin also says, "It is frequently as though the images of characters had been replaced by living people," *Speech Genres*, p. 116.

34 Bakhtin describes this type of relation as a "pure relationship" beyond referentiality: "Any truly creative voice can only be the *second* voice in the discourse. Only the second voice –

pure relationship – can be completely objectless and not cast a figural, substantive shadow." *Speech Genres*, p. 110.

35 What is being suggested here is close to the experience of creativity which Stephen Prickett finds at the basis of the poetic in the Biblical tradition. It is expressed in traditional terms as psychomachia: "the portrayal of critical events and conflicts of the soul as external occurrances." *Words and the Word* (Cambridge University Press, 1986), p. 170. The externality is, however, liminal, ambiguous and not objective. The prototypical example Prickett uses is Elijah's encounter with the "Voice" on Horeb. (I Kgs 19:12)

36 Cohn, *Transparent Minds*, p. 219.

37 *Ibid.*, p. 126.

38 Stanzel, *Narrative Situations*, p. 142.

39 Bakhtin distinguishes between the actual author who participates in the real discourse of his time, and the "image of the author" reflected in the text who only indirectly participates in that dialogue. But no absolute separation can be made between these two as Susan Lanser observes: "By whatever name, novelistic authority presumes some kind of wisdom and insight sufficient for the creation of a world that is not only internally coherent, but meaningful in the historical world as well: meaningful, not only as *mimesis* but as *diegesis* – as important discourse presenting, as its name suggests, something new." *The Narrative Act*, p. 84.

40 Bakhtin, *Poetics*, p. 45.

41 *Ibid.*, p. 226.

42 *Ibid.*, p. 52.

43 *Ibid.*, p. 81.

44 *Ibid.*, p. 69.

45 *Ibid.*

46 *Ibid.*, p. 48.

47 *Ibid.*

48 *Ibid.*, p. 70.

49 *Ibid.*, p. 69.

50 *Ibid.*, p. 63.

51 "The substitution of the 'he' for the 'I' is here obviously only a symbol, perhaps too clear a one, of which one would find a subtler, and apparently inverse, version in the way in which Proust renounces the all too well centered 'he' or *Jean Santeuil* for the decentered, equivocal 'I' of a Narrator who is not precisely either the author or anyone else, and who shows rather well how Proust encountered his *genius* at the moment when he found in his work the locus of language in which it would be possible to explode his individuality and become dissolved in the Idea." *Figures*, p. 66.

52 Bakhtin, *Poetics*, p. 72.

53 *Ibid.*

54 *Ibid.*, p. 73.

55 *Ibid.*

56 *Ibid.*, p. 74.

57 *Ibid.*, p. 80. It is curious that rhetorical references to the divine often spring up in similar contexts. Patricia Hemple, in describing Nabokov's literary inspiration, points to the "divine detail": "It comes down to faith. If, as Nabokov says, the detail is divine, there's nothing much to do but give yourself over to it as one properly does in worship." "The Lax Habits of the Free Imagination," *New York Times Book Review*, March 5, 1989, p. 38. For a curious return to the explicit intrusion of a divine Voice as a narrative technique for some recent novelists see Dan Wakefield, "And Now a Word From Our Creator," where he observes, "God is not only present in these narratives but sometimes has a 'speaking part'." *New York Times Book Review*, Feb. 12, 1989, p. 1.

58 Bakhtin, *Poetics*, p. 81.
59 *Ibid.*, p. 56.
60 Cohn, *Transparent Minds*, p. 178.
61 Bakhtin, *Poetics*, p. 48.
62 *Ibid.*, p. 32.
63 *Ibid.*, p. 33.
64 A similar process also is found by Gérard Genette to be at work in Proust's *A la Recherche du temps perdu* which he argues contains a critique of the referential and semantic illusions. The Proustian hero serves an apprenticeship that is "concerned, among other things, with the value and function of language" (*Figures*, p. 249). The development of the protagonist into maturity is depicted in linguistic terms: "the experience of 'words' ... becomes identified with the (painful) emergence from the verbal solipsism of childhood, with the discovery of the speech of the Other, and of one's own speech as an element in the relationship of otherness" (p. 250). But this engagement with the problematic of representation is never resolved giving the entire work the character of a palimpsest with "unfathomable depths" (p. 223). Thus the work takes on an ambivalence, a "double life," which denies it completeness and leaves it continually "escaping from itself" (p. 222).
65 Bakhtin, *Poetics*, p. 51.
66 *Ibid.*, p. 34.
67 Marie-Paule Laden, *Self-Imitation in the Eighteenth-Century Novel* (Princeton University Press, 1987).
68 *Ibid.*, p. 85.
69 *Ibid.*, p. 123.
70 *Ibid.*, pp. 86–87.
71 *Ibid.*, p. 131.
72 *Ibid.*
73 *Ibid.*, p. 133.
74 Genette, *Figures*, p. 73; see also Stanzel, *Narrative Situations*, p. 142, for a similar creative process reflected in the plan and character of Joyce's *Ulysses*.
75 Beryl Schlossman has found an even more profound example of this phenomenon in his Lacanian analysis of Montaigne's experience of writing. "From La Boetie to Montaigne: The Place of the Text," in *Lacan and Narration: The Psychoanalytic Difference in Narrative Theory*, ed. Robert Con Davis (Baltimore: Johns Hopkins University Press, 1933), pp. 891–909.
76 Bakhtin, *Poetics*, p. 74.
77 *Ibid.*
78 *Ibid.*, p. 178.
79 Fyodor Dostoyevsky, *The Possessed*, trans. A. R. MacAndrew (New York: The New American Library, 1962), p. 635.
80 *Ibid.*
81 *Ibid.*
82 *Ibid.*
83 *Ibid.*, p. 634.
84 For other examples of novels which explore this type of problematic relation, see Robert Siegle, *The Politics of Reflexivity: Narrative and the Constitutive Poetics of Culture* (Baltimore: Johns Hopkins University Press, 1986).

6 *The divine Voice*

1 Ortigues, *Discours*, p. 209.
2 Robert Penn Warren, *Being Here: Poetry 1977–1980* (New York: Random House, 1980), pp. 7, 8.
3 Joshua Wilner, "Romanticism and the Internalization of Scripture," in *Midrash and Literature*, ed. Geoffrey H. Hartman and Sanford Budick (New Haven: Yale University Press, 1986), p. 249.
4 Robert Penn Warren, in another poem, *Audubon: A Vision* (New York: Random House, 1969), gives expression to a view quite close to this Biblical view in his poem about the naturalist, Jean Jacques Audubon:

We never know what we have lost, or what we have found.
We are only ourselves, and that promise.
Continue to walk in the world. Yes, love it!

He continued to walk in the world.

5 The neutral "it" will be used here since the focus is upon the literary phenomenon of the Voice itself rather than upon the subject as such. It does not imply impersonality of the subject.
6 This Voice can speak through more conventional means such as dreams (28:12), visions (15:1), and appearances (17:1, 18:1, 16:2, 35:9), or through an angel calling from heaven (22:11) as is found in other ancient literature. For instance see the story of Gilgamesh where Shamash speaks to Gilgamesh and Enkidu: "Then down from heaven spoke to them heavenly Shamash: 'Draw near / fear you not' " (James Pritchard, ed., *Ancient Near Eastern Texts* [Princeton University Press, 1955], p. 83). Some typical examples from the Homeric tales are where "Minerva took the form of Laodocus ... and went through the ranks of the Trojans to find Pandarus ... [and] went up close to him and said ...," and where: "The dream went when it had heard its message ... [and] sought Agamemnon ... [and] hovered over his head in the likeness of Nestor." *The Iliad*, trans. Samuel Butler (Chicago: Encyclopaedia Britannica, 1952), Book IV, line 75, p. 24; Book II, lines 16–22, p. 10.

The occasions where it lacks such contextual clues, however, are of utmost importance to the narrative. The reason for this stylistic variation would have to be examined on a case-by-case basis, but it is clear that absence of context and medium of communication for the divine Voice is not a feature of only one source document (J and P both have it); nor is it a consistent characteristic throughout a single document, and is also not due simply to the absence of older traditions.
7 When engaging in pure third-person narration, the Biblical narrator can be more actively involved. Meir Sternberg points to the use of וְהִנֵּה (and behold) in the Biblical narrative as a sign of free indirect discourse. But, while this is an expression typical of direct speech, and represents an identification of the author with the character's perspective, as a single feature it generally does not enable narration to go beyond "vision avec" to true free indirect discourse. It does indicate a strong tendency in that direction, however, which is completely consistent with the premises of symbolic narration. *The Poetics of Biblical Narrative*, p. 53.
8 Laden, *Self-Imitation*, p. 133.

7 The micro-dialogue as the matrix of the Genesis narrative

1 Genette, *Narrative Discourse*, pp. 217, 221, 222.
2 Hermann Gunkel, *Genesis*, 6th ed. (Göttingen: Vangenhöck and Ruprecht, 1964), p. 103.
3 Gerhard von Rad, *Genesis*, trans. John H. Marks (Philadelphia: Westminster Press, 1961), p. 158.
4 *Ibid.*, p. 160.
5 Rolf Rendtorff, *Das Überlieferungsgeschichtliche Problem des Pentateuch* (Berlin: Walter de Gruyter, 1977), p. 65.
6 Gunkel, *Genesis*, p. 291.
7 *Ibid.*, p. 16, 17.
8 von Rad, *Genesis*, p. 161.
9 *Ibid.*, p. 154.

8 "Who told you that you were naked?"

1 Claus Westermann, *Genesis. Biblischer Kommentar, Altes Testament*, I,4 (Neukirchen-Vluyn: Neukirchener Verlag, 1970), pp. 287, 288.
2 *Ibid.*, p. 261.
3 *Ibid.*, p. 290; also Howard N. Wallace, *The Eden Narrative*, Harvard Semitic Monographs 32 (Atlanta GA: Scholars Press, 1985), pp. 116, 132.
4 While the most common meaning which this phrase carries is "universal knowledge," as H. N. Wallace has the most recently shown (p. 128), he also recognizes that the context in which it is used can give a more specific meaning to the phrase. I am suggesting here that the emphasis of wisdom lies not upon absolute knowledge in the sense of knowing every-thing, but upon perfect discernment between alternatives. It is this type of knowledge that can support the autonomous self. Such wisdom also assumes universal knowledge, however.
5 Barthes, *S/Z*, p. 76.
6 Westermann, *Genesis*, p. 295.
7 The argument made by D. Jobling and W. Vogels that this lack is not met until the expulsion of Adam from the garden to till the soil overstates the distinction between tilling the soil (*'adāmāh*), and tilling the garden (*gan*) mentioned in 2:15. The initial statement in 2:5b could not name the garden as man's workplace before it had been created. On the other hand, the tilling function assigned to man in verse 15 is obviously related to the absence of such a function stated in 2:5. In addition, the expulsion statement in 3:23 has ironic overtones, as will be shown below, which relate it to a different semantic field than that initiated by 2:5. David Jobling, *The Sense of the Biblical Narrative* II, Sheffield: JSOT Press, 1986), p. 23; Walter Vogels, "L'Etre humain appartient au sol. Gen. 2:4b–3:24" *Nouvelle Revue Théologique* 105 (1983), p. 532.
8 Although the term הָאָדָם used here is the same as in 2:7, I shall translate it here and below as a name rather than a generic term because a distinct character is required as the object of direct discourse. The transition of הָאָדָם to a personal name occurs quietly in 3:17 with the elision of the definite article. Since there is no English equivalent which serves both as a personal name and as the concept "humankind", I will use it here as a personal name for the purposes of this study which focuses upon the dynamics of DD. The concept "humankind" cannot properly be the subject or object of DD. See also 4:25.
9 The argument that אָדָם is neutral with regard to gender here is effectively countered by Susan Lanser on the basis of contextual inference: "Let me postulate that when a being assumed to be human is introduced into a narrative, that being is also assumed to have sexual as well

as grammatical gender. The masculine form of *hā'ādām* and its associated pronouns will, by inference, define *hā'ādām* as male ... Gendered humans are the unmarked case, it is not *hā'ādām's* maleness that would have to be marked but the *absence* of maleness." "(Feminist) Criticism in the Garden: Inferring Genesis 2–3," *Semeia* 41 (1988), p. 72.

10 Julia Kristeva, *Polylogue* (Paris: Editions du Seuil, 1977), pp. 252, 253.

11 Jean-Louis Ska, " 'Je vais lui faire un allié qui soit son homologue' (Gen 2:18) à propos du term *ezer* – 'aide,' " *Biblica* 65 (1984), p. 237.

12 *Ibid.*, p. 236.

13 The argument that woman's position in this temporal sequence implies that woman is the climax and culmination of this creative process is persuasively refuted by Susan Lanser: "For what 2:23 actually culminates is the process that begins in 2:18, when God plans to make a helper fit for *hā'ādām*. Any sense of culmination here exists within a context of inferences that have been made about the centrality of *hā'ādām*, who is the subject of this discourse and for whom, after all, this laborious act of creation and re-creation has taken place." "(Feminist) criticism in the Garden," pp. 73, 74.

14 Chatman, *Story and Discourse*, p. 228.

15 *Ibid.*, p. 243, 244.

16 The Septuagint and Syriac underscore the motif of the two being one by the insertion of שְׁנֵיהֶם, "the two of them," after the verb.

17 Other possible translations are: "they did not embarrass each other," Jack Sasson, "W^{e}lō' yitbōšāšû and Its Implications," *Biblica* 66 (1985), pp. 418–421; and "ils n'avaient pas honte l'un devant l'autre," Walter Vogels, "L'Etre humain," p. 529.

18 This is a possibility that is explicitly considered later in 6:7 and Ex. 32:10, as well as in the *Enuma Elish* where Apsu, the male creator, in response to the "overbearing" ways of his offspring, says: "I will destroy, I will wreck their ways." His female counterpart answers by saying: "Shall we destroy that which we have built?" (lines 28, 39, 45). James B. Pritchard, ed., *Ancient Near Eastern Texts*, p. 61.

19 The binary pair – naked versus clothed – anticipates diverse symbolic meanings which developed in the course of Israelite history; see Sasson, "W^{e}lō'."

20 Xavier Thévenot, "Emmaüs, une nouvelle Genèse? Une lecture psychoanalytique de Gen. 2–3 et Luc 24, 13–35" *Mélanges de Science Religieuse* 37 (1980), p. 12.

21 Contra A. S. Feilschuss-Abir, " '... da werden eure Augen geöffnet und ihr werdet sein wie Gott, wissend Gutes und Böses' (Gen. 3, 5)," *Theologie und Glaube* 74 (1984), p. 201.

22 Austin, *How to do Things With Words*, p. 40.

23 Hugh C. White, "A theory of the Surface Structure," pp. 165, 166.

24 A. S. Feilschuss-Abir, " 'da werden'," pp. 199–201, sees this visual knowledge as the origin of self-reflective consciousness. It is this form of knowledge that leads to an awareness of nakedness. For the author, however, this awareness is equated with the awareness of difference and individuality, and is unrelated to the motif of shame.

25 Cohn, *Transparent Minds*, pp. 30, 38.

26 The omission by the LXX of this word suppresses even this sublimated object of desire.

27 "This temptation impels man to pass from believing in the word to seeing," Thévenot, "Emmaüs," p. 13.

28 Dominic Crossan, "Felix Culpa and Foenix Culprit" *Semeia* 18 (1980), p. 110.

29 "Voir, c'est ... se fier a la présence plus ou moins chosifée de l'autre," Thévenot, "Emmaüs," p. 13.

30 Gunkel, *Genesis*, pp. 18, 19.

31 Alan J. Hauser shows how the use of the second-person singular ending in this direct address grammatically underscores the alienation between Adam and Issah. They are no longer one; "Gen. 2–3: The Theme of Intimacy and Alienation," in *Art and Meaning: Rhetoric in Biblical*

Literature, ed. David J. A. Clines, David Gunn and Alan Hauser, JSOT Supp. 19 (Sheffield, 1982), p. 29.

32 E.g., see Pritchard, *Ancient Near Eastern Texts*, p. 327.

33 This second naming has often been regarded as a sign of parallel accounts. Renaming, however, is a common occurrance in ancient rites of passage as an indication of a new identity. These events have constituted a rite of passage in that the parties involved have undergone a transformation, albeit a negative one. The emphasis thus is not so much upon the new identity of Issah as it is upon the new situation into which children will now be born. Thus Adam is not renamed. The irony here is thus at the expense of women (as are the peripheral implications of this story generally) due to their more direct physical role in the creation of the next generation. More recently it has been denied that the first naming of Issah constitutes a valid event of naming. Susan Lanser, on the basis of contextual arguments, shows that the deviation from the standard naming formula in 2:23 does not invalidate this as a genuine naming; "(Feminist) Criticism in the Garden," p. 73.

34 Robert A. Oden, Jr., *The Bible Without Theology: The Theological Tradition and Alternatives to It* (New York: Harper and Row, 1987), p. 104.

9 "Where is your brother?"

1 Isaac M. Kikewada, "Two Notes on Eve," *Journal of Biblical Literature* 91 (1972), p. 37.

2 For a typology of Israelite sacrificial practices see Xavier Durand, "Sacrifice et rite", *Le Point Théologique* 24 (1977), pp. 32–61. The discussion below concerns sacrifice "for the Lord" as a "total gift," i.e., the holocaust (p. 57).

3 Madeleine Biardeau and Charles Malamoud, *Le Sacrifice dans L'Inde ancienne* (Paris: Presses Universitaires de France, 1976), p. 64.

4 *Ibid.*, p. 67.

5 Audrey Hayley, "The Offering in Assamese Vaishnavism," in J. F. C. Bourdillon and Meyer Fortes, eds., *Sacrifice* (New York: Academic Press, 1980), p. 109.

6 *Ibid.*, p. 118.

7 *Ibid.*

8 Biardeau and Malamoud, *Le Sacrifice*, p. 147.

9 *Ibid.*, p. 148.

10 *Ibid.*, p. 149.

11 This form of sacrifice is structurally homologous with warfare where the contending military parties are imaged as doubles in symbolically antithetical terms. Warfare then becomes, for the society, the most material form of sacrifice through which the society renews its own symbolic order.

12 René Girard, *Violence and the Sacred*, trans. Patrick Gregory (Baltimore: Johns Hopkins University Press, 1977), pp. 193–222.

13 *Ibid.*, p. 82.

14 *Ibid.*, p. 49.

15 *Ibid.*

16 *Ibid.*, pp. 81, 82.

17 *Ibid.*, p. 306.

18 Biardeau and Malamoud, *Le Sacrifice*, p. 25.

19 Girard, *Violence*, p. 50.

20 Westermann, *Genesis*, p. 405.

21 *Ibid.*

22 Westermann articulates the view of many when he argues for its secondary nature. The duplication in content between verse 5b and the questions in verse 6, the repetition of vocabulary from 3:16 in verse 7, as well as the general moralistic tone and the personification of sin, are indications to him that it is the product of a later redactor who may have disapproved of the implications in the original version; namely, that Cain was somewhat justified in his feeling of dismay at the lack of justice in the divine decision. The original version of verse 7 may have concerned a simple warning against attack by the spirit of the dead if he murdered his brother, a widespread belief at the time. The troublesome word, רֹבֵץ , translated variously as "crouching," "being in wait," has now been accepted by many scholars as a loan word from Assyrian where it meant "demon," and often even "threshhold demon." (Westermann, *Genesis*, vol. I, p. 408; E. A. Speiser, *Genesis: Introduction, Translation and Notes* (Garden City NY: Doubleday, 1964), p. 33). Some irregularity in the text is also suggested by the lack of agreement in gender between feminine subject, חַטָּאת (sin), and the masculine verb.

23 The usual translation of שְׂאֵת as "acceptance" or "forgiveness" is less appropriate than the standard meaning of this word: lifting up, rising up, majesty, dignity, etc., which simply relates to the facial expression of Cain given in the previous sentence; see Gerhard von Rad, *Genesis* (Philadelphia: Westminster Press, 1961), p. 101.

24 This, as D. Alan Aycock points out, is not inconsistent with the preference of God for the sanguinary animal rather than the non-sanguinary offerings: "there is fine irony implied when God has rejected as a sacrifice the pious offering of Cain the farmer, expressing a preference for the products of Abel the herder, only to be offered as an alternative sacrifice the herder himself!" "The Mark of Cain," in *Structuralist Interpretations of Biblical Myths*, ed. Edmund Leach and D. Alan Aycock (Cambridge University Press, 1983), p. 124.

25 Robert C. Culley also notes the structural correspondence between the interrogation scene here and in 3:9ff.; *Studies in the Structure of Hebrew Narrative, Semeia*, Supp. 3 (Philadelphia: Fortress Press, 1976), p. 106.

26 Westermann, *Genesis*, p. 417.

27 *Ibid.*

28 See also Gunkel, *Genesis*, p. 45.

29 Patrick D. Miller, Jr. shows the extent to which the nature of human being itself in these early narratives is defined in relation to the earth: "Cain's livelihood, crime and punishment are woven into the narrative by means of the adamah motif"; *Genesis 1–11: Studies in Structure and Theme*, Supp. 8 (Sheffield: JSOT Press, 1978), p. 41.

30 Robert C. Culley has found this mitigation of the divine punishment to be a recurring feature in other narratives (II Kings 2:23–25; Num. 11:1–3; 21:4–9) though here it is the unanticipated effects, rather than the punishment itself, which are mitigated. (Such an action does not support the theory advanced by others of God as the omniscient narrator, however.) *Studies in the Structure of Hebrew Narrative*, pp. 106, 107.

31 Westermann, *Genesis*, p. 427.

10 The central micro-dialogue

1 Dickens explored the ambiguous and sometimes destructive effect of human promises of future benefits in novels such as *Bleak House* and *Great Expectations*.

2 Caryl Emerson, "The Outer Word and Inner Speech: Bakhtin, Vygotsky, and the Internalization of Language," *Critical Inquiry* 10 (1983), p. 259.

3 *Ibid.*, p. 159.

4 Emerson notes the "novelistic gap" which for Bakhtin prohibits the closure of narrative personages (*ibid.*, p. 260).

11 "Why did you say, 'She is my sister'?"

1 Westermann, *Genesis*, vol. II, p. 141.
2 See Klaus Koch, *The Growth of the Biblical Tradition*, 2nd ed. trans. S. M. Cupitt (New York: Charles Scribner's Sons, 1969).
3 John van Seters, *Abraham in History and Tradition* (New Haven: Yale University Press, 1975), p. 182.
4 Gunkel, *Genesis*, vol. II, p. 170.
5 *Ibid.*, p. 173.
6 Westermann, *Genesis*, vol. II, p. 188.
7 *Ibid.*, p. 191.
8 *Ibid.*
9 *Ibid.*, p. 194.
10 See also Robert Polzin, " 'The Ancestress of Israel' in Danger," *Semeia* 3 (1975), pp. 81–97, who argues on structuralist grounds that the fertility of Sarai was withheld by Yahweh as punishment for Abraham having improperly acquired wealth in Egypt by his deception of the Pharaoh.
11 Westermann, *Genesis*, vol. II, p. 195.
12 *Ibid.*, p. 196.
13 The parallel between the assumptions of this story about the abuse of royal power to satisfy the lust of the king is so close to the David and Bathsheba incident that this story should be viewed more as an allusion to that incident rather than to any practice in the Egyptian court. M. Augustin points out the analogous relation to the Bathsheba incident. The center of both events is the "inbesitznahme der schönen Frau durch den Mächtigen, den Herrscher." See "Die Inbesitznahme der schönen Frau aus der unterschiedlichen Sicht der Schwachen und der Mächtigen," *Biblische Zeitschrift* 27 (1983), p. 149. See also Peter Miscall's analysis of this story in relation to the Bathsheba episode in *Semeia* 15 (1979), pp. 38–42.
14 This is a rare example of indirect discourse; see Keith Crim, "Hebrew Discourse as a Translation Problem," *Biblical Translator* 24 (1973), p. 312.

12 "Where is the lamb for the burnt offering?"

1 Martin Noth, *A History of the Pentateuchal Traditions*, trans. B. W. Anderson (Englewood Cliffs NJ: Prentice-Hall, 1972), pp. 114–115.
2 Gerhard von Rad, *Genesis*, p. 238.
3 *Ibid.*, p. 239.
4 Claus Westermann, *Genesis*, vol. II, pp. 433, 434; John van Seters, *Abraham in History and Tradition*, p. 98; Gregoire Rouiller, "The Sacrifice of Isaac, Second Reading," in *Exegesis: Problems of Method and Exercises in Reading (Gen. 22 and Luke 15)*, ed. F. Bovon and G. Rouiller, trans. D. G. Miller (Pittsburgh: Pickwick Press, 1978), p. 415.
5 Gunkel found this to be basically an E legend; *Genesis*, p. 236; more recently George Coats, "Abraham's Sacrifice of Faith," *Interpretation* 27 (1973), pp. 389–412.
6 von Rad, *Genesis*, p. 238.
7 Hugh C. White, "The Initiation Legend of Isaac," *ZAW* 91 (1979), pp. 1–30.
8 "If one were to unify the various elements – pact between generations, symbolic sacrifice, future of the race – around a single emblematic element, it would undoubtedly be the initiatic circumcision of Isaac." Jeffry Mehlman, *A Structural Study of Autobiography* (Ithaca NY: Cornell University Press, 1974), p. 24; see also Guy Rosolato, *Essais sur le symbolique* (Paris: Gallimard, 1969), pp. 59–77.
9 The particle נָא, translated as "I say," or "indeed," can be considered as an entreaty or an emphasis. In either case, it is a sign of formal politeness. Because it is rarely used in connection with a divine command (elsewhere only in Is. 7:3), it seems more appropriate to

the context to translate it as a sign of polite emphasis rather than entreaty; cf. James Crenshaw, "Journey into Oblivion," *Soundings* 48 (1975), p. 254.

10 "... en fait, Isaac est 'à côté' de l'événement et 'à côté' du récit," Antoine Galy, "Une lecture de Genèse 22," *Le Point Théologique* 24 (1977), p. 126.

11 Gunkel, *Genesis*, p. 38.

12 See also Remi Lack who finds this dialogue to be the center of the narrative structure in "Le sacrifice d'Isaac: Analyse structurale de la couche elohiste dans Gn 22." *Biblica* 56 (1975), pp. 1–12.

13 The parallel construction of the mandate in 12:1–3 and here in 22:2 has been often noted; see esp. G. Rouiller, "Sacrifice," p. 17. In spite of the possibility of different sources, this passage refers directly back to 12:1–3 and seems to offer a conclusion to what was begun there.

14 G. Rouiller, "Augustine of Hippo reads Gen. 22:1–19" in F. Bovon and G. Rouiller, *Exegesis*, p. 350.

15 See also Gerald Antoine, "The Sacrifice of Isaac: Exposition of Gen. 22:1–19" in *ibid.*, p. 178.

16 G. Rouiller, "Augustine of Hippo reads Gen. 22:1–19," *ibid.*, p. 433.

17 See van Seters, *Abraham*, who argues that the use of symbolic names here serves a broader literary purpose which intentionally breaks away from the mythology of sacred places (p. 238), and sees the aetiology as "entirely ... [a] literary device" (p. 240).

18 Van Seters argues for the unity of this passage with the preceding on theological grounds (*ibid.*, p. 239). William Yarchin, noting the stylistic similarities between 22:2 and 12:1–3, finds the imperative/promise pattern repeated here; "The narrative of the sacrifice of Isaac opens with a command to part (*lek leka*, verse 2) to a location yet to be identified, and concludes with the promise of blessing *as a consequence* of what has taken place in the narrative by virtue of the opening imperative." "Imperative and Promise in Genesis 12:1–3," *Studia Biblica et Theologica* 10 (1980), p. 173.

19 Westermann, *Genesis*, vol. II, p. 445.

20 For a psychoanalytic understanding of "voice" see Guy Rosolato, "The Voice and the Literary Myth," in *The Structuralist Controversy: The Language of Criticism and the Sciences of Man*, ed. R. Macksey and E. Donato (Baltimore: Johns Hopkins University Press, 1972), pp. 201–215.

21 Also Crenshaw, "Journey," p. 246.

13 "Who then is he ..."

1 Westermann, *Genesis*, vol. II, p. 497.

2 *Ibid.*

3 Gunkel, *Genesis*, p. 307, 308.

4 *Ibid.*, p. 308.

5 von Rad, *Genesis*, p. 276.

6 Westermann, *Genesis*, p. 699.

7 *Ibid.*, p. 511; also emphasizing the conflict theme are John G. Gammie, "Theological Interpretation by Way of Literary and Tradition Analysis: Genesis 25–36," in *Encounter with the Text*, ed. Martin J. Buss (Philadelphia: Fortress Press, 1979), pp. 117–134; and Victor H. Matthews and Frances Mims, "Jacob the Trickster and Heir of the Covenant: A Literary Interpretation," *Perspectives in Religious Studies* 12 (1985), pp. 185–196; Thomas L. Thompson, "Conflict of Themes in the Jacob Narratives," *Semeia* 15 (1979), pp. 5–26.

8 Gammie, "Theological Interpretation," pp. 130, 131.

9 The Syriac inserts חיה (life) resembling the usage in 27:46.

10 E. A. Speiser, *Genesis*, pp. 194, 195.

11 Christine Garside Allen, "On Me be the Curse," in *Encounter with the Text*, ed. Martin J. Buss, pp. 170, 171.
12 *Ibid.*, pp. 163, 164.
13 The precise term אַדְמֹנִי used here is also used to describe the young David in reference to his physical beauty and robustness: I Sam. 16:12; 17:42.
14 Gunkel, *Genesis*, p. 297.
15 The LXX adds "of lentils."
16 Westermann, *Genesis*, vol. II, p. 510.
17 Bakhtin, *Problems of Dostoyevsky's Poetics*, p. 154.
18 V. N. Voloshinov, *Marxism and the Philosophy of Language*, p. 130.
19 The *pilpel* form of the verb *tā'āh*, תָּעָה, is not found elsewhere. The root means to go astray, and can be used to refer to straying from understanding (Prov. 21:16). The *pilpel* form reduplicates and therefore doubly intensifies this root meaning.
20 Here there seems to be a quasi-magical view of the felicity of a blessing which goes beyond that of secular speech acts where not only the addressor must be properly authorized, but also the addressee, e.g., not only must the figure who performs a marriage be duly authorized, the persons being married cannot already be married for the marriage to be effective.
21 One thinks also of Bathsheba's deception by which Solomon was elevated to the kingship by a senile David at the end of his life. There is no evidence that David had ever promised Bathsheba to make Solomon his successor as she asserts after Nathan's prompting (I Kings 1:11–37).
22 Westermann, *Genesis*, vol. II, pp. 535, 536.
23 Erhard Blum sees this sentence as a summary added to the oral tradition by the narrator, pointing back to what has just occurred and forward to what is about to occur. *Die Komposition der Vätergeschichte*, Wissenschaftliche Monographien zum Alten und Neuen Testament, vol. 57 (Neukirchen-Vluyn: Neukirchener Verlag, 1985), pp. 84, 85.
24 Gunkel, *Genesis*, p. 312.
25 A less sanguine case of such intervention in service of an oracle is that of Lady Macbeth in Shakespeare's play, *Macbeth*. Lady Macbeth, however, intervened at the earliest possible moment and utilized murder to achieve her ends, whereas Rebekah waited until all other possibilities were exhausted, and the only blood shed was that of a goat! For Lady Macbeth the oracle instantly inflamed desire, which totally displaced faith and operated without any moral restraint whatsoever.
26 Adele Berlin, *The Dynamics of Biblical Parallelism* (Bloomington: Indiana University Press, 1985), p. 133.
27 Speiser, *Genesis*, p. 210.
28 The translation here is uncertain with many textual variants. "Break loose" renders the MT verb *tārîyd* (תָּרִיד) which seems the most appropriate.
29 Westermann, *Genesis*, vol. II, p. 540.
30 Speiser, *Genesis*, p. 210.
31 E.g., אֶרֶץ מְגֻרֶיךָ – land of your sojournings.

14 "Where do you come from?"

1 Gunkel, *Genesis*, p. 396.
2 *Ibid.*
3 *Ibid.*, p. 397.
4 *Ibid.* Similarly, von Rad, *Genesis*, p. 433; Coats, *From Canaan to Egypt: Structural and Theological Context of the Joseph Story* (Washington DC: Catholic Biblical Association of America, 1976), p. 2.

5 Gerhard von Rad, "Josephsgeschichte und älter Chokma", in *Gesammelte Studien zum Alten Testament* (Munich: Chr. Kaiser Verlag, 1961), pp. 272–280, and *Genesis*, p. 430.

6 H. N. Whybray, "The Joseph Story and Pentateuchal Criticism," *VT* (1968), p. 526.

7 *Ibid.*, p. 525.

8 *Ibid.*, p. 528.

9 James L. Crenshaw, "Method in Determining Wisdom Influence upon 'Historical' Literature," *JBL* 88 (1969), pp. 129–137; Donald B. Redford, *A Study of the Biblical Story of Joseph* (Leiden: E. J. Brill, 1970), p. 105; George W. Coats, "The Joseph Story and Ancient Wisdom: A Reappraisal", *CBQ* 35 (1973), pp. 285–297; Claus Westermann, *Genesis*, vol. III, p. 14.

10 Redford, *A Study of the Biblical Story of Joseph*, p. 105.

11 *Ibid.*, p. 179.

12 *Ibid.*, pp. 179–180.

13 Hans-Christoph Schmitt, *Die nichtpriesterliche Josephgeschichte* (Berlin: Walter de Gruyter, 1980); for a more thorough discussion of this issue by the writer see "Reuben and Judah: Duplicates or Complements?" in *Understanding the Word*, ed. J. T. Butler *et al.*, JSOT Supplement Series 37 (Sheffield: JSOT Press, 1985), pp. 73–85.

14 Horst Seebass, *Geschichtliche Zeit und theonome Tradition in der Joseph-Erzählung* (Gerd Mohn: Gütersloher Verlagshaus, 1978); Kenneth R. Melchin, "Literary Sources in the Joseph Story," *Science et Esprit* 31 (1979), pp. 93–101.

15 White, "Reuben and Judah," pp. 80, 81.

16 Gunkel, *Genesis*, p. 396.

17 *Ibid.*, p. 399.

18 Coats, *From Canaan to Egypt*, p. 8.

19 Westermann, *Genesis*, vol. III, p. 11; also Coats, *From Canaan to Egypt*, p. 8.

20 *Ibid.*, pp. 13, 14; Westermann believes, however, that it was communicated through oral reading in its earliest forms, and thus certain oral stylistic characteristics were preserved; *ibid.*, p. 279.

21 Coats, "Redactional Unity of Genesis 37–50," *JBL* 53 (1974), p. 15.

22 Westermann, *Genesis*, vol. III, p. 9–11.

23 *Ibid.*, p. 285.

24 *Ibid.*, pp. 9, 10.

25 Redford, *A Study of the Biblical Story of Joseph*, pp. 187–243.

26 Westermann, *Genesis*, vol. III, p. 18.

27 Coats, "The Joseph Story and Ancient Wisdom," p. 296.

28 Westermann, *Genesis*, vol. III, p. 14.

29 For example, Coats, "Redactional Unity."

30 Compare B. J. Van der Merwe, "Joseph as Successor of Jacob," in *Studia Biblica et Semitica*, Th. C. Vriezen Festschrift (Wageningen: H. Veenmen Zonen, 1966), pp. 221–231.

31 The term נַעַר refers to a young assistant/apprentice attached to various professions presumably to learn the trade – a type of initiate. (See White, "The Initiation Legend of Isaac", *ZAW* 91 (1979), pp. 14, 15.)

32 The possessive ending on דִּבָּתָם makes this clearly the idle gossip (Ez. 36:3) of the brothers and not the words of Joseph about the brothers, contrary to Westermann's argument (*Genesis*, p. 26), "The suffix can only mean what one said bad about them" (the phrase in Num. 14:37 lacks this ending), and closer to Gunkel's translation: "und was man ihnen Schlimmes nachgesagte, trug Joseph ihrem Vater zu" (*Genesis*, p. 492).

33 Cohn, *Transparent Minds*, p. 14.

34 *Ibid.*, p. 52.

35 The LXX omits the narrator's statement that he recounted the story to his father, but the MT should be followed since Joseph's report of the dream to his father is presupposed by the response of his father and the private communications between Joseph and Jacob.

36 Gunkel, *Genesis*, p. 405.

37 This view is contrary to that of Westermann who, by disregarding Jacob's own resentment against Joseph's dream report, and the possibility that the "thing" which Jacob notes might include the brothers' envy of Joseph, can contend that, "Jacob suspects nothing of the danger to his son due to the commission which he gives." *Genesis*, p. 30.

38 Speiser, *Genesis*, p. 288.

39 Gunkel, *Genesis*, p. 409; for a more extensive discussion of this problem see H. White, "Reuben and Judah," pp. 78–83.

40 Jacob charges them with having "bereaved" him of his children. The piel of the term שָׁכֹל is often used with "sword" as its subject clearly meaning the murder of children and others (I Sam. 15:33; Deut. 32:25).

41 Speiser, *Genesis*, p. 321.

42 "Er hört zu, und was ihn zum Weinen rührt, ist das Schuldbekenntnis der Brüder, das eine Versöhnung, das die Heilung des Bruches ermöglicht." Westermann, *Genesis*, p. 117.

43 *Ibid.*, p. 121.

44 The lengthy debate over whether this is a duplication of the previous event in which the silver was discovered en route from Egypt will not be taken up here. Westermann's view that the silver of only one brother was reported en route while the remainder was discovered on this occasion is clearly logical (*Ibid.*, pp. 119, 120). It also does not necessarily contradict Judah's later report to Joseph which telescopes both events in a context where the report of them separately would have been both stylistically awkward and served no purpose. Westermann, nevertheless, views the second discovery as a gloss on the basis of equivocal stylistic evidence, and an aesthetic judgement that this event unnaturally intrudes between the report of the brothers and Jacob's response.

45 The habit of commentators to see this reference as a clumsy redactional intrusion stems from a general failure to recognize the narrative function of the silver in the plot. Joseph could not keep any of the brothers' money for reasons given above.

46 Speiser, *Genesis*, p. 335; see also von Rad, *Genesis*, p. 388.

47 Speiser, *Genesis*, p. 335.

48 Coats, *From Canaan to Egypt*, p. 84.

49 *Ibid.*

Bibliography

Allen, Christine Garside. "On me be the curse." In M. Buss, ed., *Encounter with the Text*, pp. 159–172.

Alter, Robert. *The Art of Biblical Narrative*. New York: Basic Books, 1981.

Anderson, Stephen R. and Paul Kiparsky, eds. *Festschrift für Morris Halle*. New York: Holt, Rinehart and Winston, 1973.

Auffret, Pierre. "Essai sur la structure littéraire de Gn 12, 1–4a(a)." *Biblische Zeitschrift* 26 (1982), pp. 243–248.

Augustin, Matthais. "Die Inbesitznahme der schönen Frau aus der unterschiedlichen Sicht der Schwachen und der Mächtigen: Ein kritischer Vergleich von Gen 12, 10–20 und 2 Sam 11, 2–27a." *Biblische Zeitschrift* 27 (1983), pp. 145–154.

Austin, John L. *How to do Things with Words*. 2nd ed. Ed. J. O. Urmson and Marina Sbisa. Cambridge MA: Harvard University Press, 1975.

Aycock, D. Alan. "The Mark of Cain." In E. Leach and A. Aycock, eds., *Structuralist Interpretations of Biblical Myths*, pp. 120–127.

Bakhtin, Mikhail. *Problems of Dostoyevsky's Poetics*. Trans. R. W. Rotsel. N.p.: Ardis, 1973.

The Dialogic Imagination: Four Essays. Ed. and trans. M. Holquist and C. Emerson. Austin: University of Texas Press, 1981.

Speech Genres and Other Late Essays. Ed. C. Emerson and M. Holquist. Trans. V. W. McGee. Austin: University of Texas Press, 1986.

Bal, Mieke. *Introduction to the Theory of Narrative*. Trans. C. van Boheemen. University of Toronto Press, 1985.

Lethal Love: Feminist Literary Readings of Biblical Love Stories. Bloomington and Indianapolis: Indiana University Press, 1987.

Murder and Difference: Gender, Genre and Scholarship on Sisera's Death. University of Chicago Press, 1988.

Banfield, Ann. "Narrative Style and the Grammar of Direct and Indirect Speech." *Foundations of Language* 10 (1973), pp. 1–39.

Unspeakable Sentences: Narration and Representation in the Language of Fiction. Boston: Routledge and Kegan Paul, 1982.

"Describing the Unobserved: Events Grouped around an Empty Center." In N. Fabb *et al.*, eds., *The Linguistics of Writing*, pp. 265–286.

Barthes, Roland. "Introduction à l'analyse structurale des récits." *Communications* 8 (1966), pp. 1–27.

Writing Degree Zero and Elements of Semiology. Trans. A. Lavers and C. Smith. Boston: Beacon Press, 1970.

S/Z: An Essay. Trans. Richard Miller. New York: Hill and Wang, 1974.

Beeston, A. F. L. "One Flesh." *Vetus Testamentum* 36 (1986), pp. 115–117.

Benveniste, Emile. *Problems in General Linguistics*. Trans. M. E. Meek. Coral Gables FL: University of Miami Press, 1971.

Berlin, Adele. *Poetics and Interpretation of Biblical Narrative.* Sheffield: The Almond Press, 1983.

The Dynamics of Biblical Parallelism. Bloomington: Indiana University Press, 1985.

Biardeau, Madeliene and Charles Malamoud. *Le Sacrifice dans l'Inde Ancienne.* Paris: Presses Universitaires de France, 1976.

Birman, Claus. *Cain et Abel.* Paris: Grasset, 1980.

Blum, Erhard. *Die Komposition der Vätergeschichte.* Wissenschaftliche Monographien zum Alten und Neuen Testament, vol. 57. Neukirchen-Vluyn: Neukirchener Verlag, 1985.

Bonhöffer, Dietrich. *Creation and Fall: A Theological Interpretation of Genesis 1–3.* London: SCM Press, 1960.

Booth, Wayne. *The Rhetoric of Fiction.* University of Chicago Press, 1961.

Bourdillon, J. F. C. and Meyer Fortes, eds. *Sacrifice.* New York: Academic Press, 1980.

Bovon, F. and G. Rouiller, eds. *Exegesis: Problems of Method and Exercises in Reading (Gen. 22 and Luke 15).* Trans. D. G. Miller. Pittsburgh: The Pickwick Press, 1978.

Brock, Sebastian. "Genesis 22: Where was Sarah?" *The Expository Times* 96 (1984/85), pp. 14–17.

Buss, Martin, ed. *Encounter with the Text: Form and History in the Hebrew Bible.* Philadelphia: Fortress Press, 1979.

Butler, J. T., *et al. Understanding the Word.* JSOT Supplement Series 37. Sheffield: JSOT Press, 1985.

Cascardi, Anthony J., ed. *Literature and the Question of Philosophy.* Baltimore: Johns Hopkins University Press, 1987.

Chatman, Seymour, ed. *Literary Style: A Symposium.* New York: Oxford University Press, 1971.

Story and Discourse: Narrative Structure in Fiction and Film. Ithaca NY: Cornell University Press, 1978.

Clark, Katrina and Michael Holquist. *Mikhail Bakhtin.* Cambridge MA: Harvard University Press, 1984.

Clines, David J. A., David Gunn, and Alan Hauser, eds. *Art and Meaning: Rhetoric in Biblical Literature. Journal for the Study of the Old Testament*, Supplement 19 (1982).

Coats, George W. "Abraham's Sacrifice of Faith: A Form-Critical Study of Genesis 22." *Interpretation 27* (1973), pp. 389–412.

"The Joseph Story and Ancient Wisdom: A Reappraisal." *Catholic Biblical Quarterly* 35 (1973), pp. 285–297.

"Redactional Unity in Genesis 37–50." *Journal of Biblical Literature* 53 (1974), pp. 15–21.

From Canaan to Egypt: Structural and Theological Context of the Joseph Story. Washington DC: Catholic Biblical Association of America, 1976.

Genesis, with an Introduction to Narrative Literature. Grand Rapids MI: William B. Eerdmans Publishing Co., 1983.

Coggins, Richard. "The Literary Approach to the Bible." *Expository Times* 96 (1984/85), pp. 9–14.

Cohen, Jonathan L. "Do Illocutionary Forces Exist?" *Philosophical Quarterly* 14 (1964), pp. 118–137.

Cohen, Norman. "The Two that are One: Sibling Rivalry in Genesis," *Judaism* 32/127 (1983), pp. 331–342.

Cohn, Dorrit. *Transparent Minds: Narrative Modes for Presenting Consciousness in Fiction.* Princeton University Press, 1978.

Connor, Steve, *Charles Dickens.* Oxford: Basil Blackwell, 1985.

Coseriu, Eugenio. *Synchronie, Diachronie und Geschichte.* Munich: Wilhelm Fink Verlag, 1974.

Couffignal, Robert. *L'épreuve d'Abraham: le récit de la Genèse et sa fortune littéraire.* Toulouse: Association de Publications de l'Université de Toulouse – Le Mirail, 1976.

Crenshaw, James. "Method in Determining Wisdom Influence upon 'Historical' Literature." *Journal of Biblical Literature* 88 (1969), pp. 129–137.

"Journey into Oblivion: A Structural Analysis of Gen. 22:1–19." *Soundings* 58 (1975), pp. 243–256.

Crim, Keith. "Hebrew Direct Discourse as a Translation Problem." *Bible Translator* 24 (1973), pp. 311–316.

Crossan, Dominic. "Felix Culpa and Foenix Culprit." *Semeia* 18 (1980), pp. 107–111.

Culler, Jonathan. "Convention and Meaning: Derrida and Austin." *New Literary History* 13 (1981), pp. 15–30.

On Deconstruction: Theory and Criticism after Structuralism. Ithaca NY: Cornell University Press, 1982.

"Problems in the Theory of Fiction." *Diacritics* (Spring 1984), pp. 2–11.

Culley, Robert C. *Studies in the Structure of Hebrew Narrative. Semeia.* Supplement 3. Philadelphia: Fortress Press, 1976.

Currie, Gregory. "Works of Fiction and Illocutionary Acts." *Philosophy and Literature* 10 (1986), pp. 304–308.

Damrosch, David. *The Narrative Covenant: Transformations of Genre in the Growth of Biblical Literature.* San Francisco: Harper and Row, 1987.

Davis, Robert Con, ed. *Lacan and Narration: The Psychoanalytic Difference in Narrative Theory.* Baltimore: Johns Hopkins University Press, 1983.

Derrida, Jacques. *Speech and Phenomena and Other Essays on Husserl's Theory of Signs.* Trans. and Introd. David B. Allison. Evanston: Northwestern University Press, 1973.

Of Grammatology. Trans. G. C. Spivak. Baltimore: Johns Hopkins University Press, 1977.

Detweiler, Robert. *Story, Sign and Self: Phenomenology and Structuralism as Literary-Critical Methods.* Philadelphia: Fortress Press, 1978.

Diengott, Nilli. "The Mimetic Language Game and Two Typologies of Narrators." *Modern Fiction Studies* 33 (1987), pp. 523–534.

Doležel, Lubomír. *Narrative Modes in Czech Literature.* University of Toronto Press, 1973.

Dostoyevsky, Fyodor. *The Possessed.* Trans. A. R. MacAndrew. New York: The New American Library, 1962.

Drewerman, Eugen. *Strukturen des Bösen: Die Jahwistische Urgeschichte in exegetischer, psychoanalytischer und philosophischer Sicht.* Paderborn, 1981.

"Exegese und Tiefen Psychologie. Von der Ergänzungsbedürftigkeit der historisch-kritischen Methode am Beispiel der Schlangensymbolik in der jahwistischen Urgeschichte." *Bibel und Kirche* 3 (1983), pp. 91–105.

Ducrot, Oswald. *Dire et ne pas dire: principes de sémantique linguistique.* Paris: Herman, 1972.

Durand, Xavier. "Sacrifice et rite." *Le Point Théologique* 24 (1977), pp. 32–61.

Eco, Umberto. *A Theory of Semiotics.* Bloomington: Indiana University Press, 1979.

Emerson, Caryl. "The Outer Word and Inner Speech: Bakhtin, Vygotsky, and the Internalization of Language." *Critical Inquiry* 10 (1983), pp. 245–264.

Emerton, J. A. "The Origin of the Promises to the Patriarchs in the Older Sources of the Book of Genesis." *Vetus Testamentum* 32 (1982), pp. 14–32.

Erlich, Victor. *Russian Formalism.* The Hague: Mouton, 1965.

Evans, Carl D. "The Patriarch Jacob: An Innocent Man." *Bible Review* 2 (1986), pp. 32–37.

Exum, Cheryl. "The Mothers of Israel: The Patriarchal Narratives from a Feminist Perspective." *Bible Review* 2 (1986), pp. 60–67.

Fabb, Nigel, Derek Attridge, Alan Durant and Colin MacCabe, eds., *The Linguistics of Writing: Arguments between Language and Literature.* New York: Methuen, 1987.

Feilschuss-Abir, A. S. " '... da werden eure Augen geöffnet und ihr werdet sein wie Gott, wissend Gutes und Böses' (Gen. 3, 5)." *Theologie und Glaube* 74 (1984), pp. 190–213.

Fish, Stanley E. *Self-Consuming Artifacts: The Experience of Seventeenth Century Literature.* Berkeley: University of California Press, 1972.

"Structuralist Homiletics." *Modern Language Notes* 91 (1976), pp. 1208–1221.

Fishbane, Michael. *Text and Texture: Close Readings of Selected Biblical Texts.* New York: Schocken Books, 1979.

Flahault, François, *La parole intermédiaire.* Paris: Editions du Seuil, 1978.

Fowler, Roger. *Linguistics and the Novel.* London: Methuen, 1977.

Literature as Social Discourse: The Practice of Linguistic Criticism. Bloomington: University of Indiana Press, 1981.

Friedman, Norman. "Point of View in Fiction: The Development of a Critical Concept." *PMLA* 70 (1955), pp. 1160–1184.

Friedman, Richard Elliott. "Deception for Deception." *Bible Review* 2 (1986), pp. 22–31.

Galy, Antoine. "Une lecture de Genèse 22." *Le Point Théologique* 24 (1981), pp. 157–177.

Gammie, John. "Theological Interpretation by Way of Literary and Tradition Analysis: Genesis 25–36." In M. Buss, ed., *Encounter with the Text,* pp. 117–134.

Gardner, John. *On Moral Fiction.* New York: Basic Books, 1978.

Genest, Olivette. "Analyse sémiotique de Gn 22, 1–19." *Science et Esprit* 33 (1981), pp. 157–177.

Genette, Gérard. *Narrative Discourse.* Trans. Jane E. Lewin. Ithaca NY: Cornell University Press, 1980.

Figures of Literary Discourse. Trans. A. Sheridan. New York: Columbia University Press, 1982.

Girard, René. *Violence and the Sacred.* Trans. P. Gregory. Baltimore: Johns Hopkins University Press, 1977.

Greimas, A.-J. *Sémantique structurale: recherche de méthode.* Paris: Librairie Larousse, 1966.

Guertichin, Herve Lenard de. "A partir d'une lecture du sacrifice d'Isaac," *Lumen Vitae* 38 (1983), pp. 303–322.

Gunkel, Hermann, *Genesis.* 6th ed. Göttingen: Vandenhöck und Ruprecht, 1964.

Gunn, David. "New Directions in the Study of Biblical Hebrew Narrative." *Journal for the Study of the Old Testament* 89 (1987), pp. 65–75.

Hancher, Michael. "Performative Utterance, the Word of God, and the Death of the Author." *Semeia* 41 (1988), pp. 27–40.

Handelman, Susan A. *The Slayers of Moses: The Emergence of Rabbinic Interpretation in Modern Literary Theory.* Albany: State University of New York Press, 1982.

Harari, Josué, ed. *Textual Strategies: Perspectives in Post-Structuralist Criticism.* Ithaca NY: Cornell University Press, 1979.

Hardmeier, Christof. "Old Testament Exegesis and Linguistic Narrative Research." *Poetics* 15 (1986), pp. 89–109.

Harris, R. Laird, S.-H. Quek, and J. Robert Vanney, eds. *Interpretation and History: Essays in Honor of A. MacRae.* Singapore: Christian Life Publishers, 1986.

Hartman, Geoffrey H. *Saving the Text: Literature/Derrida/Philosophy.* Baltimore: Johns Hopkins University Press, 1981.

Hartman, Geoffrey H. and Sanford Budick, eds. *Midrash and Literature.* New Haven: Yale University Press, 1986.

Hayley, Audrey. "The Offering in Assamese Vaishnavism." In J. F. C. Bourdillon and Meyer Fortes, eds., *Sacrifice,* pp. 106–125.

Heckelman, A. Joseph. "Was Father Isaac a Co-Conspirator?" *Dor le Dor* 13 (1985), pp. 225–234.

Hendel, Ronald S. "The 'Flame of the Whirling Sword': A Note on Gen. 3:24." *Journal of Biblical Literature* 104 (1985), pp. 671–674.

The Epic of the Patriarch: The Jacob Cycle and the Narrative Traditions of Canaan and Israel. Harvard Semitic Monographs 42. Atlanta GA: Scholars Press, 1987.

Hernadi, Paul. "Doing, Making and Meaning: Toward a Theory of Verbal Practice." *PMLA* 103 (1988), pp. 749–758.

Holquist, Michael. "Answering as Authoring: Mikhail Bakhtin's Trans-Linguistics." *Critical Inquiry* 10 (1983), pp. 307–319.

Hoy, David Cozens. *The Critical Circle: Literature, History, and Philosophical Hermeneutics.* Berkeley: University of California Press, 1982.

Huffman, Herbert. "Cain, the Arrogant Sufferer." In A. Kort and S. Morschausa, eds., *Biblical and Related Studies Presented to Samuel Iwry*, pp. 109–114.

Hunter, Alastair G. "Father Abraham: A Structural and Theological Study of the Yahwist's Presentation of the Abraham Material." *Journal for the Study of the Old Testament* 35 (1986), pp. 3–27.

Iser, Wolfgang. *The Implied Reader: Patterns of Communication in Prose Fiction from Bunyan to Beckett.* Baltimore: Johns Hopkins University Press, 1974.

Jagendorf, Zvi. " 'In the morning, it was Leah': Genesis and the Reversal of Sexual knowledge." *Prooftexts* 4 (1984), pp. 187–199.

Jameson, Fredric. *The Prison-House of Language: A Critical Account of Structuralism and Russian Formalism.* Princeton University Press, 1972.

The Political Unconscious: Narrative as a Socially Symbolic Act. Ithaca NY: Cornell University Press, 1981.

Jay, Paul. *Being in the Text: Self-Representation from Wordsworth to Roland Barthes.* Ithaca NY: Cornell University Press, 1984.

Jobling, David. *The Sense of Biblical Narrative II.* Journal for the Study of the Old Testament Supplement Series 39. Sheffield: JSOT Press, 1986.

Josipovici, Gabriel. *The Book of God: A Response to the Bible.* New Haven: Yale University Press, 1988.

Kikewada, Isaac M. "Two Notes on Eve." *Journal of Biblical Literature* 91 (1972), pp. 33–37.

Knight, Diana. "Saving the Text: Literary Theory and the Status of Fictional Events." *Renaissance and Modern Studies* 27 (1983), pp. 123–137.

Koch, Klaus. *The Growth of the Biblical Tradition.* 2nd ed. Trans. S. M. Cupitt. New York: Charles Scribner's Sons, 1969.

Kort, Ann and Scot Morschausa, eds. *Biblical and Related Studies Presented to Samuel Iwry.* Winona Lake IN: Eisenbrauns, 1985.

Kristeva, Julia. *Le Texte du roman. Approche sémiologique d'une structure discursive transformationelle.* The Hague: Mouton, 1970.

La Révolution du langage poétique. Paris: Editions du Seuil, 1974.

Polylogue. Paris: Editions du Seuil, 1977.

Kuroda, S.-Y. "Where Epistemology, Style and Grammar Meet: A Case Study from Japanese." In S. R. Anderson and P. Kiparsky, eds. *Festschrift für Morris Halle*, pp. 377–391.

Lack, Remi. "Le Sacrifice d'Isaac: Analyse structurale de la couche elohiste dans Gen. 22." *Biblica* 56 (1975), pp. 1–12.

Laden, Marie-Paule. *Self-Imitation in the Eighteenth-Century Novel.* Princeton University Press, 1987.

Lambert, Mark. *Dickens and the Suspended Quotation.* New Haven: Yale University Press, 1981.

Lanser, Susan. *The Narrative Act.* Princeton University Press, 1981.

"(Feminist) Criticism in the Garden: Inferring Genesis 2–3." *Semeia* 41 (1988), pp. 67–84.

Leach, Edmund and Alan Aycock, eds. *Structuralist Interpretations of Biblical Myths.* Cambridge University Pres, 1983.

Lecointre, Simone and Jean le Galliot. "Le Je(u) de l'énonciation." *Langages* 31 (1973), pp. 64–79.

Lemon, Lee T. and Marion J. Reis, eds. *Russian Formalist Criticism: Four Essays.* Lincoln: University of Nebraska Press, 1965.

Lodge, David. *The Modes of Modern Writing: Metaphor, Metonymy, and the Typology of Modern Literature.* Ithaca NY: Cornell University Press, 1977.

Longacre, Robert E. "Who Sold Joseph into Egypt?" In R. Harris *et al.*, eds., *Interpretation and History*, pp. 75–91.

Lotman, Yury. *Analysis of the Poetic Text.* Ed. D. Barton Johnson. Ann Arbor MI: Ardis, 1976.

McConnel, Frank, ed. *The Bible and the Narrative Tradition.* Oxford University Press, 1986.

McHale, Brian. "Free Indirect Discourse: A Survey of Recent Accounts." *Poetics and Theory of Literature* 3 (1978), pp. 249–287.

Matejka, Ladislav and Krystyna Pomorska, eds. *Readings in Russian Poetics: Formalist and Structuralist Views.* Cambridge MA: MIT Press, 1971.

Matthews, Victor H. and Francis Mims. "Jacob the Trickster and Heir of the Covenant: A Literary Interpretation." *Perspectives in Religious Studies* 12 (1985), pp. 185–196.

Medina, Angel. *Reflection, Time and the Novel: Toward a Communicative Theory of Literature.* London and Boston: Routledge and Kegan Paul, 1979.

Mehlman, Jeffry. *A Structural Study of Autobiography.* Ithaca NY: Cornell University Press, 1974.

Melchin, Kenneth R. "Literary Sources in the Joseph Story." *Science et Esprit* 31 (1979), pp. 93–101.

Miller, Patrick D., Jr. *Genesis 1–11: Studies in Structure and Theme.* Supplement 8. Sheffield: JSOT Press, 1978.

Moberly, R. W. L. "The Earliest Commentary on the Akedah." *Vetus Testamentum* 38 (1988), pp. 302–323.

Neumann, Anne Waldron. "Characterization and Comment in *Pride and Prejudice.* Free Indirect Discourse and 'Double-voiced' Verbs of Speaking, Thinking, and Feeling." *Style* 20 (1986), pp. 364–394.

Norris, Christopher. "Home Thoughts from Abroad: Derrida, Austin and the Oxford Connection." *Philosophy and Literature* 10 (1986), pp. 1–25.

Noth, Martin. *A History of the Pentateuchal Traditions.* Trans. B. W. Anderson. Englewood Cliffs NJ: Prentice-Hall, 1972.

Oden, Robert A., Jr. *The Bible Without Theology: The Theological Tradition and Alternatives to It.* New York: Harper and Row, 1987.

Orlinski, Harry M. "The Plain Meaning of Genesis 1:1–3." *Biblical Archaeologist* 46 (1983), pp. 207–209.

Ortigues, Edmond. *Le Discours et le symbole.* Paris: Aubier, Editions Montaigne, 1962.

"Les origines augustiniennes de la philosophie de l'esprit." *Kant Studien* 63 (1972), pp. 163–181.

"L'Interprétation des modalités." *Etudes Philosophique* (1984), pp. 245–264.

Pascal, Roy. *The Dual Voice.* Manchester University Press, 1977.

Patcas, Hirsch. "Akedah, the Binding of Isaac." *Dor le Dor* 14 (1985/86), pp. 112–114.

Polzin, Robert. " 'The Ancestress of Israel' in Danger." *Semeia* 3 (1973), pp. 81–97.

Moses and the Deuteronomist: A Literary Study of the Deuteronomic History. New York: The Seabury Press, 1980.

Polzin, Robert and Eugene Rothman, eds. *The Biblical Mosaic: Changing Perspectives.* Philadelphia: Fortress Press, 1982.

Pratt, Mary Louise. *Toward a Speech Act Theory of Literary Discourse.* Bloomington: Indiana University Press, 1977.

Prickett, Stephen. *Words and The Word: Language, Poetics and Biblical Interpretation.* Cambridge University Press, 1986.

Prince, Gerald. "Narrative Analysis and Narratology." *New Literary History* 13 (1982), pp. 179–188.

Pritchard, James B. *Ancient Near Eastern Texts.* Princeton University Press, 1955.

Rad, Gerhard von. *Genesis, A Commentary.* Trans. John H. Marks. Philadelphia: Westminster Press, 1961.

Gesammelte Studien zum Alten Testament. Munich: Chr. Kaiser Verlag, 1961.

Redford, Donald B. *A Study of the Biblical Story of Joseph.* Leiden: E. J. Brill, 1970.

Rendtorff, Rolf. "Genesis 8, 21 und die Urgeschichte des Jahwisten." In *Gesammelte Studien zum Alten Testament.* Munich: Theologische Bücherei, 1975, pp. 188–197.

Das Überlieferungsgeschichtliche Problem des Pentateuch. Berlin: Walter de Gruyter, 1977.

Ricoeur, Paul. "La Bible et l'imagination." *Revue d'Histoire et de Philosophie Religieuses* 62 (1982): 339–360.

Riemann, V. A. "Am I my Brother's Keeper?" *Interpretation* 24 (1970), pp. 482–491.

Rimmon, Shlomith. "A Comprehensive Theory of Narrative: Genette's *Figures III* and the Structuralist Study of Fiction." *Poetics and Theory of Literature* 1 (1976), pp. 33–62.

Rosenberg, Joel. *King and Kin: Political Allegory in the Hebrew Bible.* Bloomington: Indiana University Press, 1986.

Rosolato, Guy. *Essais sur le symbolique.* Paris: Gallimard, 1969.

Ross, Donald Jr. "Who's Talking? How Characters Become Narrators in Fiction." *Modern Language Notes* 9 (1976), pp. 1208–1221.

Rudolph, Wilhelm. "Die Josephgeschichte." In *Der Elohist als Erzähler, ein Irrweg der Pentateuchkritik?* Beihefte zur Zeitschrift für Alttestamentliche Wissenschaft 63. Giessen: Alfred Töpelmann Verlag, 1933.

Safren, Jonathan D. "Balaam and Abraham." *Vetus Testamentum* 38 (1988), pp. 105–113.

Sarda, Odette. "Le Sacrifice d'Abraham: Gn 22; Le déplacement des lectures attestées." *Le Point Théologique* 24 (1977), pp. 135–146.

Sasson, Jack M. "'w^{e}lō' yitbōšāšû (Gen 2.25) and Its Implications." *Biblica* 66 (1985), pp. 418–421.

Schedl, Claus. "Berufung Abrahams, des Vaters der Gläubigen: Logotechnische Analyse von Gen. 12.1–9." *Biblische Zeitschrift* 28 (1984), pp. 255–259.

Schmitt, Hans-Christoph. *Die nichtpriesterliche Josephgeschichte.* Berlin: Walter de Gruyter, 1980.

Schneemelcher, Wilhelm, ed. *Das Problem der Sprache in Theologie und Kirche.* Berlin: Alfred Töpelmann Verlag, 1959.

Schneidau, Herbert N. *Sacred Discontent: The Bible and Western Tradition.* Berkeley: University of California Press, 1976.

Seamon, Roger. "Acts of Narration." *Journal of Aesthetics and Art Criticism.* 45 (1987), pp. 369–379.

Searle, John. *Speech Acts.* Cambridge University Press, 1969.

Seebass, Horst. *Geschichtliche Zeit und theonome Tradition in der Joseph-Erzählung.* Gerd Mohn: Gütersloher Verlagshaus, 1978.

Shklovsky, Victor. "Sterne's *Tristram Shandy*: Stylistic Commentary." In L. T. Lemon and M. J. Reis, eds., *Russian Formalist Criticism*, pp. 25–57.

Sholes, Robert and Robert Kellog. *The Nature of Narrative.* Oxford University Press, 1966.

Siegle, Robert. *The Politics of Reflexivity: Narrative and the Constitutive Poetics of Culture.* Baltimore: Johns Hopkins University Press, 1986.

Sirridge, Mary. "Donkeys, Stars, and Illocutionary Acts." *Journal of Aesthetics and Art Criticism* 45 (1987), pp. 381–388.

Ska, Jean-Louis. "'Je vais lui faire un allié qui soit son homologue,' (Gn 2, 18): A propos du term *ezer* – 'aide'." *Biblica* 65 (1984), pp. 233–238.

Skinner, John. *A Critical and Exegetical Commentary on Genesis*. 2nd ed. Edinburgh: T. and T. Clark Ltd., 1980.

Speiser, E. A. *Genesis: Introduction, Translation and Notes*. Garden City NY: Doubleday, 1964.

Stanzel, Franz. *Narrative Situations in the Novel*. Trans. James P. Pusak. Bloomington: Indiana University Press, 1971.

Steck, Odil Hannes. "Genesis 12:1–3 und die Urgeschichte des Jahwisten." In H. W. Wolff, ed., *Probleme biblischer Theologie*, pp. 525–554.

Sternberg, Meir. *The Poetics of Biblical Narrative*. Bloomington: Indiana University Press, 1985.

"The World From the Addressee's Viewpoint: Reception as Representation, Dialogue as Monologue." *Style* 20 (1986), pp. 295–318.

Stewart, Susan. "Shouts on the Street: Bakhtin's Anti-Linguisitcs." *Critical Inquiry* 10 (1983), pp. 265–281.

Thévenot, Xavier. "Emmaüs, une nouvelle Genèse?" Une lecture psychoanalytique de Genèse 2–3 et Luc 24, 13–35. *Mélanges de Science Religieuse* 37 (1980), pp. 3–18.

Thompson, Thomas L. "Conflict of Themes in the Jacob Narratives." *Semeia* 15 (1979), pp. 5–26.

Trible, Phyllis. *God and the Rhetoric of Sexuality*. Philadelphia: Fortress Press, 1978.

Van der Merwe, B. J. "Joseph as Successor of Jacob." In *Studia Biblica et Semitica*, Th. C. Vriezen Festschrift. Wageningen: H. Veenmen Zonen, 1966, pp. 221–231.

Van Seters, John. *Abraham in History and Tradition*. New Haven: Yale University Press, 1975.

Villela-Petit, Maria da Penha. "Cain et Able: la querelle des offrandes." *Philosophie* 6 (1981), pp. 121–148.

Vogels, Walter. "L'Etre humain appartient au sol: Gn 2, 4b–3, 24. *Nouvelle Revue Théologique* 105 (1983), pp. 515–534.

Voloshinov, V. N. *Marxism and the Philosophy of Language*. Trans. L. Matejka and I. R. Titunik. New York and London: Seminar Press, 1930, 1973.

Wallace, Howard N. *The Eden Narrative*, Harvard Semitic Monographs 32. Atlanta: Scholars Press, 1985.

Warnock, G. J. "Some Types of Performative Utterance." In I. Berlin *et al.*, eds., *Essays on J. L. Austin*. Oxford: Clarendon Press, 1973.

Warren, Robert Penn. *Audubon: A Vision*. New York: Random House, 1969.

Being Here: Poetry 1977–1980. New York: Random House, 1980.

Westermann, Claus. *Genesis. Biblischer Kommentar, Altes Testament*, Neukirchen-Vluyn: Neukirchener Verlag, 1966– .

White, Hugh C. "A Theory of the Surface Structure of the Biblical Narrative." *Union Seminary Quarterly Review* 34 (1979), pp. 159–174.

"Reuben and Judah: Duplicates or Complements?" In J. T. Butler, ed., *Understanding the Word*, pp. 73–97.

"The Initiation of Isaac." *ZAW* 91 (1979), pp. 1–30.

Whybay, H. N. "The Joseph Story and Pentateuchal Criticism." *Vetus Testamentum* 18 (1968), pp. 522–528.

Wilner, Joshua. "Romanticism and the Internationalization of Scripture." In G. H. Hartman and S. Budick, eds., *Midrash and Literature*, pp. 237–251.

Wolff, Hans Walther. *Probleme biblischer Theologie*. Munich: Chr. Kaiser Verlag, 1971.

Wright, T. R. *Theology and Literature*. Oxford: Basil Blackwell, 1988.

Yarchin, William. "Imperative and Promise in Genesis 12:1–3." *Studia Biblica et Theologica* 10 (1980), pp. 164–178.

Yashar, Menahem Ben. "Zu Gen 4:7." *Zeitschrift für die alttestamentliche Wissenschaft.* 94 (1982), pp. 635–667.

Zimmerli, Walther. "Die Weisung des Alten Testamentes zum Geschäft der Sprache." In W. Schneemelcher, ed., *Das Problem der Sprache in Theologie und Kirche*, pp. 1–20.

Index – Authors and topics

Index – Biblical references